The International Series in

ELEMENTARY EDUCATION

Consulting Editor

JOHN M. KEAN

University of Wisconsin

The Teaching of Mathematics
in the
Elementary School

The Teaching of Mathematics in the Elementary School

JOHN W. STARR III

Supervisor of Elementary Education,
School City of Gary, Gary, Indiana

INTERNATIONAL TEXTBOOK COMPANY
Scranton, Pennsylvania

Standard Book Number 7002 2201 4

To

J. L. D., Jr.

*without whose faith and persistence this
book would never have been written*

Acknowledgments

The writer is deeply indebted to a great number of people who have helped and encouraged the writing of this manuscript. To the children and teachers of many elementary schools, to all others who have had a part, and especially to Pam, Christy, Elaine, and Matt, I am eternally grateful.

J. W. S. III

Gary, Indiana
January, 1969

Contents

The Teaching of Mathematics
in the
Elementary School

chapter 1

The Study of Mathematics

THE NEW APPROACH

Changes in the approach to teaching mathematics at the elementary school level require teachers and all others concerned with the child's learning of mathematics to become familiar with and prepare to make the best use of these new approaches. Essentially there is a shift in emphasis from teaching mathematics as a way of doing something to teaching it as a way of thinking. The major emphasis in the modern approach is on "understanding" of basic mathematical ideas which are sometimes hidden by computational techniques. Computation is an important part of mathematics and must be taught, but it should be taught only after the child understands the underlying mathematical ideas. The child should make use of inductive and deductive reasoning as he progresses from intuitive learning to basic information and then to an understanding of more abstract concepts. The discovery approach to learning is employed: the child is given the opportunity to discover mathematical concepts for himself.

This modern approach appears to be the result of two trends, the first of which is an awareness that the teaching of mathematics should be meaningful. In this view, which stems from psychologies holding that the most effective and efficient learning is that which emphasizes structure and understanding, elementary school mathematics is seen as a body of ideas—of concepts and relationships—to be understood. The tool-subject and analytical-drill approaches to the content are minimized and the social-utility aspect of mathematics is less emphasized. Thus mathematics is primarily conceived as working with ideas and subsequently getting right answers. Effective practice and mastery of skills are held to depend on an understanding of the meaning of numerals and of mathematical processes.

The second major trend comes from the discovery that the origin of modes of thought of most children occurs in the earlier years of life, particularly during the elementary school period. Consequently there has been a growing interest in the revision of introductory college programs, in high school curricula and methods, and finally in the educational processes of the elementary school.

Also the opinion has been developed that the learning of mathematics through all levels of instruction can be facilitated by a curricular plan which would involve a continuous and progressive development of mathematical concepts. The result of this on elementary teaching has resulted in attempts to devise for the familiar arithmetic, interpretations which are more acceptable mathematically and which are at the same time comprehensive to children. Also there have been efforts to add to the elementary curriculum elements of other traditional mathematical subjects which deal with content and ideas familiar to children in their ordinary environment.   This last development is the reason for interest in geometry, logic, and sets in the early grades.

Consequently, the efforts of the mathematics educators in emphasizing meaningful arithmetic combined with the more intellectual analysis of the mathematicians to produce a new view of the familiar grade school mathematics. For the elementary school, modern mathematics is no more than that, including ideas from the study of geometry, logic, and sets. It is characterized by teaching methods which attempt to establish, in the learner, the notion that the true significance of arithmetic today is a source of pattern—the patterns of numbers leading to higher mathematics.   The methods are based largely on a discovery approach, assuming that, in the words of Jerome Bruner, "for a child to be stimulated by his environment he must be armed with the expectancy that there is something to find out."

Classroom experience with the new mathematics in the elementary school suggests that it is learned more effectively than conventional arithmetic. In many schools in the past it has been noted that children who approach arithmetic in the primary grades in an alert and eager manner are frustrated and bored with mathematics by the end of elementary school.   Arithmetic teaching has sometimes been justly criticized as being sterile, uninspiring matter of cajoling or forcing children into a dreary memorization of facts and routines, causing the children difficulty in applying to problems of their every day lives the mathematics they have supposedly learned. Perhaps the reason for the contrast between the atmosphere created by the newer programs is due to the emphasis on the discovery of ideas and relationships rather than on special practice skills. Indeed, the very process of discovery demands an intense use of previously learned skills and provides a most vital kind of practice.

One need not be disturbed by the fact that the ideas and relationships, as studied in a variety of newer programs, are expressed in terms and symbols which are new to most of us who were trained in conventional methematics curricula. Meeting these things for the first time, one needs but to accept some modifications in the familiar vocabulary and to be willing to analyze some previously self-evident ideas in order to begin to feel at home with the new mathematics. Thus any teacher or prospective teacher, if he is willing to invest some time and effort, can prepare himself to participate in the excitement and stimulation which has been generated wherever the new mathematics has been tried in the elementary school.

TEACHING FOR UNDERSTANDING

The most significant change in the new look of mathematics is that of attitude. We are no longer seeking the one best method or technique. It has been realized that there is no one way to teach, only better ways. Variety of application toward the common goal of understanding is now the trend. This emphasizes the teaching of arithmetic in its proper perspective. To teach for understanding one must take into consideration the developmental level of the children being taught in the specific classroom, and the level of difficulty of the skill or understanding being taught. Variety in presentation and application plays an important part in this concept of teaching.

As Bruner states: "Somewhere between apathy and wild excitement there is an optimum level of aroused attention that is ideal for classroom activity. What is that level?" It is the purpose of this discussion to attempt to define these levels.

If modern-day education is going to educate the child to mathematical competency and understanding, the elementary school curriculum needs to be built upon the following basic principles:

1. The child needs to discover, understand, and master the various mathematical concepts. For example, understanding the concept of the number 4 would be indicated by such abilities as knowing that 4 is one more than 3 and one less than 5; knowing that 4 is more than 0, 1, 2, 3, but less than 5, 6, 7, 8, 9; using symbols to represent the fourth object in a series; using number symbols to represent a set (group) such as ////, or ○○○○; mastering the operation of sets of 4 in addition, subtraction, multiplication, and division. In such a manner the other concepts of "4" would be developed.

2. The child needs to discover, understand, and master the various mathematical meanings, such as knowing that 678 is six hundreds, seven tens, and eight ones; representing the number 678 with a pocket chart, place-value frame, abacus, or counters, and explaining the role of place-value in our number system and illustrating its use.

Other meanings include knowing that addition and multiplication are combining actions, whereas subtraction and division are separating actions; explaining the "equal addition" technique of compound subtraction; explaining why in subtraction of fractions, when the denominators are alike, the process is accomplished by subtracting the numerators but not the denominators; explaining the inversion or common denominator methods of dividing fractions; and understanding the relationship between the various processes in addition and multiplication, subtraction and division, addition and subtraction, and multiplication and division.

3. Once the child's understanding of the how and why of arithmetic develops, he needs to work for automatic mastery to become skillful in the use of mathematics. This means being able to compute, check results, measure accurately, describe various numerical situations, and interpret charts and graphs.

4. Throughout the entire instructional program the development of *problem-solving ability* must be carried on. Problems give purpose to the arithmetic instruction and are basic to the introduction and application of new concepts, facts, and processes. Problem solving relates to situations in all phases of the mathematical program. *All drill and practice exercises or sequences should involve problem solving.*

A mathematical problem is a challenging mathematical situation, one that requires thinking for its solution. A problem may be expressed in written form using words, or using mathematical symbols only, such as $37 + 14 = \triangle$.

Some considerations with respect to problem solving follow.

(a) Both word or verbal problems, and equations or mathematical sentences. require critical reading for their solution. The child must visualize the situation involved. This is necessarily part of the child's direct or vicarious experience.

(b) Children need to recognize what is given and what is to be found, and then think out what action is needed to solve the problem. The mathematics of each process involved must be understood clearly. For example, children who know subtraction only as "taking away" cannot be expected to recognize comparison-subtraction situations as subtraction.

(c) To encourage critical reading, discussion, or dramatization, verbal problems should be expressed in a variety of ways. For example, extraneous numerals or other information may be included. Essential information may be omitted. All numerals may be omitted. The word "left" may be used in an addition situation; the work "together" in a subtraction situation.

(d) Children need to be encouraged to write several different equations for a particular verbal problem. For example: If the temperature today rose from a low of 18 degrees to a high of 74 degrees, what was the rise? Appropriate equations are:

  (1) $18 + \triangle = 74$ (3) $74 - \triangle = 18$

  (2) $74 - 18 = \triangle$ (4) $\triangle + 18 = 74$

(e) Children need to be encouraged to write several verbal problems based upon a single equation.

(f) Where the computation involved in solving a problem is complicated, children need to be encouraged to estimate the result before computing. They should also be encouraged to use more than one algorism in computing.

Verbal Problems

These are descriptions of experience situations expressed in written form which children interpret to find the solution to the mathematical problem involved.

Dramatizing Verbal Problems. Children interpret and/or dramatize the given situation. They then write, analyze, and solve as indicated.

Example: Margaret has 35 dolls in her collection. Carol said she would bring 6 dolls that she has at home. How many dolls will they have altogether? (*Equation*: $35 + 6 = N$. *Solution*: $35 + 6 = 41$; They will have 41 dolls altogether.)

The Wirt High School football team scored 21 points during the first half. They scored 12 points during the second half. What was their total score for the football game? (*Equation*: $21 + 12 = N$. *Solution*: $21 + 12 = 33$; They scored 33 points during the football game.)

Describing Experience Situations, Based on Equations. Present a mathematical equation. Ask individual children to relate an experience situation based on the given equation.

Example: $25 + 5 = N$.
Matt had a quarter. He found a nickel. How much did he have now?

$$23 - N = 11.$$

Pam had 23 pieces of candy. She gave some to Matt. She had 11 left. How many pieces of candy did she give Matt?

$$24 - N = 12.$$

Mrs. Baker ordered 24 bottles of soda for the party. Twelve arrived. How many were missing?

Supplying Numbers. Have the children suggest various quantities for situations. Then have them write the equations to solve the situations given.

Example: Christy earned some money and then she spent part of it. How much did she have left? ($35 - 9 = N$, etc.)

Matt has a stamp collection. For his birthday his grandmother gave him an envelope of stamps. How many stamps did he have now? ($378 + 77 = N$)

Recognizing Extraneous Data. Present experience situations.

Example: In the pet shop Andrew counted 18 brown puppies, 7 black puppies, and 9 kittens. How many puppies were there?

In a baseball game 12 men struck out, 8 men hit singles, 5 men walked, and 3 men hit home runs. How many men got on base?

Completing Descriptions of Experience Situations. Children suggest ways to complete descriptions given.

Example: Matt wants to buy a 25-cent book.
Pamela put $7 in the bank yesterday.
Christy has sold 27 boxes of Girl Scout cookies.

Situations Expressed with Mathematical Symbols

Names for Numbers. Give 2 additions or subtractions. Have the children verbally or written show other names for the number expressed.

Series A	Series B
6 + 1	5 − 1
4 + 3	7 − 3
Continue	Continue

Give several additions and/or subtractions. Have the children cross out any that do not belong in the series, and then continue each series given.

Series A	Series B
6 + 3	9 + 4
1 + 9 (x)	12 + 1
5 + 4	7 + 8 (x)
2 + 7	5 + 8
Continue	Continue

Give exercises as follows. (Do not limit the exercises to just addition and subtraction.)

$$9 = (5 + 4, 24 - 15, 163 + 8 - 162), \text{etc.}$$
$$15 = \triangle + \square, \text{etc.}$$
$$0 = \square - \triangle, \text{etc.}$$

Determinations of True or False Mathematical Sentences. Give mathematical sentences such as the following. For each false sentence the children are to write 5 (or more) true sentences.

Addition

$$5 + 7 = 6 + 6 \text{ (true)}$$
$$8 + 0 = 3 + 0 \text{ (false) } (8 + 0 = 5 + 3 + 0, 8 - 5 = 2 + 1)$$

Subtraction

$$7 = 5 - 2 \text{ (false; } 7 = 10 - 3, 9 - 2 = 11 - 4, \text{ etc.)}$$
$$9 - 5 = 10 - 3 \text{ (false; } 9 - 5 = 10 - 6, 9 - 4 = 10 - 5, \text{ etc.)}$$

Number Families. A number family consists of the pair of commutative addition facts, and the inverse subtraction for each; for example:

Commutative Addition Facts	Inverse Subtraction Facts
5 + 2 = 7	7 − 2 = 5
2 + 5 = 7	7 − 5 = 2

Give an addition fact and its inverse subtraction fact. Have the children write the other two related facts.

Given	Solution
$4 + 5 = 9$	$5 + 4 = 9$
$9 - 5 = 4$	$9 - 4 = 5$

Give an addition and its commutative fact. Children write the two inverse subtraction facts.

Given	Solution
$7 + 2 = 9$	$9 - 2 = 7$
$2 + 7 = 9$	$9 - 7 = 2$

Give a single addition or subtraction fact. Have the children write the three related facts.

Given	Solution
$6 + 3 = 9$	$3 + 6 = 9$
	$9 - 3 = 6$
	$9 - 6 = 3$

Give a number. Have the children first write another name for the number (an addition or subtraction fact) and then write the four related facts.

Given	Solution
8	$6 + 2 = 8$
	$2 + 6 = 8$
	$8 - 2 = 6$
	$8 - 6 = 2$

Give three numbers, example: 4, 3, and 7. Have the children write as many facts as they can using these numbers.

Given	Solution
4, 3, and 7	$4 + 3 = 7$
	$3 + 4 = 7$
	$7 - 3 = 4$
	$7 - 4 = 3$

What is being suggested is that problem solving be treated as an integral part of the entire mathematics program. Problem solving is not the goal of all mathematics; it is only part of the entire instructional program.

How can this approach be accomplished? First of all, introduce each new concept by the use of true-to-life situations. These situations must be real, child-like, and entirely possible at the age level of the child.

Secondly, a multiple approach to the solution of the problem should be advocated. It should be realized that each child learns at a different rate in a different manner, depending upon his overall maturity and experiences. This means that varying amounts of time and thought are needed for different children to learn each new step or concept. Relating the new content or process to what the child already knows is necessary. Questions that ask the child to think through, or explore and find out, are suggested. In this manner each child finds the answer to the question or exercise from the standpoint of his own understanding. If the child understands how the processes operate and why, he will obtain the correct solution to the problem. The emphasis is placed upon the child's understanding of the problem situation and the processes involved. The correct answer is still important, but understanding and meaning are more important.

The following problem is an example of the multiple approach: "Matt has 42 apples. He wants to divide them into 6 equal sets (groups). How many apples will be in each set (group)?"

The children are told to solve the problem in any manner they can. Examples of possible solutions include:

(a)

$$42 \div 6 = N, N = 7, 42 \div 6 = 7$$

There will be 7 apples in each set (group).

(b)

$$\begin{array}{r} 7 \\ 6\overline{)42} \\ \underline{42} \\ 0 \end{array} \qquad \begin{array}{r} 7 \\ \times 6 \\ \hline 42 \end{array}$$

There will be 7 apples in each set (group).

(c) How many 6's are there in 42?

$$6N = 42$$
$$N = 7$$
$$6 \times 7 = 42$$

There will be 7 apples in each set (group).

(d)

42		18	
$\underline{-6}$	(1)	$\underline{-6}$	(5)
36		12	
$\underline{-6}$	(2)	$\underline{-6}$	(6)
30		6	
$\underline{-6}$	(3)	$\underline{-6}$	(7)
24		0	
$\underline{-6}$	(4)		
18			

There will be 7 apples in each set (group).

(e)

$$
\begin{array}{cl}
6 & (1) \\
+6 \\
\hline
12 & (2) \\
+6 & (3) \\
\hline
18 \\
+6 & (4) \\
\hline
24
\end{array}
\qquad
\begin{array}{cl}
24 \\
+6 & (5) \\
\hline
30 \\
+6 & (6) \\
\hline
36 \\
+6 & (7) \\
\hline
42
\end{array}
$$

There will be 7 apples in each set (group).

(f)

OOOOOOO   OOOOOOO   OOOOOOO   OOOOOOO   OOOOOOO   OOOOOOO

There will be 7 apples in each set (group).

Six alternative ways of solving the same problem have been presented. In each case the correct answer was obtained, but in each case the child was operating at a different level of competency. One could not expect a child operating at level (f) to be able to operate at level (a) overnight. The emphasis is placed upon understanding and meaning, not just the correct answer. Developing these various ways of solution is a common-sense teaching method, since even the most complex of mathematical understandings must develop from very simple and basic principles. Relating the unknown to what is known through a vast variety of experiences will result in the child reasoning out for himself and thereby gaining a greater understanding of the number system.

Once these various alternative methods have been explored and discussed, the child is led from his level of competency toward the more efficient ways of solving the mathematical problem. In this way the child develops an insight into better ways of solving the various processes.

The many instructional devices play an important role in the overall instructional program. The number line, abacus, pocket chart, place-value frame, hundreds board, tens blocks, and arithmetic notebooks are just a few that will lend background and meaning to the development of problem-solving ability.

Once the various concepts and processes have been taught, give the children proving problems. These are word problems that show the child that he understands the new concept or processes. Have them solve the problem in the generally accepted manner and then prove their findings by the use of an alternative method. In so doing, the child demonstrates that he understands the process or concept and is not just merely checking his work by a purely mechanical process.

There should also be experiences with problems containing no numbers, thereby emphasizing that thinking must be used in all solutions. Problems should be given that include extraneous information that must be sorted out. Problems lacking essential information should also be given. Here the child describes what information is needed in order to solve the problem.

The overall teaching of mathematics places the emphasis upon mathematically meaningful teaching but ties the mathematical aspects to its basic concepts and in turn to social applications. The "think through" approach replaces the "show and tell" approach that has been prevalent for so many years.

The characteristics of the modern mathematics program may be summarized as follows

1. Deemphasizes computation.
2. Mathematically correct.
3. The "discovery" method may be applied to all phases of the program.
4. The concept of "sets" is used throughout.
5. Emphasis is placed upon numeration and systems of numeration.
6. Emphasis of deeper thinking (logic, proof, deductive reasoning).
7. Continual use of problem-solving approach.
8. Use of precision (mathematical vocabulary).

READINESS FOR NUMBER

Children at all grade levels of the elementary school throughout the United States present a wide range of number abilities and interests. In the typical class one may find children who have a sizable amount of mathematical knowledge and readiness for new work. Others, in the same class, have a vague, inaccurate mathematical background, a lack of ability to make normal progress, and frequently living in an environment offering a limited range of mathematical and social-living experiences. The problem of improving teaching and learning mathematics in these situations remains urgent.

Today children no longer merely try to memorize symbols; they are learning at a very early age the meaning of numbers by making practical use of it at their home and school situations. They are learning to think quantitatively. Mathematics has come to have such an important place in our modern life that children need to understand it as a means of effective living. To know why and when is as necessary as to know how to perform an operation in mathematics.

The teacher's task is to direct the children to study numbers so that they may develop, enlarge, and clarify their ideas of the number system. Classroom procedure selected should instruct the children in the ways to do number thinking, and direct them into an independent study of numbers. This represents an important challenge to teachers who aim to offer guidance in the methods of studying numbers systematically.

One of the most important realizations resulting from the study of mathematics through these past years is that thinking in mathematics and an understanding of the mathematical meaning of numbers and processes must take precedence over the mechanical manipulation of numbers. Mathematical concepts and meanings should be developed over a long period of time through the use of socially significant situations before computational aspects are stressed.

The meaning theory conceives of mathematics as an organized series of related ideas, processes, and principles. It is quite the opposite of the drill theory, which holds that mathematics is a mass of separate and unrelated fragments.

Mathematics cannot be taught as an isolated subject. All school and community living have potentialities for contributing to mathematical understanding and for further mathematical thinking.

Thinking with numbers is abstract thinking, but the young child's thinking is literal and on a concrete level. He needs a great deal of help to understand the abstractions involved in the study of numbers. Plan activities that will guide the child in recognizing the numerical aspects in familiar situations, introducing a variety of objective materials suitable for developing number concepts, and assisting the individual to make the transition from concrete to abstract thinking. Gradually he will develop from simple abstractions to the more complicated abstractions.

Growth at times is difficult to measure. This transition from the concrete to the abstract is important at every point and at every grade level where a new mathematical concept or process is to be reinforced. Furthermore, when a child fails to recall a combination or method of a mathematical process it is necessary to reintroduce significant situations and objective material so that a meaningful basis is secured.

Readiness in mathematics, like readiness in any other of the fundamental learning processes, means that the child is ready to learn a new concept with meaning. Previously, readiness was considered synonymous with mental maturity and grade placement. It is now recognized that readiness in mathematics is a function not only of mental maturity and inner growth but also of previous experiences, methods of learning, interests, attitudes, and purposes. Before a child can be expected to learn computational number skills he must be exposed to many number experiences. Informal teaching situations are necessary wherein the child can develop his basic number concepts naturally. Many of these situations arise spontaneously from the child's common everyday experiences. Enumerating objects is a natural outgrowth of the child's exploring of his surroundings, and the number experiences which he will encounter in the primary grades should be an integral part of the various areas of learning. These number experiences should deal with concrete objects, as number symbols will become meaningful to him only as they are associated with tangible things. As the child develops his basic number concepts, he will also begin to acquire fundamental number skills which should be accompanied by good mathematical habits. This developmental process should be introduced when his previous experiences have brought him to the stage where he can take on the new learnings with understanding and meaning.

Readiness in mathematics should be regarded as that period in the learning situation when the child's background for learning a new concept is appraised, foundational experiences are provided, and a purpose for the new learning is established in the mind of the learner. One of the main tasks of the teacher during the period of readiness is to create a problem situation that will challenge the child's interest and provide the feeling of need that is basic to discovery and experimentation.

Readiness is a basic prerequisite for learning. The establishment of concepts and meanings, continuously and progressively, as the child matures and moves forward in the study of numbers, is what is known as mathematical readiness. This assumes that the child's mode of thinking becomes more refined as each step is taken and that he has sufficient experience to qualify him to act in more mature and systematic ways. It also implies that at his level, he has the ability to integrate or reorganize his experiences.

SUMMARY

Mathematics is more than a set of specific skills and understandings. It is a system of quantitative and qualitative thinking including facts, concepts, principles, and processes which are so closely interrelated that they cannot be separated in practice. This kind of thinking develops slowly and needs the incentive of being functional. Mathematics needs to be more of a challenge to the child's intelligence than to his memory.

It is the major goal of this book to help teachers of mathematics to teach in a more meaningful manner, both mathematically and socially. Instruction in such a program should:

1. Develop an appreciation of how numbers have facilitated human progress, and of the social significance of mathematics in the affairs of life.

2. Develop concepts and vocabularly basic to quantitative thinking.

3. Develop understanding, accuracy, and mastery of the essential skills.

4. Develop the right attitudes and interests to form a background for continued interest in and use of mathematics.

5. Develop an inquiring attitude of mind through the use of problems for which the children seek pertinent facts and numbers in the content fields, in basic texts, and in reference materials.

Based upon this philosophy the remainder of this book is organized around the following content areas:

1. Numbers and numerals
2. Sets and sentences
3. Whole numbers
4. Rational numbers
5. Measurement and geometry
6. Other systems and bases

Each of these areas is further developed by the inclusion of the mathematical concepts necessary for understanding and meaning, presented in ascending order of difficulty at the appropriate grade-level designations, together with illustrative teaching techniques of various mathematical skills and understandings with the inclusion of evaluative materials for the individual concepts.

chapter 2

Numbers and Numerals

Children when entering first grade have considerable knowledge and under-standing of number relations and experiences with concrete objects. This knowledge, obtained through eyes, ears, and hands, is real and meaningful. The first-grader is usually ready and anxious for number experiences and therefore ready for a progressively expanding number program. The teacher should use common everyday experiences of the home and school. Early instruction should deal with concrete objects that the children can see, touch, and count. Even though early instruction may seem informal and incidental, the teacher should have a planned program. Most children know something about mathematics, but need guidance in organizing what they know.

COUNTING

Counting in its simplest form is mere rote counting, but counting may be so developed as to include grouping. There are five stages in the complete process of counting: (1) rote counting, (2) rational counting, (3) comparison, (4) re-production, and (5) grouping.

1. *Rote counting* requires only the saying of the number names in correct sequences.

Example: 1, 2, 3, 4, 5, 6, 7, 8, 9, 10, etc. It does not involve the under-standing of what the number stands for. The child is merely verbalizing.

2. *Rational counting* tells how many objects there are in a set. This re-quires the child to identify the number with a specific set of objects. As the child touches each object he associates the correct number name with it.

Example: A set of four blocks are on the table. The child is asked to tell how many blocks there are in the set. As he counts 1, 2, 3, 4,—he touches one block at a time and tells you that there are a total of four blocks, not the fourth block, in this case. If the child has difficulty with rational counting lead him to see one-to-one correspondence. This involves matching, not counting. Use a set of objects and have the child match another set, one at a time to the first set.

For example, match a group of children with a set of chairs, to show in this case that for every child there is a chair.

3. *Comparison* is the noting of differences in regard to quantity, size, weight, distance, and time. Numbers are used to denote this comparison. They themselves do not possess "quantity," "weight," "size," "distance," or "time." Exercises include: Which numbers denote a larger quantity than 6: 1, 3, 8, 9, 5, 4, 7? Which numbers denote a smaller quantity than 7: 2, 5, 6, 9, 3, or 4? Comparison should be of two types: *exact*, where the child gains the understanding that there are two more in this set than in the other, or this set has three less than the other set; and *crude*, where the child develops the use of estimation in comparing the size, weight, distance, or time, of different sets of objects.

4. *Reproduction* is the selection of a certain number of objects from a larger set of objects. The child must understand the one-to-one relationship between numbers and objects to obtain the correct answer. Many experiences should be given the child in developing this ability. Such experiences might be: Show a set of 5 blocks. Give me a set of 9 sticks. Take 5 blocks from that set. Put a set of 7 clothespins on the table.

5. *Grouping* is the association of a number with a set of objects. Many varied experiences should be provided for the children to recognize numbers in different patterns. *It is very important that no one pattern become associated with any one number.* Here the child is developing the ability to separate a larger set of objects into smaller sets, and to take smaller sets of objects and combine them into one large set. Activities with materials in which the child takes a recognized set of objects—for example 5 blocks—and discovers that a set of 3 blocks and a set of 2 blocks when combined form a set of 5 blocks; a set of 2 blocks and a set of 3 blocks when combined form a set of 5 blocks; a set of 4 blocks and a set of 1 block when combined form a set of 5 blocks; a set of 1 block and a set of 4 blocks when combined form a set of 5 blocks; a set of 5 blocks and a set of 0 blocks when combined form a set of 5 blocks; and a set of 0 blocks and a set of 5 blocks when combined form a set of 5 blocks; such activities contribute to the overall readiness of mathematics instruction and develop a meaningful understanding of numbers.

Multiple counting is developed as a means of faster counting. Opportunities of many and varied experiences wherein the skill can be developed are the keys to the success of its presentation. Crayons, chalk, blocks, clothespins, books, sticks, and later the abacus, the hundreds board, and the number line are just a few of the many materials that can be used to develop meaning and understanding of the skill. As a first step in multiple counting the children must be able to count meaningfully, know that a number measures a set, understand the serial order of numbers, and be able to count by tens. The understandings and skills that should be developed are included in the succeeding overall scope and sequence of counting.

The various counting skills and understandings to be developed include the following. The child should be able to:

Grade I

1. Count by rote to 100.
2. Count by rote to 100 beginning with any numeral less than 100.
3. Count by twos, fives, tens, to 100.
4. Count by odd and even numerals through 100.
5. Count ordinal numerals through tenths.
6. Count rationally beginning with any number less than 100.
7. Use tally marks to record the number of objects in a set.
8. Determine the actual number of objects in a set of 100 or less by counting.
9. Recognize at a glance sets of 2, 3, 4, or 5 objects arranged in varying patterns and be able to tell the total number of objects in the set.
10. Recognize at a glance 6, 7, 8, 9, or 10 objects arranged in varying patterns and be able quickly to give the total of objects in the set.

Grade II

1. Count by ones, twos, fives, tens, and hundreds to 1,000.
2. Count rationally up to 1,000 by beginning with any numeral less than 1,000.
3. Determine at a glance the number of objects in randomly arranged sets (number of objects not exceeding 10) and explain how the cardinal number was determined.
4. Count the number of objects in a set and determine without regrouping whether the set can be divided into two equal parts.
5. Count by tens beyond 100 by beginning with any number from 1 through 9.
6. Count by twos, threes, fours, fives, sixes, sevens, eights, nines, tens, hundreds, 1,000's, beginning with any number that may be given.

Grades III through VI

1. Maintain previous learnings.

READING, WRITING, AND MEANING OF NUMBERS AND NUMERALS

A thorough understanding and mastery of a numeration system is essential if one is to use that system efficiently. A full understanding of its structure and of its basic principles is imperative for both teachers and pupils.

The prerequisite for gaining the meaning of numbers is the ability to count before attempting to work with the concepts of an individual number. There are many ways in which a child may be guided to discover the various understandings.

The definition between "number" and "numeral" must be understood.

1. A numeration system is a method of naming numbers. In a numeration system a set of symbols is used to represent numbers. These symbols are grouped together or combined in a special way.

2. Numerals are symbols used to represent numbers. They are something that can be read, written, seen, and erased. The symbol is used to represent a number idea.

3. Number is an abstract idea. It is an idea that is received by looking at the number of objects in a set. It is a means of communicating quantitative ideas to others. Five and 5 are numerals, but when we speak of our five fingers we speak of and think of a definite quantity; this is the number five. The idea of five is represented by writing the numeral 5 or number name 5. Later the child discovers that each number has many names—different names for the same number idea.

Number Idea	Number Names
xxxxx	5; 4 + 1; 6 − 1; 20/4; 1 × 5; etc.

Every numeration system in existence has been developed to satisfy a need— man's need for a method of counting, of communicating ideas of quantity, and a method of recording numbers. Every numeration system was developed in the same manner. The key word in the initial development of a mathematical system is *agreement*. Early man agreed upon a set of symbols, assigned a value

EGYPTIAN NUMERATION SYSTEM

Egyptian Numeral	Number Named	Meaning of Picture Symbol
I	1	Stroke
∩	10	Cattle hobble or oxen yoke
℗	100	Coil of rope
⸙	1,000	Lotus plant
⸜	10,000	Bent finger
⸜	100,000	Tadpole
⸙	1,000,000	A god with arms supporting the sky

to each symbol and set down definite ways of combining these symbols to represent numbers.

A quick look at some of the early numeration systems and their basic structure will help better understand the structure of the Hindu-Arabic numeration system.

1. The Egyptian numeration system was called an *additive system* of numeration because the number was determined by adding together the value of each numeral.

$$∩11 = 10 + 1 + 1 = 12$$

2. The position of the numeral was unimportant.

$$11∩ = 12 \qquad 1 ∩ 1 = 12$$

3. The Egyptian had no symbol for zero because there was no need for such a symbol.

ROMAN NUMERATION SYSTEM

Roman Numeral	Value of Numeral
I	1
V	5
X	10
L	50
C	100
D	500
M	1,000

The Roman system is the only older system with practical applications today. Because of its practicality, much about it is taught in elementary schools. The Roman system should be compared with the Hindu-Arabic system to provide a deeper understanding and appreciation of the system.

1. To determine the value of a numeral, the Romans added and subtracted their numerals

$$XII = 10 + 1 + 1 = 12 \qquad IX = 10 - 1 = 9$$

2. Position of symbols, except for subtraction, was unimportant and there was no symbol for zero.

CHINESE NUMERATION SYSTEM

Chinese Symbol	Value
一	1
二	2
三	3
囗	4
五	5
六	6
七	7
八	8
九	9
十	10
百	100

The Chinese used symbols to represent the numerals from 1 through 9 and separate symbols for powers of 10.

Multiplication was used to indicate number value. The multiplication avoided the repetition of symbols.

$$七 十 = 7 \times 10 = 70$$

$$三 百 八 十 = (3 \times 100) + 8(10) = 380$$

The Chinese numeration system is called a *multiplication* (or multiplicative) *numeration system*.

HINDU-ARABIC NUMERATION SYSTEM

This numeration system is also called the *decimal numeration system* or the *base-ten numeration system* because it is based on the number 10.

The Hindu-Arabic numeration system incorporates two features which make easier the representation of numbers and the performance of mathematical operations:

1. Place value (position)
2. The symbol zero

Symbols and Their Values

1. The base-10 numeration system uses ten basic numerals (0, 1, 2, 3, 4, 5, 6, 7, 8, 9) called digits.

2. The value of each digit depends on its place or position in the numeral. *Example*: The numeral 3456, is a four-digit numeral. The numeral 3456 has four place-value positions.

$$\text{Th} * \text{H} * \text{T} * \text{O}$$
$$\overline{3 \ * \ 4 \ * \ 5 \ * \ 6}$$
$$* \quad * \quad *$$

The digit 3 means 3 thousands = 3000
The digit 4 means 4 hundreds = 400
The digit 5 means 5 tens = 50
The digit 6 means 6 ones = 6
                                          3456

Number and Number Names (combining symbols to represent numbers)

1. The numeral 3456 means

$$3000 \quad + \quad 400 \quad + \quad 50 \quad + \quad 6$$
$$(3 \times 1000) \quad + \quad (4 \times 100) \quad + \quad (5 \times 10) \quad + \quad (6 \times 1)$$

2. To make numerals with five or more digits easier to read, the numerals, are separated into sets of 3 digits called *periods*. Periods are separated by the use of commas:

		PERIODS		
Trillions	Billions	Millions	Thousands	Ones
H T O	H T O	H T O	H T O	H T O
5 6 7,	0 1 0,	9 7 2,	6 0 4,	3 7 2

To read this numeral, read the numeral in each period and say the period name. Avoid use of "and" in reading numerals. Read: 567 trillion, 10 billion, 972 million, 604 thousand, 372.

The various reading, writing, and meaning skills and understandings as regards number and numeral to be developed include the following. The child should be able to:

Grade I

1. Begin to develop the concept that number is an idea we get by looking at sets of objects. Numeral is something we can read, write, see, and erase.
2. Read and write numerals by ones, twos, fives, and tens, to 100.
3. Read and write number words through 100.
4. Read ordinal words through tenth.
5. Identify odd and even numbers.
6. Read ordinal names through twentieth.

Grade II

   1. Write thousands, hundreds, tens, and ones in correct columns.
   2. Read number words through thousands.
   3. Relate "teens" and decade number words.
   4. Use symbols and words for one-half, one-third, two-thirds, three-fourths, one-fourth, and one-fifth.
   5. Use ordinals correctly as needed in mathematical situations.
   6. Read numerals through 1,000.
   7. Read numerals through 1,000 without using the word "and."

Grade III

   1. Review previous learnings.
   2. Write thousands, hundreds, tens, and ones, in correct columns.
   3. Read and write fractions.
   4. Read number words through thousands.

Grade IV

   1. Review previous learnings.
   2. Read and write numerals and number words through billions.
   3. Read and write fractions, decimals, percents.

Grade V

   1. Review previous learnings.
   2. Read and write numerals and number words through billions.
   3. Read and write decimal fractions through hundredths.
   4. Explain composite numbers and review prime numbers.

Grade VI

   1. Review previous learnings.
   2. Read and write decimal numerals through thousandths.
   3. Read and write numerals for positive and negative integers.
   4. Explain the meaning of number bases.

POSITIONAL VALUE (PLACE-VALUE)

The basic structure of the decimal numeration system is that of place value. Every place-value numeration system has a method of grouping called its *base*. It is possible to use any number as a base in building a numeration system. "Ten" is the base of the Hindu-Arabic numeration system. That is, "ten" is the basis for grouping the system. For example:

1. The number of digits used in a system is always equal to the base. Ten is the Hindu-Arabic base, therefore, ten digits (0, 1, 2, 3, 4, 5, 6, 7, 8, 9) are used.

2. Each place-value position has a name that tells its value in terms of ten.

3. Each place-value position has a value 10 times greater than the position to its right and 1/10 of the value of the position to its left.

The following diagram will help children see the importance of ten and make clear the above statements.

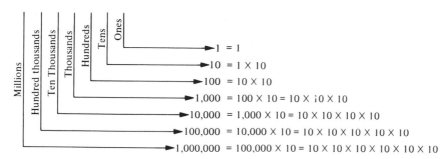

Example: 3,000 may be written 3 × 1,000 or 3 × 100 × 10 or 3 × 10 × 10 × 10

Example:

$$3,000 \text{ may be written } 3 \times 1,000$$
$$\text{or } 3 \times 100 \times 10$$
$$\text{or } 3 \times 10 \times 10 \times 10$$

4. Another way of expressing place value is through the use of *exponents*.[1] The exponent, therefore, expresses the power of the numeral. In 3^4, 3 is the base; 4 is the exponent.

3^4 says: Multiply 3 by itself four times, or $3 \times 3 \times 3 \times 3$
3^4 is read: 3 to the fourth power

5. Using Exponents in Naming Numbers:
By agreement, mathematicians have assigned the following values:
Base 10.

$$1 = 1 \times 10^0$$
$$10 = 1 \times 10^1$$
$$100 = 10 \times 10 = 10^2$$
$$1,000 = 10 \times 10 \times 10 = 10^3$$
$$10,000 = 10 \times 10 \times 10 \times 10 = 10^4$$
$$100,000 = 10 \times 10 \times 10 \times 10 \times 10 = 10^5$$

[1] The definition of an exponent is: a^n is the number having n factors of a. This implies $n - 1$ multiplications, not n multiplications.

Example: 136,456

100,000 +   30,000   +   6,000   +   400   +   50   +   6
(1 × 100,000) + (3 × 10,000) + (6 × 1,000) + (4 × 100) + (5 × 10) + (6 × 1)
(1 × 10^5) +   (3 × 10^4)   +   (6 × 10^3)   + (4 × 10^2) + (5 × 10^1) + (6 × 10^0)

Values Less Than One

In the Hindu-Arabic numeration system numerals with values less than 1 can be recorded. The decimal point separates the ones from units having a value less than 1. All the principles of the decimal system that have been discussed apply to decimal fractions also. Study the following example.

Example: 4.444

$$4 \text{ thousandths} = .004 = \frac{4}{1,000} = 4 \times \frac{1}{1,000} = 4 \times \frac{1}{10^3}$$

$$4 \text{ hundredths} = .04 = \frac{4}{100} = 4 \times \frac{1}{100} = 4 \times \frac{1}{10^2}$$

$$4 \text{ tenths} = .4 = \frac{4}{10} = 4 \times \frac{1}{10} = 4 \times \frac{1}{10^1}$$

$$4 \text{ ones} = 4.0 = 4 = 4 \times 1 = 4 \times 10^0$$

Sum   = 4.444

1. The value of each digit depends on its place or position.
2. The numeral can be expressed to show the additive property of the decimal numeration system.

$$.004 + .04 + .4 + 4 = 4.444$$

$$\left(4 \times \frac{1}{1,000}\right) + \left(4 \times \frac{1}{100}\right) + \left(4 \times \frac{1}{10}\right) + (4 \times 1)$$

Exponents can be used in renaming numbers.

$$\left(4 \times \frac{1}{10 \times 10 \times 10}\right) + \left(4 \times \frac{1}{10 \times 10}\right) + \left(4 \times \frac{1}{10}\right) + (4 \times 1)$$

$$\left(4 \times \frac{1}{10^3}\right) + \left(4 \times \frac{1}{10^2}\right) + \left(4 \times \frac{1}{10^1}\right) + (4 \times 10^0)$$

3. In reading decimal fractions, the numeral is read exactly as any whole number is read. Then the place-value position of the last digit at the right is named.

.956 is read: 956 thousandths

.0019 is read: 19 ten thousandths

4. That every place-value position has a name which tells its value in terms of 10 can be seen from the expanded notation.

5. Each place-value position has a value 10 times greater than the position to its right and 1/10 of the value of the position to its left:

$$\frac{1}{100} \times 10 = \frac{10}{100} = \frac{1}{10}$$ One-tenth is 10 times greater than one-hundredth,

$$\frac{1}{1,000} \times 10 = \frac{10}{1,000} = \frac{1}{100}$$ One-hundredth is 10 times greater than one-thousandth

$$\frac{1}{100} = \frac{1}{10} \text{ of } \frac{1}{10} = \frac{1}{10} \times \frac{1}{10} = \frac{1}{100}$$

$$\frac{1}{10} = \frac{1}{10} \text{ of } 1 = \frac{1}{10} \times 1 = \frac{1}{10}$$

SUMMARY

The teaching of 10 as the first two-place numeral is important because it lays the foundation for understanding that our number system is based on ten. If a child can associate the idea of units with the numbers 0 through 9, as 4 units, 7 units, 9 units, he will be able to understand the meaning of zero in the numeral 10. By combining ten sticks into a set of 10, the child discovers that he has one ten and no units; hence he writes this in abstract form as 10. In this case, the zero denotes absence of "unit" quantity.

As he adds a stick at a time to his set of ten, he discovers that he has 10 + 1 = 11, 10 + 2 = 12, etc. This is the beginning of the understanding of positional value. He could write the 12 sticks as 12 units, but with our number system with its base of ten he writes abstractly the numeral 12, showing that he has one set of ten sticks and a set of two sticks more. Other materials, such as pictures or dots and dashes on cards or on the chalkboard, could be used to develop the idea of grouping tens and ones.

Encourage the children to record their findings in picture form: 16 might call to mind ////////// //////, ///// ///// ///// /. Further understanding would lead to the following exercises:

16 is ____ ten and ____ units.   ____ is 1 ten and 6 units

With this basic foundation of 10 as the first two-place numeral and the understanding of the "teens numbers," the successive decades can be developed. The children will continue to use the same materials that were used in objectifying the numbers, and in addition will use the abacus, the hundreds chart, and the number line.

The specific place-value skills and understandings that should be developed include the following. The child should be able to:

Grade I

1. Change any number of objects (not exceeding a hundred) into as many sets of ten as possible.

2. Write the appropriate numeral (10, 20, 30, etc.) when it is evident that there is one set of ten, two sets of ten, and so on up to nine sets of ten.

3. Attach the written numeral to any number of objects from 1 through 100 when objects are arranged in groups of tens and units:

```
. . . . .      . . . . .
. . . . .      . . . . .      . . . .
```

depicts 24 (without counting by ones).

4. Count by tens and finish by counting by units the number of elements in a set one hundred of less (if number is not divisible by ten).

5. Reproduce with counters or other objects in units of tens and ones, any numeral from 1 to 100.

6. Use tally marks or equivalent in a specially designed place to record the number of subsets of ten in a set and another group of tally marks in a different place to record the remaining subset of elements.

7. Determine by inspection of a two-digit number the greatest number of tens it contains and how many units as a remainder.

8. Use zero as a place-holder.

Grade II

1. Write the appropriate numeral (110, 120, etc.) when it is apparent that there are 11 groups of 10, 12 groups of 10, and so on.

2. Write the appropriate numeral when it is apparent that there are 2–5 hundreds. Use of place-value chart and abacus as means of showing.

3. Represent on the abacus, place-value chart, etc., and number of elements up to 500 by the least number of beads or tally marks.

4. Reproduce with counters or other objects in units of hundreds, tens, and units, any numeral through 500.

5. Determine by inspection the number of hundreds, tens, or units in a given number up to 500 when the number is given in numerals or represented on an abacus. For example, 152 contains:

1 hundred	52 left over
15 tens	2 left over
152 units	

Grade III

1. Show correctly on a money place-value chart any amount of pennies through 500.

2. Show correctly on a place-value chart the number of pennies on a specific amount of money given in dollars and cents.

3. Write the appropriate numeral when it is apparent that there are 51–500 sets of ten; that there are 6–50 sets of hundreds; that there are 1–5 sets of thousands.

4. Correctly use the zero symbol when writing the numerals corresponding to the number represented by the presence or absence of beads in the columns on an abacus.

5. Write the appropriate numeral when it is apparent that there are 0–5 thousands, 0–9 hundreds, 0–9 tens, and 0–9 units.

6. Reproduce with counters or other objects in sets of hundreds, tens, and units any numeral through 5,000.

7. Represent on an abacus, place-value chart, etc., any number of objects or any numeral up to 5,000 by the least number of beads or tally marks.

8. Determine by inspection the number of units, tens, hundreds, or thousands in a given number up to 5,000 when the number is given in numerals or represented on an abacus.

Grade IV

1. Determine by inspection of a three- or four-digit numeral, the equivalence of values when the digits represent:

Example:

728 is equal to 7 hundreds and 2 tens and 8 units or 72 tens and 8 units. 7936 equals 793 tens and 6 units or 79 hundreds and 36 units or 7 thousands and 936 units.

2. Same as above but with a five-digit numeral.

3. Read, write, and recognize zero as a symbol representing at least two meanings:

> the absence of quantity—"Not any"
> to hold a position open

Grade V

1. Determine by inspection a six-digit numeral; how many tens there are in the tens place, hundreds in the hundreds place, thousands in the thousands place, etc.

Grade VI

1. Representative five or more digit numerals on an open-end abacus, place-value chart, etc., in several ways.

2. Reconstruct a five- to ten-digit numeral by any method to illustrate the principle used when regrouping.

TEACHING SUGGESTIONS

Concept: Counting—finding the number of elements in a set

Procedures. 1. Have a child point to objects about the room and count them (windows, children, coat hangers, books on one shelf, desks, erasers at the chalkboard, boys, girls).

2. Arrange objects in sets of one to ten. Have one child count to see how many there are in a set (books in a pile, milk cartons, pencils.) Have another child write on the board the figure that stands for or tells the number. The class acts as judge of correctness of the figure written. Counters may be disks, sticks, clothespins, cards, or any easily obtainable objects. Each pupil should keep a supply of some kind of counters in a bag or box for counting practice.

3. Let the children arrange counters in patterns. Then have them make dot pictures of the pattern and write beside the figure that tells how many counters were used. Domino dot cards are useful for practice in "counting" and may be used later on for practice with the addition combinations. They can easily be made by stamping pieces of construction paper 6 X 10 inches with the cut side of a half-potato dipped in paint. Use the domino cards for "counting on" practice. Hold the card with the larger group of dots at the top. Ask the pupil to tell without counting how many dots are at the top, then count on to give the total.

4. In the classroom situation there are many opportunities for the children to count to find the number of elements in a set. The teacher should take advantage of these numerous occasions: How many children are here today? How many rulers do we have? How many books are needed for our reading group?

5. Use ten heavy cardboard sheets with fasteners to display sets (groups) of one to ten toy whistles, cars, boats, dolls, shovels, etc. Call upon pupils to place the correct number of each group in front of it or to say the correct number of elements in the set.

6. Place several objects in a small sugar sack. Let the pupils guess how many objects are in the sack. The sack can then be emptied and the objects counted. Later the pupils can count by feeling the objects in the sack. This can then be checked by visual count.

7. Put a group of erasers on the table in the front of the classroom. Ask the pupils how many erasers are on the table. They count the erasers aloud and say that there are three erasers. Then add two more to the set, and then ask them to

count the group of erasers again. They count and the answer is five erasers. Keep adding erasers to the original set, thereby increasing the size of the set. Repeat this for several days with various materials such as blocks, books, or pencils, but using different numbers. This shows the children that they can find out how many elements are in a set by counting.

8. Give directions that require children to identify a certain set of elements:

Bring the box that has five flowers in it.
Put these books on the second shelf.
What is the number on the last page of our reading book?
Bring five pieces of paper.
Put three chairs at this table.

9. Give the children practice in discovering that the last number in the counting process gives the total in the series of objects counted.

Concept: Counting—starting with "one" and enlarging the size of the set by successive addition of elements

Procedures. 1. Using objects that the children can handle and count, place one of the objects on the table, have the children tell how many objects they see. After they have answered correctly, have a child come up and add another element to the one already on the table. Ask the class again how many elements are there. Repeat the procedure again with another element being added to the group. Note with the children that as one element is added, the original set becomes larger and thus each successive number represents a larger set.

2. The same technique can be used in counting children. Have one child stand up. The children are asked to tell how many children are standing. Have another child stand. Again the children are asked to tell how many there are. Repeat the procedure until ten children are standing. Show how the original set becomes larger with the addition of a new person.

3. Give each child some clay and ask him to make a nest. Tell a story of a robin who laid an egg a day for five days; as the story progresses, the children make the appropriate number of eggs and place them in the nest.

4. Finger games such as the Five Chickadees, Here's the Beehive, Where Are All the Bees?, and Ten Little Soldiers Standing in a Row, can be used to teach this skill. Poems and songs involving counting can also be used. Counting in unison the number of children present, tables, chairs, or milk cartons, develops a rhythm sound and order for the children as they hear the numbers chanted. Children will discover that as things are counted, as the numbers are pronounced, each single addition of child or element indicates the next number in the sequence.

5. As the children count in unison, move the beads on the abacus to denote the number value. Have the children take turns counting and moving the beads

of the abacus. Later ask which is larger, three or four, and have the children demonstrate with blocks. Then ask how many more blocks are necessary to form a set of four from a set of three blocks. Do this with various sets of elements, demonstrating in each case that just one more element will make the next number in the number sequence.

6. Make a counting chart step by step with the class. First develop the number "one" by having the children point to "one" of anything in the room, one desk, one chair, one book, one pencil, or one window. Then transfer their thinking from the concrete objects to the abstract number names and symbols, such as "one" and "1," by printing them on the chalkboard or the flannelboard. Then put the idea on the counting chart. Begin to develop the number 2. Are there 2 of anything in the room? To stimulate thinking, ask the class what is the difference in value between the number "1" and the number "2." Put the squares and names on the chart so that they can see that there is just one more of something added to 1 to make a set of 2 elements. The rest of the numbers to 10 can be developed and added to the counting chart as the first two were. There is no end of examples and questions one can use to stimulate the thinking of the children. Have the children make counting charts using pictures. Have them make counting charts from different materials, such as blocks or beads, or use the chalkboard. Be sure to ask questions such as "How many more books are in row 5 than there are in row 4?" "How can we make a set of 7 elements from a set of 6 elements?"

7. The following suggestions are word problems that can be used as a basis for understanding or as supplementary exercises. They are strengthened by the use of concrete and semiconcrete examples as shown. (In this case the children have worked with the numbers 1, 2, 3. The number 4 is being developed). "Matt was walking to school and picked up Bob, then Rick, and then Mike. How many boys are there now? Each time Matt stopped to pick up a friend, another boy (element) was added to the set (group). When Mike joined the set, there were already 3 boys (elements) in the set (group). How many boys are there in the group now? Is it true that one more than 3 is 4? Complete the following to make a set of 4 elements and tell what you did, first with words then with numbers. Each of you have 3 pieces of gum. How many more pieces shall I give you so that you will have 4 pieces of gum?" Let the children draw a picture to show their answers.

Concept: Comparisons—big, bigger; large, larger; small, smaller; and the same size as

Procedures. 1. Use geometric shapes previously learned, square, circle, and triangle, and let the children compare to see if the figures are the same size or is one bigger than the other. When comparing any two objects in regard to size, one of the following three relationships exists:

(a) The first square may be the same size as the second. In this case, the second square is the same size as the first.

(b) The first object may be larger than the second. In this case the second object is smaller than the first.

(c) The first square may be smaller than the second. In this case the second square is larger than the first.

2. Develop worksheets and have the children color the larger ball green; the smaller ball red; etc.

3. Play the game Big or Bigger. To play this game you must first fold your paper in half the long way (demonstrate). Next fold it in thirds the short way (demonstrate). Now you have six squares, just as are shown on the chalkboard. In each square are two pictures. One is big and the other is bigger. Draw these two pictures. Under each picture print the word "big" or "bigger," depending upon the size of the picture. (Write the words "*big*" and "*bigger*" on the board to help the children.)

4. A good comparison of the size of objects is found in the use of nested boxes or cans. Here the child opens a box and finds a smaller one inside, opens that and finds another smaller one, until he at last finds the smallest box. After the children have seen the boxes opened and noted that each is smaller than the one seen before, "scramble" them in a large box or bag and have as many children as there are boxes pick out one without seeing the size. Allow a certain length of time for the "team" to put the boxes together correctly.

5. Classroom equipment and materials brought into the room by the children offer excellent opportunities for the comparison of length, width, and size. For example: My jump rope is longer than yours. You have the biggest ball. You aren't as tall as I am. Give me a piece of paper the same size as Bill's. There are many other typical classroom experiences which can lead naturally into a situation calling for on-the-spot comparison.

6. Speak in comparative terms of objects in the room. For example: the tallest child, the largest block. Stress words such as over, under; short, shortest; largest, longest; smaller and smallest.

7. Reproduce a sheet of paper on which you have drawn a circle and square. Have the children draw a circle and a square which is larger (or smaller) than the one on the page. Then let them color the shapes.

Concept: Patterns

Procedures. 1. Display one ball and three blocks. Discuss the four objects and have the children identify which one is different from the rest. When someone decides that the ball is not like any of the other objects, discuss why. Display other sets of objects that are different in some manner from all the other objects in the set. Continue discussing why one is different from all the others.

2. Provide auditory experiences in noticing patterns. For example: The

teacher would display a pattern on the board. She then orally names the objects in the pattern to give the child experiences in hearing the pattern sequence. The child could then repeat the made-up pattern.

3. Let the children string beads and develop patterns of their own design. Question them about their patterns to see if they can explain what the pattern is. If they string beads in a helter-skelter way with no apparent pattern, ask them to try again according to a pattern that you might suggest.

4. Encourage children to discuss patterns they have made with beads and blocks by displaying several interesting patterns on the chalkboard, flannelboard, or bulletin board.

5. Provide duplicated sheets with triangles, circles, and squares printed on them. Have the children color the triangles one color, and all the circles another color, and all the squares a third color. Have them cut out these shapes and form patterns by pasting them onto another sheet of paper.

Concept: Positional relationships—over, under, on, above, below, beside, top, inside, outside, lower, and lowest

Procedures. 1. Have the children come to the chalkboard and place a mark *under* the smaller object. Have another child place a mark *on* the larger object. Continue this activity until the children master the skill. Then move onto comparison of three or more subjects.

2. Have a child describe the position of some object in the classroom, and the other children try to guess what object is being described.

3. Have the children hold a block and as the teacher says the word "over," "under," and "on," they move the block into the position stated (*over* their head, *under* their chair).

Concept: Number concepts 1-10

Procedures. 1. Have several different objects which show a set of one. Let the children match them to see that they are equivalent sets. Discover together that a name is needed to show how many are in each set. Ask the children if they know a name to show this. Anticipate someone saying the word *one*. Write the symbol for *one* on the chalkboard and explain to the children that it is called the numeral 1. Look for other sets of *one* and associate the numeral 1 with the name *one*.

2. Use the flannelboard, place-value chart, or chalkboard and place a numeral 1 on it. From pictures on a table, let the children decide if any belong to the ones family. If the picture does, let them place it on the chalktray. If it does not, have them place it elsewhere.

3. Have several pictures on the chalkboard and have the children identify those that show the numeral 1.

4. Have displays about the room showing a set of *one* and the numeral 1.

5. String beads to emphasize sets of a numeral that the teacher writes on the chalkboard.

6. Draw pictures showing a set of one, two, three, and placing the correct numeral on the appropriate picture.

7. Show cards with various sets represented and have the children tell the number of elements in each set.

8. Have each child make a Number Book which contains a page for each numeral from 1 to 10. On each page have him mount clippings from newspapers and magazines illustrating that number concept. Included could be the figure itself as well as the illustration.

9. Give each child a paper with numerals in squares to play Can You Find Me? As you call out, "My name is seven; can you find me?" each child should cover the seven with a square of construction paper. To introduce the numerals you can show a card or write the figure on the board as you speak the words so the children can begin to associate the name with the shape of figure. This activity can be used with progressively advanced numerals.

10. Bounce a ball while the children count the number of beats. Have one child select the card which tells how many beats there were. (Having the other children write the figure also.)

Concept: Ordinal counting

Procedures. 1. Write the numerals 1 through 10 on the board, then write the ordinal form beneath:

1	2	3	4	5	6	7	8	9	10
first	second	third	fourth	fifth	sixth	seventh	eighth	ninth	tenth

Have the children repeat and discuss. Erase the words (ordinal names) and ask questions such as, "Matt, which is the fifth numeral? Can you show me the tenth numeral? Which is the third?" Have ten children stand in line. Then ask, "Who is tenth in line? What is the sixth person doing? Will the second child come to me?

2. Introduce the concept by asking questions like these: "What grade are you in? This is the _____ year you have been in school." Discuss the children's brothers and sisters at the several grades and decide how many years they have been in school according to whether it is third, fourth, fifth, sixth. From this children will begin to see the ordinal concept of numbers.

3. The children have had experience in counting many things and know that each number has a fixed place in the number sequence. To help them understand the ordinal concept of numbers, have the children sit or stand in line. (Use a small number first.) Have each child give his position, as "I am first," "I am second," "I am third." Make simple requests of the children. "The fourth child in the row—please clap your hands." The third child is asked to bring the

fourth book in the pile to the second child in the row. The second child is asked to jump.

4. Have the children point to the first number in the number line, the second, and so on. Have them point to the first letter in the alphabet, and go on to the tenth letter.

5. Give many opportunities during classroom activities to use the number names to denote location. "Pam, you may be first." "Christann you may be second." "Matt, bring the book that is fourth from the left end of the row." Discuss which is the first row of chairs in the room, then the second, the third, Ask the children, "Who is the first child in the second row?" "Who is the third child in the fourth row?" Make a chart with all the pictures alike and label them first, second, third, fourth, fifth, sixth, seventh, eighth, ninth, tenth. Discuss these grades. Discuss why Grade I is called first grade, why Grade II is called second grade, and so on.

6. Choose five children and have them come to the front of the room. The teacher should stand behind them and she should read the following poem:

> Five little squirrels sat in a tree.
> The first one said, "What do I see?"
> The second one said, "A man with a gun."
> The third one said, "Then we better run."
> The fourth one said, "Let's hide in the shade."
> The fifth one said, "I'm not afraid."
> Then bang went the gun!
> And how they did run!

As the teacher reads the second line of the poem, she should stand behind the first child and put her hand on his shoulders. On the next line she should be behind.the second one and touching him. This should be continued on down the line until the last two lines of the poem. On the last line of the poem each child can run and tap another child and go to his seat. The children chosen should then go to the front of the room and the same process should be repeated. This should be done until everyone in the room has had a chance to be a squirrel. After the children know the poem, the teacher should stop taking an active part in it. The first child should step out when it is his turn, the second when it is his turn, the third, the fourth, and the fifth in their respective turns. Another way to add variety would be to have one of the children stand behind the squirrels and touch each child on the shoulder on the words first, second, third, fourth, and fifth.

7. Place ten objects on the table. Have a child come up and pick up the third block, the second block, the fifth block. If he does it correctly he may tell the next child which block he is to pick up. After using five blocks for awhile, change objects. The objects should be large enough for the children still in their

seats to see. Objects which may be used include books, chalkboard erasers, milk cartons, individual paste jars, crayon boxes, and tempera paint cans.

8. Have ten chairs lined up in the front of the room. Make one child the engineer. He in turn chooses ten children to sit in the cars of the train. As he chooses a child, he designates which chair the child is to take—first, second, third, etc. He does not fill the chairs in order. The child chosen must decide where to sit. If the child sits in the wrong chair, he must go back to his seat and the engineer chooses someone else to sit in that chair. After all of the cars are filled, the engineer tells two children to change places with each other, designating first, second, third, fourth, etc. He must check each time to be sure the right children changed places. If a child moves when he shouldn't or doesn't move when he should, he must go back to his own seat and the engineer chooses someone else to take his place. After a period of time a new engineer is chosen and fills the train and proceeds as before.

9. This technique is built around the use of two charts. The first one has pictures of ten animals. They are the butterfly, the squirrel, the lion, the skunk, the rabbit, the kangaroo, the monkey, the elephant, the fox, and the bird—in that order. The second chart has ten fish that are of different colors. On both the charts a child can be asked to come and point to the second, fifth, or seventh creature on that chart. On the first chart he can later be asked what the second animal is or in which place is the lion or the elephant. On the second chart, the child should be asked what the color of the first fish is or in what position the blue fish or red fish is. The words first, second, third, fourth, fifth, sixth, seventh, ninth, and tenth are lettered under the pictures.

10. If the children are still having trouble with this concept, labels may be put on the windows telling which window is first, second, third, and on up through tenth. One row of coat hangers could be marked in the same way. The drawers in the filing cabinet, each shelf in a group of shelves, the doors on the closed shelves, and the bulletin boards could all have these same labels on them. This would also help the child recognize the printed words and associate them with the spoken ones.

11. Illustrative situations in which ordinals are used follow:
    (a) Days of the month, holidays, birthdays, dates of trips, etc.
    (b) Pages in a book, or lines on a page, as the 87th page, the 21st line, etc. (Page "numbers" are ordinals although cardinal names, as "page 34," are ordinarily used)
    (c) Order in which children bring in materials, as Matt was the 29th one to bring in his book-rental money.
    (d) Order of rows in the multipurpose room.
    (e) Order of position in line for going to lunch.
    (f) Street signs, as 32nd Street, 53rd Street.

12. Have children indicate ordinal positions of particular beads on the tens frame:

34th bead, 46th bead, 67th bead, 89th bead

13. As the child counts collections of small objects have him indicate particular objects.

Example: 26th, 46th, 68th

Concept: Sequence of number names for counting—one, two, three, four, five, six, seven, eight, nine, ten

Procedures. 1. Have the children count aloud. With the use of the flannelboard put the numbers on the board and put the right number of objects under the number. Repeat this several times using different objects each time so that the children begin to get the concept of "2" as meaning two of anything.

2. Have the children start to collect objects for their individual counting box, such as rocks, nuts, popsicle sticks, etc. Then as the children count have them pick up an object for each number.

3. Ask different children to count aloud. As the child counts have another child point to the number on the number line. This will be repeated many times and will also bring up questions as to what numbers come after each number.

4. Let several children go to the board. The rest of the class takes turns counting and the children at the board write the numbers. Ask the children at their desks if the work on the board is correct.

5. Practice counting in play periods by counting off into teams of different numbers. For example, play Squirrel In a Tree and count off in threes, then later count off "by the numbers," 1, 2, 3, 4, 5, or 1, 2, 3, 4, 5, 6, 7, 8, 9, 10.

6. During a music lesson, practice counting the tones on the piano. Sing songs about counting. Let a child play the tones on the piano and the others count the tones. Have a child play the tones and count as he plays.

7. Make a number chart. Practice putting the correct number of objects under the numbers on the flannelboard.

8. Draw pictures about animals. For example, draw a certain number of animals and after the drawings have been made, decide what numbers to put under the picture to tell how many animals there are.

9. *Number Games.* The children form a line at the side of the room, facing the front of the room, the first child playing the engine and the last child the caboose. The child who is the caboose says "one" and moves to the head of the train, becoming the engine. The rear child says "two" and becomes the engine. Each child says his number quickly and moves to the front of the train. The game is played until the train has circled the room back to its starting place.

10. *Rhythm Instrument Game.* Each child in turn picks any rhythm instru-

ment of his choice and after whispering a number (1 to 10) to the teacher, taps the number on his instrument, then asks the class, "How many taps did you hear?" He then chooses a child who tells the number he heard and reproduces it by clapping or tapping. The child then becomes "it." Tapping must be done slowly so that the children can count the taps. This game gives further practice in the ordinal position of numbers as well as teaching the cardinal values by the question "How many?" The teacher then asks, "Did Pam tap the same number Christann tapped?" If the children noticed a difference in the numbers, Pam is asked to listen as Christann retaps her number, counting orally with the taps, if she wishes, to discover the correct answer. She then becomes "it."

11. Reading-readiness books, seatwork and activities offer daily opportunities to use such questions as; "Which one is different from all the others?" "Which one of the books is the same as this one?" Instead of answering the question by describing the objects, the child may refer to them by number. He may be given oral directions such as "Color eight balloons blue," or "Color ten apples red." While he learns the sequence of the numbers as he counts the apples he is also learning to recognize the words "red" and "blue" as the teacher writes them on the chalkboard.

Concept: Rational counting (one-to-one correspondence between elements being counted)

Procedures. 1. Seeing one-to-one correspondence between related elements is necessary before the child can understand, in counting, the one-to-one correspondence between numerals and the elements being counted. *One* refers to the first element counted, *two* to the second element counted, and so on. Experiences involving matching should be confined to groups of not more than ten objects, because the pupils are to match the two sets of objects instead of counting them. Places may be set at the table for five or six children. The pupils determine whether or not there is a chair for each child, a cookie for each child, a straw for each child, a bottle of milk for each child, and so on. Art paper and crayons may be distributed to each row or group of children. One child may determine whether or not there is a piece of paper for each child, a book for each child, a box of crayons for each child, or a pair of scissors for each child. Plan a variety of these experiences. For example, it should sometimes be necessary to put away extra art material or get some more out. This would show the need and worth of counting.

2. Show the children pictures of children with pets. Ask them if there is a pet for each child in the picture. Utilize the opportunities for counting that arise from classroom activities.

3. Have the children count objects by touching each object as they count. Count windows, books, boys, girls, or number of children in each row.

4. The children match the objects of one group with those of another:

Match children with chairs, books, etc.
Match boys with hats.
Place dolls in beds.
Plant plants in their flower pots.
Draw a chair for each doll.
Draw an apple for each child.

5. The children compare sets by matching to see whether the sets contain the same number of elements, or if one set has fewer elements than the other, or one set has more elements than the other.

6. Use and encourage the children to use, words such as "enough," "too many," "more than," "less than," "as many as," or "not enough." Daily practice in following simple directions is useful: Bring enough chairs for the reading circle. Get enough science books for everyone.

7. All primary books have many pictures. Take advantage of these pictures to do rational counting. How many babies did the mother rabbit have? How many eggs did the robin have in the nest? How many puppies are there?

Concept: Counting by twos

Procedures. 1. To introduce the vocabulary of counting by twos, 10 triangles may be drawn on the board. The children count the triangles by ones. Lines encircling the triangles in sets of two are drawn. As the teacher points to each set successively, the teacher and the children count the sets, saying: 2, 4, 6, 8, 10.

2. Ten girls may come before the class and arrange themselves in pairs. The children count them by twos.

3. Ask the children to draw 10 elements of their choice and encircle them in sets of two. The children are to count their own drawings and write down the total number of elements.

4. Use the flannelboard. Show two elements such as balls or ducks, and explain as you add two more elements that the set is increased by two elements. Then have different members of the class go through the process on the flannelboard. How many ducks are there now? (4) Add two more ducks. How many are there now? (6) How many ducks did I add to the set?

5. Use the abacus. Move two beads down. How many are down? Add two more. How many are in the set now? (4) How many elements (beads) were added to the set? Have the children work with this device to further the understanding of counting by twos.

6. Illustrate by drawings on the board. In all of these techniques, the children must count the elements to get the answer. Illustrations on the board can also be done by using the abstract numbers and combinations of drawings and numerals.

7. Use the number line. Have the children mark off on the board under the

number line as they count by twos. Here they can also see how many more 4 is than 2, then 4, 8 than 6, 10 than 8, etc.

8. Have the children place 10 counters on their desks in a line at the top. Then ask them to pull down 2 of the counters from the line of 10 to the bottom of their desk. How many counters do they have at the bottom of their desk? (2). Bring down 2 more (4). Bring down two more (6). And so on.

9. Let the children leaf through a book to page 10, finding pages 2, 4, 6, and 8 as they progress. Be sure that the children realize they skip a page number for each numeral.

10. Place two balls in a two-row egg carton. The children count 2. Add 2 more, the children count 4 and so on until you have reached 12.

Concept: Counting by fives

Procedures. 1. In order to have a proper background of readiness to be introduced to the concept of multiples of five, the children should have been first familiarized with the concepts of tens. They should know how to count by tens to 100 in terms of ten. The idea of counting and grouping by fives should be presented on the concrete level where the pupils can see five actual elements in each group as they count. For example, have someone bring his piggy bank to school, containing at least 100 pennies; or ask a child to bring his bank for counting because it is getting too full or to see whether enough money has been saved for a certain purchase, e.g., (savings stamps at school). As the bank is emptied, the children are led to discover that by grouping the pennies into piles and keeping track of the total number as each group is counted, they are not so apt to lose their place or get mixed up and have to start over again. The children could keep this record of the number counted by the use of tally marks to represent the number of piles of pennies each containing five pennies. Refer to these groups of pennies as "fives" and ask the class why it is a good name for the groups. This is the beginning of the development of the meaning of fives. As the children begin counting the first group, each penny is restacked as it is counted and the sign "5" is set by the pile. The next pile is counted 6, 7, 8, 9, and 10, and the sign "10" is set by the pile, and so on up to 100. When all the fives are counted, comment that counting by ones is very slow when there are large amounts to count. Ask the pupils to try and find a quicker way to recount the stacks of pennies. Lead them by questioning and discussion to discover that, since they already know that the first pile is "5," the second pile is "5" more or 10 in all, the third pile is "5" more or 15 in all, as the signs indicate. They can count by fives by reading the sign by each stack.

2. Pennies are used to introduce counting by fives so that the children could actually see and feel the groups of five and could abserve that the total increased by 5 as each group was counted. Now suggest that since the bank is getting very heavy and full, the children try to think of a coin that each stack

of 5 pennies could be exchanged for. (Review the meaning of "coin" here.)
Discussion and questioning lead to the discovery that they can get a nickel in
exchange for each 5 pennies and refill the bank with nickels. A trip to the
school office (previously arranged) can be made for this purpose, each child
carrying 5 pennies and making the exchange with the school secretary or a play
bank may be set up in the classroom for the purpose, especially is a store or
money unit is in progress. The children count the nickels by fives several times
to be sure none are lost and refill the bank, each child saying the number as his
turn comes to drop his nickel. Be sure that the children understand that a person who wishes could exchange a nickel for 5 pennies just as easily as he can exchange 5 pennies for a nickel; that their values are equal; that each is worth 5
cents. This experience teaches them the meaning of "nickel."

Other concrete objects should be grouped by fives and counted: children,
desks, pencils, blocks, or chairs. The elements should be counted by ones also
to prove that the total will be the same but that counting by fives is more efficient and just as accurate.

3. See two sets of five in a set of ten. The children should become aware of
the relation between counting by fives and counting by tens. Two devices which
are especially helpful in showing this are (1) the 100 spool or pegboard that contains two colors of spools or pegs in each row, five of one color and five of
another, and (2) the 100-bead abacus containing a similar color scheme. The
abacus is especially helpful in seeing multiples of five because each five beads
can be moved on the rod as a group as they are counted. If the children are
asked to count on these devices by tens, then by fives, they will soon discover
that there are two fives in each ten; that counting by ten increases the total by
tens and counting by fives increases the total by five; that counting by tens
always ends in "0" and counting by fives always ends in "5" or "0." Counting
charts should be made to show these relationships. Coin-value charts should also
be made to show the relationship between the values of pennies, nickels, and
dimes.

4. Count by fives in semiconcrete form to tell time. After the children
have learned to tell time efficiently by hours they may learn to count the minutes on the clock to discover how many minutes in an hour; what is meant by
such expressions as eleven-thirty (lunch time), two forty-five (bus time), etc. A
large clock face should be made ready by the teacher so that the minutes may be
pictured large enough to be seen and counted. Instead of showing the hours, this
clock may show only the minutes in order not to be too confusing. As each 5-
minute period is counted, the numbers by five are written around the clock.
Now the hours may be placed on the clock face in case a child may forget the
location of 1 o'clock, etc. The children work as a group at first, setting the
clock at 5 minutes after 1, 10 minutes after 1 and so on until 2 o'clock is
reached. Then, being careful to go clockwise, they may try counting by fives to

find out what the clock says after it has been set randomly by the teacher. Later, individual clocks can be made and folded in halves and quarters to discover the meaning of "half past" and "quarter past."

5. Apply the skill of counting by fives. There are few arithmetic skills put to greater practical use than counting by fives. Each day as the milk money or funds such as saving-stamp money, hot-lunch money, or Red Cross money is collected the children are required to count their nickels and stacks of 5 pennies by fives. They will often pass supplies to their tables, groups, or rows of fives. They can learn how to tally scores for recess games by fives.

6. Picture the fives and tens. Two charts showing the actual values of the numbers by fives and by tens to 100 should be made and displayed side by side so that the relationship between the numbers on each individual chart may be shown. If actual groups of objects such as packages of toothpicks could be fastened to the chart, the children could easily be led to see that counting by five enlarges the group by fives and counting by tens enlarges the group by tens.

Concept: Any number has a value of one less than the succeeding number

Procedures. 1. Teach the meaning of the word "less." Use books, a set of four and a set of two. Ask which set contains more books, which set has less. Explain that "less" means "not as many," or "less than." Make several sets using other elements, asking which set has more and which has less elements. Ask a student to draw a picture of three apples, ask another to erase one of the apples to make a set containing one less apple.

2. Introduce a new game in reading class called One Less. Write words for reading drill all over the chalkboard. Now let's see how fast we can read all these words. Take turns, point to a word, read it. If the word is identified correctly, the class may say "one less," which allows the one reading the word to erase the word from the board, thereby making "one less" word to read.

3. Work with counters. Each child has 6 counters. Lay them in a row, take one counter away. How many counters are left? Encourage the children to say, "There are 5 counters left because 5 is one less than 6."

4. Use the number line. Have the children plan a racing game. Three children with pointers race to find the numeral that is one less in value than the numeral called by the teacher. Use large and small numerals.

5. Have a relay race. Divide a group of 16 children into two teams. The first child in each group runs to the chalkboard, writes a numeral, hands the chalk to the second child in line who writes the numeral that is one less in value than the first numeral written. Write the second numeral to the left of the first numeral. The third child writes a new numeral, the fourth child writes the numeral which is one less in value than the third numeral beside it, etc. The team that finishes with the most correct answers wins.

Concept: The value of a digit in a number is determined by its position

Procedures. 1. Write the "teen" numerals on the chalkboard. Explain to the children that they are called "teen" numerals because all of the numerals end in "teen." Say the names and write them. Ask the children what they think 14 means. Count out 14 blocks. Then count out 24 blocks. Ask the children what the difference is. They will arrive at 10 as the difference. Then look at the way the "teen" figures are written. Why is the 4 on the right-hand side? Why is the left-hand number different? Ask the children what happens if 14 is changed to put the 4 on the left-hand side (41). Does the placement of the digits make any difference? Use blocks with the children to figure out the answers to these questions. Lead them to the concept that the value of a digit in a number is determined by its position.

2. Develop a chart such as the following:

	Tens		Units
15 =	1	+	5
25 =	2	+	5
62 =	6	+	2

Set up a problem with the children such as this: What difference does the position of these digits make on their value? Divide the children into groups. Let each group work on the problem. Have counters, blocks, egg cartons, and other instructional aids for them to use. Help them set up other questions which help answer the problem, such as: What does the "1" in "15" mean? How many groups of "10" are there in "25"? Are there any tens in "62"? Will "62" have any units left over? After the groups have arrived at answers to the various problems, bring the groups together to explain their solutions. Lead the children to the desired generalization.

3. Begin by asking how many children there are in the room. The children will state that there are 32 pupils in the room. Ask if there are any tens in 32? How can we find out? Have the children see by getting into groups of 10 themselves. How many ones are left over? Is this the reason "2" is written on the right-hand side of the "3"? Develop a chart like this:

	Tens		Units
32 =	3	+	2
23 =	2	+	3

Have the children group according to the 23. They will see that some children are left. Therefore it does make a difference where we place the digits in our numbers to have them represent what they stand for.

4. Study a hundreds board. Discuss and make the following discoveries from the hundreds chart.

(a) In each column in the ones place the numeral is the same.

(b) In each row the numeral in the tens place is the same, except in the last column.

(c) Each number in a column is 10 more than the one above it.

(d) We count to see how many times a numeral is used in the chart. We find that "4" has been used 20 times. It is used 10 times in the ones place and 10 times in the tens place. Follow the same procedure with several other numbers.

(e) Develop a place-value chart.

The children show that 22 is 2 tens and 2 ones; that 44 is 4 tens and 4 ones. Do the same with many other numerals.

The children place the number cards in the pocket chart to represent 22, 44, 66, etc. The children can soon tell you that they know the meaning of the number 44 because there are 4 in the tens place and 4 in the ones place.

5. Play money (dimes and pennies) is spread on the table, and the children are given turns to pick up certain amounts and tell how much they have, then write the amount on the chalkboard. When it is Matt's turn to pick up 6 dimes and 9 pennies, he does so, counts, and writes 69¢ on the board. Among other amounts that are given is 96¢. Now make drawings of several of the numerals, including the 69¢ and the 96¢. Discuss the drawings, deciding which is of more value, 69¢ or 96¢. There are 6 dimes and 9 pennies in 69¢, whereas in 96¢ there are 9 dimes and 6 pennies. Dimes are worth more than pennies, so 96¢ has more value than 69¢. The pennies are worth only 1 cent each, and dimes are worth 10 cents each. Discuss how to show that dimes have more value than pennies when you write the 69¢ and 96¢. The number of dimes or tens is shown by the digit in the tens place and the number of pennies or ones is shown by the digit in the ones place.

Concept: Zero used as a place holder when there is no frequency to record in a position in a numeral

Procedures. 1. For a long time people made marks in columns to show numerals. What do these marks show? (Draw the diagram below on the board.)

Hundreds	Tens	Ones		Hundreds	Tens	Ones
—	—	—		—	—	—
—	—	—		—	—	—
		—			—	
	— -					
		—				

When people wrote figures in columns the numbers looked like this:

Hundreds	Tens	Ones		Hundreds	Tens	Ones
1	2	5		3	1	2

We write like this: 125, 312.

Here is the number two hundred three. (Put the following on the board.)

Hundreds	Tens	Ones		Hundreds	Tens	Ones
___		___		2		3
___		___				
		___				

How many tens are there? The figures without lines look like this, 2 3. Can you tell whether this 2 is in the tens place or the hundreds place? Now you can tell if we write 203. Who can give us a rule about zero as a place holder? We use zero to keep the figures in their proper position (place). Now let us write numerals without marks.

Hundreds	Tens	Ones		Hundreds	Tens	Ones
6	3			8		4

Some have hundreds and ones but no tens. For example, one hundred five. It means 1 hundred and 5 ones. We write the 1 in the hundreds place and the 5 in the ones place. We have no tens to record, but we must write 0 in the ten place so that the number will be 105 instead of 15. We sometimes write numbers that have hundreds and tens but no ones, as six hundred thirty.

2. Have a list of three-place numbers on the board. The children read the munerals first as so many hundreds, so many tens, and so many ones. Then they read the number in the usual way. The same process can be used in reading four-, five-, and six-digit numbers.

3. On the board, have a child write all the figures we use in writing numbers 0, 1, 2, 3, 4, 5, 6, 7, 8, 9. Have the children write such numbers as 41, 40, 22, 20, 100, and 204 on the board and tell how many hundreds, tens, and ones, are in each. They should tell that the zero in the 20, 40, 100, means "not any," or "none." The teacher asks, "What numerals would we have instead of 20, 40, or 100 if the zeros weren't there?" The expected answer would be 2, 4, and 1. The children should explain in their own words the value of zero in 20, 40, and 100.

4. Use an abacus on which you place the beads to present various place values. Each child is given an opportunity to place beads to show the number given, then to write the numeral on the board. When there are no beads in the ones place, a zero must show on the board (or tens place or hundreds place, as the case may be). The class should discuss why zeros are not necessary unless other figures are further to the left. After the discussion, the conclusion should be reached that zero holds the place in a numeral where there is no frequency to record.

Concept: In a two-digit numeral the numeral on the left represents "tens"

Procedures. 1. Use tongue depressors, meat skewers, drinking straws, or any solid objects that can conveniently be fastened together into bundles. Begin by asking a child to set one object in the chalk tray and write the number "1" on the board above it. The next child puts up two objects and writes the number "2." Continue until "10" is reached. Put the ten objects together in a bundle. Remove all sticks except the bundle of ten from the chalk tray and erase all numbers except "10" from the board. Explain that the number "10" on the board tells how many objects are contained in the bundle of ten. Go ahead with the lesson, asking the children to watch the digit on the left to see when it changes. The children now come up to the time to add one more stick and change the number on the board until there are "19." Now ask if they notice anything about the numbers on the board and the bundle of tens? (The bundle of ten and the left-hand digit of "one" has remained the same, only the separate sticks and the digit on the right have changed.) Put up another stick. How many sticks do we have now? Are there enough to make another bundle of ten? Now we have two bundles of ten. What does this do to the numeral on the board? What can we say that the digit on the left tells us?

2. Go through the same procedure using play money (pennies and a dime). When 10 pennies are reached, we change the 10 pennies to one dime. Add more pennies until another dime in value is reached. Children discover the digit on the right tells how many pennies, the one on the left how many dimes.

3. Reverse the process by putting sets of ten or dimes and single sticks or pennies up and ask the children to write the number represented by them.

4. Write a numeral and have the children put out the proper number of bundles and single sticks or dimes and pennies, always noticing and discussing that the digit on the left tells how many tens to put out and the digit on the right tells how many units.

5. Place on the table 11 blocks in two sets, one set of 10 blocks, and the other set of 1 block. Ask how many blocks there are together? (11) How many are there in this group? (10) How many here? (1) Explain that the group with 10 blocks can be called 1 ten. How many extra blocks or ones are on the table? (1) Add 1 ten and 1 one (11). Now adding one block at a time to the group of ones (units, elements), have the children continue counting: 1 ten and 2 ones, 1 ten and 3 ones, etc., until they reach 1 ten and ten ones. Unless someone in the class notices by himself, ask whether the two groups aren't now of equal size or value. Now how many tens do we have? (2) Show how this is written in abstract form. (20) Ask different children to go to the board and write one 10. What does the zero stand for? (There are no units—ones—to record, the zero being a place-holder in this case). How would you write 1 ten and 4 units (ones)? (14) Continue working with other numbers in the same manner.

6. Ask one of the children to go to the board and write a number that is larger in value than 10 but smaller in value than 20. Then ask the class, "Do you know why the number 14 is written as it is?" Why wasn't it written as 41? To make the numbers more meaningful, a question such as the following might be

asked: "If Judy had 14 kittens at her house and Matt had 41 kittens at his house, would each of the children have the same number of kittens?" Analyze the numbers presented to determine their make-up. After having one of the children go to the board and write the numbers 1 through 10, discuss the difference of the number 10 from the other numbers written. (10 is a two-digit numeral). How is (10) different from (1)? (It has a zero on the right side of the 1.) Explain that the 1 stands for 1 ten and the zero tells us that there are no units (ones) to record. Continue with other numbers (11 means 1 ten and 1 one, 13 means 1 ten and 3 units, etc.). Have a student write on the board the numerals from 10 to 20. Pointing to the numerals, ask what they mean. Continue working with the numbers up to 100, showing that each time there are 10 ones, the digit in the tens column increases in value by one.

7. Use a number pocket chart to show the orderliness of the number system. The numerals 20 to 30 will be presented first. As the children count to see how many tens are in 20, they will discover that there are 2 tens and no units. Each numeral to 30 is presented and divided into tens and units. Concrete objects should be used to show how many tens and ones are in each number. For example, one child may demonstrate 20 with pencils, counted and bundled into 2 tens; another may show 20 with play pennies, stacked into 2 tens, or blocks piled into 2 tens. These new numbers 20 and 30 should then be concretely compared to familiar smaller numbers 1 to 19. Comparison should then be made at the semiconcrete level, using the flannelboard cutouts, markers, a 100-bead counting board, 100-spool or pegboard, pictures, a hundreds board (disks being used to cover the numbers), the abacus, counting blocks, drawings, and so on. By guiding the children in reading and counting the number chart to 100, the teacher can through questioning lead them to discover such concepts as the repetition of the digits 1 to 9, the increased value of each number as the number progresses in size or value, the fact that the left-hand digit refers to the tens and therefore can be used as a clue to estimating the value or size of a number as compared to another number.

8. Such games as bingo and lotto are good for extra practice, not only because they give practice in recognizing two-digit numbers, but because they help make the child aware of the relative positions of the numbers in the scale from 1 to 100.

9. I'm thinking of a number. The child may describe his number in one of several different ways for another child to find or identify. He may say, "It is 2 more than 60," or "It has 3 tens and 9 units," or "It comes after 21 and before 23."

10. Which is more? Two children may close their eyes and "fish" for two-digit number cards from a container. Winner is the child whose two-digit number has the greatest size or value. He fishes again until defeated.

11. Baseball. Each child progresses from the picture's box to the batter's position and around the bases by writing the two-digit numbers named orally by the teacher or a member of the opposing team.

Concept: Place value

Procedures. 1. Display a set of nine objects and have the children count together as you point to each object in turn. Put one more object with the set and count together again. When you reach ten, observe with the children that there are ten objects in this set. Write the word ten on the chalkboard, and tell the children that this is the number word for the number ten. Count several other sets containing ten objects.

2. Let children do some grouping by tens themselves. Either on the children's desk or on a demonstration table, provide sets containing 30, 40, or 50 objects.

3. Choose a child before the group and make a statement such as this: "I am thinking of a number that is one ten and seven ones. Those who think they know the number raise your hands." The leader calls on someone to write the number which in this case is 17. If what the latter writes is correct, he becomes the leader. This may be done with other numbers too.

4 Provide sets of objects which can be grouped by tens with no objects left over. For example, display a set of 50 objects and have the children come to the front of the room and group this set into five sets of ten. At this time do not call attention to the numeral 50 but rather attention to the number of sets of ten. Continue this activity until the children are thoroughly acquainted with the idea of grouping by tens.

5. Now provide sets which have objects left over after grouping by tens. For example, display a set of 24 objects for the children to group by tens. When they have discovered that there are two groups of ten and four objects left over, write on the chalkboard 2 tens and 4 ones. Repeat this several more times with other sets.

6. Display 47 pencils and have the children group them by tens. When they see there are four tens and seven, display the numeral.

7. Conduct an oral exercise in which you give a number and the children tell the number of tens and the number left over.

8. Have children group by tens to get groups of 10 tens. They may begin with groups less than 100. Give the children opportunity to discover what number to write. Many are able to write 100.

9. Write several three-digit numerals on the chalkboard and then point in turn how many ones, how many tens, or how many hundreds.

10. Emphasize that only ten basic numerals are needed to represent all the whole numbers greater than nine. Choose three teams of ten players each. Distribute to each team a set of large cards bearing the numerals 0 through 9. Designate one team the "hundreds" team, another team the "tens" team, and the third team, the "ones" team. Call out a numeral, for example seven hundred forty-seven. The members of the hundreds team who holds the digit 7, the member of the tens team who holds the digit 4, and the member of the ones team who holds the digit 7 must come quickly forward and stand beneath the proper

words to form the numeral 747. Use different numerals until each child on each team has had a turn.

11. Use the bead frame to strengthen the children's understanding of three-digit numerals. Label the rods on the bead frame "hundreds," "tens," and "ones." Have the children number 729 on the frame. They should place seven beads on the hundreds rod, two beads on the tens rod, and 9 beads on the ones rod. Repeat the activity with other numbers from one hundred through nine hundred and ninety-nine.

12. Play a matching game. Present a column of numerals on the chalkboard and to the right of this column write a column of phrases which describe the place-value meaning of these numerals. Ask a child to read the first numeral in the column and then identify the phrase in the second column which matches the numeral read. Have him draw a line from the numeral to the selected phrase. Continue in a similar manner to have the other numerals matched with the correct phrase.

13. Write several four-digit numerals on the chalkboard. Have the children read these numbers together; then call attention to the first numeral. Select one of the digits and ask the children what this digit represents. Continue this until children are thoroughly acquainted with the concept of place value.

14. Provide the children with experience in comparing pairs of four-digit numbers. Follow this by giving them an opportunity to do some counting starting with larger numbers. For example start the children with a number such as 5678 and have them count forward for ten or twenty whole numbers.

15. Review place value of three- and four-digit numbers. Write a four-digit number such as 7894 and ask the children to identify the number represented by the various digits. Follow this by giving some exercises which require the children to give a number that is either 10, 100, or 1,000 more or less than a given number.

16. Have children write three-digit numerals for these numbers:

> a number greater than 175
> a number less than 300
> a number between 230 and 240
> a number between 470 and 475

17. Write numerals for:

> three hundred ninety-six
> one hundred twenty-six
> five-hundred seventy-nine

18. Write several rows of numerals on the chalkboard. Instruct the children to think of the numbers represented by these numerals and rewrite them on their own paper from the smallest to the largest. (Also reverse the order—from the largest to the smallest.)

19. Show on the chalkboard several four-digit numerals for the children to read. Then show a five-digit numeral and give the children an opportunity to read it. Some of them will know how this should be read. Emphasize that the two digits in front of the comma, or left of the comma, name the number of thousands. Following the work with five-digit numerals, show some six-digit numerals and give the children an opportunity to read them. Extend this activity into seven-, eight-, and nine-digit numbers when the children are ready.

20. Instruct the children to write the correct numeral for the number name you write on the board. Example: eight hundred million, nine hundred twenty-six thousand, four hundred twelve (800,926,412).

21. Write several pairs of numbers on the chalkboard and have the children write just the larger or smaller number in each pair according to the teacher's directions.

22. Have the children tell the meaning of the numerals by writing several numerals on the board and the children tell you what a particular digit means.

In 126,789, the 6 stands for 6,000.
In 345,987, the 4 stands for 40,000.

23. Write a series of numerals on the chalkboard. Have the children number their paper and write the numerals from the smallest to the greatest.

24. Conduct an activity in which the children compare several pairs of large numbers. You might show on the chalkboard two five-digit numbers and ask the children to tell which number is larger. Repeat this with several examples.

PRACTICE AND EVALUATION

Numbers and Numerals

1. Take the card with the numeral that shows how many boats there are in the picture, and place it under the picture. Concrete objects also can be used (cars, trucks, boats, trains).
2. Have various members of the class construct block formations up to ten. Then have them point to the stacks of blocks in order, tell how many blocks in each stack, and note that the number in each stack is one larger than in the preceding stack. Call on various children to choose the appropriate number card and place it at the bottom of each stack.
3. Using dittoed or photocopied sheets, ask the children to draw a line between the two sets with the same number of elements in them.
4. Have pictures of various groups of objects with a list of numerals following each. Ask the children to circle the numeral that tells how many elements that are in each set.
5. Picture a set of three children. Ask the pupils to make a set of four children.
6. Picture one ball. Ask the children to make a set of five balls.
7. Picture domino dots up to 10 with a blank at the bottom of each picture.

Ask the children to write the numeral denoting how many dots on each domino.

8. Develop a picture test and give directions such as the following: Pamela is seven years of age. There are seven candles on her cake. Put a mark on her cake. Put a mark on the nest with three eggs in it. Put a circle around the tree with seven apples on it.

9. Give problems orally and have the children write the answer only. "There are this many trees in a yard (Draw four trees on the chalkboard). Write the number that tells how many there are. Draw four squirrels on your paper. Is there a squirrel for each tree? Write yes or no. Draw four more squirrels. Write the numeral that tells how many squirrels can live in each tree." "Eight children are going to a picnic. They each had an apple. Draw the apples. Write the numeral that tells how many apples you drew."

10. Provide pictures of sets of related objects. Have the children discover whether there is an object in the second set for each object in the first set. This is done by drawing a line from each object of one set to an object in the related set. Make pictures of several sets of toys and several sets of stick figures; have the children match the toys with the stick figures.

11. Give each child four blocks. Ask the children to make a set out of them. Next have them make their sets one smaller, and then check to see if this has been done. Again have them make the set one smaller, then larger again.

12. Ask the question: Do you know how to make a set larger or smaller? If I add two birds to a set of birds in a tree, how much larger will the set be than it is now?

13. Make a picture showing a group of four balls. Now make the group two balls larger. How many balls did you make in all?

14. Hold up four lollipops. Have four children stand up. Ask the question: If you each get part of this set of lollipops, how many will each of you get? (1)

15. Place a set of 8 erasers on the table. Ask the children to tell how many erasers are in the set. Place a set of 5 blocks on the table. Have the children tell how many single elements are in the set.

16. Draw on the chalkboard a group of objects and have a child write the correct number of single objects in the group beside the picture. Repeat the same procedure with a group containing a different number of single objects.

17. Children are asked to draw pictures to make sets match given number symbols.

18. Have a chart with elements placed in sets and ask the children to circle the sets containing a specific number of elements.

19. Give each child ten counters and tell him to make two groups, three groups, four groups, etc. Have him tell how many in each group.

20. Add enough boxes to the pictured set of boxes to make a set of seven boxes.

21. What numerals are missing: 1, 2,___, 4,___,___, 7,___,___, ___.

22. Match the numeral and the number picture:

1	XXXX
2	X
3	XXXXX
4	XXX
5	XX

23. What numeral comes after each of these numbers:

         1, _____   5, _____

         2, _____   6, _____

         8, _____   3, _____

24. Put the following on the chalkboard:

         2 and 1 are _____

         3 and 1 are _____

         4 and 1 are _____

25. Put these equations on the chalkboard:

      3 and 1 are _____   6 and 1 are _____

          N = _____   N = _____

      3 and 1 are _____   6 and 1 are _____

26. Using counters have the children say as they put one counter down at a time, one and one are two, two and one are three, three and one are four, etc.

27. Chalkboard instruction or worksheets should be given for coloring or making objects.

      Make the first hat blue.

      Put three flowers on the third hat.

      Make the fourth hat green.

      Put an X on the sixth tree.

      Make the seventh circle yellow.

28. Give directions such as these:

      Draw five apples. Color the third one red.

      Draw four houses. Color the second one green.

      Draw six flowers. Color the sixth one blue.

      Draw three trees. Color the first one green.

29. Draw lines from each numeral to its two number names:

three	1	sixth
seven	2	second
one	3	eighth
five	4	first
six	5	seventh
two	6	third
four	7	fourth
nine	8	ninth
eight	9	fifth

30. On the chalkboard have ten pictures of dogs drawn or cut out from a magazine. The numerals 1, 2, 3, 4, 5, 6, 7. 8, 9, and 10 are written on the chalkboard and are held in the dog's mouth. Give each child a mimeograph copy of the following questions. They are to fill in the answers.

      The tenth dog is holding what card? _____

      The first dog is holding what card? _____

      The second dog is holding what card? _____

      The fifth dog is holding what card? _____

31. Place a certain number of elements on the flannelboard and then ask different children to place the correct numeral by the set on the flannelboard.
32. Say numbers for the children at the board to write down. This oral test can also be given with elements. As you count, the children are to pick up the corresponding number of elements.
33. Give each child a card with a numeral on it. (No two cards having the same numeral.) Ask the child to tell you what numeral he had and where it would come if he were counting. Then have the children line up in numerical order.
34. Sample problems:
    How many candles are on the cake? (picture of a cake with candles)
    Make a ring around the numeral that tells how many balls:

    (a) OOOO   (b) OO   (c) OOOOOOOOO
        5436   21   754869213

    One more than 7 is _____
    One more than 9 is _____
    One less than 5 is _____
    One less than 9 is _____
    Draw seven balls.
    Draw three hats.
    Draw a line to the correct numeral:

XX	3
XXXX	2
XXX	5
X	7
XXXXX	4
XXXXXX	1

    How many are:

    OOOO   O   OOOOOO   OOO   OOOOOOO   OOOOOOOOO

    _____   _____   _____   _____   _____   _____

35. Hold up mounted picture-questions:

    Here I have 3 apples and on this side I have 5 apples. Which set has fewer apples?

    On this side we see 2 green popsicle sticks, on the other side we see 6 red popsicle sticks. Are these sets the same size?

    On this side we have 1 pencil, on the other side two pencils. Which is the larger set?

36. Have children circle the number which represents the greatest number of elements in each row.

2	5	7
1	3	8
9	2	8
5	7	1

37. On worksheets, the children are asked to draw a line around a set that has more or fewer or the same as elements in the same "picture frame" which has two pictured sets.

38. Ask the children to draw more elements or fewer elements than you do on the board. Example: "Draw 3 more apples than I do."

39. Solving problems:

>Anna Louise has three apples, her brother has one less. How many apples does her brother have?

>Christy has 9 cents but she lost 1 cent. Now she has 1 cent less. How many cents does she have now?

>In Mary's class there are 20 children but one is absent so we have one less. How many children are present today?

40. Have the children point to numerals on the number line. Then have them point to the numeral that is one less than the first number identified.

41. Write the numeral that comes before each of the following:

_____ 7   _____ 4   _____ 3

_____ 2   _____ 5   _____ 8

42. Write the number that is one less in value than:

two _____   three _____   four   five

15_____   33_____   14_____   10 _____

43. In each set take one element away, how many elements are left:

OO _____ ,   OOOO _____ ,   OOOOOOOOO _____ ,

OOO _____ ,   OOOOOOO _____ ,   OOOOO _____ ,

44. Count the circles by two orally. How many circles did you add each time you counted?

45. How much larger in value is 4 than 2? How much larger in value is 6 than 4? How much larger in value is 8 than 6? How much larger in value is 10 than 8?

46. Write to 20 by twos. After writing to 20 by twos in a column, make drawings to show that 4 is 2 more in value than 2, 6 is 2 more in value than 4, etc.

47. Have children illustrate on paper counting by twos. He may use the abstract numerals, pictures, picture story, or any other way he can think of.

48. Count the stars by twos:

* *   * *   * *   * *   * *   * *   * *   * *   * *

_____   _____   _____   _____   _____   _____   _____   _____   _____

49. Write the missing numeral:

1,___, 3,___, 5, ___, 7,___, 9,___ , 11,___ , 13.

50. The main testing of the child orally will be observation by the teacher of his ability to use his skill of counting by fives when an actual need arises: counting his own money by fives, counting school supplies, or counting any other set of objects by fives.

51. The child may be asked to count by fives on the hundreds board, spool board, or pegboard showing the fives as he goes either by spanning them with both hands or sweeping the pointer along each group.

52. Pictures or tally marks by fives may be arranged at random for the child to count, identifying the total orally as in the following:
How many?

///// ///// _____

///// ///// ///// ///// _____

///// _____

///// ///// ///// _____

53. Story problems can be given involving sets of five as:

   Andrew had 8 nickels in his bank. How much money did he have?

54. The numerals by fives to 100 may be counted out, scrambled and arranged, or placed in correct sequence.
55. Story problems involving fives may be illustrated by drawings.
56. Write the following numbers giving the positional value: (64 as 6 tens and 4 ones) 39, 84, 20, 98, 55.
57. Show on the abacus the following: 1 one, 6 tens, 8 hundreds.
58. Tell whether the 7 in the following numbers is 7 ones, 7 tens, 7 hundreds: 742, 7, 76, 07, 407, 704.
59. Write the tens and ones under the right name in the numbers: 36, 87, 49, 72, 15.

	Tens	Ones
15 =	____	____
36 =	____	____
87 =	____	____
49 =	____	____
72 =	____	____

60. Draw a picture to show how many dimes and pennies you would take to the store to get a loaf of bread if the bread costs 32 cents.
61. Oral problems such as the following: What is the number that is 2 tens and 4 ones? How much is 5 dimes and 3 pennies?
62. Underline the tens in the following numbers:
82, 57, 91, 63, 83, 20.
63. Have the children show with concrete or semiconcrete materials what various numbers mean.
64. Write these numbers in figures and tell what each one means.
eighty-seven, thirty-eight, fifty-six, ninety-two, fourteen, sixteen.
65. The teacher places beads on the abacus, using none in different places. The children tell what number is being represented, and give the place name of each figure in each number. Numbers are written on the chalkboard by one child, and he chooses another to give the place names to each figure and say the number.
66. Tell in your own words why we need zero in our system. How many of these numbers change in value if we do not use zero?

20	102	470	160
100	90	800	504

67. Write these numbers in figures: two hundred and seven; nine hundred and four; fifty; twenty-six.
68. Tell what numeral belongs in each blank:

407 means ____ hundreds ____ tens ____ ones

209 means ____ hundreds ____ tens ____ ones

420 means ____ hundreds ____ tens ____ ones

300 means ____ hundreds ____ tens ____ ones

69. Write the numerals from 99 to 110.
70. There are some numbers to add on the board. Who will add the ones column? Who will add the tens column?
71. Have the children make a tens and units chart on paper and show various numbers considered by indicating the number of tens and the number of units.
72. Illustrate the meanings of a two-digit number by drawings that show tens and units.
73. Show a two-digit number on an abacus or counting blocks. Have the children identify and write the number.
74. Mark the number representing the smallest value or size: 24, 86, or 74.
75. Mark the number representing the largest value or size: 96, 57, or 62.

NONDECIMAL SYSTEMS OF NUMERATION

One reason alone provides the basis for using a valuable segment of or time in examining numeration systems other than the Decimal Numeration System. The fact that our system derives its superiority from its utilization of the principle of place-value makes imperative the full understanding of this principle by all who guide the mathematical growth of elementary children. A clear understanding of place-value thus becomes one of the most important objectives of mathematical teaching. Without such an understanding there is no hope of meaningfully teaching the algorithms of arithmetic and decimal notation.

An important judgment which comes from every experimental project in mathematics is that children must from the beginning (1) be exposed to the structure of mathematics, (2) led to discover and make use of patterns and relationships, and (3) taught to think analytically.

Teaching in this manner is virtually impossible for the majority of us who fail to understand why children continue to have difficulty with a problem such as $9 + 4 = 13$. The teacher who is sensitive to the children's difficulty is one who has met this same frustration while working in a similar situation such as base-4 numeration and failing to understand that $3 + 3 = 12$.

A brief review of what we know concerning numeration systems is the starting point for working in bases other than ten.

THIS WE KNOW

I. When we speak of base 10, we simply mean that we are thinking about grouping by tens.

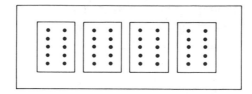

II. The decimal system, with its orderly grouping by sets of tens and powers of ten, produces regular and logical patterns.

Thousands	Hundreds	Tens	Ones	
		1	0	Ten ones or one ten
	1	0	0	Ten tens or one hundred
1	0	0	0	Ten hundreds or one thousand

III. When we refer to place value we mean that the number a digit represents depends on the place it occupies in the symbol.

IV. A numeral in any column has ten times the value of that same numeral in the column to its right.

10 × 10 × 10	10 × 10	10	1
Thousands	Hundreds	Tens	Ones

V. Distinct symbols from zero up to but not including the base are needed.

$$0, 1, 2, 3, 4, 5, 6, 7, 8, 9$$

VI. The decimal point is a separator: it separates the whole number part of the number from the fractional part. More significantly, its role is that of fixing the ones digit, enabling us to extend the number to the right of the ones position.

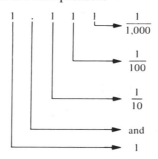

MAKING OUR DECIMAL SYSTEM CLEAR

In our attempts to make these and other properties of our decimal system clear to children, we have discovered that we can (for example)

I. *Use expanded notation*, in which numbers are broken up into particular component parts before performing an operation, to help children see the direct relationship of the component parts to the decimal. Consider the number 2146 written in expanded notation:

  A. $2,000 + 100 + 40 + 6$

  B. $(2 \times 1,000) + (1 \times 100) + (4 \times 10) + (6 \times 1)$

II. *Use exponents* to simplify the expanded notation and tell how many times 10 is used as a factor.

$$(2 \times 10^3) + (1 \times 10^2) + (4 \times 10^1) + (6 \times 10^0)$$

III. *Use a grid* to illustrate how exponential notation and place value are related.

Thousands	Hundreds	Tens	Ones
$10 \times 10 \times 10$	10×10	10	1
10^3	10^2	10^1	10^0

Should the question arise concerning how much and to what depth elementary children should be expected to acquire knowledge and understanding of bases other than ten we conclude that the concept of individual differences must be respectfully used in a teacher's determination of whether individuals or groups of children can handle the idea without the risk of confusing what was previously clear.

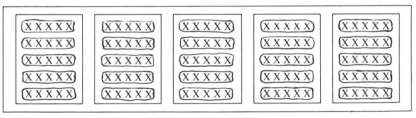

Five 25's or one 125

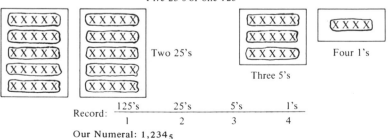

Two 25's

Three 5's

Four 1's

Record:	125's	25's	5's	1's
	1	2	3	4

Our Numeral: $1,234_5$

The subscript is used to indicate the base of the numeral.

To avoid confusion, nondecimal numerals should be read by pronouncing the name of each digit and naming the base. Example: 1234_5 is read one-two-three-four, base 5.

To show the additive property, we can use expanded notation:

$$1,234_5$$
$$\text{one } 125 + \text{two } 25\text{'s} + \text{three } 5\text{'s} + \text{four } 1\text{'s}$$
$$1,000_5 + 200_5 + 30_5 + 4_5$$
$$(1 \times 5^3) + (2 \times 5^2) + (3 \times 5^1) \times (4 \times 5^0)$$

Changing Base-5 Numeral to a Base-10 Numeral

To change any base numeral to a base-10 numeral, use your place-value chart or exponential notation. Using the above exponential notation:

$$(1 \times 5^3) = 1 \times 125 = 125$$
$$(2 \times 5^2) = 2 \times 25 = 50$$
$$(3 \times 5^1) = 3 \times 5 = 15$$
$$(4 \times 5^0) = 4 \times 1 = \underline{4}$$
$$\text{Sum} = 194_{10}$$

Counting all of the X's in our original diagram, you will find there are 194.

Using Place-value chart and same base-5, and with numeral $1,234_5$,

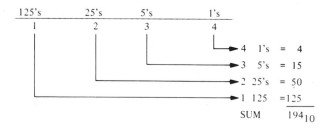

Changing Base-10 Numerals to Base-5 Numerals

We know that $194 = 1,234_5$.

1. Set up base-5 place-value chart:

125's	25's	5's	1's
1	2	3	4

2. Determine how many 125's there are in 194 and record on chart.

$$\begin{array}{r} 194 \\ -125 \\ \hline 69 \end{array} \qquad \begin{array}{r} 1 \\ 125\overline{)194} \\ \underline{125} \\ 69 \end{array}$$

3. How many 25's are there in our remainder? Record on chart.

$$\begin{array}{r} 69 \\ -50 \quad \text{(2-25's)} \\ \hline 19 \end{array} \qquad \begin{array}{r} 2 \\ 25\overline{)\,194} \\ \underline{50} \\ 19 \end{array}$$

4. We have 19 left so we need to take all 5's from 19 and record.

$$\begin{array}{r} 19 \\ -15 \quad \text{(3-5's)} \\ \hline 4 \end{array} \qquad \begin{array}{r} 3 \\ 5\overline{)\,19} \\ \underline{15} \\ 4 \end{array}$$

5. There are no sets of 5 in 4, so the 4 means the number of ones.

The repeated-division method may also be used to change nondecimal numerals to base-10 numerals.

The divisor is always the base to which one intends to change the numeral.

Changing 194_{10} to base 5

1. We take out all the 5's and the remainder tells us the number of 1's we will have in our new base.

$$\begin{array}{r} 38 \\ 5\overline{)\,194} \\ \underline{190} \\ 4 \quad \text{ones} \end{array}$$

2. We now divide 37 by 5 and take out all of the 5^2. The remainder will tell us the number of 5's.

$$\begin{array}{r} 7 \\ 5\overline{)\,38} \\ \underline{35} \\ 3 \quad \text{fives} \end{array}$$

3. Dividing our new quotient by 5 we take out all of the 5^3. Our remainder tells us the number of 5^2 that will be left.

$$\begin{array}{r} 1 \\ 5\overline{)\,7} \\ \underline{5} \\ 2 \quad \text{twenty-fives} \end{array}$$

4. We take out all of the 54 and the remainder gives us the number of 5^3.

$$\begin{array}{r} 0 \\ 5\overline{)\,1} \\ \underline{0} \\ 1 \quad \text{one hundred twenty-five} \end{array}$$

Our numeral: $1,234_5$

Changing 194_{10} to base 6

1.
$$\begin{array}{r} 332 \\ 6\overline{)\,194} \\ \underline{192} \\ 2 \quad \text{ones} \end{array}$$

2.
$$\begin{array}{r} 5 \\ 6\overline{)\,32} \\ \underline{30} \\ 2 \quad \text{6's} \end{array}$$

3.
$$\begin{array}{r} 0 \\ 6\overline{)\,5} \\ \underline{0} \\ 5 \quad \text{36's} \end{array}$$

When the quotient becomes 0, the process is ended.

Our numeral: 522_6

NONDECIMAL OPERATIONS

Addition:

32_5 = 3 fives + 2 ones
11_5 = 1 five + 1 one
———
43_5 = 4 fives + 3 ones

43_7 = 4 sevens + 3 ones
12_7 = 1 seven + 2 ones
———
55_7 = 5 sevens + 5 ones

Regrouping:

14_5 = 1 five + 4   ones
21_5 = 2 fives + 1   one
———
40_5 = 4 fives + 0   ones

(4 ones + 1 one = 5 ones)
(5 ones = 0 ones and 1 five)

Regrouping:

35_6 = 3 sixes + 5   ones
14_6 = 1 six   + 4   ones
———
53_6 = 5 sixes + 3   ones

(5 ones + 4 ones = 9 ones)
(9 ones = 1 six   + 3 ones)

Numeral Systems on the Number Line

The different numeral systems can be shown very clearly with the number line. The simple requirement is that the units on the number line be numbered in the base being used.

This is by no means a complete treatment of the number line in various bases. No attempt has been made to treat multiplication or division in the various bases. It can be done but other concrete illustrations appear to be much clearer to the student. An example is given on page 59. See part (a).

Numbers in different bases can be compared directly by the use of the number line. Thus:

$$8_{10} = 1,000_2$$
$$20_{10} = 10,000_2$$
$$32_{10} = 1,000,000_2$$
etc.

To construct a number line that shows this comparison of any base to base 10, we construct the number line with the numbers to base 10 on one side and the numbers in the other base on the other side of the line. Examples are given on page 59. See parts (b) and (c).

Number Systems Basic Operations (See example on page 60.)

Examples:

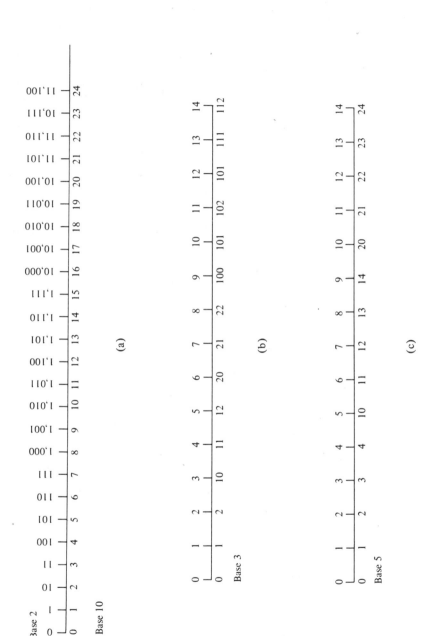

(a)

Base 2

Base 10

(b)

Base 3

(c)

Base 5

Number Systems Basic Operations

Addition.
Example: $4_5 + 3_5 = 12_5$

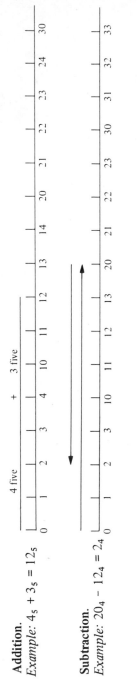

Subtraction.
Example: $20_4 - 12_4 = 2_4$

Multiplication.
Example: $3_6 \times 5_6 = 23_6$

Division.
Example: $110_3 \div 12_3 = 2\,\dfrac{2}{12_3}$

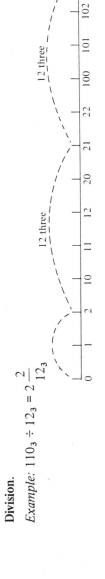

Base 12

An interesting variation of the comparison of bases on the number line is the comparison of numbers in base$_2$ and base$_8$.

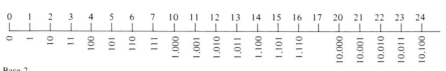

Base 8

Base 2

Notice that:

$$2_8 = 10_2$$
$$4_8 = 100_2$$
$$10_8 = 1,000_2$$
$$20_8 = 10,000_2$$
$$40_8 = 100,000_2$$

Fractions can also be represented on the number line in any base:

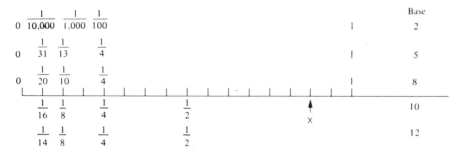

Point X on the line can be read in each base:

For base$_2$ it is $1/10 + 1/100 + 1/1000 = \dfrac{111}{1000} = .111$

For base$_5$ it is $1/2 + 1/4 + 1/13 = \dfrac{12}{13}$

For base$_8$ it is $7/10$

For base$_{10}$ it is $7/8$

For base$_{12}$ it is $7/8$

The specific skills and understandings regarding other systems and bases include the following. The child should be able to:

Grade II

1. Understand and use roman numerals to 10 (optional).

Grade III

1. Understand and use roman numerals through 39.

Grade IV

1. Review roman numerals through 39.
2. Understand and use roman numerals through "C" (100).

Grade V

1. Understand and use roman numerals through "D" and "M."
2. Recognize the importance of the lack of a symbol for zero with roman numerals.
3. Understand "base 5" (optional).
   (This skill is undertaken so that structure of the base 10 system can be better understood)
   (a) Count by groups of 5.
   (b) Convert from base 10 to base 5.

Grade VI

1. Understand and use roman numerals through "M" (1,000).
2. Understand the additive and subtractive principles involved in the use of roman numerals.
3. Understand "base 8."
   (a) Understand grouping principle.
   (b) Understand the use of digits and their use.
   (c) Count in base 8.
   (d) Add and subtract on base 8.

TEACHING SUGGESTIONS

Concept: Roman Numerals

Procedures. 1. Write the arabic numerals on the board in white chalk. Beside each one, write the roman numeral in red. Discuss the difference with the children for numbers through ten and let the children take turns writing them on the board as you call out the numerals.

2. Have the children match the arabic and roman numerals.

Example:

VII _____	10 _____
X _____	2 _____
V _____	7 _____
II _____	5 _____

3. Have the children write the roman numerals that stand for each of these arabic numerals:

Example:

10 _____		33 _____	
13 _____		60 _____	
42 _____		8 _____	
15 _____		4 _____	

4. Reverse the above activity and write the arabic numerals that stand for each of the roman numerals.

Example:

XIII _____		IX _____
III _____		V _____
VII _____		X _____

5. Write the roman numerals for these number words:

Example:

Seven _____
One _____
Four _____
Ten _____
Eight _____
Two _____
Five _____
Three _____

SELECTED READINGS

Numbers and Numerals

Banks, Houston J. *Learning and Teaching Arithmetic.* Boston: Allyn and Bacon, 1959, pp. 20-30, 29-41, 50-63.

Bell, Clifford, Cleia Hammond, and Robert Herrera. *Fundamentals of Arithmetic for Teachers.* New York: Wiley, 1962, pp. 20-35, 52-53, 75-77.

Brumfield, Charles, Robert Eicholz, and Merrill Shanks. *Fundamental Concepts of Elementary Mathematics.* Reading, Mass.: Addison-Wesley, 1962, pp. 24-49.

Evenson, A. B. *Modern Mathematics: Introductory Concepts and Their Implications.* Chicago: Scott, Foresman, 1962, pp. 25-32.

Johnson, Donovan A., and William H. Glenn. *Understanding Numeration Systems.* St. Louis: Webster, 1960, pp. 2-44.

Meserve, Bruce E., and Max A. Sobel. *Mathematics for Secondary School Teachers.* Englewood Cliffs, N. J.: Prentice-Hall, 1962, pp. 11-31.

Morris, Dennis E., and Henry D. Topfer. *Advancing in Mathematics.* Chicago: Science Research Associates, 1963, pp. 3-45.

Osborn, Roger, Vere DeVault, Claude Boyd, and Robert Houston. *Extending Mathematical Understanding.* Columbus, Ohio: Merrill, 1961, pp. 12–24, 20–24, 129–141.

Peterson, John A., and Joseph Hashisaki. *Theory of Arithmetic.* New York: Wiley, 1963, pp. 1-13, 59-69, 69-80.

Schaaf, William L. *Basic Concepts of Elementary Mathematics.* New York: Wiley, 1963, pp. 47-52, 173-183.

Smith, D. E. *History of Mathematics,* Vol II. New York: Dover, 1958, pp. 36-77.

Williams, Sammie, Garland H. Read, Jr., and Frank L. Williams, *Modern Mathematics in the Elementary and Junior High Schools.* New York: Random House, 1961, pp. 1-10, 15-25.

chapter 3

Sets and Sentences

SETS

A set may be regarded as a collection of clearly defined things—boys, girls, people, animals, numbers, lines, ideas, etc. In developing the properties of sets and various operations with sets, a special language is used involving:

(a) Capital letters as symbols of sets: Set $A = \{a, b, c\}$.

(b) Symbols for operations: $\cup$, union; and $\cap$, intersection.

(c) Symbols for showing relations unique to sets include:

$\subset$ "is a subset of"

$\not\subset$ "is not a subset of"

$\in$ "is an element of"

$\notin$ "is not an element of"

$=$ "is equal to"

$\neq$ "is not equal to"

$\sim$ "is equivalent to"[1]

Each thing in a set is called an element of that set, or a member of that set. A set may have many elements, one element, or even no elements. A set with no elements is called an empty set $\{\}$, or null set $\emptyset$. For example: All the two-headed boys in Matt's class could be written:

$$\text{Set } A = \{\} \quad \text{or} \quad \text{Set } A = \emptyset$$

Commas are used to separate the elements of a set. The elements or members are enclosed by curly brackets or braces. In defining a particular set, the equal symbol (=), is placed between the name of the set and the members of the set.

$$\text{Set } B = \{4, 8, 12, 16\}$$

[1]Sets that have the same number of elements, but whose elements are not identical, are equivalent.

Example:

$$\text{Set } A = \{1, 2, 3, 4\}$$
$$\text{Set } B = \{5, 6, 7, 8\}$$
$$\text{Set } A \neq \text{Set } B \text{ but Set } A \sim \text{Set } B$$

If one wanted to direct attention to all the counting numbers that are multiples or factors of four, three dots are added after the last element indicating
"and continues in a like manner."

Example:

$$\text{Set } C = \{4, 8, 12, 16, \ldots\}$$

Equal Sets are two sets whose elements are identical, regardless of their
order. An example of equal sets is:

$$\text{Set } D = \{\text{ Matt, Pam, Christy }\}$$

$$\text{Set } E = \{\text{ Pam, Christy, Matt }\}$$

$$\text{Set } D = \text{Set } E \quad \text{Set } D \sim \text{Set } E$$

Equivalent Sets have the same number of elements, but the elements need
not be identical. The elements of the sets below have been put into one-to-one
correspondence.

$$\text{Set } F = \{\text{ Andrew, Mary, Anna }\}$$

$$\updownarrow \qquad \updownarrow \qquad \updownarrow$$

$$\text{Set } E = \{\text{ Pam, Christy, Matt }\}$$

$$\text{Set } F \neq \text{ Set } E \quad \text{Set } F \sim \text{Set } E$$

Equal sets are equivalent sets, but equivalent sets are not equal sets.

Subsets are sets within sets. If the elements of one set are contained in another, the contained set is called a subset of the other. Every set is a subset
of itself, and an empty set is a subset of every set. For example:

$$\text{Set } A = \{\square, \triangle, \bigcirc, \lozenge, \square\}$$

$$\text{Set } B = \{\square, \triangle\}$$

$$\text{Set } C = \{\}$$

Set A is a set which contains five elements: a square, a triangle, a circle,
a diamond, and a polygon.

Set B is a set which contains two elements: a square and a triangle. Set C is
an empty set and therefore has no elements.

By examining the elements of sets A, B, and C, we can make the following
mathematical statements:

$B \subset A$	(B is a subset of A)
$C \subset A$	(C is a subset of A)
$A \subset A$	(A is a subset of A)
$B \subset B$	(B is a subset of B)
$C \subset C$	(C is a subset of C)

$A \not\subset B$ (A is not a subset of B)
$B \not\subset C$ (B is not a subset of C)
$\square \in A$ (the $\square$ or square is an element of A)
$\square \in B$ (the square is an element of B)
$\square \notin C$ (the square is not an element of C)
$\bigcirc \in A$ (the circle is an element of A)

The above sentences are all true mathematical statements; however, with sets as with numbers, we could have made a false statement such as:

$A \subset B$ (A is a subset of B)   Not true

However, true or false, it is still a mathematical sentence just as $4 + 3 = 5$ is a mathematical sentence.

So far, only relation symbols have been used. Let us now take a look at symbols of operation on sets.

Union of Sets ($\cup$). If two or more sets are joined, the new set is described as the union ($\cup$) of their elements. Note the word "dissimilar" when the union of sets is spoken of. Sets are joined. But numbers are added (operation).

In union the word "set" is dropped and only the capital letter is used:

Set $H = \{ a,c,d, \}$ Set $J = \{ 7, 8, 9 \}$

Set $I = \{ b,d,e \}$ [2]   Set $K = \{ 9, 10, 11 \}$ [2]

$H \cup I = \{ a,b,c,d,e \}$ $J \cup K = \{ 7, 8, 9, 10, 11 \}$

Although there is agreement on the meanings behind the operational symbols used in set mathematics, there is lack of agreement on exactly how these symbols should be read. For example:

$$H \cup I = \{ a,b,c,d,e \}$$

This sentence could be read as any one of the following:
"H union I has elements a, b, c, d, and e."
"The union of sets H and I has five elements: a, b, c, d, and e."
"The union of H and I is the set containing the elements a, b, c, d, and e."

Regardless of how the sentence is to be read, the meanings all imply the same and all contain the same elements.

The Intersection ($\cap$) *of Two Sets* is the set containing the elements common to both sets. For example:

Set $K = \{ 1, 3, 5, 7, 9 \}$

Set $L = \{ 7, 8, 9, 10 \}$

$K \cap L = \{ 7, 9 \}$

[2]Note that in the union of H and I the "d" is not repeated, and that the "9" is not repeated in the union of sets J and K. The union of two sets contains all the elements of both sets, but one does not repeat an element common to both sets.

This sentence could be read as any one of the following:

"The intersection of K and L is 7 and 9."

"K intersection L is 7 and 9."

"The intersection of sets K and L has 7 and 9 as its common elements."

"In K and L, we have 7 and 9."

Examples of the work of "union" and "intersection" in the same problem are:

$$\text{Set } A = \{\text{Matt, Pam, Christy}\}$$

$$\text{Set } B = \{\text{Pam, Andrew, Mary}\}$$

$$A \cup B = \{\text{Matt, Christy, Pam, Andrew, Mary}\}$$

$$A \cap B = \{\text{Pam}\}$$

or

$$\text{Set } A = \{1, 2, 3, 4, 5,\}$$

$$\text{Set } B = \{2, 4, 6, 8, 10\}$$

$$A \cup B = \{1, 2, 3, 4, 5, 6, 8, 10\}$$

$$A \cap B = \{2, 4,\}$$

The mathematical sentence $2 < \square < 6$ may be thought of as stating two conditions: (1) Two is less than the variable, $2 < \square$; (2) The variable is less than six, $\square < 6$. Let A name the solution set to $2 < \square$ and B name the solution set to $\square < 6$; the set problem and solution set would look like this:

$$A = \{3, 4, 5, \dots\} \quad \text{(all whole numbers greater than 2)}$$

$$B = \{0, 1, 2, 3, 4, 5\} \quad \text{(all whole numbers less than 6)}$$

$$A \cap B = \{3, 4, 5\}$$

To help understand the properties of sets, a pictorial representation called a *Venn diagram* could also be used. By definition, a rectangle with a large $\cup$ is the universal set. With the aide of a Venn diagram, solve the same set problem as above, $2 < \square < 6$. The shaded area shows the solution set for $A \cap B$ or $2 < \square < 6$.

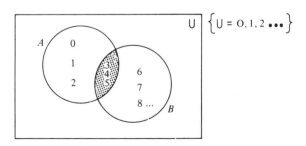

Diagrams are also helpful in understanding and discussing subsets. For example:

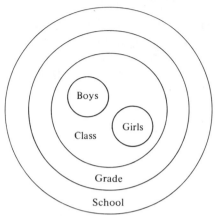

In this diagram, boys are subset of the class, the class is a subset of the grade, the grade is a subset of the school, etc. Likewise the boys, for example, may be broken into subsets of brown-haired, blue-eyed, left-handed, etc., and combinations of these. Such combinations would be intersections. The shaded area is $A \cap B \cap C$ (Intersection).

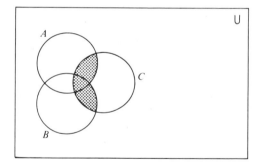

Set A = Brown-haired boys in school
Set B = Blue-eyed boys in school
Set C = Left-handed boys in school
$A \cap B \cap C$ = Brown-haired, blue-eyed, left-handed boys in school
$A \cap B$ = Brown-haired, blue-eyed boys in school
$A \cap C$ = Brown-haired, left-handed boys in school
$C \cap B$ = Left-handed, blue-eyed boys in school

The idea of "sets" is not new. In everyday living, sets have been thought of in terms of dishes, tires, books, blocks, etc. In the traditional mathematics, when groups of things (apples, money) were worked with to establish number concepts, sets were actually worked with without naming them as such. The thoughts and expressions were not well defined.

The "modern" mathematics clarifies and extends these ideas with the early introduction to set language and ideas. The set language is used throughout the study of mathematics as a means of making more precise statements, developing the ability to visualize, analyze, and relate various parts of a problem, solving equations, and describing geometric figures. The language and concept of sets are begun in kindergarten and carried through all further study of mathematics as a unifying thread.

The specific skills and understandings regarding sets that should be developed include the following. The child should be able to:

Grade I

1. Develop the idea that a set is a collection or group of things.
2. Know that things in a set are called its elements or members.
3. Know the number assigned to a set is determined by counting the elements or members of the set.
4. Know that the empty set has no elements. Zero is the number assigned to the empty set.
5. Do the following activities:
    (a) Find and name sets.
    (b) Compare sets.
    (c) Complete sets.
    (d) Match elements of sets in one-to-one correspondence.
    (e) Join sets (set union).
    (f) Separate sets (subtraction) It is permissible to use "take away" in the *beginning* to develop the subtraction concept.
    (g) Discover equal and unequal sets.
    (h) Explore subsets.

Grade II

1. Build on concepts introduced in the previous grades.
2. Continue to:
    (a) Match sets in one-to-one correspondence.
    (b) Compare sets.
    (c) Complete sets.
    (d) Find and name sets.
    (e) Join sets (set union).
    (f) Separate sets.
    (g) Discover equal and unequal sets.
    (h) Explore subsets.

Grade III

1. Build on concepts introduced in the previous grades.
2. Continue to:
   (a) Explore and recognize sets.
   (b) Compare and complete sets.
   (c) Combine and separate sets.
   (d) Work with sets and subsets.
3. Use the new term *element*, which has the same meaning as member. (Member is the term used in the first two grades.)
4. Use braces { } to enclose sets.

Grade IV

1. Review set concepts and notation.
   (a) Define sets and subsets.
       Set A: the set of even numbers—i.e., {2, 4, 6, 8, . . . }
       Set B: subset of set A—i.e., the set of even numbers to six, {2, 4, 6}
   (b) Define elements of sets: the elements of a set are its members, the things, objects, numbers that belong to it. (2 and 4 are elements of set B above.)
   (c) Define *equal* sets: sets that are identical in size, shape, color, and number of elements.
   (d) Define one-to-one correspondence: it exists when sets have the same number of elements. Sets having one-to-one correspondence are *equivalent*.
   (e) Use braces { } to enclose sets.
   (f) Use *null set* as a synonym for *empty set*.
   (g) Use the symbol for empty set, $\emptyset$. Remember the empty set is a subset of all sets.

Grade V

1. Review set concepts and notation as developed in previous grades.
2. Understand *finite* and *infinite* sets.

Grade VI

1. Review set concepts and notation as developed in previous grades.
2. Understand *disjoint* sets. These are sets which have no common element.
3. Understand intersection of sets. The intersection of two sets is a set consisting of only those elements which are common to both sets, for example: Set A = {4, 5, 6, 7}; set B = {6, 7, 8, 9}. The elements 6 and 7 are common to both sets. The set 6, 7 which contains only the elements common to set A and set B is called the intersection of these sets.

SENTENCES

Early in mathematical study children learn to translate or express word problems in a form now referred to as a "number sentence." Such expressions, written horizontally, using frames, provides readiness for use of the equation pattern of thinking in finding an unknown number. Besides calling attention to the missing quantity, use of frames seems to stimulate curiosity; and it challenges the child to find the missing part.

Use of number sentences offers many opportunities for developing understanding of interrelationships in equations and for making general concepts of mathematics more meaningful. The child discovers that number sentences, like word statements, may be true or false according to the quantity replacing the place holder.

The number sentence is an aid to problem solving in that it provides a convenient way of organizing or relating the known to the unknown in the problem. To develop a number sentence a child has to *think* about the problem situation—to visualize it—before he performs the computation. The child's number sentence then reveals to his teacher *his* (the child's) interpretation of the problem situation and the action taking place. The number sentence can be used to provide drill or practice which call for more than rote memorization.

One of the most important ways in which people communicate with each other is through language. In language arts the child learns to construct complete, meaningful English sentences. To express a complete idea, the English sentence must contain a subject and a predicate.

Mathematics, too, is concerned with expressing complete, meaningful ideas in a definite pattern. In developing the properties of numbers and various operations on numbers, we use a rather special language involving:

(a) Symbols for numbers $(1, 3, 5, 7, 9)$
(b) Symbols for operations $(+, -, \times, \div, \ldots)$
(c) Symbols showing relations between numbers $(=, >, <, \neq, \ldots)$

A number may be named by many numerals. For example: $5 + 4$, $11 - 2$, IX, $18/2$, 9, all name the same number. This being true, go a step further: $5 + 4 = 11 - 2$, or $11 - 2 = IX$, or $18/2 = 9$, etc., to show that these are numerals for the same number. In this manner mathematical sentences are formed, where the relation symbol $(=)$, acts as the verb, the numerals to the left act as the subject, and the numeral or numerals to the right act as the predicate noun.

In mathematical sentences the following relation symbols (verbs) are used to relate one expression to another:

$=$	"is equal to" (the same)	$5 + 2 = 4 + 3$
$\neq$	"is not equal to"	$4 + 3 \neq 4 + 1$
$<$	"is less than"	$8 < 9$
$>$	"is greater than"	$14 > 8 + 4$

$\leqslant$ "is less than or equal to" $9 \leqslant 10, 9 \leqslant 10 - 1$
$\geqslant$ "is greater than or equal to" $12 \geqslant 10 + 2$

A statement such as "$8 - 3 = 5$" is in mathematical form (a mathematical sentence), but it can be put into words in the sentence, "If three is subtracted from eight, the result is five." A great deal of modern mathematics is in the form of sentences about numbers or "number sentences" as they are called. These sentences may make true statements, such as "$5 + 3 = 8$," or they may be untrue, such as "$5 + 3 = 6$." However, whether it is true or false, no more disqualifies the fact that it is a sentence than the statement, "John F. Kennedy was the first president of the United States" is disqualified as a sentence. In grammar, "a sentence is a group of words that gives a complete thought." Whether the thought is true or false is immaterial; the same reasoning applies in mathematics. Beyond being classified as either true or false, they can be classified as *closed* and *open*, and as *direct* and *indirect* sentences.

A *closed* mathematical sentence is synonymous with a mathematical statement, in that the sentence contains enough information for us to judge whether or not the sentence is true. Some examples of closed mathematical sentences:

$7 \times 6 = 42$ True statement, but a closed sentence
$6 \times 5 = 3 \times 15$ False statement, but a closed sentence
$9 < 8$ False statement, but a closed sentence

Open sentences are not statements in that they do not contain enough information to determine whether they are true or false. Some examples of open sentences are:

$$\triangle + 5 = 19$$
$$15 - N = \; 7$$
$$(3 \times 4) + 6 = \square$$
$$a + b = b + a$$

The task for the child is to find a number to replace the variable ($\triangle, N, \square$) to make the sentence true. Once the child has rewritten the open sentence, replacing the variable with a number, then he has formed a closed sentence, which will be either a true or a false mathematical statement depending on the child's computational skill.

Direct number sentences are sentences where the operation to be performed is directly indicated and will provide the answer. For example:

$18 + 7 = \triangle$ Add as indicated.
$18 - 7 = \square$ Subtract as indicated.
$N = 18 \div 7$ Divide as indicated.

Indirect sentences are mathematical sentences where the operation symbol does *not* indicate the direct operation to be performed in solving the equation.

Example:

$$18 + \triangle = 25$$

This equation cannot be solved by adding. However, there is a sum (25) and an addend (18). To find the unknown addend, subtract: $25 - 18 = \triangle$. Now there is a direct sentence and proceed to solve the equation.

When presented with an equation, the child should not have to guess how to solve it. Number sentences (closed and open, direct and indirect) are aids in helping the child organize both the data given in a problem and his thoughts in a logical manner that will lead him to the correct method of solving the problem, and the correct answer. In short, mathematical sentences lead to better problem-solving ability.

Note that in modern mathematics many other operational symbols are used than were used with traditional mathematics. In traditional mathematics only the equality operation was really stressed. For example, "If Mary weighs 83 pounds and Anna Louise weighs 78 pounds, how much more does Mary weigh than Anna Louise?" The problem is usually solved in the following manner:

$$\begin{array}{r} 83 \\ -78 \\ \hline 5 \end{array}$$

Mary weighs 5 pounds more than Anna Louise. In traditional mathematics, the variety of ways to express this problem would not have been stressed. The most logical manner to express the problem would be an open, direct sentence: $83 - 78 = \square$. However, the same number relationship could also be expressed by $83 - \square = 78$, or $83 = 78 + \triangle$.

The following true statements could also be made showing number relationships:

$83 - 78 = 5$	Mary is 5 pounds heavier than Anna Louise
$83 - 5 = 78$	Mary's weight less 5 pounds is equal to Anna Louise's weight
$83 = 78 + 5$	Mary's weight is equal to Anna Louise's weight plus 5 pounds
$83 > 78$	Mary's weight is larger than Anna Louise's weight
$78 < 83$	Anna Louise's weight is less than Mary's weight
$78 \neq 83$	Anna Louise's weight is not equal to Mary's weight

The specific skills and understandings regarding mathematical sentences that should be developed include the following. The child should be able to:

Grade I

1. Use open sentences with one and two place-holders.

$$3 + 3 = \square \qquad \triangle + \square + 2 = 9$$

2. Use frames to indicate place-holders.
    (a) Know if two or more frames are the same in a problem, the like frames represent the same numeral.

$$\triangle + \triangle = 12 \qquad \square + \square = 8$$

    (b) Know if frames are different in the problem, they may represent different numerals.

$$\triangle + \square = 9$$

3. Use equations and inequalities.
    (a) Know that equations may exist when expressions on both sides of the equal sign (=) are names for the same numeral.

$$7 = 5 + 2 \qquad (2 + 1) + 3 = \square \qquad 2 + 3 = 6 - \triangle$$

    (b) Use symbols for inequality—*greater than* and *less than*.

$$10 > 9, \quad 4 < 8, \quad 5 + 3 > 6, \qquad 2 + 2 < 8 - 3$$

Grade II

1. Use open sentences with one and two place-holders.

$$8 - \square = 5 \qquad 9 + \square + \triangle = 15$$

2. Use frames to indicate place-holders.
    (a) Know if the frames are the same in a problem; the numerals are the same.

$$\boxed{4} + \boxed{4} = 8$$

    (b) Know if the frames are different in the problem; they represent different numerals.

$$\boxed{5} + \boxed{2} = 7$$

3. Use equations and inequalities.
    (a) Build on equation concepts introduced in previous grades.
    (b) Build on inequality concepts introduced in previous grades.
    (c) Continue to use symbols for greater than (>), for less than (<), is equal to (=), the place-holder ($\triangle$).
    (d) Use the parentheses in equations. Everything within ( ) is a name for one number.

$$2 = (1 + 1) = 4$$

    (e) Understand the symbol of $\neq$ as meaning "not equal to."
4. Use story problems as another means of stating mathematical sentences.
5. Select means of solving these sentences by using subtraction or addition.

Example:

$$9 + \triangle + \square = 12 \qquad 8 - \triangle = 5$$

Grade III

1. Use open sentences with one or two place-holders.
   (a) Build on concepts introduced in previous grades.
2. Use frames to indicate place-holders.
   (a) Build on concepts introduced in previous grades.
3. Use the number line to prove addition and subtraction facts.

4. Use number sentences for word problems, using addition, subtraction, multiplication, and division.

$$
\begin{array}{ll}
34 + 38 = N & N = 72 \\
36 - N = 49 & N = 13 \\
9 + 3 = N & N = 12 \\
15 \div 3 = N & N = 5 \\
9 \times 3 = N & N = 27
\end{array}
$$

Grade IV

1. Use frames and letters as place-holders.
   (a) Know that frames or letters are used to hold the place of the missing numeral.

$$
\begin{array}{ll}
\square \times \square = 36 & n \times n = 36 \\
\square \times 10 = 90 & y \times 10 = 90
\end{array}
$$

   (b) Know that open sentences contain place-holders that cannot yet be judged to be true or false.

$$\triangle \times 52 = 624 \qquad \text{Is the following true or false?}$$
$$12 \times 52 = 624$$

2. Use equations and inequalities.
   (a) Know that equations are number sentences which express an equal relationship. Number represented on one side of equal sign must be the same as that represented on the other side of the equal sign.
   (b) Know that inequalities are number sentences that do not express an equal relationship.
3. Use the following symbols in sentences to determine relationship of numbers.

equal to $=$ greater than $>$

not equal to $\neq$ not greater than $\ngtr$

less than $<$ not less than $\nless$

4. Use number sentences when solving two-step problems.

$$24 - (2 \times 3) = n \quad \text{or} \quad 24 - (3 + 3) = n$$
$$24 - 6 = n \qquad\qquad 24 - 6 = n$$
$$n = 18 \qquad\qquad\quad n = 18$$

Grade V

1. Build on previous learned concepts.
2. Use the symbol $\leq$ as meaning "is less than or equal to."
3. Use the symbol $\geq$ as meaning "is greater than or equal to."
4. Use letters, frames, or any other suitable symbol which stands for the missing numeral as place-holders.
5. Recognize true and false number sentences.
6. Write number sentences when solving problems.

$$501 - 263 = n \qquad n = 238$$

Grade VI

1. Review previous learnings.
2. Derive formulas and generalizations from ideas of geometric formulas.

addend + addend = sum   factor $\times$ factor = product

$\quad x \quad + \quad y \quad = z$ $\quad A \quad \times \quad B \quad = \quad C$

3. Write number sentences when solving word problems and rate problems.

TEACHING SUGGESTIONS

Concept: Sets are made up of single elements

Procedures. 1. The children who wish to buy a complete lunch and the children who wish to buy only milk are asked to stand in separate groups to be counted. The children learn that when the groups are counted the last number named tells how many are in a group, but they can see that the groups are made up of individuals. The children in each group are separated, then brought together again to further the understanding. Later, children are arranged in groups of different patterns, but with the same number of children in each arrangement. Chairs are also placed in groups with varying arrangements, separated and then regrouped, so that children can see that each group is made up of single elements.

2. Blocks, spools, bottle caps, and books can be used to make sets of various numbers of elements.

3. Put 7 erasers on the table. This is considered a set of 7 erasers. In this set there are 7 single elements. The set can be broken down to 7 separate elements; then put together, these elements for a set of 7 erasers.

4. Have several children stand in a group at one side of the room. Ask: Here we see a group of children. How many are in the group? Again emphasize that there are single objects in a group and these objects must be counted to obtain the size of the group.

5. Display a string of beads. Show how you can make the group (set) of beads on the string smaller by removing a bead at a time from the string. Put them all back on the string to show the original group (set). Here it is the set of "group" of beads that is being considered. But there still exists the original "group" of "all the beads we had."

6. Explain the meaning of sets by the use of cutouts and the flannelboard. Put five apples in a group and ask a child to count each element (apple) in the set (group). It is called a set (group) of 5 apples. A set (group) is made up of a number of elements (objects). Show that a set (group) can be made up of anything—apples, pencils, books, chairs, tables, or pens. Now divide the flannelboard into five sections and place an apple in each section. Point out that there is no longer a set of five apples, but now there are 5 sets of 1 element each. Each of these sets are a subset of the original set of five apples. This is true because we can combine the elements into one set of 5 elements. Continue this instruction by separating the original set of 5 apples into subsets of 3 apples and 2 apples; 4 apples and 1 apple; 2 apples and 3 apples; 1 apple and 4 apples; 5 apples and an empty set; and an empty set and 5 apples. Use other cutouts (balls, triangles, squares, and circles) and let the children manipulate them showing how sets (groups) are made up of elements (objects).

7. Present physical objects such as a set of dishes, a set of dominos; etc. Draw from the children the understanding that a collection of things is called a set. Explain to the children that the mathematical name for a collection of objects is "Set."

8. Display and discuss sets of objects. Include some examples in which the elements are dissimilar, for example, a book, a block, and a piece of chalk.

9. Have the children use available objects to create their own sets on their desks and then describe their set.

10. Have the children describe sets of similar things. Make sure that they understand that each thing is a discrete object.

11. Have the children follow the same procedures as in (j), but this time use dissimilar objects. Develop a discussion as to why these objects are considered as sets.

12. Develop the meaning of "element" and "member" of a set by having the children name elements in displayed sets; in sets of similar objects; in sets of dissimilar objects.

13. Develop the understanding that a set may have only one element in the following manner. Ask the children to think of and discuss sets that have only one element.

14. Develop the understanding of the null set in the following manner. Ask the lions in the room to stand. When no one stands, ask: "Is there a set of lions?" (Yes) "Is there a set of lions in the room?" (No) (The set of lions is an empty set or null set.)

Concept: Sets differ in the number of elements they contain

Procedures. 1. After the room leader has taken the lunch count and the milk count, determine whether more children are taking lunch than milk. Use terms such as: as many as, less than, how many more, how many less, the same as, equal to, more than. Then when you go to lunch, the ones taking lunch stand in one line and the ones having milk stand in another line. Compare the length of the two lines.

2. Have two pupils stand on one side of the room and three stand on the other side. Determine which set has more children, which set has fewer children. This can also be done with the boys standing on one side of the room and the girls standing on the other side of the room. Which set is larger, which set is smaller, are they the same size?

3. Dominos can be used to teach the fact that sets may differ in size. One set may have more or fewer elements than another set. The sets may be the same size, each containing the same number of elements. Have someone take a domino out of the box and compare the number of dots (elements) at each end of the domino. Which set of dots contain more, less than, the same as, the set of dots at the other end of the domino?

4. Playing cards, with the face cards omitted may also be used to teach set comparison. Start pairs of children with 20 cards each. With the pack face up, have the children alternately give the difference between the exposed cards. A correct response wins the opponent's card. The child gaining the most cards is the winner.

5. Have the children move elements (objects) such as blocks, sticks, books, and toys to show groups (sets) of varying sizes.

6. Use pictures showing groups (sets) of more, fewer, the same number of objects (elements).

7. Use stacks of books. Have a child bring you the stack with the most books. Use two stacks at first and then increase difficulty by having three or four stacks of books.

8. Exercise: Which is greater?

2 or 6	5 or 2 or 7
4 or 8	3 or 6 or 9
1 or 3	7 or 4 or 2

9. Start by making the differences very obvious by putting 6 elements in one set and 18 elements in another set. Now take 4 elements from the larger set and put them in the smaller set. Are the sets the same size? Keep varying the sets, watching how different children decide, some by actual counting, others by observation.

Concept: Recognition of subsets

Procedures. 1. Introduce term of *subset* by stressing there are groups within groups. For example, a subset of boys may consist of boys with blond hair, brown hair, black hair, and red hair. The boys can be grouped into these subsets but they still are a set of boys. Use other examples: During the regular classroom activities, there will be many opportunities to use and reinforce the concepts of removing a set and having a remaining set. Children in the room can form the original set. The set removed can be those children going to a work area for the free-activity period. Other children are members of the remaining set.

2. Children on their rugs at rest time can form the original set, or a set removed can be described as children who are asked to put away their rugs. At dismissal time, attention can be called to the set of children, to designated subsets that are removed, and to the remaining set.

3. Put the wheeled toys together in a group and ask to have the set described. Show the set of cars without moving them from the larger set.

Is this set of cars a subset of these wheeled toys? (Yes)

Can we remove these cars from the set of toys? (Yes)

Pull the cars to one side, off the rug, but do not take them entirely away.

What set do we have *remaining* here on the rug? (the other wheeled toys) We call this the *remaining set*. The remaining set is the set that is left when we remove a subset from the set we had at first.

Concept: Equivalent sets

Procedures. 1. Discuss with the children the fact that sets can be compared according to number.

2. Match objects to show that they have the same number of elements and discuss the fact that because objects can be matched one to one, we know that the two sets have the same number of elements.

3. Give children opportunity to compare more than just one pair of sets. For example, display a set of erasers, four pencils, and four pieces of chalk. Tell children to compare these sets without discussing the number of each set. Point out that they can do this by one-to-one matching. When they have completed the matching, point out that these sets are *equivalent* to each other, and therefore have the *same number*.

PRACTICE AND EVALUATION

Sets and Sentences

1. Give each child four blocks. Ask the children to make a set out of them. Next have them make their sets one smaller, and then check to see if this has been done. Again have them make the set one smaller, then larger again.
2. Ask the question: Do you know how to make a set larger or smaller? If I add two birds to a set of birds in a tree, how much larger will the set be than it is now?
3. Make a picture showing a set of four balls. Now make the set two balls larger. How many balls did you make in all?
4. Hold up four lollipops. Have four children stand up. Ask the question: If you get part of this set of lollipops, how many will each of you get? (1)
5. Place a set of eight erasers on the table. Ask the children to tell how many erasers are in the group. Place a group of five blocks on the table. Have the children tell how many single elements are in the set.
6. Draw on a chalkboard a set of objects and have a child write the correct number of single objects in the group beside the picture. Repeat the same procedure with a set containing a different number of single elements.
7. Children are asked to draw pictures to make sets match given number symbols.
8. Have a chart with elements placed in sets and ask the children to circle the sets containing a specific number of elements.
9. Give each child ten counters and tell him to make two sets, three sets, four sets, etc. Have him tell how many are in each set.
10. Name as many words as you can that mean set.
11. Write the set of odd numbers from 13 through 27.
12. Record next to the following sets, using set notation, those that have no elements.

    The sets of cats that fly.
    The set of dishes in the kitchen cabinet.
    The set of children in the sixth grade who have blue hair.
    The set of letters in the alphabet.
    The set of even whole numbers having a value less than 1.

13. List the elements of the following sets.

    The set of the Great Lakes.
    The set of the capital city of Indiana.
    The set of players on the baseball team.

14. Consider the following sets:

    $$B = \{Matt, Pam, Christy\}$$

    $$F = \{Sunday, Tuesday, Thursday\}$$

    $$R = \{1, 3, 5, 7, 9\}$$

    Write these sentences in set notation:

    Matt is an element of set A.
    Saturday is an element of set F.
    Bill is not an element of set A.
    7 and 9 are elements of set R.

15. Use set notation to write:

> The set of numbers that are less than 7.
> The set of letters in your name.
> The set of numbers between 50 and 60.

16. Think of five examples of the empty set. Use set notation to write these examples.

17. Describe the following sets:

$$A = \{2, 4, 6, 8, 10\} \qquad C = \{a, e, i, o, u,\}$$

$$B = \{January, June, July\} \qquad D = \{1, 3, 5, 7, 9\}$$

18. List the elements of each set:

> The set of whole numbers greater than 20 and less than 29.
> The set of odd numbers less than 18.
> The set of prime numbers less than 45.

19. List the elements of the following sets, if possible, with the information given.

> set of cards   set of book in your desk
> set of stamps   set of letters
> set of names of the states

20. Make a list of five examples of pairs of sets that are in one-to-one correspondence.

21. Describe the following sets in words:

$$Set\ P = \{Wednesday, Thursday, Friday\}$$

$$Set\ R = \{7, 8, 9, 10, 11, 12, 13, 14, 15, 16\}$$

$$Set\ S = \{blocks, ball, truck, car\}$$

22. Set $A = \{2, 4, 6\}$ Set $B = \{3, 5, 7\}$ Set A _____ Set B (=, ≠)

23. Set C = square, circle, star, triangle   Set B = triangle, star, circle, square

Set C _____ Set D {=, ≠}

24. Draw diagrams to show the following sets and subsets:

> The set whose elements are 3, 5, 7, 9, 11 and set whose elements are 5, 7, 9.
> The set whose elements are the counting numbers between 5 and 10 and the set whose elements are 6 and 7.

SELECTED READINGS

Sets and Sentences

Banks, Houston J. *Learning and Teaching Arithmetic.* Boston: Allyn and Bacon, 1959, pp. 73-78, 369-373.

Bell, Clifford, Cleia Hammond, and Robert Herrera. *Fundamentals of Arithmetic for Teachers.* New York: Wiley, 1962, pp. 16-20.

Brumfield, Charles, Robert Eicholz, and Merrill Shanks. *Fundamental Concepts of Elementary Mathematics*. Reading, Mass.: Addison-Wesley, 1962, pp. 3-13, 63–67, 169–186.

Educational Research Council of Greater Cleveland. *Key Topics for the Primary Teacher*. Chicago: Science Research Associates, 1962, pp. 9-14.

Evenson, A. B. Modern Mathematics: *Introductory Concepts and Their Implications*. Chicago: Scott, Foresman. 1962, pp. 9-22, 199-210.

Fujii, John N. *An Introduction to the Elements of Mathematics*: New York; Wiley, 1961, pp. 16-17, 69-73, 78-84.

Howard, Charles F., and Enoch Dumas. *Basic Procedures in Teaching Arithmetic*. Boston: Health, 1963, pp. 53-56.

Johnson, Donovan A., and William H. Glenn. *Sets, Sentences, and Operations*. St. Louis: Webster, 1960.

Marks, John L., Richard C. Rurdy, and Lucien B. Kinney. *Teaching Arithmetic for Understanding*. New York, McGraw-Hill, 1958, pp. 310-337.

Meserve, Bruce E., and Max A. Sobel. *Mathematics for Secondary School Teachers*. Englewood Cliffs, N. J.: Prentice-Hall, 1962, pp. 77-79.

Morris, Dennis E., and Henry D. Topfer. *Advancing in Mathematics*. Chicago: Science Research Associates, 1963, pp. 49-58, 217-223.

National Council of Teachers of Mathematics. *Insights into Modern Mathematics*. (23rd Yearbook) Washington: the Council, 1957, pp. 36-45.
_____ . *The Growth of Mathematical Ideas*: Grades K–12. (24th Yearbook) Washington: The Council, 1959, pp. 11-17.

Osborn, Roger, Vere DeVault, Claude Boyd, and Robert Houston. *Extending Mathematical Understanding*. Columbus, Ohio: Merrill, 1961, pp. 97-101.

Peterson, John A., and Joseph Hashisaki. *Theory of Arithmetic*. New York: Wiley, 1963, pp. 20-32, 97-108.

Schaaf, William L. *Basic Concepts of Elementary Mathematics*. New York: Wiley, 1960, pp. 10-24.

School Mathematics Study Group. *Studies in Mathematics*. Vol. IX: *A Brief Course in Mathematics for Elementary School Teachers*. Stanford, Calif.: Stanford U. P., 1963, pp. 1-20.

Shipp, Donald, and Sam Adams. *Developing Arithmetic Concepts and Skills*. Englewood Cliffs, N. J.: Prentice-Hall, 1964, pp. 33-65.

Thorpe, Cleata B. *Teaching Elementary Arithmetic*. New York: Harper, 1962, pp. 86-89.

Williams, Sammie, Garland H. Read, Jr., and Frank L. Williams. *Modern Mathematics in the Elementary and Junior High Schools*. New York, Random House, 1961, pp. 74-86, 103-105.

chapter **4**

The Teaching of Whole Numbers (Addition and Subtraction)

The importance of teaching the basic addition and subtraction properties cannot be overemphasized. The study of these processes is begun as soon as the child enters school, where they tell about having two blocks in one hand and three blocks in the other hand, and putting both hands together they have five blocks. This can further be represented by the use of the flannelboard where the blocks are represented by drawings or pictures to show that there are five blocks altogether. In the same manner the basic concept of subtraction is shown by separating two objects from a group of five objects to show that $5 - 2 = 3$. Most of the concepts and skills concerned with addition and subtraction are introduced by the end of the third grade.

Understanding what is meant by addition and subtraction means more than memorizing answers and combinations. Complete understanding means that in working with these processes, students will employ previous learnings to arrive at the use of abstract symbols.

The important fact to remember is that instruction must be systematic. This means that at the beginning much time must be spent for the children to understand the meaning of these two processes. Then and only then do you teach for mastery of the processes. Systematic instruction is introduced through pupil solution of various problem situations. At this stage the children solve these problems by the use of drawings and the use of objects. The basic combinations are developed from the solution of these problems. Appropriate activities such as dramatization, the movement of children, the manipulation of large objects and smaller concrete materials, and imagined situations help to make the concepts clear.

The requiring of children to prove their answers by the use of drawings and other devices is a very important aspect of this instruction. The child is developing understanding and meaning as well as skill in the mastery of the various combinations. Instruction must be such that the children are able to discover relationships between the basic combinations. In subsequent grades the children review, expand, and maintain the various skills and understandings.

This is a suggested sequence for the learning of the basic number combinations:

1. *Show the combination in concrete or picture form.* For example, be able to show $3 + 2 = 5$ by holding 3 blocks in one hand, 2 blocks in the other, then combining the two sets of blocks in one hand and counting the resulting larger set.

2. *Objectify the combination with markers or objects.* For example, represent 3 cookies by 3 markers on the flannelboard, and similarly for 2 cookies, combine the two sets, and count.

3. *Reproduce the combination by drawings.* For example, draw a picture of 3 cookies and a picture of 2 cookies, combine the sets and count.

4. *Write the combination in symbolic form.* For example, $3 + 2 = 5$.

5. *Verify the combination by using a previously known combination.* For example, I already know that $3 + 1 = 4$, so I recognize $3 + 2$ as being one more than $3 + 1$.

6. *Use the combination in a problem.* For example, Matt had 3 cookies in one hand and 2 cookies in the other. How many cookies did Matt have altogether?

In the beginning exercises, the student works with concrete materials. As he begins to understand he should proceed to the use of semiconcrete materials, and later on to the use of abstract symbols. As his number experiences increase, he will begin to discover the new combinations through associations with already known combinations or through other number relationships. At this point he shows his readiness to develop new skills in addition and subtraction through the use of abstract forms rather than concrete materials.

Systematic instruction in the more efficient ways of adding or subtracting multidigit numbers does not begin until the children have mastered the basic combinations. The various problems are presented and the children directed to obtain the answer for each question, and show by diagram, picture, or drawing that the answer is correct. Discussion follows with the teacher guiding the children to see the more efficient ways of solving the problems, such indirect means of solving as the number line, tens blocks, counters, flannelboard, and other concrete and semiconcrete materials are used as a check on the correctness of the number solution.

Three important principles must be developed and understood by the children in regard to multiplace addition and subtraction:

1. Only digits in like places can be added/subtracted.

Example: In adding $23 + 21$, the 3 units and the 1 unit are added together to get 4 units; then the 2 tens and the other 2 tens are added together to get 4 tens, giving the answer 4 tens and 4 units or 44.

2. The understanding of place value.

Example: In the number 256, the 2 stands for 2 hundreds; the 5 for 5 tens; and the 6 for 6 ones. $200 + 50 + 6 = 256$.

3. When adding, add from the right to the left.

Example: $234 + 453$; add the 4 ones and the 3 ones, then the 3 tens and the 5 tens, then the 2 hundreds and the 4 hundreds. Answer, 687. This same principle holds for subtraction.

Another difficult concept for the children to understand concerns column addition. Here the child has to develop the ability to add to a seen and an unseen number. The difficulty arises through the fact that one of the numbers added after the first addition is not visible.

Example: $3 + 4 + 5 + 6 = n$. In the first addition you can see the 3 and the 4 giving the sum of 7, but you cannot see the 7 when in turn you add it to the 5 getting a sum of 12, nor do you see the 12 when you add it to the 6 giving you the answer 18.

There are many methods suggested for teaching advanced addition and subtraction. Regardless of what method is used, children need continual practice and study in this phase of mathematics.

PROPERTIES AND RELATIONSHIPS

Addition is a binary operation in which an ordered pair of numbers is operated on to yield a third number called the *sum*. Each number in the ordered pair is called an *addend*.

Example:

addend		addend		sum
2	+	7	=	9

Subtraction is a binary operation on an ordered pair of numbers. It is the operation of finding a missing addend when the sum and the other addend are known.

Example:

addend		addend		sum
4	+		=	9

In terms of subtraction this is *finding the difference*. Properties of operation of addition and subtraction are:

1. Associative Property. When three numbers are to be added in a stated order, the way in which they are grouped does not effect the sum. In its abstract generalized form, this may be stated:

$$(a + b) + c = a + (b + c)$$
$$(6 + 2) + 1 = 6 + (2 + 1)$$

Subtraction is not associative:

$$(5 - 3) - 1 \neq 5 - (3 - 1)$$

Other applications include:
   Children add the second number in steps by reaching 10.

$$9 + 7 \text{ as } 9 + (1 + 6) = (9 + 1) + 6 = 16$$

Extended to higher-decade additions:

$$17 + 6 \text{ as } 17 + (3 + 3) = (17 + 3) + 3 = 23$$

Extend to adding to numbers in the hundreds and thousands, etc.

$$126 + 8 = (126 + 4) + 4 = 134$$
$$2{,}167 + 9 = (2{,}167 + 3) + 6 = n$$

Complete the equations below. Regroup as needed.

$$6 + 8 = \quad (6 + 4) + 4 = n$$
$$26 + 8 = \quad (26 + 4) + 4 = n$$
$$226 + 8 = \quad (226 + 4) + 4 = n$$
$$1{,}226 + 8 = (1{,}226 + 4) + 4 = n$$

2. Commutative Property. The order in which two numbers are added does not affect the sum. In its abstract generalized form, this may be stated for each replacement of a and b.

$$a + b = b + a$$
$$6 + 2 = 2 + 6$$

Subtraction is *not* commutative.

$$a - b \neq b - a$$
$$8 - 2 \neq 2 - 8$$

Other applications include:
   Higher-decade addition:

$$7 + 35 = 35 + 7; 9 + 67 = 67 + 9$$

Adding to numbers in the hundreds:

$$4 + 119 = 119 + 4$$

Adding to numbers in the thousands:

$$6 + 2,245 = 2,245 + 6$$

From this presentation the children may summarize that the order of the addends may be interchanged without changing the sum. Reversing the addends sometimes helps to make an addition easier:

$8 + 5$ is easier than $5 + 8$
$1,126 + 6$ is easier than $6 + 1,126$

3. Inverse Operations. The inverse operation of "adding" a number is "subtracting" that number.

$$a + b = c; \quad c - b = a$$
$$3 + 6 = 9; \quad 9 - 6 = 3$$

The inverse of adding 6 is subtracting 6. The additive inverse of 6 is $- 6$. Other applications include:

Child relates adding and subtracting.

$$7 + 4 = 11 \qquad 17 + 4 = 21$$
$$11 - 4 = 7 \qquad 21 - 4 = 17$$

Extend to adding and subtracting from numbers in hundreds and thousands.

$$137 + 8 = n \qquad 5,679 + 6 = n$$
$$n - 8 = 137 \qquad n - 6 = 5,679$$

4. The Identity Element for addition is zero.

$$a + 0 = 0 + a = a$$
$$7 + 0 = 0 + 7 = 7$$

5. Closure. The set of whole numbers is closed with respect to addition. When whole numbers are added, the sum is always a whole number.

The set of whole numbers is *not* closed with respect to subtraction.

Example:

$$4 - 6 = - 2$$

where 4 and 6 belong to the set of whole numbers; $- 2$ does not belong to the set of whole numbers.

The specific skills and understanding regarding the various properties and relationships with whole numbers as regards the operations of addition and subtraction include the following. The child should be able to:

Grade I

1. Understand the commutative property of addition. (The order of addends does not change the sum.)

$$2 + 4 = 6 \qquad 4 + 2 = 6$$

2. Understand the associative property of addition. (When three or more numbers are to be added in stated order, the way in which they are grouped does not effect the sum.)

$$7 + 2 + 1 + 6 = (7 + 2 + 1) + 6 = 16$$

3. Understand the inverse operation with addition and subtraction.

$$3 + 1 = 4 \qquad 4 - 1 = 3$$
$$1 + 3 = 4 \qquad 4 - 3 = 1$$

4. Understand the relationships between facts (patterns).
   (a) Show that when 1 is added to a number, the sum is the next counting number.

$$
\begin{array}{cccccc}
1 & 2 & 3 & 4 & 5 & 6 \\
\underline{+1} & \underline{+1} & \underline{+1} & \underline{+1} & \underline{+1} & \underline{+1} \\
2 & 3 & 4 & 5 & 6 & 7
\end{array}
$$

   (b) Show that when 1 is subtracted from a number, the remainder is the next lower counting number.

$$
\begin{array}{cccccc}
2 & 3 & 4 & 5 & 6 & 7 \\
\underline{-1} & \underline{-1} & \underline{-1} & \underline{-1} & \underline{-1} & \underline{-1} \\
1 & 2 & 3 & 4 & 5 & 6
\end{array}
$$

   (c) Show that when 0 is added or subtracted from a number, the number remains the same.

$$
\begin{array}{cccc}
2 & 3 & 2 & 3 \\
\underline{+0} & \underline{+0} & \underline{-0} & \underline{-0} \\
2 & 3 & 2 & 3
\end{array}
$$

5. Explain that zero is the identity element for addition. The sum of zero and any other number is the same number.
6. Understand that zero is the cardinal number of the empty set.

Grade II

1. Review the commutative property of addition.

$$2 + 1 = 3 \qquad 5 + 4 = 9$$
$$1 + 2 = 3 \qquad 4 + 5 = 9$$

2. Review the associative property of addition.

$$1 + (4 + 2) = 7$$
$$(1 + 4) + 2 = 7$$

3. Use the associative property with teen combinations.

$$12 + 5 = (10 + 2) + 5 = 10 + (2 + 5) = 17$$

4. Discover experiences which give readiness for division by joining sets, separating sets, and recording your findings. A flannelboard is very useful in teaching these concepts.

Grade III

1. Review previous learnings.
2. Continue to develop concepts of the associative property of addition.
3. Continue to develop concepts of the commutative property of addition.

$$4 + 3 = \triangle \qquad 3 + 4 = \triangle$$

Grade IV

1. Review previous learning.
2. Continue to develop concepts of the associative property of addition.

$$(4 + 2) + 6 = 6 + 6 = \square$$

or

$$4 + (2 + 6) = 4 + 8 = \square$$

3. At this level, the children should be taught to use the precise vocabulary for these concepts and be expected to use it.

Grade V

1. Review previous learning.
2. Understand and use each of the basic properties:
   (a) Use the commutative property of addition.
   (b) Use the associative property of addition.
   (c) Use inverse operation (addition-subtraction)
3. Use the properties of zero:
   (a) Additive identity: $0 + C = C$
   (b) Zero as a place-holder.

Grade VI

1. Review previous learnings.
2. Express properties in algebraic form.
3. Understand closure under addition.
4. Continue to develop concepts concerning associative and commutative property of addition.

The specific relationship, skills, and understandings between addition and subtraction that should be developed include the following. The child should be able to:

1. Demonstrate by using number chart, etc., that subtraction has a definite relationship to addition. Addition is the inverse of subtraction.

Example:

$$6 + 2 = 8 \qquad 8 - 2 = 6$$

2. Write the family of 4 relationships which exist between a given set of 3 members.

Example: For the set 3, 4, and 7, the relationship would be

$$3 + 4 = 7 \qquad 4 + 3 = 7$$
$$7 - 4 = 3 \qquad 7 - 3 = 4$$

3. Show that subtraction can be proved by addition.

Example:

$$
\begin{array}{cc}
8 & 5 \\
-5 & +3 \\
\hline
3 & 8
\end{array}
$$

4. Demonstrate by using manipulative material that each basic process can be interpreted as the rearranging or regrouping of a collection of elements and that all basic processes are interrelated.

5. Show the correctness of addition exercises with up to 5 addends by subtraction.

$$
\begin{array}{cccc}
9 & 14 & 6 & 15 \\
+5 & -5 & 4 & -6 \\
\hline
14 & 9 & 5 & 9 \\
& & \hline
& & 15 & -4 \\
& & & \hline
& & & 5
\end{array}
$$

6. Demonstrate the correctness of subtraction exercises by:
   (a) Subtract remainder from minuend and the difference should be equal to the subtrahend of the original problem.

Example:

$$
\begin{array}{cc}
54 & 54 \\
-21 & -33 \\
\hline
33 & 21
\end{array}
$$

   (b) The sum of the subtrahend and the remainder should equal the minuend.

Example:

$$
\begin{array}{cc}
54 & 21 \\
-33 & +33 \\
\hline
21 & 54
\end{array}
$$

TEACHING SUGGESTIONS

Concept: Associative property

Procedures. 1. Show three sets of objects on the demonstration table, making sure that the total number of objects is ten or less. For example, exhibit a set of two, a set of three, and a set of four. Have the children identify the number of each set. Write these numbers on the chalkboard so that a definite order is established. The left to right order is established and should be the same as on the demonstration table.

2. Have a short oral drill on the meaning of place value.

Example: Give the children the number 48 and have them tell how many tens and how many more are there. Following this write it on the chalkboard and have the children fill in the answers. $48 = \_\_\_$ tens and $\_\_\_$.

3. Have children regroup the following problems in terms of tens and ones. For example:

$$12 + 7 = 10 + (2 + 7) = 10 + 9 = 19$$
$$13 + 5 = 10 + (\_ + 5) = 10 + \_ = \_\_$$

4. Show three addends; 3, 4, 5 (any will do). Explain to the children you can add $3 + 4$, and then add $7 + 5 = 12$. Or, show them you can add $4 + 5$ first, which is 9, and then $9 + 3 = 12$, $3 + 9 = 12$. Be sure that the children understand that any grouping which helps them is acceptable, and will give them the same answer.

5. Place a series of numerals on the chalkboard, then have the children take turns writing different numerals for the numbers represented.

$$24 + 3 = 20 + (4 + 3)$$
$$80 + 17 = 80 + 10 + 7$$
$$55 + 3 = 50 + 5 + 3$$
$$50 + 5 + 3 = 50 + 7$$
$$30 + 8 + 10 + 2 = 50$$

6. Give an oral presentation of chain problems. Make the problems as simple or as complex as they need be to challenge the children's abilities. For example: "Ten plus seven" (pause) "plus forty." Or say, "Twenty plus thirty" (pause) "plus nine."

7. Provide a list of numbers on the chalkboard such as 7, 11, 5, 8. Choose a child to come up and add these in any order he likes and write his order for these numbers. Conduct a discussion with the children to show that although the orders in groupings have been changed, the sums remain the same.

8. Place five strips of blue paper, one strip of brown paper, and two strips of red paper in the reading pocket chart. Have the children read the grouping of sets they see, from top to bottom. Have a child write the related column addi-

tion on the chalkboard. Have the children read from bottom to top. Have the related column addition read this way. Change the order of the top two sets and have the related column addition written on the chalkboard and read two ways. Continue in this manner to have children scramble the sets until all possible combinations of the three sets are discovered and the related column additions written on the chalkboard. Follow the same procedure with other sets and numbers.

9. Give three children cards with numerals representing numbers whose sum is no greater than nine. Have them stand in a straight line in front of the class. Have the numbers added, reading from left to right. Have the related equation written on the chalkboard and read aloud, "Two plus one equals three; three plus six equals nine." Have the class decide upon a different arrangement of these numbers. Direct the children to change places accordingly. Have the equation related to this new grouping written on the chalkboard and read. Continue in this way until the class discovers all possible combinations for these three addends. Change the numerals and call upon three different children to begin the activity again.

10. Prepare number cards on which are written placeholder equations involving three addends. Have the place-holder appear in various positions. Expose the cards to view, one at a time, and have the children read each completed equation.

Concept: Commuting the addends does not change the sum

Procedures. 1. Have 5 boys on one side of the room, and 3 boys on the other. Point to one set of boys and ask: "How many are there on this side? (5) How many on that side? (3) Five boys and 3 boys are how many boys altogether?" Have the children count the total and write the number problem on the board. 5 boys + 3 boys = 8 boys. Next have the boys change sides of the room and go through the same procedure. Have another child write: 3 boys + 5 boys = 8 boys. Next compare the two examples side by side: 5 boys and 3 boys are 8 boys; 3 boys and 5 boys are 8 boys. Do this same technique with girls; you may use three groups, interchanging them.

2. On a table lay 7 counting sticks or other easy-to-handle objects, such as tongue depressors, jacks, or clothespins. Have the children count them. Then call on various children to show how many different ways the objects can be picked up in two-hand combinations: 6 and 1, 1 and 6, 5 and 2, 2 and 5, 4 and 3, 3 and 4. Emphasize that the entire group is contained in the two parts whose total is 7. Write the number picked up in each hand on the chalkboard and total for each pupil. Show that all are equal, no matter in what order they are picked up.

3. Place 5 objects on a table in this fashion: XX   XXX. Have the children approach the table from one side, showing left to right sets 2 + 3 and ask, "How

many are there?" (5) Write the answer on the board and have the children re-turn to their desks and write the combination. Now have the children approach the table from the opposite side of the table, showing right to left sets, 3 + 2, and ask, "How many are there;" (5) Write the answer on the board or have the children write the combination at their desks. Emphasize that we have not touched the objects—just looked at them or thought about them in a different manner or order. The total is still the same (5).

4. Place three objects on the table. Show the order principle of addition by manipulation of objects and have the children identify the number of this set. Then place with these three objects a set of four objects, and have the children identify both the number of the set of objects put with the first set and the total number of objects. Follow this by exhibiting the equation 3 + 4 = 7, calling at-tention to the fact that you started with three objects joined them with four more objects and now have a total of seven objects in the new set. Repeat the demonstration by reversing the order of the sets presented, and then exhibiting the equation 4 + 3 = 7. Emphasize that here you start with four objects, joined them with three more, and now have a total of seven objects in the new set. Ob-serve with the children that the result is the same in both equations.

5. Draw a picture of the joining of two sets and let the children draw a pic-ture of joining the two sets in a different way. Then have the children write the two equations representing the two pictures.

6. Have the children rewrite problems another way. Fill in the blanks. For example:

$$4 + 3 = 3 + 4 \qquad 27 + 32 = \underline{\quad} + \underline{\quad}$$
$$8 + 9 = 9 + 8 \qquad 0 + \ 6 = \underline{\quad} + \underline{\quad}$$

7. Draw a number line on the chalkboard to use in reviewing this mathe-matical principle. Let the children work problems and see how the principle works. For example:

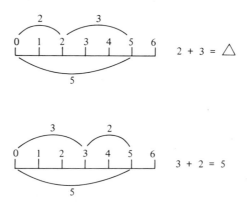

8. Use the number line and involve three jumps rather than two. Help children to see that the order of grouping does not make any difference. For example:

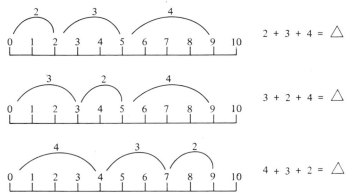

9. Have children associate a number sentence with the joining of two sets. For example, draw on the board:

Let the children discuss and write the number sentence that tells about it underneath.

10. When children understand how to add three numerals horizontally, present the vertical arrangement.

11. Give the children several exercises which would show the order principle for addition as:

$$22 + 5 = 5 + \underline{\quad} = \underline{\quad}$$
$$7 + 6 = \underline{\quad} + \underline{\quad} = \underline{\quad}$$

Concept: Zero added to a number does not change the value (identity element of addition)

Procedures. 1. Place two boxes on the table, one containing a set of four elements (spoons), the other containing an empty set. Ask the class to count the spoons in the one box (4) and the other box (0). Then put the 4 spoons from the first box into the second box and ask the class what the sum of the spoons this made by combining the elements together into a new set (4). Repeat using different amounts of elements in the box. On the board write:

$$0 = \underline{\quad\quad\quad}$$
$$4 = \underline{\quad\quad\quad}$$

Ask the class how many pictures of spoons should be drawn to represent (0) spoons. Ask the class how many pictures of spoons should be drawn to represent (4) spoons.

$$0 =$$
$$4 =$$

marks or spoons. Have the children put 4 crayons on the desk. Ask them how they would have to group the crayons to have 4 crayons in one set and 0 crayons in another set $4 + 0 = 4$.

2. Teach the use of (0) in addition only after the children have had many experiences with other types of addition. Place three chairs in one group and put a chair all by itself. Have three children come and sit in the three chairs (3). How many children are sitting in the chair over there by itself? (none) Explain that the number symbol for none, not any, nothing, or zero is (0). Write (0) on the board. Now if we add the zero and the three, how many do we have? (3). Continue until all numerals from 1 to 10 have been used.

3. Ten sticks and two cans shorter than the sticks are needed. Place the two cans on a table in the front of the room and put two sticks in one can and none in the other. There are now two sticks in one can and none in the other. Ask the class to add the contents of the two cans. Write on the board $2 + 0 = 2$. Have the children write the other combinations as you change the number of sticks in the can. Talk each problem over before going on to another. Use different kinds of elements—blocks, toys, pencils, or chairs.

4. Play the following game with the children. Cut out circles and give each child four circles. Then go to each child and merely stand before him for a moment, not giving him anything, and return to your desk. Next, ask them how many circles you gave them the first time. (4) Write the 4 on the board. Now ask them how many circles you gave them the second time (0). Write = 0 alongside the 4. Now ask them how many circles they have altogether. (4) The presentation in this manner allows the children to see the entire development of the combination $4 + 0 = 4$. Have them work this type of problem with other elements and combinations.

5. The class plays a game which requires score keeping. When a child misses the peg, as in bean bag or ring toss, you can teach the meaning of zero in keeping score. It shows that you scored nothing—you missed—but you did have your turn. It shows that you added nothing to your score, since zero means nothing, or "not any" in this case.

Score:

Pamela	Christy	Matt
3	2	2
0	1	0
1	0	1
4	3	3

6. Each child has number cards 0 through 9. Write $2 + 5 =$ ____ on the board and ask the children to hold up the card with the correct answer, then write $2 + 0 =$ ____ , on the board and ask them to hold up the card with the correct answer. Continue testing the various combinations including those involving "0." Illustrate with concrete elements (materials).

Concept: The related facts in addition and subtraction:
$(2 + 5, 5 + 2, 7 - 5, 7 - 2)$

Procedures. 1. On the flannelboard or chart have the shapes of 5 cars. Then add 2 more cars so that there is now a group of 7 cars. Remove 2 cars from the group and there are 5 cars left. Go through the same procedure with 2 and 5, and 5 from 7. Have some children go to the front of the room and manipulate the flannelboard as you have shown them to. At their seats, have the class draw 5 cars, then 2 more. Ask how many there are now. Have the children write the problem under the picture. Now if you cross out 2 cars, how many will be left? If you cross out 5 cars, how many will be left? From these exercises, the class will see that 2 and 5 = ____ , 5 and 2 = ____ , 7 - 5 = ____ , and 7 - 2 = ____ are related.

2. Each child is given seven blocks. Have them count their blocks in as many different combinations as they wish. *Conclusion*: In any way that I count, there are still 7 blocks. Now group the blocks, 2 blocks in your left hand and 5 blocks in your right hand. *Conclusion*: 2 blocks and 5 blocks equal 7 blocks. Switch hands, now you have 5 blocks in your left hand and 2 blocks in your right hand. *Conclusion*: 5 blocks and 2 blocks are 7 blocks. Therefore the addition combinations are related. Can you use these three numbers (2, 5, and 7) in subtractions? Write the problems we have just done. Then using only the numbers 7, 5, and 2, write the two subtraction problems. You will find that $2 + 5 = 7$; $5 + 2 = 7$; $7 - 5 = 2$; and $7 - 2 = 5$ are related addition and subtraction combinations.

3. Have the children make story problems concerning the four related number combinations. Then have them dramatize these stories.

4. Have the children use paper plates with a line drawn across the center. Have them place eight counters on the left side of the plate and one counter on the right side. Have them place the related addition equation under the plate. Tell them to remove the set of nine and to place the equation representing this activity under the addition equation. Have the children tell two sets of stories and read the related equations. Continue the activity using other number combinations.

5. Have the children use their ten-frames to illustrate that addition and subtraction are inverse operations. Use the number strips on the flannelboard to guide the activity. Follow the procedure suggested for development of the inverse concept related to sums of eight.

6. Mark off nine 9-in. squares on the floor. Have the class sit in a circle

around the strip of nine blocks. Have one child be "It." Ask the rest of the children to close their eyes during this game. The child who is "it" chooses a numeral as his starting point and tells the rest of the class where he is. He may say, "I am standing on the 8." Have him walk backward, stepping on one numeral after another, and tell the class how many steps he has moved. For example: "I have walked backward five steps." Call on a child to tell what square the walker has stopped on. Have the related subtraction equation written on the chalkboard: $8 - 5 = 3$. As a variation of this activity, a child may combine forward and backward steps. In each instance have the children determine whether an addition or subtraction idea was involved.

PRACTICE AND EVALUATION

Associative Property of Addition

1. Activities with different concrete objects or groups of children, can be used to help establish this concept:
    (a) $(3 + 2) + = $ _____ $+ 4$
    (b) $(4 + 1) + 0 = $ _____ $+ 0$
    (c) $5 + (1 + 2) = 5 + $ _____
    (d) $(0 + 4) + 2 = $ _____ $+ (4 + 2)$
    (e) $5 + (3 + 1) = $ _____ $+ $ _____
    (f) $(6 + 2) + 1 = $ _____ $+ $ _____
2. Complete the mathematical sentences.
    (a) $(4 + 4) + 1 = $ _____ $+ 1$
    (b) $(2 + 1) + 4 = $ _____ $+ 4$
    (c) $(3 + 5) + 1 = $ _____ $+ 1$
    (d) $3 + (4 + 6) = 3 + $ _____
    (e) $2 + (4 + 3) = 2 + $ _____
    (f) $(7 + 3) + 5 = $ _____ $+ 5$
    (g) $(6 + 4) + 4 = $ _____ $+ 4$
3. Complete the mathematical sentences.
    (a) $13 + 5 = (10 + 3) + 5$
             $= 10 + ($ _____ $+ 5)$
    (b) $16 + 3 = (10 + $ _____ $) + 3$
             $= 10 + ($ _____ $+ 3)$
    (c) $33 + 7 = (30 + 3) + 7$ _____ $= 30 + $ _____
             $= 30 + (3 + $ _____ $) = $
    (d) $23 + 5 = ($ _____ $+ 3) + 5$
             $= $ _____ $+ (3 + 5)$
    (e) $21 + 4 = ($ _____ $+ 1) + 4$
             $= $ _____ $+ $ _____
             $= $ _____
    (f) $38 + 2 = (30 + 8) + 2$
             $= $ _____ $+ (8 + 2)$
             $= $ _____ $+ $ _____
             $= $ _____ . _____

4. Group the addends in any manner. *Do not change* the order of the addends. By the use of parentheses show the addends that you group.

(a) $7 + 3 + 8 =$
(b) $28 + 29 + 1 =$
(c) $18 + 2 + 7 =$
(d) $36 + 4 + 9 =$
(e) $48 + 22 + 59 =$
(f) $65 + 5 + 9 =$
(g) $88 + 25 + 45 =$
(h) $64 + 27 + 33 =$

5. Place the correct sign $(+, -)$ in each placeholder.

(a) $7 + 8 = 10 \triangle 5$
(b) $(13 - 3) - 2 = 6 \triangle 2$
(c) $23 \triangle 9 = 10 + 4$
(d) $(16 - 6) - 3 = 3 + (2 \triangle 2)$
(e) $8 + 4 = 15 \triangle 3$
(f) $8 + 4 = 6 \triangle 6$
(g) $(3 + 8) + 4 = 8 \triangle 7$
(h) $(22 - 6) + 4 = 14 \triangle 6$

Commutative Property of Addition

1. Look at the sets pictured below. Solve each problem.

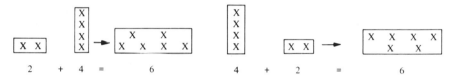

$$2 \quad + \quad 4 \quad = \quad 6 \qquad\qquad 4 \quad + \quad 2 \quad = \quad 6$$

$$6 \quad + \quad 3 \quad = \qquad\qquad 3 \quad + \quad 6$$

$2 + 4 = \square$		$3 + 2 = \square$
$3 + 6 = \square$		$4 + 2 = \square$
$2 + 3 = \square$		$6 + 3 = \square$
$5 + 2 = \square$		$2 + 5 = \square$

2. Complete:

$4 + 3 = 3 + 4$
$8 + 9 = \underline{\quad} + \underline{\quad}$
$4 + 0 = \underline{\quad} + \underline{\quad}$
$0 + \underline{\quad} = \underline{\quad} + 0$
$6 + \underline{\quad} = \underline{\quad} + 6$
$24 + 35 = \underline{\quad} + \underline{\quad}$

3. Decide which of the following mathematical sentences are true:

$27 + 48 = 48 + 27$
$215 + 215 = 251 + 251$
$6^2 + 4^2 = 4^2 + 6^2$
$16_{four} + 46_{four} < 46_{four} + 16_{four}$
$7 + 4 > 7 + 3$
$a + 7 = 7 + a$
$a^2 + b = b^2 + a$
$4^2 + n = n^2 + 4$

UNION OF SETS AND ADDITION OF NUMBERS

Two sets may be combined or joined to form a new set. The new set is called the union of the two sets. The term "union" is applied both to the operation and to the resulting set. Understanding of the union of two sets is basic to the understanding of addition of whole numbers.

The term "union" applies to sets and the term "addition" applies to numbers.

Example:

$$\text{Let } A = \{a,b,c,d\}$$
$$B = \{q,r,s,t\}$$

Then $A \cup B = C$ where

$$C = \{a,b,c,d,q,r,s,t\}$$

and

$$N(A) + N(B) = N(C)$$
$$4 + 4 = 8$$

This is the way we can define the operation of the addition of two whole numbers which will be called "*a*" and "*b*."

If $N(A) = a$, and $N(B) = b$; where A and B are disjoint sets; then $a + b$ is equal to $N(A \cup B)$. By applying this definition we can verify each of the properties that is noted earlier in this chapter.

Basic Addition Facts

Basic addition facts are statements about the addition of two numbers, each less than 10. Examples of addition facts are:

$$7 + 2 = 9 \qquad 3 + 2 = 5 \qquad 4 + 4 = 8 \qquad 5 + 5 = 10$$

There are 45 basic addition facts with sums in the first decade, that is, sums of 10 or less than 10. There are 36 basic addition facts with sums in the second decade—that is, sums from 11 to 18. There are 19 "zero facts." This makes a total of 100 basic addition facts.

Teachers must aim for automatic response to basic facts by their children. Automatic response is achieved through periodic drill.

All drills should be organized according to specific patterns which emphasize one type of relationship at a time. When facts are presented in random order this is considered "testing," rather than drill. A few minutes of each lesson should be devoted to drill. It must be related to the major topic under consideration, whenever possible. All drill and practice exercises or sequences should involve problem solving.

Adding by Grouping "Tens"

This is an application of the "associative property of addition." This property states that three numbers may be combined (associated) in two different ways without affecting the sum.

This property is applied in a drill on addition facts, and in learning higher-decade addition, etc., where the second number is added in steps, as follows:

1. *Addition Facts*: $9 + 8 = n$. The three sets to be added are 9, 1, 7. Drill by relating to 10 involves this association: $(9 + 1) + 7$. To arrive at the sum, children count forward: 10, 17.

Automatic response involves this association: $9 + (1 + 7)$. Thus will eventually respond automatically to $9 + 8$ as: 17.

2. *Higher-Decade Addition*: $74 + 8 = n$. The three sets to be added are: 74, 6, 2.

Adding by relating to tens involves this association: $(74 + 6) + 2$. To arrive at the sum in this way, children count forward: 80, 82. Later, children will make the association: $74 + (6 + 2)$, responding automatically to $74 + 8 = 82$.

3. *Adding Numbers in the Hundreds*: $363 + 9 = n$. The three sets to be added are 360, 7, 2.

Adding by relating tens involves this association: $(363 + 7) + 2$. To arrive at the sum in this way, children count forward: 370, 372. Later, children will automatically make the association: $363 + (7 + 2)$, responding automatically to $363 + 7 = 392$.

4. *Adding Numbers in the Thousands*: $1,267 + 5 = n$. The three sets to be added are 1,267, 3, 2.

Adding by relating tens involves this association: $(1,267 + 3) + 2$. To arrive at the sum in this way, children count forward: 1,270, 1,272. Later, children will automatically make the association: $1,267 + (3 + 2)$, responding automatically to $1,267 + 5 = 1,272$.

Emphasize Mathematical Relationships

Throughout the entire instructional program of teaching the operation of addition, emphasize the following mathematical relationships:

1. *Application of Commutative Property*:

$$2 + 3 \text{ thought of as } 3 + 2$$
$$7 + 36 \text{ thought of as } 36 + 7$$
$$9 + 346 \text{ thought of as } 346 + 9$$

2. *Deriving Near-Doubles from Doubles*:

From $6 + 6$ we derive, $6 + 5$, $6 + 7$, $5 + 6$, and $7 + 6$.
From $33 + 33$ we derive, $33 + 34$, $33 + 32$, $34 + 33$, and $32 + 33$.

3. *Application of Associative Property*:

8 + 7 thought of as
$$8 + (2 + 5) = (8 + 2) + 5 = 10 + 5 = 15$$
46 + 9 thought of as
$$46 + (4 + 5) = (46 + 4) + 5 = 50 + 5 = 55$$
275 + 8 thought of as
$$275 + (5 + 3) = (275 + 5) + 3 = 280 + 3 = 283$$

Column Addition

Usually, the term "column addition" is used to refer to additions involving three or more addends arranged in a column, that is vertically. Teachers should use a variety of procedures to make sure that children add "in order" and that they add both up and down. These procedures are important in order to:

1. Provide continuous emphasis on higher-decade additions.

2. Encourage the habit of checking a column by adding in the reverse direction.

There are four basic levels of instruction in regard to the teaching of column addition.

1. *Presentation of Additions Orally*: Children record only the total.

Examples:

$$2 + 3 + 2 \quad (7)$$
$$4 + 2 + 1 + 3 \quad (10)$$
$$3 + 5 + 1 + 0 \quad (9)$$
$$2 + 3 + 0 + 1 + 3 \quad (9)$$

2. *Presentation of Additions in Column Form.* Children record the successive sums.

Instruct the children to record sums in steps as illustrated below. (Statements in parenthesis are for teacher's information only).

(Step 9: 8 + 2)	10	2	↓	
(Step 8: 5 + 3)	8	3	5	(Step 1: Add 3 + 2. Write 5)
(Step 7: 5 + 0)	5	0	5	(Step 2: Add 5 + 0. Write 5)
(Step 6: 1 + 4)	5	4	9	(Step 3: Add 5 + 4. Write 9)
	↑	1	10	(Step 4: Add 9 + 1. Encircle final sum)
		10		(Step 5: Record final sum in column)
				(Step 10: Check all final sums. Encircle 10 in column)

3. *Presentation of Additions in Horizontal Form*

(a) Have children record successive sums as follows:

$$3 + 2 + 1 + 2 + 0 + 2 = n$$

1. Adding forward ───────────→ 5   6   8   8   10
2. Adding backward ←───────── 10   7   5   4   2
3. Recording final sum after "=" sign   = 10

(b) Have the children point to successive numerals but do not record successive sums.

4. *Another Presentation of Additions in Column Form.* Children are not to record successive sums as was done in part "2."

Regrouping in Addition

When regrouping in addition is to be learned, the children are guided to discover ways of solving the given problem. The more ways suggested, the higher is the indicated level of understanding numbers. Manipulative materials are provided to aid in finding the solutions. The solutions are then written in symbolic form. The process should be followed by a verification of the answer by approximating the result and then correcting. This can be done by rounding the numbers to the nearest ten and adding or subtracting as the case may be.

When the children are ready to duplicate the solution of the problem with symbols, there are steps of procedure by means of which the better representations can be developed. In the example $25 + 46 = n$, the quantities may be written:

2 tens and 5 ones
4 tens and 6 ones
─────────────────────
6 tens and 11 ones

or 6 tens plus 1 ten plus 1 one or 7 tens and 1 one equal 71.

Words would be eliminated in the next step and the numbers written in conventional form:

$$
\begin{array}{ccc}
25 & & 25 \\
\underline{46} & \text{or} & \underline{46} \\
11 & & 60 \\
\underline{60} & & \underline{11} \\
71 & & 71
\end{array}
$$

At this time the shorter form of solving the problem can be presented:

$$
\begin{array}{c}
25 \\
\underline{46} \\
71
\end{array}
$$

Add the units (ones), change the 11 ones to 10 ones and 1 one. Change the 10 ones to 1 ten and add to the other tens. Sum 7 tens and 1 one or 71.

It is recommended that the regrouped 1 ten be written in the initial work with the understanding:

$$
\begin{array}{r}
{}^{1}25 \\
46 \\
\hline
71
\end{array}
$$

This same kind of understanding is carried on with more difficult forms of addition where regrouping is involved in the tens, hundreds, thousands (or more) place or places.

Concepts from Algebra

1. Development of meaning and understanding of various mathematical symbols. Symbols such as $\Box$, $\triangle$, $\Diamond$, n, etc. in a mathematical sentence are called *place-holders* or *variables*.
Mathematical statements containing variables are called *open sentences.*

2. Have the children replace the variable to complete a true statement.

$$8 + \Box = 14$$
$$15 + \Box = 28$$
$$7 + \Box = 16$$

Which of the statements below are true? Which are false? Which are open?

$$4 + 7 = 11$$
$$7 + 7 = 15$$
$$\triangle + 4 = 11$$
$$5 + 3 = 8$$

3. Have the children make an open sentence true: $456 + \triangle = 465$ (9) 9 is the truth set for the open sentence $456 + \triangle = 465$.

4. Have the children make the following open sentences true.

Commutative Property
$$3 + 76 = 76 + n$$
$$9 + n = 235 + 9$$
etc.

Associative Property
$$1,345 + 7 + \Box = 1,360$$
$$4 + 1,546 = 1,540 + \triangle$$
etc.

5. Replacement Set. Given the set $\{3, 4, 7, 8, 9\}$ the children choose the values for "n" to make the following statement true.

$$8 > \{n + 2\} \qquad [n = 3]$$

Develop the understanding that the set of numbers from which one or more numbers can be chosen to replace a variable is called a *replacement set*.

Note that more than one choice is possible for the *truth set* or *solution set*.

6. Develop the skill to find the truth set for the following:

Open Sentence	Replacement Set
(a) $4 < \Box < 10$	The set of whole numbers
(b) $\Box + \triangle = 7$	$\{1, 2, 3, \ldots 10\}$
(c) $36 + 6 > n$	$\{43, 41, 29, 50\}$
(d) $9 + 8 < n$	$\{18, 19, 20 \ldots\}$

The Use of the "Number Line" in the Operation of Addition

On a drawing representing a line, some point is taken as an origin and to the right of this, a dot is placed. The distance between the origin and this dot to the right represents the unit length. Zero is associated with the origin, and the positive integers are associated with other dots placed at intervals equal to the unit length along the drawing to the right of zero as shown. Points to the left of zero are associated with negative numbers. This is called a number line.

Prior to the time children study negative numbers, only that segment of the number line which contains points associated with the whole numbers is used. Later segments of the number line to indicate certain rational numbers are introduced, the segment of the line which shows a point associated with 2 may be used.

One of the concepts which children should learn early in the primary grades is that numbers may be "ordered," or placed in a certain relationship to each other on the number line so that any given number represented on the line will be larger than any number represented on the line to the left of this given number. Thus "5" is associated with a point to the right of the point associated with 4, 3, or any smaller whole number. When children are introduced to negative numbers at higher levels, they will see that points associated with negative numbers are represented on the number line to the left of zero. Thus – 5 is less than – 4, it is associated with a point to the left of – 4.

It should be realized that even though much work with the operation of addition is done in grades one through four, there is still a great deal of need for additional attention to the basic facts and concepts in grades five and six and even in grades seven and eight. A large part of this review of the various concepts and understandings in the upper-grade arithmetic books is presented in the same manner in which the work was first presented in grades I through IV. No wonder children are not challenged by the arithmetic review at the beginning of the year! The teacher's job is to find meaningful ways for the child to gain mastery of the facts and procedures. One such interesting technique is the use of the number line in the teaching of as well as the review of the operation of addition.

In the primary grades the teacher uses discretion in the number of units which are shown on a line at a given time for facts and understandings develop gradually. In the early stages it is important that some degree of concreteness be retained as long as it is needed for understanding. One of the concerns of the primary teacher will be that determining points on the line is not merely a counting exercise. This has already been of concern while dealing with concrete objects in learning about numbers.

In the teaching of addition facts a set of segments of the line to represent the length of each of the numbers 1-10 may be made and used. Colored segments may be most useful.

The line may appear like this (the number of units shown will vary):

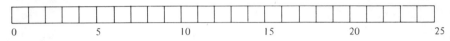

Segments appear as shown in the first example on page 107. Later these segments may be used in an extended line to show how "facts" hold in bridging decades (second example on page 107).

Objects lined up provide the first experience of the child with a number line. As he moves to a more formal line, the following illustrate the types of problems he will find in the operation of addition. In the early experiences line segments, hands as frames, or other methods are needed to avoid mere counting.

1. Application of associative property:

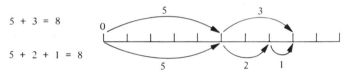

2. Application of commutative property:

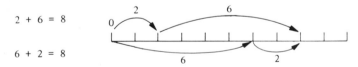

3. Addition and subtraction as inverse operations:
   (a) Beginning with addition

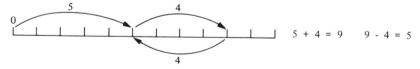

   (b) Beginning with subtraction

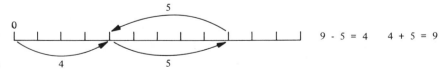

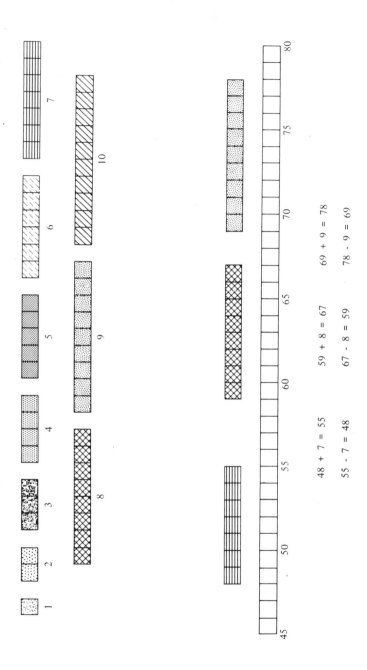

4. Principles of equality applied:
   (a) Adding 5, adding 6

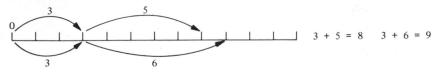

$$3 + 5 = 8 \qquad 3 + 6 = 9$$

   (b) Doubles and near-doubles

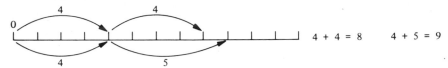

$$4 + 4 = 8 \qquad 4 + 5 = 9$$

$$4 + 4 = 8 \qquad 4 + 3 = 7$$

   (c) Inverses of doubles and near-doubles

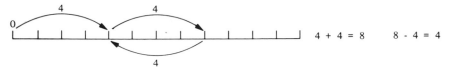

$$4 + 4 = 8 \qquad 8 - 4 = 4$$

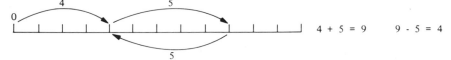

$$4 + 5 = 9 \qquad 9 - 5 = 4$$

5. Identity property applied to addition:

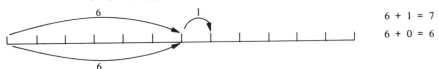

$$6 + 1 = 7$$
$$6 + 0 = 6$$

6. Combinations of numbers to make the sum of 8:

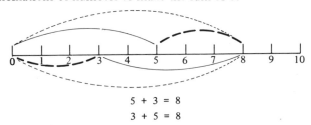

$$5 + 3 = 8$$
$$3 + 5 = 8$$

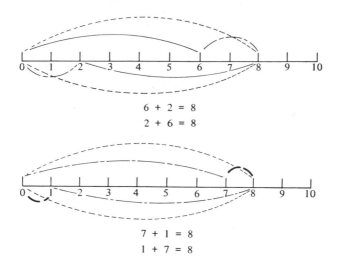

$$6 + 2 = 8$$
$$2 + 6 = 8$$

$$7 + 1 = 8$$
$$1 + 7 = 8$$

7. The facts hold when bridging decades:

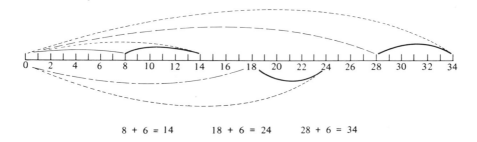

$$8 + 6 = 14 \qquad 18 + 6 = 24 \qquad 28 + 6 = 34$$

8. Addition involving two or more digits:

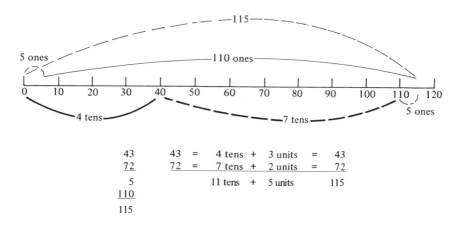

43	43 =	4 tens + 3 units =	43
72	72 =	7 tens + 2 units =	72
5		11 tens + 5 units	115
110			
115			

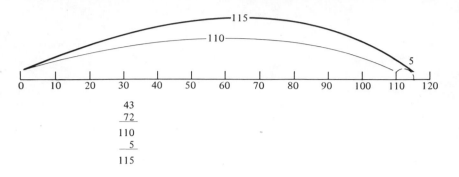

```
43
72
110
 5
115
```

9. Use of number line in checking column addition:

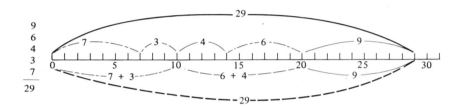

```
9
6
4
3
7
29
```

10. Addition of two-digit numbers, with no renaming:

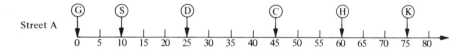

Street A

(a) Line is Street A.
(b) Locate Christy's house, grocery, school, etc.
(c) How far is Christy's house from the grocery? How many tens of blocks, etc.?
(d) How far is Christy's house from Karen's house?
(e) If Christy rides her bike from school, how far will she ride to her house?
(f) If she proceeds to Karen's house after stopping at home, how many blocks will she have ridden? Develop algorism horizontally and vertically.
(g) If she returns to school to play ball, how many blocks will she have ridden then?

Key to Number Line: G-Grocery, S-School, D-Debbie's House, C-Christy's House, H-Hal's House, K-Karen's House.

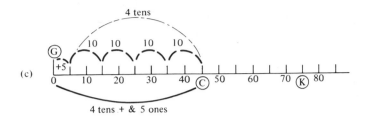

(c)

4 tens + & 5 ones

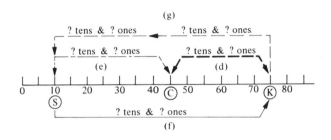

(g)

? tens & ? ones

(f)

(e)	3 tens	&	5 ones	=	35	(g)	30
(f)	3 tens	&	0 ones	=	30		+35
	6 tens	&	5 ones	=	65		65

11. Addition—two-digit number, renaming
    (Refer to number line on page 112.)
    (a) Christy is at the grocery store. From there she rides her bike to Debbie's to deliver a package. She continues to Hal's house. How many blocks does she ride? How many ways can this problem be shown? (e.g., $25 + 35 = N$,

$$\begin{array}{r} 2 \text{ tens } 5 \text{ ones} \\ + \ 3 \text{ tens } 5 \text{ ones} \end{array}$$

etc.)

    (b) Suppose she were to reride this trip in the opposite direction, how far would she ride?
    (c) Continue on types similar to the following:

$$36 + 27 = N$$

    (d) Ask for examples from the children.
    (e) Show the associative by G to D to C to H, or $25 + 20 + 30 = 25 + (20 + 30) = (25 + 20) + 30 =$ etc.

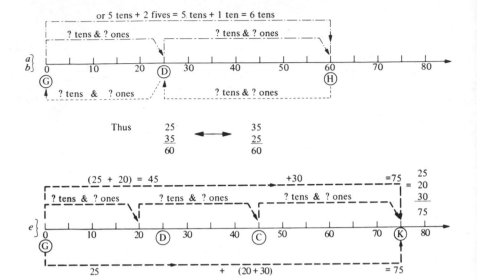

Thus
        25   35
        35   ⟷   25
        60   60

12. Enrichment activities: Games may be developed which will provide practice and add fun to such practice through the use of the number line. These should be simple thinking exercises such as "I am thinking of a number that is three times more than 27. What is it?" Or more complicated games may be devised by the teacher and/or pupils.

The number line should help develop mental computation by illustrating the jumps in decades or decades and units.

Example:

$$29 + 46 = N$$

Think: Go to 29, jump 40, jump 6. Where are you?

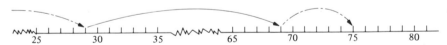

Children will enjoy diagraming some problems by use of the number line and adaptations of the line.

Example:

"Judy walked 8 blocks east, 7 blocks south and 9 blocks east. How many blocks did Judy walk? How far east had Judy walked? Suppose the blocks are the same size and show where Judy was when she finished her walk."

This may be used and extended as children get ready for signed numbers.

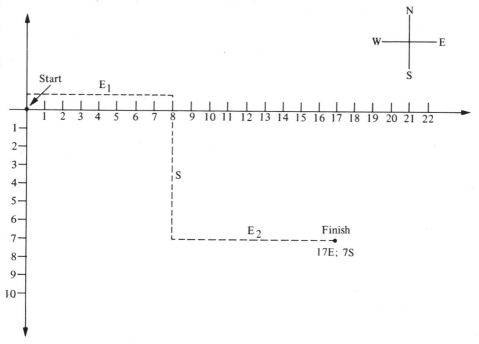

Example:

The operator of a parking lot noted that there was a car in space 58 and one in space 73. The spaces between were empty. Can a fleet of 12 trucks be parked between cars 55 and 73 if one truck occupies two spaces? If not, how many more spaces would be needed? If so, did he have any spaces left for cars?

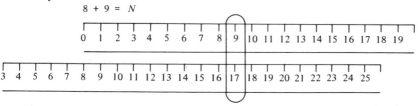

Two number lines may be used as a simple slide rule to add or subtract. Two yard sticks will provide considerable practice.

Example:

$8 + 9 = N$

To add $8 + 9 = N$, place the "0" of the top line by the 8 on the lower line and read the number of the lower line which meets the 9 on the top line—this gives you the sum.

Example:

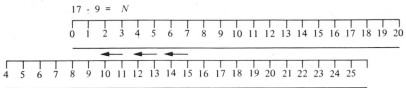

$$17 - 9 = N$$

To subtract $17 - 9 = N$, start with the "0" on the top line at 17 in the lower line; move top line to the left until 9 is at 17 (the starting point) on the lower line. The "0" falls at 8, which is the difference.

The specific addition skills and understandings that should be developed include the following. The child should be able to:

Grade I

1. Demonstrate with counters or other objects what is meant by "counting-together" groups.

2. Use concrete objects to arrive at answers to the addition combinations with sums through 10.

3. Symbolize in arithmetic language when a "counting-together" action is demonstrated by another person.

$4 + 2 = 6$ or $\begin{array}{r} 4 \\ +2 \\ \hline 6 \end{array}$ is written after counting-together action takes place.

4. "Count-together" groups when (+) is shown.

$2 + 3 = 5$ or $\begin{array}{r} 2 \\ +3 \\ \hline 5 \end{array}$

5. Tell a story problem to illustrate a number combination.

Example: Given $2 + 3 = 5$. Matt tells "I have two cookies in one hand and three cookies in the other. How many cookies do I have altogether?"

6. Give the answer to a combination such as $2 + 5$ immediately after obtaining the sum of $5 + 2$ by the use of concrete or semiconcrete materials.

7. Demonstrate mastery of addition combinations with sums through 10 by responding automatically and using correctly in problem situations.

8. Use (=) as meaning "are" or "equal."

Example: 2 and 2 are 4; 2 and 2 equal 4; read facts such as $2 + 2 = 4$, and 2 and 2 equal 4, or 2 and 2 are 4.

9. Write $2 + 2 = 4$ when 2 and 2 equal 4, or 2 and 2 are 4 is read or is heard.

10. Use concrete objects to arrive at answers of the addition combinations through 18.

11. Find the sum of a single column of addends not exceeding 3 whose sum does not exceed 10.

12. Demonstrate mastery of addition combinations with sums through 18 by responding automatically and using correctly in any situation.

13. Demonstrate mastery of the doubles with sums through 18.

$$7 + 7 = 14 \qquad 9 + 9 = 18$$

14. Demonstrate the mastery of ten in groups of ten plus any number.

$$10 + 3 = 13 \qquad 30 + 6 = 36$$
$$10 + 7 = 17 \qquad 50 + 3 = 53$$
$$10 + 9 = 19 \qquad 90 + 7 = 97$$

15. Transform more difficult combinations whose sums are not more than 18 into simpler sums that are already known.

Example:

$$7 + 8 - 10 + 5 - 15$$
$$7 + 8 = 7 + 7 + 1 = 15$$
$$7 + 8 = 8 + 8 - 1 = 15$$

16. Show with counters or other materials how many objects are in 1 through 10 groups of 2; and how many groups of 3 are in any given number 1 through 9.

17. Use concrete objects to arrive at answers to those subtraction combinations which correspond to the addition combinations with sums through 18.

18. Find the number which takes the place of the symbol N, $\triangle$, $\bigcirc$, $\square$ etc., which will make statements like the following true.

Example:

$$n + 3 = 9$$
$$9 - \square = 3$$
$$6 + 3 = n$$
$$9 - \triangle = 6$$

Grade II

1. Add a two-digit number and a one-digit number where the sum of end digits is the same as when the end digits are added alone.

Example:

$$\begin{array}{cc}
26 & 6 \\
+3 & +3 \\
\hline
29 & 9
\end{array} \qquad \text{(adding by endings)}$$

2. Determine by use of concrete objects sums when the algorism containing three addends are given in both vertical and horizontal form.

Example:

$$2 + 3 + 1 = n \qquad \begin{array}{r} 2 \\ 3 \\ \underline{1} \end{array}$$

is given and sum determined by "counting together"

3. Determine quickly the sum of any one-digit number and any two-digit number divisible by 10.

Example:

$$\begin{array}{r} 30 \\ \underline{+8} \\ 38 \end{array} \qquad 70 + 6 = 76$$

4. Determine quickly the sum of any two-digit number less than 20 and any number (through 80) divisible by 10.

$$\begin{array}{r} 30 \\ \underline{+17} \\ 47 \end{array} \qquad 60 + 15 = 65$$

5. Find the sum of double column of addends whose sum exceeds 10 (involving only combinations they have mastered).

Example:

$$\begin{array}{r} 43 \\ \underline{+27} \\ 60 \\ \underline{10} \\ 70 \end{array} \qquad \begin{array}{r} 43 \\ \underline{+27} \\ 10 \\ \underline{60} \\ 70 \end{array}$$

6. Find the sum of a double column of addends not exceeding 3, whose sum does not exceed 10.

Example:

$$\begin{array}{r} 13 \\ 21 \\ \underline{+14} \\ 48 \end{array} \qquad \begin{array}{r} 13 \\ 21 \\ \underline{+14} \\ 40 \\ \underline{8} \\ 48 \end{array} \qquad 13 + 21 + 14 = 48$$

7. Add two- or three-digit addends when the sum of all the tens is greater than 10.

Example:

$$\begin{array}{r} 40 \\ +80 \\ \hline 120 \end{array} \qquad \begin{array}{r} 34 \\ 91 \\ +32 \\ \hline 157 \end{array}$$

8. Add with zeros in the addends.

Example:

$$\begin{array}{r} 20 \\ +29 \\ \hline 49 \end{array} \qquad \begin{array}{r} 3 \\ 0 \\ +2 \\ \hline 5 \end{array} \qquad \begin{array}{l} 3 + 0 + 2 = 5 \\ \\ 29 + 20 = 49 \end{array}$$

Grade III

1. Demonstrate mastery of the addition facts whose sums are less than 19 by responding automatically and using correctly in practical situations.

2. Add by endings in column addition, using not more than five addends.

Example:

$$\begin{array}{r} 3 \ (17) \\ 5 \ (14) \\ 4 \ (9) \\ 1 \ (5) \\ 4 \\ \hline 17 \end{array} \qquad \begin{array}{c} (8) \ (12) \quad (13) \qquad (17) \\ 3 + 5 + 4 + 1 + 4 = 17 \end{array}$$

3. Place each numeral of the addends and sum in its correct position (place).

Example: The ones in the ones place, tens in the tens place, hundreds in the hundreds place, etc.

4. Add two or three addends (two digits) when the sum of the digits in the ones place is greater than 10. Use the partial-sum method.

$$\begin{array}{r} 14 \\ +27 \\ \hline 11 \\ 30 \\ \hline 41 \end{array} \qquad \begin{array}{r} 14 \\ +27 \\ \hline 30 \\ 11 \\ \hline 41 \end{array} \qquad \begin{array}{r} 34 \\ +89 \\ \hline 13 \\ 110 \\ \hline 123 \end{array} \qquad \begin{array}{r} 34 \\ +89 \\ \hline 110 \\ 13 \\ \hline 123 \end{array}$$

5. Add with renaming in the ones place, changing ones to tens.

Example:

$$
\begin{array}{r} 14 \\ +27 \\ \hline 41 \end{array}
\qquad
\begin{array}{r} 98 \\ 46 \\ +52 \\ \hline 196 \end{array}
$$

6. Add a column of numbers with zero as a digit.

Example:

$$
\begin{array}{r} 213 \\ 210 \\ +17 \\ \hline 440 \end{array}
$$

7. Place cent point and dollar sign correctly when adding.

Example:

$$
\begin{array}{r} \$1.25 \\ +1.19 \\ \hline \$2.44 \end{array}
\qquad
\begin{array}{r} \$\ .78 \\ +.34 \\ \hline \$1.12 \end{array}
\qquad
\begin{array}{r} \$\ .78 \\ +.12 \\ \hline \$\ .90 \end{array}
$$

8. Find sums of two and three addends when the sum of the digits in the tens place is greater than 10, and the sums of the digits in the ones place and hundreds place may or may not be greater than 10.

Example:

$$
\begin{array}{r} 183 \\ 135 \\ +281 \\ \hline 9 \\ 190 \\ 400 \\ \hline 599 \end{array}
\qquad
\begin{array}{r} 183 \\ 135 \\ +281 \\ \hline 400 \\ 190 \\ 9 \\ \hline 599 \end{array}
\qquad
\begin{array}{r} 682 \\ 175 \\ +281 \\ \hline 8 \\ 230 \\ 900 \\ \hline 1,138 \end{array}
\qquad
\begin{array}{r} 682 \\ 175 \\ +281 \\ \hline 900 \\ 230 \\ 8 \\ \hline 1,138 \end{array}
$$

9. Add with renaming (regrouping) in the tens place, changing the tens to hundreds with three-digit numbers.

Example:

$$
\begin{array}{r} 146 \\ +271 \\ \hline 417 \end{array}
\qquad
\begin{array}{r} 247 \\ 352 \\ +171 \\ \hline 770 \end{array}
$$

10. Add one- or two-digit numbers with not more than five addends by forming decades.

Example:

$10 + (4 + 3) = 17$	35	$20 + 6 = 26$
	68	$10 + (3 + 7) = 20$
$4 + 4 + 2 = 10$	44	
	+29	$9 + 1 = 10$
	176	

11. After determining the answer to an addition exercise, respond quickly when an addend is increased or decreased by some multiple of ten.

Example: Determine that $27 + 7$ is 34 after knowing $17 + 7 = 24$.

12. Add 2, 3, 4 or more place numbers with at least four addends.

Grade IV

1. Add two-place numbers to one-place numbers when the sum falls:

        (a) within the decade, $22 + 5 = 27$
        (b) at the decade, $22 + 8 = 30$
        (c) into the next decade, $22 + 9 = 31$

2. Use addends which are composed of dollars and cents.

Example:

$106.59	(Stress importance of keeping the decimals
75.24	in a straight column so that uneven column
.64	may be added.)
$182.47	

3. Add two-place, three-place, and four-place numbers in regular and irregular columns with and without regrouping.

Example:

$$
\begin{array}{r}
1,986 \\
27 \\
357 \\
4 \\
\hline
2,374
\end{array}
$$

Grade V

1. Estimate the reasonableness of the answer in an addition problem.

Example:

725	(is about 700)
+352	(is about 400)
	(answer is less than 1,100, answer = 1,077

2. Add five- (or more) digit numbers with five addends, involving both regular and irregular columns.

Example:

$$\begin{array}{r} 62,784 \\ 470 \\ 29 \\ 8,784 \\ +55,576 \\ \hline 127,643 \end{array}$$

Grade VI

1. Maintain previously learned skills and understandings.

TEACHING SUGGESTIONS

Concept: Two or more sets of elements can be joined to form a larger set

Procedures. 1. Each child has 10 sticks which are kept in a bundle in his desk. With them he has learned the numbers from 1 to 10 and the meaning of each of the numbers. Change the objects (elements) with which they are to count from time to time, using bottle caps, counters made of beads, the abacus, and the pegboard. Ask the children to take 4 sticks and put them in a set, then take 2 sticks and put them in another set, now combine the elements of the two sets into one larger set and count. Write the problem on the chalkboard that 4 sticks and 2 sticks equal a set of 6 sticks, 4 sticks + 2 sticks = N, N = 6 sticks, 4 sticks + 2 sticks = 6 sticks. With the use of the flannelboard have one of the children put 3 apples in one set, and another set of 2 apples. Count the first set, then count the second set, and then count the two sets together, and write the problem on the chalkboard, 3 apples + 2 apples = N apples, N apples = 5 apples, 3 apples + 2 apples = 5 apples. Have the children draw a story with 3 ducks in one set and 5 ducks in the second set, and then have the children count the two sets together to find that there are a total of 8 ducks.

2. Have two tall boys stand before the class. Then choose a short boy to stand beside them. On the board write the number story about these boys in the following way: 2 boys + 1 boy = N boys, N boys = 3, 2 boys + 1 boy = 3 boys.

3. Have the children take 6 of their counter sticks or disks and put 4 counters in one hand and 2 counters in the other. Then, putting their hands together, they discover that they have a larger group of 6 sticks. Write on the chalkboard 4 and 2 are 6. Then ask them to put the hand with 4 counters in it behind them and hold up the hand with the 2 counters. Then ask them to join to the set of 2 sticks the hand containing the 4 sticks. Ask someone to tell how

this number story should be written: 2 and 4 are 6. Ask for other combinations of sets. They will develop 3 and 3 are 6, 5 and 1 are 6, 1 and 5 are 6, and sometimes 6 and 0 are 6, and 0 and 6 are 6.

4. Draw on the chalkboard simple pictures in sets such as:

> 2 cats and 3 cats are _____ cats
> 4 boxes and 2 boxes are _____ boxes
> 2 apples and 1 apple are _____ apples

Have the children tell what numbers are to be written. Develop thoroughly that 2 and 3 are 5, just as 3 and 2 are 5. Stress verbalizing the whole statement: 3 and 2 are 5. Do not accept the answer alone.

5. The use of the flannelboard and pegboard will give the children many opportunities to see that combining (putting objects together) elements into larger sets is adding.

Concept: In combining two sets, the total may be found by counting the elements of the new set

Procedures. 1. Children may be taught to combine sets and count the total as soon as they have learned how to count rationally. Example: Four children stand in the front of the room, four at the side. Each group is counted separately to find out "how many." The two groups are combined. Ask "How many are there in this new group?" Since the children already know that to find out "how many," they must count; count the total (8). Ask, "How did we discover that 4 children and 4 children are eight children?" Answer growing out of the discussion would be by counting the new group. Repeat with other groups of children, varying the numbers of children in each group.

2. On the table are 3 sets of blocks: a set of 4 blocks, a set of 3 blocks, and a set of 5 blocks. Have in each hand a set of 2 blocks, which the children count; the left hand (2), the right hand (2). Present the following problem; If these sets of blocks in my hands were combined, how many sets would I have then? (One set) The sets are combined into a single set. Then have the children compare this new set with the 3 sets already on the table to see which of the sets is equivalent in value or size. After a tentative decision is reached, the children are asked to prove the sets of 4 are of the same size or value. Repeat with books, pencils, erasers, etc., until the children show the understanding that they must count to find how many are in the new set.

3. *The numbers 1-10, expressed in sets of geometric figures, dot, or balls, arranged at random along the chalk tray.* One child builds on the flannelboard 2 groups of semiconcrete objects, for example 5 trees and 2 trees. He says, "If I wish to combine (add) 5 trees and 2 trees, how many trees will I have in all?" The child chosen to answer selects a card from the chalk tray containing the number of elements he believes to represent the new set. He must then com-

bine the sets of 5 trees and 2 trees and count the new set in order to find out whether he selected the right card. The number (7) should match. Then he takes his turn to form a new pair of sets for the next player. Show the problem in the following forms:

$$\begin{array}{r} \text{XXXXX trees} \\ \underline{\text{XX trees}} \end{array} \quad 5 \text{ trees} + 2 \text{ trees} = 7 \text{ trees}$$

$$\begin{array}{l} 5 \text{ trees} + 2 \text{ trees} = N \text{ trees} \\ \underline{N = 7} \\ 5 \text{ trees} + 2 \text{ trees} = 7 \text{ trees} \end{array}$$

4. Many opportunities will arise daily where two groups are put together, such as two groups combining for reading. Their total number needs to be known for the purpose of passing out books, paper, pencils, chairs, and the like. Two children may wish to combine their small groups of spending money into one group to buy a popsicle and share it. In these cases, the simple question "how many" will direct the children's thinking to discovering the total by counting the new set.

5. Each child has a supply of 10 counters at his desk, such as markers, flannelboard figures, or popsicle sticks. Two children select objects to hold, the total of which should not exceed 10. This total is counted privately by the two leaders. As each child tells how many elements he is holding, the pupils represent the elements at their desks with markers, forming a separate group for each of the two leaders. The leaders then combine their sets and ask, "How many do we have altogether?" The children combine their two representative sets and discover the total by counting the new set.

6. A helpful technique to make the meaning of addition clearer is to suggest that as the children build their separate sets, they build them at the opposite sides of their desk or on the opposite sides of their flannelboards. Then when they combine the two sets they manipulate and actually move the two sets into one. Some children will tend to count the total without combining their sets, in order to be first with the answer. But the meaning of addition will be clearer to them if they are made to realize that 2 sets of 4 do not become a set of 8 *unless they are added together or combined.*

7. Simple addition story problems may be presented orally, using the children's names to increase interest. The students may be asked to draw the separate sets and "combine" them by drawing a circle around both sets to give the feeling of putting them together. The question "how many" will direct them to count the total.

8. Another technique of showing two sets combined is to use a different color for each set. In this way, the children can see two original sets, and also see them combined as they count the total.

9. Put each set of elements in a different row when combining them, so that the children can see them as two sets combined. Example: 6 as two sets of 3, or sets of 4 and 2, sets of 5 and 1, as the case may be.

Concept: When the sum of the ones column is ten or more the sum is regrouped into tens and ones and tens are added to digits in the tens column

Procedures. (a) Problem situations: Christy is saving her money to buy Christmas gifts. In her bank she has 37 cents. She has just earned 25 cents. How many dimes does she have now? (5) How many pennies? (12) Set up the number problem on the chalkboard:

In her bank:	3 dimes and 7 pennies
Just earned:	2 dimes and 5 pennies
	5 dimes and 12 pennies

Now change the 12 pennies to 1 dime and 2 pennies. Put the dime over with the 5 dimes. Keep the 2 pennies in the cents column. Then Christy has 6 dimes and _____ pennies, or _____ ¢.

(b) Using toy dimes and pennies, have the children prove that:

3 dimes and 14 pennies = 4 dimes and 4 pennies or 44¢
2 dimes and 12 pennies = 3 dimes and 2 pennies or 32¢
5 dimes and 13 pennies = 6 dimes and 3 pennies or 63¢

(c) *Answering questions in addition by the discovery method.* Write the answers to the questions in the problem. If you don't know the answer, make a drawing to show what the problem tells in words. *Problem*: We have 14 boys and 18 girls in our classroom. What is the total number of children in our room? *Examples of possible diagrams and number solutions*: The use of the number line.

14 boys + 18 girls = 32 children

Picture Solution:

	Tens	Ones	Tens	Ones	
14	x	xxxx	x	x	14
+18	x	xxxxxxxx	x	x	+18
			x		32

12 ones = 1 ten and 2 ones. Change   Now we have 2 tens and
10 ones to 1 ten and place the 1 ten   1 ten = 3 tens
in the tens place.   3 tens and 2 ones = 32.

Estimation:

Pam thinks that 14 is nearly 15 and 18 is nearly 20. 15 and 20 are 35. Take away the 1 she added to make 15, and the 2 she added to make 20, and she has 32.

4. *Use the pocket chart. Problem:* $25 + 9 = N$ Put 25 in the top row of the place-value chart; the 2 tens and 5 ones. Put 9 ones in the second row. Add the two rows. This equals 2 tens and 14 ones. Take 10 of the 14 ones, bundle them to make 1 ten and put it with the other tens.

5. Write the example $18 + 45 = N$ on the chalkboard. Use tens blocks and ones blocks to demonstrate. Place 1 tens block and 8 ones blocks in a set on the table. Place 4 tens blocks and 5 ones blocks in a set on the table. Write beside the example on the chalkboard:

$$
\begin{array}{l}
18 = 1 \text{ tens block and } 8 \text{ ones blocks} \\
\underline{+45 = 4 \text{ tens blocks and } 5 \text{ ones blocks}} \\
5 \text{ tens blocks and } 13 \text{ ones blocks}
\end{array}
$$

Change 13 ones blocks to 1 tens block and 3 ones blocks. Now you have:

$$
\begin{array}{l}
5 \text{ tens blocks} \\
\underline{+1 \text{ tens block and } 3 \text{ ones blocks}} \\
6 \text{ tens blocks and } 3 \text{ ones blocks} = 63
\end{array}
$$

Concept: Addition of multidigit numbers: (no regrouping)

Procedures. 1. Review the addition of a one-digit addend to a two-digit addend, such as $12 + 3$. Have the children use materials that can be grouped in tens. On the chalkboard build the expanded notation from $10 + 2 + 3$. Have the children building a corresponding picture with their set material. Guide the children in discussing what is occurring in the process.

2. Write $24 + 5$ on the chalkboard. Ask the children how they would group this.

Example:
$$(20 + 4 + 5) = 20 + (4 + 5)$$

3. Develop chalkboard, flannelboard, and seatwork activities to help the children understand the regrouping principle necessary in adding of two-digit numbers.

4. Review addition of multiples of ten:

Examples:
$$20 + 40 = n \qquad 60 + 30 = n \qquad 70 + 20 = n$$

After the equations have been completed, have one of the children explain the equations in terms of tens. In the first problem, for example, a child might say: "Two tens (or twenty) plus three tens (or thirty) equals five tens (or fifty)." Have the child write the related vertical form for the problems on the chalkboard.

5. Write an equation on the chalkboard. Example: $22 + 35 = N$. Have a child place twenty-two paper strips (two bundles of ten and two singles) in the pocket card. Ask him to join a set of thirty-five paper strips (three bundles of ten and five singles) to the set of twenty-two strips. Have him show how many strips there are altogether. Have him first put the ones together, then put the tens together, and finally the ones and tens together. Ask another child to write the related equations under the pocket chart.

6. Place a series of numerals on the chalkboard, then have the children take turns writing different numerals for the numbers represented.

Examples:

$$34 + 5 = 30 + 4 + 5$$
$$84 + 22 = 80 + 10 + 4 + 2$$
$$53 + 4 = 50 + 3 + 4$$
$$41 + 38 = 40 + 30 + 1 + 8$$

7. Have a short oral session with the class. Ask a child to give the sum of 6 and 3. When the child replies 9, ask him how much are 6 tens and 3 tens. When he replies 9 tens, ask him how much are 60 and 30. Call on another child, and continue the sequence, first asking the adding of one-digit numbers, then finding the number of tens, then solving the problem involving the multiples of ten. This sequence will develop mastery of the addition of multiples of tens.

8. Provide children with other activities of sums of multiples of ten.

9. Place 25 objects and 13 more objects on a table. Let a child group each set into groups of tens and ones. Write on the chalkboard how many ones. Show the children how to add these to get the sum. Do the same with the groups of tens. Combine the number of ones and the number of tens to get the total sum. Provide as many demonstrations as needed until the children are familiar with the process.

10. Use the pocket chart as a place-holder device. Put a piece of yarn down the center; label the left side "tens" and the right side "ones." Place four bundles of ten strips in the tens place and four separate strips in the ones place. In the pocket beneath the one holding the bundles of tens place two bundles of strips. Ask a child to write the related vertical-notation form for this activity on the chalkboard. Have the problem read in terms of ones and tens. Continue in this way to build set stories related to two-digit addition with no carrying. Have the children write the corresponding algorism for the activity they viewed.

Example:

$$44 + 20 = 64 \qquad \begin{array}{r} 44 \\ +20 \\ \hline 64 \end{array}$$

11. Have the children work with two-digit addition problems through a play store. Increase the prices and let each child purchase something which would involve adding two-digit numerals.

12. Developing addition involving three- and four-digit numbers. Begin with a short oral game in which the children discover the number that comes next, after you read a sequence of numbers. For example, 40, 50, 60, 70, and ask a child to tell what number comes next.

Repeat this several times, using multiples of ten; then move on to multiples of 100; then to multiples of 1,000.

13. Provide oral exercises similar to these:

> What number is 100 more than 500?
> What number is 10 more than 70?
> What number is 1,000 more than 6,000?
> What number is 300 more than 400?
> What number is 2,000 more than 4,000?

14. Draw a number line on the chalkboard similar to below. Show the children how to find a sum of hundreds or a sum of thousands by drawing the appropriate arrow.

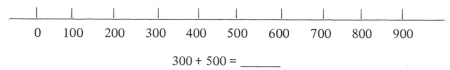

| 0 | 100 | 200 | 300 | 400 | 500 | 600 | 700 | 800 | 900 |

$$300 + 500 = \underline{\hspace{2cm}}$$

15. Present exercises on the chalkboard involving three one-digit addends, then three multiples of ten, and then three multiples of 100 and so on. Develop with the children the procedure of solving these problems and let the children do similar ones on the chalkboard.

Examples:

```
  3      40      500     1,000
  1      20      100     3,000
 +4     +30     +200    +4,000
```

16. When the children have an understanding of the concepts involved in additions with two three-digit addends without carrying, give them opportunities to try to adapt their skill to column additions involving three to five two- and three-digit addends. Have them work several sample problems orally. Place four or five problems on the chalkboard. Have one child add from top to bottom; have another add from bottom to top; have a third child add in the most convenient way for him. Lead the children to see that the commutative and associative properties of addition are still effective.

Examples:

```
        310     505     200
        125     11       22
        244     40       13
       +20     +133    +743
```

17. Challenge some of the children by presenting oral chain problems involving hundreds, tens and ones. Say "Two hundred plus three hundred (pause) plus twenty." Call on someone to give the sum. Present another problem similar to that suggested to develop mastery.

Concept: Addition of multidigit numbers: (involving regrouping)

Procedures: 1. Begin to think about ideas involved in regrouping in addition with problems involving estimations. Work problems such as examples below and think whether the answer would be greater than or less than the numeral given. Put the correct symbol in the circle.

$$7 + 5 \bigcirc 10 \qquad 36 + 25 \bigcirc 50$$
$$3 + 6 \bigcirc 10 \qquad 58 + 30 \bigcirc 80$$
$$7 + 6 \bigcirc 10 \qquad 42 + 21 \bigcirc 65$$

2. Provide other activities where the children estimate the sum.

3. Show the children a set of 35 objects and a set of 8 objects. Write on the chalkboard the combination $35 + 8 = N$. The set of 35 objects should be grouped by tens to show that there are three tens and five ones. Then ask the children to take enough from the eight ones to place with the set of 35 to make a set of four tens. On the chalkboard show the equation $35 + 8 = 40 + 3$, and show the new arrangement of the sets, that now shows 4 tens and 3 ones. Repeat this until the children understand the idea of going from one decade to another in this regrouping process.

4. Show the children a set of 44 objects and a set of 26 objects which are grouped by tens so that the children can see four sets of ten and four ones, and two sets of ten and six ones. Now observe that if all the objects that are not grouped by ten are put together, another set of ten will be formed, to make seven tens in all. Write on the chalkboard the equation $44 + 26 = (40 + 20) + (4 + 6) = 60 + 10 = 70$. Develop how this equation represents the grouping principle shown by the sets.

5. Have the children work problems involving this regrouping process such as the following:

Example:

$$48 + 39 = (40 + 30) + (8 + 9) = 70 + 17$$
$$= 70 + (10 + 7) = (70 + 10) + 7 = 80 + 7 = 87$$

6. You may wish to develop an intermediate step between the expanded notation and the algorism. This method can be used to help some children make the transition more easily. For others it will be an interesting new approach to the problem. A problem such as $65 + 8 = N$ would be worked in three steps. First, 5 and 8 are added, and the 13 recorded under the line. Then the tens are added, and recorded under the 13. As a final step, 13 and 60 are added to get the sum of 73.

Example:

$$
\begin{array}{r}
65 \\
+8 \\
\hline
13 \\
60 \\
\hline
73
\end{array}
$$

SEPARATION OF SETS AND SUBTRACTION OF NUMBERS

In the operation involving set separation we are concerned with the *elements* of a set.

If $A = \{a, b, c, d, e\}$ and we wish to remove the elements of a subset, $B = \{d, e\}$ from A, we are left with a set $C = \{a, b, c\}$. Set C is said to be the complement of Set C with respect to Set A.

These complements may be diagramed as follows:

Set A

$\{a, b, c\}$	$\{d, e\}$
Set C	Set B

In the operation involving subtraction we are concerned only with the numbers of the sets.

$$N \{a, b, c, d, e\} - N \{d, e\} = N \{a, b, c\}$$
$$5 \quad - \quad 2 \quad = \quad 3$$

The concept of operating on the number of the set (subtraction) is more abstract than the concept of operating with the elements (objects) of the sets. In subtraction, we are not concerned with what particular elements of the set are, but only in how many there are.

Basic Subtraction Facts

A basic subtraction fact involves three numbers, at least two of which are selected from 0 to 9.

Example:

$14 - 6 = 8$ is a basic subtraction fact.

$27 - 5 = 22$ is not considered a basic subtraction fact. It is an extension of a basic subtraction fact.

Subtraction facts should be presented concurrently with their related addition facts.

$$9 + 6 = 15 \qquad 15 - 6 = 9$$

There are 45 basic subtraction facts with minuends in the first decade, that is, minuends 10 or less than 10. There are 36 basic subtraction facts with minuends in the second decade—that is, minuends from 11–18, as: $15 - 8 = 7$ (minuend, 15; subtrahend, 8) There are 19 "zero facts." This makes a total of 100 basic subtraction facts.

Teachers must aim for automatic mastery of basic facts by their children. Automatic mastery is achieved through periodic drill.

All drill should be organized according to specific patterns which emphasize one type of relationship at a time. When facts are presented in random order this is considered "testing," rather than drill. A few minutes of each lesson should be devoted to drill. It must be related to the major topic under consideration, whenever possible. All drill and practice exercises or sequences should involve problem solving.

Types of Subtraction Experience Situations

Children should develop the understanding that there are various types of experience situations involving subtraction.

1. *Take-Away Situation, to find the remainder*
Six birds are on a wire, 4 flew away. How many are left?

$$6 - 4 = n \qquad 6 - 4 = 2$$

2. *Comparing Two Numbers, to find how many more or less in one, (difference)*
Six birds are on the wire, 4 on another. How many more (or less) birds are on one wire than the other. (Compare 6 birds with 4 birds.)

3. *How-Many-More-Are-Needed Situations, to find the difference between the number we have and the number we need*
Four birds are on the wire. How many more are needed to have 6 birds on the wire? (Compare 4 birds with 6 birds.)

4. *Change-Making Situations, to find the difference between the purchase price and the amount of money given*
The model car costs $.98. How much change will Matt get from a dollar? (Compare 98 pennies with 100 pennies.)

Suggested terminology for take-away subtraction as follows:
Take (away) from 7, 36, 104, etc.
From 9, take 6, 2, 5, etc.
Subtract from 22: 14, 9, 5, etc.
Subtract 4 from: 10, 16, 9, etc.
22 minus 5, 38 minus 26, etc.

Suggested terminology for comparison subtraction as follows:
How many more are there in 46 than in 12 (things)?
How many less (fewer) are there in 12 than in 46 (things)?

Find the number less (or fewer) in 12 (things) than in 46?

What is the difference between 46 and 12 (things)?

Compare 46 (things) with 12.

Compare 12 (things) with 46.

How much more is 46 than 12 (units of length on a number line)?

What is the difference between 46 and 12 (units)? between 12 and 46 (units)?

Compare 46 (units) with 12.

Compare the number of dimes we have with the number of dimes we need? How many more do we need?

Compare the amount it cost with the amount you gave him. How much money does he give you? How much change do you get?

46 minus 12

Regrouping in Subtraction

The major issue in subtraction is "regrouping." This term is applied where a change in form is indicated before the problem can be solved. *Example:* $\begin{array}{r} 82 \\ -26 \end{array}$. Like the teaching of most other areas of mathematics, it is best indicated with problem situations. The children are asked to solve the problem in as many ways as they can. From there you guide them to the more effective ways of working the problem.

Examples of this method are shown below. In each, the minuend has been regrouped or changed in form if subtraction is impossible in the column under consideration. For example, in the second problem 264 was regrouped from 200 + 60 + 4 to 200 + 50 + 14, since it was not possible to subtract 8 from 4 in the whole numbers.

Example	Regrouped form	Explanation
$\begin{array}{r} 91 \\ -54 \end{array}$	$\begin{array}{r} 8\,^{1}1 \\ -5\ \ 4 \end{array}$	91 regrouped to 8 tens, 11 ones 54 unchanged
$\begin{array}{r} 264 \\ -147 \end{array}$	$\begin{array}{r} 2\,5\,^{1}4 \\ -1\ 4\ 7 \end{array}$	264 regrouped to 2 hundreds, 5 tens, 14 ones 147 unchanged

In the problem $\begin{array}{r} 91 \\ -54 \end{array}$ a pocket holder containing bundles of tens and ones to represent the 91 could be used. Since the 4 ones cannot be subtracted from 1 one, it is necessary to regroup one bundle of ten to 10 ones. Now there are 11 ones. The indicated subtraction can now be completed. The 4 ones are subtracted from the 11 ones, leaving 7 ones. Then, because 1 ten was taken from 9 tens, there are now only 8 tens in the tens place. Five tens from 9 tens leaving 4 tens. The remainder is 4 tens and 7 ones or 47.

Much experience with concrete materials is needed before the child should be expected to do abstract work. In the initial work, various "crutches" might be used to facilitate learning and understanding of the process. However, once the skill has been developed and understood by the children, the various "crutches" should be discouraged.

The following might be helpful in developing the overall understanding of compound subtraction:

1. Changing tens to ones:

$$\begin{array}{r} 91 \\ -36 \\ \hline \end{array}$$

Thought process that the pupil might use in rationalizing this example:

$$\begin{array}{r} 91 \\ -30 \\ \hline 61 \\ -6 \\ \hline 55 \end{array}$$

Thirty-six is made up of 3 sets of ten and a set of 6 ones. The 30 separated from the 91 leaves 61. There are still the set of 6 ones to be subtracted; now separate 6 from 61. Six ones cannot be taken from 1 one, so 1 ten is taken from the 6 tens, leaving 5 tens. The 1 ten is regrouped with the 1 one equaling 11 ones. The computation then becomes:

$$\begin{array}{r} {}^{8}\not{9}{}^{1}1 \\ -3\ \ 6 \\ \hline \end{array}$$

2. Changing hundreds to tens:

$$\begin{array}{r} 817 \\ -365 \\ \hline \end{array}$$

Thought process: Take 5 ones from 7 ones, Six tens cannot be taken from 1 ten so 1 hundred is taken from the 8 hundreds. One hundred is regrouped into 10 tens; 10 tens added to 1 ten equals 11 tens. Separate 6 tens from 11 tens and 3 hundreds from 7 hundreds:

7 hundreds	11 tens	7 ones	817	${}^{7}\not{8}17$
−3 hundreds	6 tens	5 ones	−365	−365
4 hundreds	5 tens	2 ones −	452 −	452

3. Changing tens to ones and hundreds to tens:

$$\begin{array}{r} 924 \\ -889 \\ \hline \end{array}$$

Thought process: Here the 9 ones cannot be separated from the 4 ones so 1 ten is taken from the 2 tens and regrouped to make 14 ones. Eight tens cannot be taken from 1 ten so 1 hundred is separated from the 9 hundreds. One hundred regrouped to 10 tens; 10 tens added to 1 ten equals 11 tens. Subtract 9 ones from 14 ones, 8 tens from 11 tens, and 8 hundreds from 8 hundreds.

8 hundreds	11 tens	14 ones	8	11	14	924
−8 hundreds	8 tens	9 ones	−8	8	9	−889
	3 tens	5 ones −		3	5 =	35

4. Changing tens to ones and hundreds to tens with 0 tens:

$$702$$
$$-368$$

Thought process: Eight ones cannot be separated from 2 ones. There are no tens, regroup 1 hundred to 10 tens, so 10 tens are added to 0 tens. One ten is separated from the 10 tens and regrouped to 10 ones making 9 tens and 12 ones in all. Subtract 8 ones from 12 ones, 6 tens from 9 tens, and 3 hundreds from 6 hundreds.

6 hundreds	9 tens	12 ones	6	9	12	702
−3 hundreds	6 tens	8 ones	−3	6	8	−368
3 hundreds	3 tens	4 ones −	3	3	4 −	334

Checking by addition should be taught along with each step in regrouping tens to ones, hundreds to tens, etc.

Equal-Additions Method of Subtraction

This method is being presented here so that you can compare this method with the "regrouping" method which has been discussed and which is in wide use. The "equal-additions" method involves the adding of the same amount to the minuend that is added to the subtrahend. The mathematical principle used is that the adding of the same amount to the subtrahend and the minuend does not change the difference. See examples below:

Original Example	Crutches	Explanations
91 − 54	$9^1 1$ −6 4	10 ones added to original minuend to give 11 ones. 1 ten added to the original subtrahend, giving 6 tens.
264 −187	$2^1 6^1 4$ −2 9 7	10 tens and 10 ones added to the original minuend, giving 2 hundreds, 16 tens, 14 ones. 1 hundred and 1 ten added to original subtrahend, giving 2 hundreds, 9 tens, 7 ones.

The following may be helpful in developing the overall understanding of this form of compound subtraction.

1. Given the example:

$$814$$
$$-365$$

Thought process: Five ones cannot be separated from 4 ones, so 10 ones are added to 4 ones giving 14 ones. Six tens cannot be separated from 1 ten, so 10 tens are added to the 1 ten giving 11 tens. Ten tens and 10 ones were added to the minuend, so their equivalent must be added to the subtrahend. One hundred is added to the 3 hundreds in the subtrahend, giving 4 hundreds. (10 tens equal 1 hundred.) One ten is added to the 6 tens in the subtrahend, giving 7 tens. (1 ten equals 10 ones.) Subtract the 5 ones from the 14 ones, the 7 tens from the 11 tens, and the 4 hundreds from the 8 hundreds.

$$
\begin{array}{r}
8 \text{ hundreds } {}^{1}1 \text{ tens } {}^{1}4 \text{ ones} \\
-{}^{4}\cancel{3} \text{ hundreds } {}^{7}\cancel{6} \text{ tens } \quad 5 \text{ ones} \\
\hline
3 \text{ hundreds } \quad 4 \text{ tens } \quad 9 \text{ ones}
\end{array}
\qquad
\begin{array}{r}
8 \; {}^{1}1 \; {}^{1}4 \\
-{}^{4}\cancel{3} \; {}^{7}\cancel{6} \; 5 \\
\hline
4 \quad 4 \quad 9
\end{array}
$$

Example:

$$702$$
$$-368$$

Thought process: Eight ones cannot be separated from 2 ones, 10 ones are added to 2 ones, giving 12 ones. Six tens cannot be separated from 0 tens, so 10 tens are added to 0 tens, giving 10 tens. Ten tens and 10 ones were added to the minuend, so their equivalent must be added to the subtrahend. One hundred is added to the 3 hundreds in the subtrahend giving 4 hundreds. (10 tens equal 1 hundred). One ten is added to the 6 tens in the subtrahend giving 7 tens. (10 ones equal 1 ten.)

Subtract the 8 ones from the 12 ones, the 7 tens from the 10 tens, and the 4 hundreds from the seven hundreds.

$$
\begin{array}{r}
7 \text{ hundreds } {}^{1}0 \text{ tens } {}^{1}2 \text{ ones} \\
-{}^{4}\cancel{3} \text{ hundreds } {}^{7}\cancel{6} \text{ tens } \quad 8 \text{ ones} \\
\hline
3 \text{ hundreds } \quad 3 \text{ tens } \quad 4 \text{ ones}
\end{array}
\qquad
\begin{array}{r}
7 \; {}^{1}0 \; {}^{1}2 \\
-{}^{4}\cancel{3} \; {}^{7}\cancel{6} \; 8 \\
\hline
3 \quad 3 \quad 4
\end{array}
$$

Regrouping (take away) vs. Equal Additions

When the criteria of speed and accuracy are considered, neither method has been found to be superior to the other. But the regrouping method has wider acceptance because it is more easily rationalized, and it is more a natural procedure to use.

The Use of the "Number Line" in the Operation of Subtraction

Subtraction is the inverse of addition:

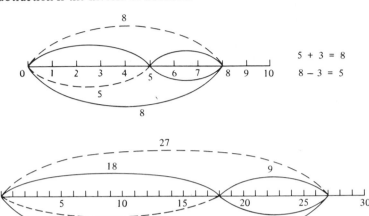

$$5 + 3 = 8$$
$$8 - 3 = 5$$

$$18 + 9 = 27$$
$$27 - 9 = 18$$

Types of Subtraction Problems

Example: Matt has seven books on his bookshelf. 3 are taken away. How many are left?

Example: Christy's reading group needs 7 chairs. They have 3. How many more do they need?

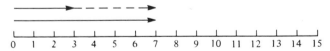

Example: Pamela needs only 6 pennies for the candy. She has 13 pennies. How many will she need to take away?

The specific subtraction skills and understandings that should be developed include the following. The child should be able to:

Grade I

1. Demonstrate with counters or other objects what is meant by separating (counting away) sets (groups).
2. Solve a story problem involving separating groups when a story is told by someone else.
3. Separate groups when the (−) sign is shown.

Example:

$$5 - 2 = 3 \qquad \begin{array}{r} 5 \\ -2 \\ \hline 3 \end{array}$$

4. Use concrete objects to arrive at answers to the subtraction combinations which correspond to the addition combinations with sums through 10.
5. Indicate immediately after obtaining the answer to a subtraction combination, such as $4 - 2 = n$, that $2 - 4 = n$ does not make sense.
6. Symbolize in mathematical language the separating of a subset from the total set as demonstrated by another person.

Example:

$$7 - 4 = 3 \qquad \text{or} \qquad \begin{array}{r} 7 \\ -4 \\ \hline 3 \end{array} \qquad \begin{array}{l} \text{written after counting-} \\ \text{away action takes place} \end{array}$$

7. Demonstrate mastery of subtraction combinations by responding automatically and using correctly in any situation (those corresponding to addition combinations through 6).
8. Solve by picture or manipulative material a story problem involving the comparison concept of subtraction.

Example: I have a brother who is 8 years old. I am 6 years old. How much older is my brother than I? (How much younger am I than my brother?)

9. Solve by picture or manipulative materials a story involving the "lack" concept of subtraction.

Example: We have ten children in our group. Here are three books. How many more do we need?

Grade II

1. Identify and demonstrate the three meanings of subtraction (a) Remainder: 6 birds are on a wire, 4 flew away. How many are left? (b) Comparison:

6 birds are on a wire, 4 on another. How many more (or less) birds are on one wire than the other? (c) Lack: 4 birds are on a wire. How many more are needed to have 6 birds on the wire?

2. Demonstrate mastery of subtraction combinations through 10 by responding automatically and using correctly in all situations.

3. Transform the more difficult subtraction combinations (corresponding to the addition combinations whose sums are no more than 18) into simpler combinations already known.

Example:

$$17 - 9 = 10 - 9 + 7 = 8$$
$$17 - 8 = 10 - 8 + 7 = 9$$
$$17 - 9 = 18 - 9 - 1 = 8$$

4. Indicate from a list of number pairs separated by a minus sign those pairs in which subtraction is possible and those which are not.

Example:

$$9 - 8 = n \text{ possible}$$
$$7 - 10 = n \text{ not possible}$$

5. Subtract two-digit numbers without regrouping.

Example:

$$\begin{array}{r} 26 \\ -13 \\ \hline 13 \end{array}$$ including zero in the ones column

6. Solve together with the teacher a simple problem that arises from group situations involving regrouping in subtraction or renaming in addition.

Example: There are 24 children in our room. Only 19 are here today. How many are absent?

7. Demonstrate mastery of subtraction combinations by responding automatically and using correctly in all situations.

8. Place each numeral of the minuend, subtrahend, and remainder in its correct place.

Example:

Ones in the ones place, tens in the tens place,
hundreds in the hundreds place, etc.

Grade III

1. Subtract by endings:

Example:

$$
\begin{array}{cc}
18 & 46 \\
-6 & -2 \\
\hline
12 & 44
\end{array}
$$

2. Subtract with zeros in subtrahend and minuend involving no regrouping:

Example:

$$
\begin{array}{cc}
205 & 235 \\
-105 & -101
\end{array}
$$

3. Place cents point and dollar sign correctly when subtracting:

$$
\begin{array}{c}
\$2.36 \\
-1.22 \\
\hline
\$1.14
\end{array}
$$

4. Recognize that ones in subtrahend cannot be subtracted from ones in the minuend if the ones in the subtrahend are greater than ones in the minuend. Decrease the tens by one ten and convert this ten to ones. Combine these ones with those already in the ones place.

5. Recognize that the tens in the subtrahend cannot be subtracted from tens in the minuend if the tens in the subtrahend are greater than the tens in the minuend. Decrease hundreds by one hundred and convert this hundred into ten tens. Combine these tens with those already in the tens place.

Example:

$$
\begin{array}{c}
314 \\
-142 \\
\hline
172
\end{array}
$$

6. Determine the answer to a subtraction exercise and quickly respond when the minuend is increased or decreased by some multiple of ten:

Exercise:

Determine that $26 - 3 = 23$
after knowing that $16 - 3 = 13$

Grade IV

1. Subtract four-place numbers with regrouping in tens, hundreds, and thousands column:

5,132	4 thousands,	10 hundreds,	12 tens,	12 ones
-4,875	4 thousands,	8 hundreds,	7 tens,	5 ones
		2 hundreds,	5 tens,	7 ones

2. Use minuends and subtrahends involving the use of money.

Example: Pam has $7.80, Matt has $5.90. How much more money does Pam have than Matt?

$7.80 minuend
-5.90 subtrahend
$1.90 Pam has more than
           Matt

Grade V

1. Use amounts of money in subtraction up to five-place figures with regrouping in various positions.

Example:

$311.16
-    4.89
$306.27

Grade VI

1. Subtract whole numbers of 4 to 6 digits to include numbers with all types of difficulties; zero in the tens or (and) hundreds place in either (or both) the minuend and subtrahend.
2. Orally find the difference between two numbers of two or three digits each; round the minuend to hundreds then add or subtract. *Example:*

468	round to	500	216
-284		-284	- 32
		216	184

3. Examine a problem in subtraction and identify it as (a) take away, (b) comparison, or (c) addition:

(a) Christy had $15.00, and lost $4.00.
(b) This board is how much longer?
(c) Matt has $6.00 and he needs $10.00.

TEACHING SUGGESTIONS

Concept: Subtraction is the process of separating one set into two or more smaller sets

Procedures. 1. Each child is provided with a set of 10 bottle caps or similar small uniform elements. These elements (objects) have become familiar through many counting and addition experiences. The child is asked to move four of the bottle caps to a separate place and count the remaining caps to see how many are left. The words "take away" and "are left" are used; the children learning to verbalize the process. Fewer than 10 caps may be used in the initial work. Later the process and vocabulary become familiar and the child learns to write the problem given.

2. Using a group of 10 children, separate some of the children, showing now that you have two sets. Combine the two sets again to prove that the two smaller sets when combined equal the larger set of 10 children that you started with.

3. Have 6 balloons on strings in the front of the room. Take them around the room and have the children count the balloons. One child writes the number of balloons on the board. Ask the children what would be left if 3 balloons were separated from the larger set of 6 balloons. Pop three of the balloons. How many are left? Repeat this procedure of finding out how many are left with a small group of children separated from a larger group. Each time, a child writes the problem on the board. This will be done many times and with a variety of elements such as blocks, books, and other counting materials. Continue to relate the concrete to the abstract symbols on the board.

4. Use a flannelboard with a variety of elements such as ducks, apples, houses, and balls. For example, have the children count the apples as you put them on the flannelboard. Then show them what happens to the set of apples when you separate four of the apples from the set on the flannelboard. What is the size of the set that remains? Do this several times with different elements. Let the children make up their own problems with the use of the flannelboard. Others may write down the problems at their desks.

5. One day before the class is over, ask the children to remember to bring some objects, such as pebbles, to add to their counting boxes. Then as the children work with the objects at their desks the next day, write problems about a small group separated from a larger group to find out how many remain, and ask the children to do these problems with their various counting objects.

6. Dramatize the process of having groups of boys and girls standing in the front of the room. If 5 boys are standing in a group and 2 boys go and stand by the window, how many boys are left in the group? Is the group smaller?

7. Use the number line to show how a larger set of objects is separated into two smaller sets.

8. Starting with actual situations arising from roll check and lunch count each morning, questions like the following can be developed: "Is everyone here this morning?" Actual observation and count will show whether anyone is not present and how many are gone. "Seven brought lunches today. Six brought lunches yesterday. Did more bring lunches today or yesterday?"

9. *In the reading circle:* "How many are there in our reading circle? If we let Mary, Andrew, and Anna Louise go to their seats, how many will be left in our group?"

10. *Illustrative kinds of seatwork:* The children may illustrate subtraction stories by drawings of actual objects or tally marks or geometric representations on the chalkboard, crossing out or erasing the objects separated from the group, counting the number remaining, and writing the problem in abstract form. Seatwork may be used in which the problem is already represented pictorially and the children write the answer in abstract form. Other seatwork may be used in which the children see the original group already pictured and must cross out the group that is separated, counting the remaining group, and writing the answer. A story or a problem may be presented in which the pupil must illustrate the story entirely by himself, drawing the original group, crossing out the group to be separated, counting to discover the remaining group, and writing the answer.

11. The following three types of subtraction situations may be dramatized: (a) the remainder situation, (b) the additive or how-many-needed situation, and (c) the comparative or how-many-more situation. The *remainder* situation is presented first. Example: "Matt has 6 marbles. He gave Andrew 4 marbles. How many marbles does Matt have left?" The *comparative* or how-many-more situation is next: "Matt has 6 marbles. His little cousin has 4 marbles. How many less does his little cousin have?" Or "How many more marbles does Matt have? What is the difference?" The *additive* or how-many-needed situation: "Matt has 6 marbles. He dropped some. He still has two in his hand. How many should he look for?" This situation is best handled by using empty spaces to represent things not actually shown, as with an egg carton having some of the egg-holes filled and some empty. These story problems may be oral, or at times may be read and dramatized. The work "subtraction" may be used casually by the teacher, just as the word "add" is used, but the meaning of the process should be made clear first.

Concept: The minuend is equal to the sum of the subtrahend and the remainder

Procedures: 1. *Use blocks.* Have the children start with the number 36. Ask them to take 15 of the blocks away from the set of 36 blocks. They will find that they have 21 left. Ask, "What happens when the 21 blocks and the 15 blocks are put back together to form the original set?" Do you have 36 blocks again? Why? Write the example on the chalkboard:

$$\begin{array}{r} 36 \text{ blocks} \\ -15 \text{ blocks} \\ \hline 21 \text{ blocks} \end{array} \qquad \begin{array}{r} 15 \text{ blocks} \\ +21 \text{ blocks} \\ \hline 36 \text{ blocks} \end{array}$$

2. *Use counters.* Count off 12 objects. Take 5 of the objects away from the group of 12. Ask, "How many are left?" Then ask the children how many can be put with the 7 objects left to get the original group of 12 again. Ask them if they could write this:

$$\begin{array}{r} 12 \\ -\ 5 \\ \hline 7 \\ +\ 5 \\ \hline 12 \end{array} \qquad \text{///////////} - \text{/////} = \text{///////} \qquad \begin{array}{r} 12 \quad 7 \\ -\ 5 \ +5 \\ \hline 7 \ \ 12 \end{array}$$

$$\text{///////} + \text{/////} = \text{//////////}$$

$$\begin{array}{r} 12 \text{ blocks} \\ -\ 7 \text{ blocks} \\ \hline 5 \text{ blocks} \end{array} \qquad \begin{array}{r} 7 \text{ blocks} \\ +5 \text{ blocks} \\ \hline 12 \text{ blocks} \end{array}$$

3. *Problem situation.* Matt started to the movies. He had 36 cents. He did not count his money. He did not know whether he got the right change back after he had paid for his ticket. What should Matt have done first so that he would know whether his change was correct? Discuss the various answers. (Counted his money, subtracted the price of the movie ticket from his money to see how much was left.) Through these various methods comes the generalization that subtraction may be checked by adding the number left (the remainder) to the number subtracted (the subtrahend), this should result in the original amount (the minuend).

4. Have a child get any number of counters, say nine. Have him place them in a straight line across the flannelboard. Have another child count the number of counters (9). Write the number on the chalkboard. Have another child take 2 counters away from the set of 9 and write the example on the board: $\begin{array}{r} 9 \\ -2 \end{array}$. Ask the children what kind of example this is (subtraction). What is the answer to the problem? $7, \begin{array}{r} 9 \\ -2 \\ \hline 7 \end{array}$ How do we know that the answer is 7? (by counting) This is one way of checking our problem, but there is another way. Suppose Pam goes to the flannelboard and circles the two counters with her arms. Matt circles the other group of 7 counters with his arms. Have another child write the example shown on the flannelboard. ($2 + 7 =$ _____.) Now we have two examples: $\begin{array}{r} 9 \\ -2 \end{array} \begin{array}{r} 2 \\ +7 \end{array}$ In what ways are they alike? (We have used the same 3 numerals in both examples, 2, 7, and 9.) How do they differ? (One

example is addition and the other subtraction.) Have the children rearrange the two combinations:

$$
\begin{array}{cc}
9 & 2 \\
-2 & +7 \\
\hline
7 & 9
\end{array}
\qquad \text{to show} \qquad
\begin{array}{cc}
9 & 7 \\
-7 & +2 \\
\hline
2 & 9
\end{array}
$$

This should be recognized as a number family. Ask the children what has been done in each set of examples. In the first example, the bottom number (subtrahend) was subtracted from the top number (minuend) and the remainder found. In the second example the remainder and the subtrahend were added together and the sum was found to be equal to the minuend (the value of the original set).

5. Have the children copy the example $\begin{array}{r} 36 \\ -15 \\ \hline \end{array}$ on their papers to subtract and check

$$
\begin{array}{lr}
\text{Number had at first} & 36 \\
\text{Number taken away} & -15 \\
\hline
& 21
\end{array}
\qquad
\begin{array}{lr}
15 & \text{number taken away} \\
+21 & \text{remainder} \\
\hline
36 &
\end{array}
$$

Have them draw dotted lines connecting the two 21's and the two 15's. Connect the two 36's with an arrow.

Concept: Regrouping is a process of changing a ten into 10 ones, a hundred into 10 tens, a thousand into 10 hundreds, etc.

Procedures: 1. *Answering questions in subtraction by the indirect method.* Write the answers to the questions of the problems. If you do not know an answer, make a drawing to show what the problem shows in words. Think of as many ways as you can to show how you can solve the problem.

Problem: Christy had 52 cents. She spent 35 cents for lunch. How much money did she have left? Examples of diagrams and number solutions that children may possibly make:

(a) ///
          Fifty-two cents minus 35¢ equals 17¢

(b) Number line:

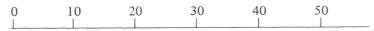

    35¢ from 52 ¢ equals 17¢.

(c) Thinking the difference:
       Fifty-five is 3 more than 52. Thirty-five from 55 is 20. Three from 20 is 17.

(d)

5 tens and 2 ones = 4 tens and 12 ones	52
−3 tens and 5 ones = 3 tens and 5 ones	−35
1 ten and 7 ones	17

(e)

	tens	ones	tens	ones
52 =	xxxxx	xx = xxxx	xxxxxxxxxxxx
−35 =	xxx	xxxxx =	xxx	xxxxx
		x	xxxxxxx = 17

2. Pam had 6 dimes and 2 pennies, but she spent 25¢ for Christmas cards. How much did she have left? A child is asked to put the problem on the board and indicate the process:

$$\begin{array}{r} 62¢ \\ -25¢ \\ \hline \end{array}$$

As the solution is started, the children will note that you cannot separate 5 from 2. Point out that 62¢ is more than 25¢, so it is possible to subtract, and if it were worked out with dimes and pennies, the amount left could be found. As others watch and check, one child will change one of the dimes into pennies so that there are 5 dimes and 12 pennies from which to subtract 2 dimes and 5 pennies. The next step is to write on the chalkboard what has been done:

62¢	6 dimes and 2 pennies = 5 dimes and 12 pennies
−25¢	−2 dimes and 5 pennies = 2 dimes and 5 pennies
	3 dimes and 7 pennies = 37¢

Several examples are given, and the solution written out. After the children can explain what they are doing, ask them to see if they can develop a shorter method to subtract without writing out the whole solution.

$$\begin{array}{r} 62¢ \\ -25¢ \\ \hline 37¢ \end{array}$$

Christy cannot separate 5¢ from 2¢, so she changes one of the 6 dimes into 10 pennies. Then she has 10 pennies and 2 pennies, which equals 12¢. She has 5 dimes left. Five cents separated from 12¢ equals 7¢, which is written in the ones column. Two dimes from 5 dimes equals 3 dimes, which is written in the tens place (62¢ − 25¢ = 37¢). After practice on dimes and pennies, tens and ones can be introduced. Note that "change" and "regroup" mean the same operation. Dollars, dimes, and cents (hundreds, tens, and ones) can be presented by comparing subtraction of two-place money and numbers.

46¢ = 4 dimes and 6 pennies = 3 dimes and 16 pennies
−19¢ = 1 dime and 9 pennies = 1 dime and 9 pennies
2 dimes and 7 pennies

$3.15 = 3 dollars, 1 dime, and 5 pennies = 2 dollars, 11 dimes, 5 pennies
-1.72 = 1 dollar, 7 dimes, and 2 pennies = 1 dollar, 7 dimes, 2 pennies
_____
                                        1 dollar, 4 dimes, 3 pennies
                                        or $1.43

3. Use the abacus in the initial work, showing that 3 tens and 4 ones are the same as 2 tens and 14 ones. Give many examples, having the children change the tens and ones. Write the equal tens and ones on the chalkboard. 3 tens and 4 ones = 2 tens and 14 ones.

Give the following problem: Matt has 34 marbles, but he lost some of them. How many does he have left? Develop the understanding in the same manner as in the above technique.

4. Use the abacus in solving problems such as the following: Fifty-two children will be in the audio-visual room. There are 27 chairs in the room. How many more chairs are needed so that everyone will have a chair?

5. Use of the pocket chart in a problem: If Christy has 42¢ and buys a package of cookies for 18¢, how much money will she have left? To work out this problem, use the pocket chart with play-money pennies and dimes Scotch-taped to cards.

Concept: Subtraction of multidigit numbers: (no renaming)

Procedures. 1. Display a set of 27 objects and ask the children how many would be left if 4 were removed. Write the equation on the board. Follow this with an illustration of expanded notation.

Example:

$$
\begin{array}{ccc}
27 & 20 + 7 & 27 \\
-\ 4 & -\quad 4 & -\ 4 \\
\hline
 & 20 + 3 & 23
\end{array}
$$

2. Provide the children with mimeograph materials involving simple subtraction with two-digit problems.

3. Write related placeholder equations on the chalkboard. Have children complete each equation.

$$
\begin{array}{ll}
n - 5 = 4 & 8 - n = 12 \\
n - 5 = 14 & 18 - n = 22 \\
n - 5 = 34 & 88 - n = 82
\end{array}
$$

Have children understand the relation among the three equations and to realize that knowing how to work the equation involving only ones will help them work equations involving tens and ones.

4. Use the pocket chart, which was introduced in addition. Instead of adding bundles, take some away.

5. Create story problems for children involving two-digit subtraction. Let the children make their own stories and have the children write the problems on the chalkboard.

6. Introduce the children to comparison of numbers involving two-digit additions and subtractions without regrouping or renaming. Place on the chalkboard a series of equations and inequalities in which the relation symbol is missing. Have the children compare the numbers represented by the numerals and write the correct symbol ($>$, $<$, or $=$) in the circle. Have them explain why they chose the symbol.

$$12 + 3 \bigcirc 13 + 2$$
$$10 + 2 \bigcirc 10 + (2 + 1)$$
$$15 + 3 \bigcirc 10 + (3 + 5)$$

7. Review subtraction of tens in problems such as $70 - 30 = n$, $90 - 20 = n$, $60 - 10 = n$. Have the children explain the solutions in terms of tens. In the first problem, for example, a child may say: "Seven tens (or seventy) minus three tens (or thirty) equals four tens (or forty)." Have the children write and solve the related vertical form for each problem on the chalkboard.

8. Write the equation $42 - 20 = n$ on the chalkboard; then have a child place 42 paper strips (four bundles of ten and two ones) in the pocket chart. Ask him to remove 20 strips (two bundles of ten). Ask how many ones and how many tens he has now, and have him complete the place-holder equations. Use expanded notation, write the problem in vertical form. Explain to the children that the parentheses around the numeral $(20 + 0)$ will help them think of the number that is to be subtracted. Remind them that the plus sign between the twenty and the zero is part of the expanded notation numeral for twenty. The minus sign in front of the numeral $(20 + 0)$ means that both ones and tens are to be subtracted in the problem.

9.

$$\begin{array}{r} 40 + 2 \\ -(20 + 0) \\ \hline 20 + 2 = 22 \end{array}$$

Write the standard algorism on the chalkboard and have the children solve it. Remind the children that the same steps are involved in thinking out a problem in this form as in each of the other forms. Provide additional exercises of this type.

10. Put the following equation on the chalkboard: $68 - 42 = n$; then have the children place 68 paper strips (six bundles of ten and eight ones) in the pocket chart. Now remove 42 strips (four bundles of ten and two ones). How many ones and how many tens remain? Now have a child work the same problem on the chalkboard using expanded notation in vertical form and the related subtraction algorism.

Example:

$$
\begin{array}{ll}
60 + 8 & 68 \\
-(40 + 2) & -42 \\
\hline
20 + 6 = 26 & 26 \\
\end{array}
$$

11. Write the following on the chalkboard and have the children participate in finding the differences.

Examples:

$$
\begin{array}{ll}
7,000 + 400 + 50 + 6 & 7,456 \\
-3,000 + 200 + 30 + 4 & -3,234 \\
\hline
4,000 + 200 + 20 + 2 & 4,222 \\
\end{array}
$$

Let the children have other similar activities to work on the chalkboard.

12. Relate the different forms that can be used in working problems of this type. Discuss the fact that the numbers involved remain the same—only the symbolism and approach change.

Examples:

$$
\begin{array}{lll}
437 = & 400 + 30 + 7 = & 437 \\
-316 = & -300 + 10 + 6 = & -316 \\
\hline
& 100 + 20 + 1 & 121 \\
\end{array}
$$

$$
\begin{array}{llll}
437 & 437 & 437 & 437 \\
-316 & -6 & -10 & -300 \\
\hline
& 431 & 421 & 121 \\
\end{array}
$$

$$
\begin{array}{c}
437 \\
-316 \\
\hline
121 \\
\end{array}
$$

13. Continue further development of this concept.

Concept: Subtraction of multidigit numbers: (involving renaming)

Procedures. 1. On the chalkboard write the expanded notation for the problem $32 - 17 = N$. On the flannelboard, place sets to represent the first number in this subtraction. Circle each set of ten with a piece of yarn. Have the children explain what they must do first in this problem: they must try to subtract seven from two. Tell them to remove seven disks from the two loose disks on the board. They will immediately discover that this is impossible. Ask how may they make the removal possible. They should say that one of the sets of ten can be thought of as ten ones. Remove the yarn from around one set of ten. Explain that three tens and two ones can be thought of as two tens and twelve ones. It is then possible to remove seven from twelve. Develop other subtraction problems of this kind in the same way.

2. You may wish to present some children with a variation in the writing and working of subtraction involving renaming. Show the children how to subtract "in pieces" in problems involving numbers represented by two-digit numerals. In this method ones are subtracted from the number represented by the first numeral, then tens are subtracted from this difference for the final result.

3. Provide a lot of practice for children in two-digit renaming.

4. Present set demonstrations which illustrate ideas of equations. For example, if you present the equation $42 - 5 = N$, show on the chalkboard:

$$
\begin{array}{ccc}
40 + 2 & 30 + 12 & 42 \\
-\quad\quad 5 & -\quad\quad 5 & -\ 5 \\
\hline
 & & 37
\end{array}
$$

5. Exhibit for the children a set of 34 objects. Have these objects grouped by tens so that the children can clearly see three tens and four. Now have them subtract 17 objects and to begin by subtracting 7 objects. Observe that to subtract 7 objects, 4 objects must be taken, then one of the sets of ten must be broken to remove three more. That is, seven is subtracted from 14. Now observe with the children that in order to take away 17 in all, they must take away ten in addition to the seven that has already been removed. Have someone remove a set of ten. Now repeat this demonstration for another pair of numbers and show the corresponding equation on the chalkboard.

6. Review any ideas with which the children have had particular difficulty. Follow this review with a short oral practice session.

7. The inverse operation is important in developing the idea of renaming in subtraction. The child makes use of the different numerals for the same number in his work with regrouping. He learned to rewrite a problem such as $25 + 8 = N$ in the following ways.

$$
\begin{array}{ll}
25 + 8 = 20 + 13 & \quad\quad 20 + 5 \\
\quad\quad\ = 30 + 3 & \quad + \quad\quad 8 \\
\quad\quad\ = 33 & \quad\overline{20 + 13 = 33}
\end{array}
$$

To "undo" this problem, the child will learn to begin subtracting at the place where he finished adding. The equation $33 - 8 = N$, can be written in expanded notation.

$$
\begin{array}{c}
30 + 3 \\
-\quad\quad 8 \\
\hline
\end{array}
$$

The child will observe that it is impossible to subtract eight from three. Then he will learn to think of another way to write $30 + 3$; he will use the numeral that was used in the addition problem: $20 + 13$.

It is now possible for the child to perform the subtraction. He is now back where he started in the related addition problem.

Example:

$$\begin{array}{r} 30 + 3 \\ - \quad 8 \\ \hline \end{array} = \begin{array}{r} 20 + 13 \\ - \quad\quad 8 \\ \hline 20 + 5 = 25 \end{array}$$

The main emphasis in developing subtracting with renaming will be placed on the approach just described. There is, however, a second method, just as there is a second method in addition with regrouping.

8. This second method lends itself best to subtraction of a number represented by a one-digit numeral from a number represented by a two-digit numeral with renaming involved. In doing problems such as $13 - 7 = N$, the child learned to think of the problem as $(13 - 3) - 4 = N$. It is possible for him to adopt an analogous approach for $23 - 7 = N$. He can first subtract 3 from 23 to get 20 and subtract 4 from 20 and get the answer 16.

Example:

$$\begin{aligned} 23 - 7 &= (23 - 3) - 4 \\ &= 20 - 4 \\ &= 16 \end{aligned}$$

PRACTICE AND EVALUATION

Addition and Subtraction of Whole Numbers

1. $\boxed{\text{X X X}}$ $\boxed{\text{X X}}$ $\boxed{\text{X X X X X}}$
      $\triangle$ + 2 + $\triangle$ = $\boxed{}$

2. Solve:

$$\triangle + \square = 8 \qquad\qquad \triangle + \square = 6$$
$$\triangle + \square = 5 \qquad\qquad \triangle + \square = 7$$

$$\begin{array}{r} \square \\ +5 \\ \hline 9 \end{array} \qquad \begin{array}{r} 9 \\ -\triangle \\ \hline 4 \end{array} \qquad \begin{array}{r} \square \\ +3 \\ \hline 5 \end{array} \qquad \begin{array}{r} 10 \\ -\triangle \\ \hline 6 \end{array}$$

3. Solve each problem:

$$15 - 4 = \square \qquad 38 - 6 = \triangle \qquad 26 - 3 = \triangle$$
$$\triangle + 6 = 12 \qquad 42 + \square = 49 \qquad \square + 9 = 29$$

4. Solve:

$$\begin{aligned} 32 + 4 &= (30 + \underline{}) + 4 \\ &= 30 + (\underline{} + 4) \\ &= \underline{} + \underline{} \\[2mm] &= \underline{} \end{aligned} \qquad\qquad \begin{aligned} 38 - 6 &= (30 + 8) - 6 \\ &= 30 + (8 - 6) \\ &= 30 + \underline{} \\[2mm] &= \underline{} \end{aligned}$$

5. Use the correct comparison ($<, >, =$) in each circle:

$$3 + 2 \bigcirc 2 + 4 \qquad 6 + (4 + 3) \bigcirc (7 + 3) + 4$$
$$8 + 4 \bigcirc 7 + 5 \qquad 4 + 7 \bigcirc 12$$
$$16 - 7 \bigcirc 15 - 9 \qquad 8 - (4 + 2) \bigcirc (8 - 4) + 2$$

6. Use the correct sign of operation (+ or −) in each triangle:

$$5 \triangle 9 = 14 \qquad 19 \triangle 18 = 1$$
$$14 \triangle 5 = 9 \qquad 3 \triangle 8 = 11$$

7. Complete each equation:

$$7 + 9 = \underline{\quad} + 7$$
$$11 + (8 + 2) = 11 + \underline{\quad} = \underline{\quad}$$
$$653 = \underline{\quad} + 50 + \underline{\quad}$$
$$96 = \underline{\quad} + 6 = 80 + \underline{\quad}$$

8. Indicate the correct symbol ($<, >,$ or $=$) in each circle:

$$24 - 5 \bigcirc 20 + (4 + 5)$$
$$251 - 51 \bigcirc 200$$
$$79 - 47 \bigcirc (70 - 40) + (9 - 7)$$
$$(13 - 3) - 2 \bigcirc 11 + 3$$

9. Complete each mathematical sentence:

$$\square + 7 = 19 \qquad 47 - \square = 24$$
$$24 + \square = 37 \qquad 19 - 7 = \square$$
$$\square + 23 = 47 \qquad \square + 13 = 37$$

10. Solve:

12	$\square$	6	73	$\square 9$	$3 \square$	98
4	5	7	$\square \square$	$2 \square$	$\square 2$	$\square 6$
$\square$	8	16	93	65	16	72
19	16	$\square 9$				

11. Solve:

$$\begin{array}{l} 32 \\ +6 \\ \hline \end{array} \qquad 32 + 6 = 30 + \underline{\quad} = \underline{\quad} \qquad \begin{array}{l} 30 + 2 \\ +\ 6 \\ \hline 30 + \underline{\quad} \end{array}$$

$$\begin{array}{l} 14 \\ +23 \\ \hline \end{array} \qquad \begin{aligned} 14 + 23 &= (10 + 4) + (20 + 3) \\ &= (10 + 20) + (4 + 3) \\ &= 30 + 7 \\ &= \underline{\quad} \end{aligned} \qquad \begin{array}{l} 10 + 4 \\ 20 + 3 \\ \hline \underline{\quad} + \underline{\quad} \end{array}$$

$$\begin{array}{l} 37 \\ -\ 5 \\ \hline \end{array} \qquad \begin{aligned} 37 - 5 &= (30 + 7) - 5 \\ &= 30 - (7 - 5) \\ &= \underline{\quad} \end{aligned} \qquad \begin{array}{l} 30 + 7 \\ -\quad 5 \\ \hline \underline{\quad} + \underline{\quad} = \underline{\quad} \end{array}$$

$$27 + 23 = (20 + 7) + (20 + 3)$$
$$= (20 + 20) + (7 + 3)$$
$$= \underline{\quad} + \underline{\quad}$$
$$= \underline{\quad\quad}$$

$$\begin{array}{r} 27 \\ +23 \\ \hline 10 \\ 40 \\ \hline \end{array}$$

$$34 + 22 + 16 = 34 + 16 + 22$$
$$= (34 + 16) + 32$$
$$= \underline{\quad} + \underline{\quad}$$
$$= \underline{\quad\quad}$$

$$75 - 9 = (70 + 5) - 9$$
$$= (60 + 15) - 9$$
$$= 60 + (15 - 9)$$
$$= \underline{\quad} + \underline{\quad}$$

$$\begin{array}{r} 75 = 60 + 15 \\ -\ 9 = \underline{\quad} -\ 9 \\ \hline \underline{\quad} + \underline{\quad} = \underline{\quad} \end{array}$$

12. Replace each letter with the missing number:

$$243 + 789 = n \qquad\qquad (729 + 201) - 174 = g$$
$$497 - 76 = h \qquad\qquad 98 - a = 27$$
$$36 + f = 158 \qquad 986 + 52{,}198 + 23{,}410 + 25 = t$$

13. Fill in each blank:

$$315 + 539 = 900 - \underline{\quad\quad}$$

$$975 - 432 = \underline{\quad\quad} + 195$$

$$12{,}789 + 11{,}234 = 22{,}000 + \underline{\quad\quad}$$

$$67{,}564 - 42{,}123 = 24{,}743 + \underline{\quad\quad}$$

14. Place the correct sign of operation in each of the squares:

$$1{,}743 + \quad 228 = 1{,}824 \ \square \ 147$$
$$5{,}526 + 1{,}478 = 7{,}500 \ \square \ 496$$

15. Add from left to right as shown:

7,493	2,468	9,876	12,964
4,211	+ 1,357	+ 4,789	+ 86,734
11,000			
600			
100			
+ 4			
11,704			

16. What number must be added to the first number to give the second?

74,893	156,847
173,594	387,654

17. Solve each problem using expanded notation, indicating the properties used in each step:

$$
\begin{array}{cccccc}
 & & & 120 & & \\
26 & 87 & 124 & 768 & 4{,}190 & 69{,}375 \\
+45 & -59 & +456 & +109 & -2{,}893 & +16{,}902
\end{array}
$$

Example:

$$
\begin{array}{llll}
137 = 100 + & 30 + & 7 & \text{renaming} \\
+576 = 500 + & 70 + & 6 & \\
\hline
600 + & 100 + & 13 &
\end{array}
$$

$(600 + 100) + 13$	associative property
$700 + 13$	associative property
$700 + (10 + 3)$	renaming
713	addition

$$
\begin{array}{llll}
479 = 400 + 70 + 9 = (300 + 170 + 9) & \text{renaming} \\
-\ 184 = \underline{100 + 80 + 4} = \underline{100 + \ \ 80 + 4} & \\
\qquad\qquad\qquad\qquad 200 + \ \ 90 + 5 = 295 &
\end{array}
$$

SELECTED READINGS

Addition and Subtraction of Whole Numbers

Banks, Houston J. *Learning and Teaching Arithmetic.* Boston: Allyn and Bacon 1959, pp. 83–85, 113–139.

Bell, Clifford, Cleia Hammond, and Robert Herrera. *Fundamentals of Arithmetic for Teachers.* New York: Wiley, 1962, pp. 38–60, 78–90.

Brumfield, Charles, Robert Eicholz, and Merrill Shanks. *Fundamental Concepts of Elementary Matiematics.* Reading, Mass.: Addison-Wesley, 1962, pp. 20–32, 69–78.

Educational Research Council of Greater Cleveland. *Key Topics in Mathematics for the Primary Teacher.* Chicago: Science Research Associates, 1962, pp. 36–57.

Evenson, A. B. *Modern Mathematics: Introductory Concepts and Their Implications.* Chicago: Scott, Foresman, 1962, pp. 33–43.

Fujii, John N. *An Introduction to the Elements of Mathematics.* New York; Wiley, 1961, pp. 113–114.

Johnson, Donovan A., and William H. Glenn, *Sets, Sentences, and Operations.* St. Louis: Webster, 1960, pp. 30–34.

Morris, Dennis E., and Henry D. Topfer. *Advancing in Mathematics.* Chicago: Science Research Associates, 1963, pp. 65–78, 84–87.

Osborn, Roger, Vere Devault, Claude Boyd, and Robert Houston. *Extending Mathematical Understanding.* Columbus Ohio: Merrill, 1961, pp. 1–11, 25–33.

Peterson, John A., and Joseph Hashisaki. *Theory of Arithmetic.* New York: Wiley, 1963, pp. 45–51, 86–98.

Schaaf, William L. *Basic Concepts of Elementary Mathematics.* New York: Wiley, 1960, pp. 107–118.

School Mathematics Group. "Studies in Mathematics," Vol. IX: *A Brief Course in Mathematics for Elementary School Teachers.* Stanford, Calif.: Stanford U. P., 1963, pp. 5–19, 41–76.

Shipp, Donald, and Sam Adams. *Developing Arithmetic Concepts and Skills.* Englewood Cliffs, N. J.: Prentice-Hall, 1964, pp. 40–43, 162–171.

chapter 5

The Teaching of Whole Numbers (Multiplication and Division)

Multiplication is a short efficient way of adding when addends are of the same size. Division is a series of subtractions. There are two kinds of division problems:

1. You know the size of a group and the total and you need to find the number of groups.

Example: In Pam's class there are 35 children. Seven children sit in each row of desks. How many rows of desks are there in the room? This is called *measurement division.*

2. The other is when you know the total and the number of groups and you need to know the number in each group.

Example: Pamela's class has 35 children. There are five rows of desks in the room. How many children sit in each row? This is called *partition division.*

In the initial instruction of multiplication, show the relationship between multiplication and addition, as well as the relationship between multiplication and division. As they learn the facts, build the multiplication tables as reference charts, not just memorizing; showing that if he knows one fact (7 × 5) the student can find any other fact he wishes. The basic facts should be mastered by the end of Grade IV.

In the initial instruction of division, show the relationship of division and multiplication as well as the relationship between division and subtraction. Each fact should be developed with concrete and manipulative materials. One of the better ways is to have pupils show the meaning of the process by dramatizing it. If the pupil understands the reason for the correct placement of the quotient figure, it is probable he has learned division through meaning. In teaching division, teach the long form from the beginning and the short form only as a short cut. Teach the short form only after the students have fully mastered the long form.

Long Form   Short Form

$$\begin{array}{r} 4 \\ 6\overline{)24} \\ \underline{24} \end{array} \qquad \begin{array}{r} 4 \\ 6\overline{)24} \end{array}$$

If the students are taught the long form from the start, they have a greater chance of fully understanding the meaning of the process. Also, they know and have mastered the fact if they can reproduce it in the long form—which is not the case if they reproduce it in the short form. True, this means more work and more time to introduce and master the facts, but in the long run it will pay off for the student.

Current practice is sharply divided on a number of issues relative to the teaching of multiplication and division. The major ones are procedures used in initial instruction, the order and number of facts presented, and the reading of multiplication and division problems.

INITIAL INSTRUCTION

It is felt that a number of facts should be developed from problem settings and number questions before you teach work for the mastery of the basic facts. This procedure is opposite to common practice found in current textbooks where only a few facts are presented at a time with the suggestion that you learn them before going on. No matter what method you use, a variety of study procedures makes for more efficient learning.

The same general plan that has been previously outlined in addition and subtraction is recommended for the initial instruction for multiplication and division, this being the presentation of the various processes through a problem situation with the children solving the problem in any way that they can.

Order and Number of Facts

In general, the easier facts where the divisor and the factors are 2, 3, 4, or 5, are introduced in the third grade, and the harder facts are introduced and studied for mastery in the fourth grade. These include 1, 6, 7, 8, and 9 in multiplication and 6, 7, 8, and 9 in division. The order of introduction of the facts is not an important issue.

Reading of Multiplication and Division Problems

It is felt that 4×3 should be read as four 3's, not 4 times 3. You are not multiplying a single group of 3 four times; rather you are multiplying 4 groups of 3.

In view of the difficulties involved in the reading of the basic division facts, care needs to be taken when they are developed from illustrative problems. The following are examples of how we read $12 \div 3 = 4$. "In 12, there are four 3's." "12 divided by 3 equals 4." "How many 3's are in 12?" "How many 3's equal 12?" The expression, "How many 3's equal 12?" presents the complete mathematical concept of the actual operation.

Advanced Multiplication and Division

Multiplication and division of two or more digits by a one-digit number is usually introduced *before* all the basic facts are taught. But multiplication with a two-digit multiplier and division with a two-digit divisor is not introduced until *after* all the basic facts have been studied and mastered. The importance attached to these two areas is clearly seen by the amount of time spent in Grades IV and V developing the mastery of the necessary understandings and skills.

The exact tens technique could again be used in the initial development of this division and multiplication. The introductory problems should be solved by several means and then careful study directed toward arriving at the best number way of solving the problem.

The teaching of how to divide with a two-figure divisor has long been considered as the most difficult part of the entire mathematical curriculum in the elementary school. True, it is a process that is inherently difficult to teach, but if children are given the opportunity to acquire an understanding and meaning of the process they will not find it difficult to learn. This means the extensive use of illustrative problems to initiate the instruction and of instructional procedures where the emphasis is placed upon already known computational procedures. Then the process becomes meaningful to the student as well as the teacher.

PROPERTIES AND RELATIONSHIPS

In addition, an ordered pair of numbers is operated on to yield a third number called the *sum*:

$$\begin{array}{ccc} \text{addend} & \text{addend} & \text{sum} \\ 3 & + \quad 5 & = \quad 8 \end{array}$$

In *multiplication*, a unique third number, called the *product*, is similarly assigned to an ordered pair of numbers:

$$\begin{array}{ccc} \text{factor} & \text{factor} & \text{product} \\ 3 & \times \quad 5 & = \quad 15 \end{array}$$

There are at least two interpretations involving the operation of multiplication on the set of whole numbers. In the early instruction children have interpreted multiplication as repeated additions. This interpretation is shown below by the use of rectangular *arrays*. An array is an orderly arrangement of sets of things, numerals, or other symbols. Consider the following arrays:

$$3 \times 5 = 15 \qquad 4 \times 5 = 20 \qquad 5 \times 5 = 25$$
$$\text{or} \qquad\qquad \text{or}$$
$$5 \times 3 = 15 \qquad 5 \times 4 = 20$$

.   In each of the arrays above the product may be computed by successive additions. Thus the product for 4×5 may be interpreted by considering 5 as an addend 4 times; $5 + 5 + 5 + 5 = 20$ or 4 as an addend 5 times as $4 + 4 + 4 + 4 + 4 = 20$.

Another interpretation of multiplication of whole numbers involves a situation such as the following:

Matt has a set of three new shirts; a blue one, a green one, a brown one.

He has a set of two new pairs of pants; a gray one and a tan one.

He wants to know how many different outfits he can have.

Possible matchings:

Gray pants, blue shirt
Gray pants, green shirt
Gray pants, brown shirt

Tan pants, blue shirt
Tan pants, green shirt
Tan pants, brown shirt

The *product set* (also called cartesian product) of two sets A and B is denoted by $A \times B$ and is defined as the set of all ordered pairs (a, b) where a is an element of Set A and b is an element of Set B. Therefore if

$$A = \{ \text{blue, green, brown} \} \text{ and}$$
$$B = \{ \text{gray, tan} \}$$

then the six ordered pairs above list the elements of $A \times B$. Notice that

$$N(A \times B) = 6$$
$$N(A) \quad = 3$$
$$N(B) \quad = 2$$

and that $N(A \times B) = N(A) \times N(B)$, which is the reason $A \times B$ is called the *product* set. Thus $A \times B$ in the above illustration can be represented on a chart as

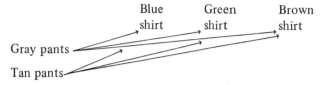

and represented as an array:

Shirts

	Blue	Green	Brown
Gray	·	·	·
Tan	·	·	·

(Pants)

There are then six matchings possible, and we see that by this interpretation of multiplication of the ordered pair $(2, 3)$ we arrive at the same array with 6 elements as in the first interpretation. The numbers operated on, 3 and 2, are called *factors*. The result of operation, 6, is called the product:

Factor $\times$ factor = product

In *division* we continue to operate on two numbers to obtain another number. Division is the operation of finding one factor when the other factor and the product are known.

Factor $\times$ $\square$ = product

Example:

5 $\times$ 3 = $\square$ requires the operation of multiplication for solution
$\square$ $\times$ 3 = 15 requires the operation of division for solution
5 $\times$ $\square$ = 15 requires the operation of division for solution

The relationship of the arithmetic operations is shown in the diagram:

Addition $\xrightarrow{\text{Related}}$ multiplication
$\uparrow$ Inverse $\qquad\qquad$ $\uparrow$ Inverse
Subtraction $\xrightarrow{\text{Related}}$ division

1. **Associative Property.** The order of associating a product involving more than two factors does not affect the product. For example:

$$8 \times 5 = (4 \times 2) \times 5 = 4 \times (2 \times 5) = 4 \times 10$$

Division is *not* associative.

$$(8 \div 4) \div 2 = 1$$

but

$$8 \div (4 \div 2) = 4$$

2. **Commutative Property.** The reversing of the order of the factors does not affect the product. For example:

$$8 \times 5 = 5 \times 8$$

Division is *not* commutative.

$$8 \div 4 \neq 4 \div 8$$

3. **Inverse Operations.** The inverse operation of "multiplication" of a number is the "division" of that number.

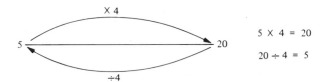

$$5 \times 4 = 20$$
$$20 \div 4 = 5$$

Develop and drill division facts by relating them to associated multiplication facts.

4. **Identity Element for Multiplication.** The number "one" has a special property with respect to multiplication. The product of "one" and any number is that same number. For example:

$$1 \times 8 = 8 \qquad 8 \times 1 = 8$$

5. **Multiplicative Property of Zero.** The product of zero and any number is zero.

Example:

$$0 \times 7 = 0 \qquad 7 \times 0 = 0 \qquad 0 \times 0 = 0$$
$$0 \times y = 0 \qquad y \times 0 = 0$$

6. **Distributive Property of Multiplication with Respect to Addition.** This operation combines addition and multiplication.

Example:

$$8 \times 25 \ = n$$
$$8 \times (20 + 5) = (8 \times 20) + (8 \times 5) = 160 + 40 = 200$$
$$a \times (b + c) = (a \times b) + (a \times c) = ab + ac = n$$
$$25 \times 8 = n$$
$$(20 + 5) \times 8 = (20 \times 8) + (5 \times 8) = 160 + 40 = 200$$

7. **Distributive Property of Division with Respect to Addition.** In division the dividend can be renamed.

Example:

$$36 \div 6 = (30 \div 6) + (6 \div 6)$$

However, the divisor cannot be renamed to apply a distributive property.

Example:

$$36 \div 6 \neq (36 \div 4) \neq (36 \div 2)$$

8. **Closure.** The set of whole numbers is closed with respect to multiplication; that is, when multiplying any two whole numbers, the product is *always* a whole number.

The set of whole numbers is not closed with respect to division.

Example:

$12 \div 4$ is a whole number (3)
$12 \div 5$ is not a whole number.

9. **Factors and Factorization.** The idea and terminology—factors—are introduced with the formalized instruction of multiplication. The concept is enlarged upon at each succeeding grade level so that the sixth-grade child has a clear understanding of the concept.

$4 \times 5 = 20$
4 and 5 are factors of 20
20 is the product of the factors 4 and 5
20 is a multiple of 4
20 is a multiple of 5

The factors of a number, are pairs of whole numbers that when multiplied result in that number. Thus the factors of 20 are 4 and 5, 10 and 2, 20 and 1.

A multiple of a number is a number that can be divided evenly by that number.

20 is a multiple of 5 and 4, 10 and 2, 20 and 1, because it
can be divided evenly by all those numbers.

Thus, 20 is a multiple of all its factors.

Factorization or factoring is the process of expressing a number in terms of its factors.

Factorization of 20 is: {20, 1, 10, 2, 5, 4} .
Some numbers have only two factors, itself and 1.

The factors of 3 are { 3, 1} .
The factors of 7 are { 7, 1} .
The factors of 19 are {19, 1} .

A number that has only two factors, itself and 1, is called a *prime number.*

A number that is not a prime number and has more than two factors other than itself and 1 is called a *composite number*.

The number one is neither prime nor composite.

> The factors of 1 are {1, 1}.
> Thus one has only one factor not two different factors.

As a result of the examples above the following conclusions can be made:
(a) Every number is a factor of itself.
(b) One is a factor of every number.
(c) Not all even numbers with the exception of 2 are composite numbers.
(d) *Not all* odd numbers are prime numbers.

Prime factorization may be developed as follows. Factor trees are helpful at the elementary level for picturing prime factorizations.

The prime factorization of 20   The prime factorization of 20

As a result of the examples above the following conclusions can be made:
(a) Regardless of the two factors that are used, the prime factorization is the same. The order of the numerals is unimportant because it does not effect the product.
(b) Multiplying the prime factors gives the initial product.
(c) Every composite number has one and only one prime factorization.

Common and greatest common factors may be developed as follows. The factors of 20 are {20, 1, 10, 2, 5, 4}. The factors of 30 are {15, 2, 10, 3, 6, 5, 30, 1}. By examination it is seen that 1, 2, 5, and 10 are common factors of 20 and 30. Therefore 1, 5, 2, and 10 are common factors of 20 and 30. Common factors are those factors which are the same for each of two given numbers.

The factors of 20 are {20, 1, 5, 4, 10, 2}. The factors of 30 are {30, 1, 15, 2, 10, 3, 6, 5}. The common factors of 20 and 30 are {1, 2, 5, 10}. The greatest common factor is the largest factor that is common to each of two given numbers. Therefore 10 is the greatest common factor of 20 and 30.

The concept of the intersection of two sets may be used to define common factors and greatest common factor.

Factors of 20: Set A = {20, 1, 5, 4, 10, 2}.
Factors of 30: Set B = {30, 1, 15, 2, 6, 5, 10, 3}.
$A \cap B$ = {1, 2, 5, 10}.
10 is the greatest of the common factors.

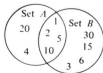

The greatest common factor may also be found by the following technique:

Take the prime factorization of each number,

$$20 = \boxed{5} \cdot \boxed{2} \cdot 2$$
$$30 = \boxed{5} \cdot \boxed{2} \cdot 3$$

Multiply the common prime factors. Their product is the greatest common factor: $5 \times 2 = 10$.

10 is the greatest common factor.

Common multiple and least common multiple may be developed as follows:

20 is a multiple of 5 and 4 because 20 can be divided by 5 or 4 with a zero remainder.

Least common multiple means the smallest number that can be divided evenly by both 5 and 4.

Multiples of 5: 5, 10, 15, 20, 25, 30, 35, 40, 45, 50.

Multiples of 4: 4, 8, 12, 16, 20, 24, 28, 32, 36, 40.

20 and 40 are multiples of 5 and 4.

20 is the *least* common multiple of 5 and 4.

Set intersection may be used to define common multiples and least common multiples. Develop the technique in the same manner as it was used to define common factors.

Prime factorization of numbers can be used to find the least common multiple.

Prime factorization of $2 = 2 \cdot 1$; of $3 = 3 \cdot 1$.

Least common multiple of 2 and $3 = 2 \cdot 1 \cdot 3 = 6$.

Note that $\boxed{2 \cdot} \boxed{1} \boxed{\cdot 3}$ includes the complete prime factorization of both 2 and 3. If the same factor appears in both factorizations, it is written only once in the new prime factorization.

$7 = 7 \times 1$
$14 = 7 \times 2$

LCM $= \boxed{1 \times \enclose{circle}{7} \times 2} = 14$

$\downarrow \quad \downarrow$
$7 \quad 14$

$6 = 2 \times 3$
$25 = 5 \times 5$

LCM $= \enclose{circle}{2 \times 3} \times \enclose{circle}{5 \times 5} = 125$

$\downarrow \quad \downarrow$
$6 \quad 25$

$8 = 2 \times 2 \times 2$
$24 = 2 \times 2 \times 2 \times 3$

LCM $= \left(\enclose{circle}{2 \times 2 \times 2} \times 3 \right) = 24$

$\downarrow \quad \downarrow$
$8 \quad 24$

The specific skills and understandings regarding the various properties and relationships with whole numbers as regards the operation of multiplication and division include the following. The child should be able to:

Grade II

1. Understand the relationship of multiplication to addition. (Multiplication can be shown by repeated additions.)

$$2 + 2 + 2 + 2 = 8 \qquad 4 \text{ two's are } 8$$

2. Show that the identity element of multiplication is 1. (One times any number is the same number.)

$$1 \times 3 = 3 \qquad 1 \times 4 = 4 \qquad 1 \times 5 = 5$$

Grade III

1. Review previous learnings.
2. Understand the distributive property of multiplication over addition.

$$(4 \times 8) = 4 \times (5 + 3) = (4 \times 5) + (4 \times 3)$$
$$= \quad 20 \quad + \quad 12$$
$$= \quad 32$$

3. Understand the relationship of division to subtraction. (Division can be shown as repeated subtractions.)

$$
\begin{array}{ll}
12 & \\
\underline{-3} & (1) \\
9 & \\
\underline{-3} & (2) \\
6 & \qquad\qquad 12 \div 3 = 4 \\
\underline{-3} & (3) \\
3 & \\
\underline{-3} & (4) \\
0 &
\end{array}
$$

4. Understand the inverse operations of multiplication and division. (Division "undoes" multiplication and multiplication "undoes" division.)

$$
\begin{array}{ll}
4 \times 3 = 12 & \qquad 12 \div 3 = 4 \\
3 \times 4 = 12 & \qquad 12 \div 4 = 3
\end{array}
$$

Grade IV

1. Review previous learnings.
2. Understand the commutative property of multiplication. (The order of the factors does not change the product.)

$$4 \times 3 = 12 \qquad 3 \times 4 = 12$$

3. Understand the associative property of multiplication. (Factors may be grouped in any way without changing the product.)

$$(2 \times 3) \times 4 = 24 \qquad \text{or} \quad 2 \times (3 \times 4) = 24$$

so

$$(2 \times 3) \times 4 = 2 \times (3 \times 4) = 24$$

and

$$2 \times (3 \times 5) = 2 \times 15 = 30$$

4. Understand the distributive property of multiplication over addition.

$$4 \times 26 = 4 \times (20 + 6)$$
$$= (4 \times 20) + (4 \times 6)$$
$$= 80 + 24$$
$$= 104$$
$$4 \times 67 = n, 4 \times (60 + 7) = n, (4 \times 60) + (4 \times 7) = n,$$
$$240 + 28 = n, 268 = n$$

5. Develop meaning and usage of factors.

$$1 \times 9 = 9$$
$$9 \times 1 = 9 \qquad \text{Factors 1, 3, 9.}$$
$$3 \times 3 = 9$$

Grade V

1. Review previous learnings.
2. Understand factors and primes.
   (a) 3, 4; 6, 2; 12, 1; are all factors of 12 since $3 \times 4, 6 \times 2, 12 \times 1 = 12$.
   (b) 3 is a prime number, prime because its only factors are itself and one (only $3 \times 1 = 3$).
   (c) Use tests for divisibility.
3. Understand and use each of the following basic properties:
   (a) Use commutative property of multiplication.
   (b) Use associative property of multiplication.
   (c) Use distributive property of multiplication over addition.
   (d) Use inverse operations (multiplication-division).
   (e) Use properties of zero and one.
       Multiplicative identity: $1 \times A = A$.
       Zero is a place-holder.
   (f) Understand the relationship of division to subtraction.
   (g) Understand the relationship of addition to multiplication.

Grade VI

1. Review previous learnings.
2. Express properties in algebraic form.
3. Understand closure under multiplication.

TEACHING SUGGESTIONS

Concept: Associative property—multiplication

Procedures. 1. Write three factors on the chalkboard: 2, 5, 7. Show the children the ways in which these can be multiplied by different groupings. For example: $(2 \times 5) \times 7$ or $2 \times (5 \times 7)$. Provide a discussion period where the children can explain the associative principle in their own words.

2. Be sure to go over the mathematical meaning of parentheses. Children should understand it shows which operation is to be performed first.

3. Provide story problems, worksheets, and oral experiences to develop further the associative principle.

Concept: Commuting the factors does not change the product ($a \times b = b \times a$)

Procedures. 1. This can be done quite well by showing rectangular arrays and having the children consider them first in columns and then in rows.

2. Prepare cards on which pictures are arranged in rows and columns to represent multiplication combinations. 5×6 through 5×9 and 6×5 through 9×5. Distribute the cards to the children and give them time to determine how many pictures appear in each row and how many rows there are on the cards. Call on a child to stand, display his card, describe the sets, and give the related multiplication combination. If, for example, he displays the first card illustrated above, he should say, "I have eight rows with six pictures in each row. Eight sixes are forty-eight." Now have him turn the card 90 degrees. He should say, "Now my card shows six rows with eight pictures in each row. Six eights equal forty-eight." Have the two equations $8 \times 6 = 48$ and $6 \times 8 = 48$, written on the chalkboard and the commutative property discussed.

$$8 \times 6 = 48 \qquad\qquad 6 \times 8 = 48$$

3. Construct a multiplication table on a large piece of chart paper. Guide the children as they fill in the table. Ask one child to suggest a product to record. If he suggests 9×3, have him record 27 in the proper box. Call on a second child to record the related product which illustrates the commutative property. If a child suggests 5×5, have him record the product 25; then ask whether the commutative property applies with this product.

4. Draw on the chalkboard a set of objects arranged in a rectangular array. You might begin by choosing a 4×3 array (four rows with three in each row).

Call the childrens' attention to the four rows with three objects in each row. Have one of the children relate this to the idea of four sets of three; then write the multiplication equation $4 \times 3 = 12$. Now call attention to the columns and notice with the children that there are three columns with four objects in each column and that they can think of three sets of four. Exhibit the multiplication equation $3 \times 4 = 12$. Following this, observe with the children that $4 \times 3 = 3 \times 4$.

5. To review the commutative property of addition, place two felt cutouts joined to a set of three cutouts. Have the children tell how many are in the set union and have them use their plastic numerals and other symbols to build the related addition equation $2 + 3 = 5$. Now reverse the procedure by having a set of two joined to a set of three and have the related equation built: $3 + 2 = 5$. Discuss the meaning of the commutative property of addition. Ask the children whether they think multiplication might be commutative. Some children may suggest that since addition is commutative and multiplication can be thought of as repeated addition, multiplication may also be commutative.

6. Construct a set of tagboard cards to illustrate different multiplication combinations. Mark off rows of 3 inch $\times$ 3 inch squares. To show the product 1×4, for example, cut a card 3 inches $\times$ 12 inches and mark off four squares as illustrated. To show 2×4, cut a card 6 inches $\times$ 12 inches and mark off two rows of four squares each. Glue bits of flannel or sandpaper on the back of each card so that they will adhere to the flannelboard.

7. Place a card which has two rows of three squares each on the flannelboard. Ask a child to tell how many squares are in each row, and how many squares there are altogether. Have him use the felt numerals and ($\times$) and (=) signs to build the related multiplication equation: $2 \times 3 = 6$. Rotate the card 90 degrees so that three rows of two blocks each are displayed. Ask a child to build the related multiplication equation $3 \times 2 = 6$. Remove the card from the flannelboard and have both equations read and discussed. Some child might point out that the order of the factors has been changed but the product is the same.

8. Construct a set of cards bearing multiplication placeholder equations involving single-digit factors. Distribute these cards to the children. Have a child come to the front of the room, display his card and say, "I am looking for a partner." The child who holds the equation that illustrates the application of the commutative property to the given multiplication comes to the front of the room and holds his card alongside of the first card. The children must then give the product of the two equations. Call upon another child to come to the front of the room and continue the activity.

$$2 \times 3 = n \qquad 3 \times 2 = n$$

9. Construct one set of cards bearing multiplication placeholder equations, and another set bearing the same problems in vertical notation. Place the vertical-notation cards on the chalk tray. Display one of the equation cards to two

children, and have them race to see who can find the related vertical-notation card on the chalk tray and tell the product of the given factors. The winner becomes the leader and displays a card for the next two contestants.

$$5 \times 3 = n \qquad \begin{array}{r} 5 \\ \underline{\times 3} \end{array}$$

10. Have the children draw pictures of rockets at different altitudes on the chalkboard. Write a multiplication combination in vertical notation on each rocket. Have one child act as rocket booster and point to one rocket at a time. Each child in turn has a chance to fire a rocket by quickly reading the problem and giving the product. His reward for success is a successful space shot. If he misses he must use counters to work out that combination.

Concept: Distributive property and multiplication-addition

Procedures. 1. The children can be prepared for these types of activities by a review of equations involving multiplication and addition.

Example:

$$(2 \times 5) + (2 \times 6) =$$

Be sure that the children do the two multiplications first and then add the products.

2. To help the children understand the concept of "breaking apart" numbers, make several large domino-type cards:

. . . .
. . . .
. . . .

The problem is $3 \times 12 = 36$.

Either cut or fold a part of the card to show the following:

. . . .
. . . .
. . . .

$$(3 \times 5) \quad + \quad (3 \times 7) = 36$$

3. Have five sets of two beads and one set of two beads placed on the bead frame. Have the children tell the story in terms of sets and relate it to the ideas expressed in equation form. Point out that the distributive property allows them to use two easy combinations to find the product. Ask whether there are other combinations they could use to find 6×2. Lead them to say that $6 \times 2 = (3 \times 2) + (3 \times 2)$ and that also $6 \times 2 = (4 \times 2) + (2 \times 2)$. Repeat the activity to develop the multiplication combinations.

4. Have the children use the sets of rectangles cut from squared paper to reinforce the ability to work with the multiplication combinations, and to strengthen the understanding of the distributive property. Ask the children to place their rectangles on their desks. Have them find the two rectangles which taken together will represent 6 X 2. Various combinations may also be used. Write the multiplication combination 6 X 2 on the chalkboard. Ask one of the children to show the class the two rectangles he used to show 6 X 2.

5. Have the children create simple story problems to illustrate these equations.

$$6 \times 3 = (4 + 2) \times 3 = (4 \times 3) + (2 \times 3)$$
$$7 \times 4 = (6 + 1) \times 4 = (6 \times 4) + (1 \times 4)$$

6. Write brief story problems that involve the use of the distributive property of multiplication over addition. Prepare cards, each containing a different equation, and display them on the chalk tray or in chart pockets. Read a story and have a child select an equation that would be used to find the solution.

Example:

$$5 \times (3 + 4) =$$
$$(3 + 4) \times 5 =$$

Concept: The product of 1 and any other factor is that factor itself (identity element of multiplication)

Procedures. 1. Have a number of like objects such as blocks, clothespins, sticks, and books. Have two children go to the table and each take an object. Ask another child how many objects do the two children have together. (2) Have the number problem written on the board:

$$\begin{array}{r} 1 \\ \underline{\times 2} \\ 2 \end{array} \qquad 2 \times 1 = 2$$

Ask the children how many objects each child is holding. (1) How many children are holding an object? (2) Write the number problem on the board:

$$\begin{array}{r} 1 \\ \underline{\times 2} \\ 2 \end{array} \qquad 2 \times 1 = 2$$

Now have one child go to the front of the room and pick up two objects. How many objects is the child holding? (2) How many children are holding two objects? (1) Write the number problem on the board:

$$\begin{array}{r} 2 \\ \underline{\times 1} \\ 2 \end{array} \qquad 1 \times 2 = 2$$

Notice that the answers are the same:

$$\begin{array}{cc} 1 & 2 \\ \underline{\times 2} & \underline{\times 1} \\ 2 & 2 \end{array} \qquad \begin{array}{l} 2 \times 1 = 2 \\ 1 \times 2 = 2 \end{array}$$

Use other numbers and further develop the concept that the product of 1 and any other number is the number itself.

2. *Use the flannelboard.* Have one child go to the flannelboard and place 7 stars on it. How many stars were placed on the flannelboard? (7) How many times were the stars placed on the flannelboard? (1) Write the problem.

$$\begin{array}{ll} 7 \text{ stars} & 7 \\ \underline{1 \text{ time}} & \underline{\times 1} \qquad 1 \times 7 = 7 \\ 7 \text{ stars} & 7 \end{array}$$

How many times were the stars put on the flannelboard? (1) How many stars are there on the flannelboard? (7) Write the number story.

$$\begin{array}{ll} 1 \text{ time} & 1 \\ \underline{7 \text{ stars}} & \underline{\times 7} \qquad 7 \times 1 = 7 \\ 7 \text{ stars} & 7 \end{array}$$

Continue the same procedure with different numbers of objects.

3. *Problem.* How many cartons of milk will it take if each child in the first row is given one bottle of milk? Since there are seven children in the first row, the example will be seven times one. Place the cartons and find that it does take seven cartons of milk. Do the same thing with the third row which has six children in it and we find that $6 \times 1 = 6$. Do this with other objects.

Place one child in each corner of the room. How many children are in each corner? How many corners in the room? $4 \times 1 = 4$. Then place four children in a corner and find that $1 \times 4 = 4$. "In our room there are 9 windows. If an Easter bunny is placed in each window, how many bunnies do we need?" ($9 \times 1 = 9$.)

Each child has the bottom half of an egg carton. The child works out the problem. A block in each of four cups is how many blocks? ($4 \times 1 = 4$.) Four blocks in one cup is how many blocks? ($1 \times 4 = 4$.)

4. Direct the children to place one set of one counter on their desk. Have them use plastic numerals and other symbols to build the related multiplication equation: $1 \times 1 = 1$. Now have the children lay out two sets with one counter in each set and determine how many counters in both sets. Have them build the related multiplication equation: $2 \times 1 = 2$.

5. Write place-holder equations on the chalkboard. Have the children complete each equation by recording the product in the place-holder. When all of the equations have been completed, discuss the pattern that has been formed. Lead them to generalize that any number times one is that same number. Some

children may wish to try this idea out with larger numbers. Encourage them to do so by using their sets of counters.

6. Draw a picture of a large daisy on the chalkboard. Write a numeral 0 through 5 on each of the six petals and the numeral 1 in the center of the daisy. Call on a child to multiply the number named by the numeral on each petal by one. Success is achieved when one child "picks" all the petals off the daisy by naming each product correctly.

PRACTICE AND EVALUATION

Commutative Property of Multiplication

1. Observe the sets pictured below. Then complete the equations.

$$
\begin{array}{l}
\text{XXX} \\
\text{XXX} \text{XXX} = \text{XXXX}\quad \text{XXXX}\quad \text{XXXX} \\
\text{XXX} \\
\underline{} \times 3 = 3 \times 4
\end{array}
$$

2. XXXXXX   XXXXXX = XX   XX   XX   XX   XX   XX
3. 4 X 1 =   3 X 6 =   2 X 5 =
   1 X 4 =   6 X 3 =   5 X 2 =

Associative Property of Multiplication

1. Flannelboard and chalkboard diagrams, as well as rectangular arrays, are used in the introduction of this property.

X X X	X X X	X X X
X X X	X X X	X X X
6 sets of 1	3 sets of 2 sets of 1	3 sets of 2 sets of 1
6 X 1 = 6	3 X (2 X 1)	(3 X 2) X 1

2. Do not change order—select most efficient grouping, and parentheses to show the factors:

$$
\begin{array}{ll}
2 \times 5 \times 6 = & 20 \times 5 \times 3 = \\
7 \times 2 \times 5 = & 3 \times 10 \times 5 = \\
10 \times 10 \times 9 = & 2 \times 9 \times 5 =
\end{array}
$$

3. Rearrange factors for easier grouping:

$$
\begin{array}{ll}
5 \times 4 \times 2 = & 18 \times 6 \times 3 = \\
100 \times 2 \times 2 = & 4 \times 35 \times 5 = \\
20 \times 3 \times 5 = & 19 \times 3 \times 10 =
\end{array}
$$

4. Complete equations:

$$
\begin{array}{ll}
5 \times 50 = 5 \times (10 \times 5) & 8 \times 60 = 8 \times (10 \times 6) \\
 = (5 \times 5) \times 10 & = (8 \times 6) \times 10 \\
 = \underline{} \times 10 & = \underline{} \times \underline{} \\
 = \underline{} & = \underline{}
\end{array}
$$

5. Complete equations:

$$4 \times 300 = 4 \times (3 \times 100)$$
$$= (\underline{} \times \underline{}) \times \underline{}$$
$$= \underline{} \times 100$$
$$= \underline{}$$

Distributive Property of Multiplication over Addition

1. $2 \times 2 = (1 + 1) \times 2$ $5 \times 2 = (4 + 1) \times 2$
    $= (1 \times 2) + (1 \times 2)$ $= (4 \times 2) + (1 \times 2)$
    $= 2 + 2$ $= 8 + 2$
    $= 4$ $= 10$

Find the pattern in each of the examples above. In the second example, think of any other way the factor 5 could be renamed. Do you get the same result? Now do the ones below:

$3 \times 2 = \underline{}$, $7 \times 2 = \underline{}$, $9 \times 3 = \underline{}$, $4 \times 8 = \underline{}$.

2. Use rectangular arrays:

```
X X X X X X X X              X X X X | X X X X
X X X X X X X X              X X X X | X X X X
X X X X X X X X              X X X X | X X X X
     3 X 8 = ____           (3 X 4) |  + (3 X 4)
X X | X X X X X X            X X X X X X X X
X X | X X X X X X            X X X X X X X X
    |                        _ _ _ _ _ _ _ _ _
X X | X X X X X X            X X X X X X X X
   (3 X 2) + (3 X 6)         (2 X 8) + (1 X 8)
```

3. Solve.

$3 \times 25 = 3 \times (20 + 5)$ $2 \times 136 = 2 \times (100 + 30 + 6)$
$= (3 \times 20) + (3 \times 5)$ $= (2 \times 100) + (2 \times 30) + (2 \times 6)$
$= \underline{} + \underline{}$ $= \underline{} + \underline{} + \underline{}$
$= \underline{}$ $= \underline{}$

MULTIPLICATION

Historically, the multiplication of whole numbers probably came into being to satisfy a basic counting need—that of determining how many or how much under certain circumstances. Such circumstances, then, as now, were probably based on situations in which the number of elements in a given set was known, as was the number of such equivalent sets. What was needed was the number of elements in "all" given sets. There are, of course, many applications of this problem and thus the operation of multiplication was developed to find this count, since previous methods (successive additions) were probably very time-consuming.

Successive additions were probably used as the basic method before the development of multiplication. Today in the primary grades successive additions are used as the method by which multiplication is introduced. From this experience the children are led to discover that the count of the number of addends can be used for one factor while the other factor is the number representing each addend. Through the use of the decimal-numeration system, and through the use of the property of closure and other properties the count can be found without rational counting or the process of addition. The process used is "multiplication."

Another explanation of multiplication is one which employs the use of the set idea to make the operation logical and meaningful. Multiplication is the process of pairing every element of a first set with every element of a second set. Here the total number of pairs would represent the product. Thus if the sets $\{a,b,c,\}$ and $\{1,2,3,\}$ are paired, every element in one set with every element in the other, the following would prevail:

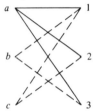

The resulting pairs are $1a$, $2a$, $3a$, $1b$, $2b$, $3b$, $1c$, $2c$, and $3c$. Thus there are nine unique pairings in the two sets illustrated.

It must be understood that multiplication is an operation on "numbers." Whether abstracted from the repeated addition point of view, or from the pair of elements of sets, or from concrete presentations, the symbolism for depicting the multiplication operation may be the same.

Some ways of indicating the multiplication operation are as follows:

$$3 \times 3 = 9 \qquad\qquad (3)\ 3 = 9$$
$$3 \cdot 3 = 9$$
$$(3)(3) = 9 \qquad\qquad \begin{array}{r} 3 \\ \times 3 \\ \hline \end{array}$$
$$3(3) = 9$$

No matter the way the operation is indicated, two numbers are operated on and as such there is a binary operation. These two numbers are called *factors*—or to distinguish between them, *multiplicand* and *multiplier*, and the result of the operation is called the *product*.

Modern programs in mathematics do not use the term "carrying" but are substituting the term "renaming." Rather than "carrying" in addition and multiplication, and "borrowing" in subtraction, the concept of renaming can be taught and applied to all four fundamental operations.

The Use of the "Number Line" in the Operation of Multiplication

1. Multiplication—the commutative law:

$$a \times b = b \times a \qquad\qquad 3 \times 4 = 4 \times 3 = 12$$

2. Multiplication—the associative law:

$$a(bc) = c(ba) \qquad\qquad 4 \times (3 \times 2) = 2(4 \times 3) = 24$$

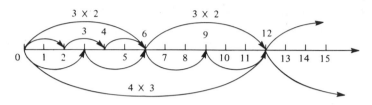

3. Multiplication—the distributive law:

$$x(y + z) = xy + xz \qquad\qquad 2(3 + 4) = (2 \times 3) + (2 \times 4)$$

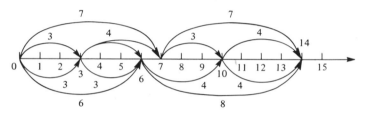

4. Prime factors of a number: The prime factors may be found by use of the number line. Other methods will be more efficient, however.

Problem: Find the prime factors of 28.

(a) Begin division by 2, the first prime. There are 14 two's in 28, and two is a prime factor of 28.

(b) Secondly, find the prime factors of 14. Begin with 2.

(c) Thirdly (if necessary), try 2, 3, and 5 as factors of 7. Since 7 is a prime, then

$$2 \times 2 \times 7 \text{ are the prime factors of 28}$$

5. Common multiple and LCM: The concept of common multiple and least common multiple can easily be shown on a number line. For the numbers 3, 4, and 6 the CM's and LCM are shown thus (the CM's being found where the

"paths" coincide):

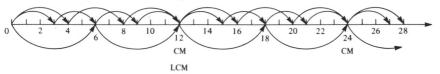

CM

LCM

Twelve and 24 are two of the CM's for the three numbers. The smaller of the two CM's shown (12) is the *least* CM (LCM).

The specific multiplication skills and understandings that should be developed include the following. The child should be able to:

Grade II

1. Understand the meaning of multiplication through the use of the following discovery techniques:
   (a) Set concepts
   (b) Number line
   (c) Array
   (d) Skip counting
   (e) Repeated additions
2. Discover (not master) facts and reverses through the use of the discovery techniques and commutative property.

2's through 20	Reverses
3's through 18	
4's through 20	two 4's and four 2's
5's through 20	
7's through 14	4 + 4 = 2 + 2 + 2 + 2
8's through 16	
9's through 18	

3. Understand that the order of numerals does not affect the product. The symbol for multiplication (X) is not introduced at this level.
4. Discover facts for 5's through 50 and 10's through 100.

Grade III

1. Understand presentation methods of multiplication.
   (a) Array
   (b) Repeated addition
   (c) Partial products
   (d) Number line
   (e) Expand form

$$\begin{array}{r} 123 \\ \underline{\times 5} \end{array} \qquad \begin{array}{r} 100 + 20 + 3 \\ \underline{\times 5} \end{array}$$

2. Discover facts through presentation methods.
  (a) 6's through 60
  (b) 7's through 70
  (c) 8's through 80
  (d) 9's through 90
3. Understand the meaning and use of signs for multiplication:

$$(\times) \text{ multiply: } 3 \times 2 = n, \ 3 \text{ times } 2, \text{ three } 2\text{'s}$$

4. Multiply numbers up to 3 digits by 1 digit with and without renaming.

```
  214
  X2
   8    (2 X 4)      214 X 2 = (200 X 2) + (10 X 2) + (4 X 2)
  20    (2 X 10)
 400    (2 X 100)
 428
```

5. Further development: Multiply one-, two-, and three-place multiplicands by a one-place multiplier without regrouping (partial-product method).

```
   4     14     14     214     214
  X2     X2     X2      X2      X2
   8     20      8     400       8
          8     20      20      20
         28     28       8     400
                       428     428
```

6. Further development: Multiply two- and three-place multiplicands by a one-place multiplier with carrying (regrouping) tens to tens.

```
  126     126     126
   X2      X2      X2
  252      12     200
           40      40
          200      12
          252     252
```

7. Further development: Multiply two- and three-place multiplicands by a one-place multiplier with regrouping hundreds to hundreds.

```
  173     173
   X3      X3
  300       9
  210     300
    9     210
  519     519
```

8. Multiply a three-place multiplicand with a cent point by a one-place multiplier.

$$\begin{array}{r} \$1.12 \\ \underline{\times 2} \\ \$2.24 \end{array}$$

Grade IV

1. Rediscover and learn the facts through the use of arrays, repeated addition, number line, etc.
2. Relate facts—multiplication and division.

$$3 \times 4 = 12 \qquad\qquad 12 \div 4 = n$$

factor x factor = product   product ÷ factor = missing factor

3. Multiply a four-digit number by a one-digit number.
4. Multiply a two-digit number by a two-digit number.
5. Multiply by tens.
6. Understand multiplication algorithm.
   (a) By expanded notation.
   (b) By partial products.
   (c) By standard algorithm.

$$32 \times 2 = 30 + 2$$
$$\underline{\times 2}$$
$$60 + 4 = 64$$

partial   partial   product
product   product

$$2 \times (30 + 2) = (2 \times 30) + (2 \times 2)$$
$$= 60 + 4$$
$$= 64$$

$$\begin{array}{r} 32 \\ \underline{\times 2} \\ 64 \end{array} \quad \text{standard algorithm}$$

Grade V

1. Review and maintain patterns, facts, and arrays.
2. Review skills for finding missing factors in multiplication.
3. Review multiplication by tens, hundreds, thousands.
4. Change the order of multiplication of factors, thus making the process easier.
5. Estimate the number of places in the answer in multiplication by rounding off the numbers.

6. Multiply a two-digit multiplicand by a two-digit multiplier with zero in both.

7. Multiply a three-or-more-digit multiplicand by a two-digit multiplier.

Example:
Matt made 34 trips to the paper stand to pick up his newspapers. If he traveled 786 yards each trip, how many yards did he travel?

$$
\begin{array}{rl}
786 & \text{yards per trip} \\
34 & \text{trips} \\
\hline
3144 & \\
2358 & \\
\hline
26{,}724 & \text{yards traveled}
\end{array}
$$

8. Multiply a five digit multiplicand by a one-digit multiplier.
9. Multiply a three-digit multiplicand by a three-digit multiplier.
10. Multiply mentally a two-digit multiplicand by a one-digit multiplier.

Grade VI.

1. Review and maintain patterns, facts, and arrays.

2. Multiply by three-digit multipliers using a four-place multiplicand and include those processes with zero difficulties.

3. Determine by use of an abacus and later by inspection, the product of a seven-digit number by 10; six-digit number by 10 or 100; a five-digit number by 10, 100, or 1,000; a four-digit number by 10, 100, 1,000, or 10,000, etc.

4. Multiply by ten or power of ten, orally, by mentally adding zeros or placing a decimal point.

5. Multiply a two-place number by a two-place number mentally

Example:
Matt bought 12 tickets to a hobby show. Each ticket cost 24¢. How much did he spend for tickets?

Procedures:
(a) You know that 25¢ is 1¢ more than 24¢. Four tickets would cost about $1.00, so tickets would cost 3 X $1.00 or about $3.00. But 12¢ too much has been added, so subtract 12¢ from $3.00, giving $2.88.

(b) You know that 12 is one ten and two ones. So first multiply 24¢ by 2. That's 48¢. Then multiply 24¢ by 10. That is $2.40. Then add $2.40 and 48¢, obtaining $2.88.

(c) You know that 24¢ is about 25¢. Four tickets would cost $1.00 so tickets would cost 3 X $1.00 or about $3.00. Now find the exact amount by using paper and pencil.

TEACHING SUGGESTIONS

Concept: Product sets and their relationship to multiplication

Procedures. 1. Make a set of partial multiplication tables from tagboard or construction paper. Distribute these to the children and have them use plastic numerals to record the products of the given factors. After each card has been checked, have the children exchange cards and repeat the activity.

2. Write numerals 0 through 25 in a long horizontal row on the chalkboard. Give one child a piece of colored chalk. Have him begin with 1 and circle the numeral which represents each multiple of one through five times one. As he circles each numeral in turn he should say, "One times one equals one, two times one equals two, three times one equals three," and so on. Give a second child a different colored piece of chalk. Have him begin by circling 2 and the numeral for each successive multiple of 2 through 5 X 2. Have three other children follow the same procedure by beginning with 3 and counting by threes, beginning at 4 and counting by fours, and beginning at 5 and counting by fives, until they have circled five multiples of each number.

3. Exhibit two cups of different colors and three saucers of different colors. For example, you can exhibit a green and a yellow cup and green, yellow, and brown saucers. Now ask the children to think about the number of different color combinations they can get by pairing each cup with each saucer. Have a child come forward to show different ways of pairing cups with saucers. Help the children see that by thinking about the fact that each cup can be paired with three different saucers, they are really thinking about the idea of two 3's, so they can pair these objects six different ways.

4. Provide additional demonstrations of product sets. You can do this by connecting dots on the chalkboard or by using various objects cut from colored paper.

Concept: Multiplication is related to groups of equivalent sets

Procedures. 1. Display 12 identical objects. Demonstrate to the children how these can be arranged in many equivalent sets, such as 3 sets of 4's; 4 sets of 3's; 2 sets of 6's, and 6 sets of 2's. Children should understand how these same 12 objects can be arranged in various sets.

2. Put 18 blocks on a table. Ask the children who can arrange these into equivalent sets. Every time a child arranges the blocks in an equivalent set, write the arrangement on the board. *Example:* 2 sets of 9's; 9 sets of 2's; etc.

3. Give the children a set of paper that has been folded in 12 blocks. Give the children instructions such as "In the first box make 2 sets of 4's; in the second box make 3 sets of 1's."

4. Discuss the many things in the child's everyday environment which come

in twos or in pairs: shoes, mittens, twins. Have one child stand in front of the class. Ask another how many eyes the first child has. Tell a second child to stand beside the first, ask, "How many sets of eyes do you see?" Continue the activity.

5. Present some demonstration of groups of equivalent sets and related multiplication equations. You can do this by drawing groups of equivalent sets on the chalkboard or by exhibiting sets of objects grouped in a special way. Be sure to accompany each set demonstration with the related multiplication equation. Use the phraseology, "Three fives are 15," at this point. This phraseology will help the children understand the association of a multiplication equation with groups of equivalent sets. The phrase "three fives" suggests the idea of three sets of five.

6. Place three sets with two felt cutouts in each set, on the flannelboard. Ask the children to tell how many sets they see and how many are in each set.   Place the multiplication equation $3 \times 2 =$ beneath the sets.   Read the equation: "Three twos equal how many?"   Remind the children that the 2 in the equation tells how many are in each set and that the 3 tells how many sets of two there are. Ask one of the children to tell how many there are altogether in three sets of two. Have another child place 6 in the place holder and read the completed equation. Remind the children that multiplication is used to find the number of objects in a group of equivalent sets. Point out that in the completed equation 3 and 2 represent *factors* of six and 6 represents the *product* of three and two. Repeat this procedure with four sets of two, five sets of two, two sets of one, one set of two, and so on. For each set story, have the children build the related multiplication equation.

7. Place two sets with two felt cutouts in each set on the flannelboard. Ask the children to tell how many sets there are, how many in each set, and how many cutouts there are all together. Call on one child to write the corresponding multiplication equation: $2 \times 2 = 4$. Ask who remembers another way to find out how many there are altogether. After some child suggests adding two and two, have the equation $2 + 2 = 4$ written below the multiplication equation $2 \times 2 = 4$. Discuss the difference between the operations of multiplication and addition. Remind the children that in addition the numbers of the sets they join need not be the same, but that in multiplication each set must have the same number. Repeat this activity with three sets of two, four sets of two, five sets of two. Have the related multiplication equation written each time and have each multiplication interpreted as *repeated addition*.

8. Have the children work with sets of counters at their desks. Direct them to lay out five sets of two:

$$0 \ \ 0 \ \ 0 \ \ 0 \ \ 0$$
$$0 \ \ 0 \ \ 0 \ \ 0 \ \ 0$$
$$2 + 2 + 2 + 2 + 2 = 10$$
$$5 \times 2 = 10$$

Ask them how many they have all together. Have them build two different equations which tell the set story. Repeat the activity with four sets of two, one set of two, two sets of two, zero sets of two, and three sets of two.

Concept: Interchanging the factors in a multiplication fact does not change the product

Procedures: 1. Put 3 groups of four erasers on a table in front of the classroom. Count them. The answer is 12. How many groups are there? (3) How many erasers are there in each group? (4)

Now rearrange to have four groups of 3. How many groups do we have? (4) How many erasers in each group? (3) How many do we have altogether? (12) Is our answer the same as it was before? Repeat this same procedure many times with other objects and combinations.

Now have 12 children stand in front of the room and divide themselves into 3 groups of 4. How many are there in each group? (4) How many groups are there? (3) Write the number problem on the board.

$$\begin{array}{r} 4 \\ \times 3 \\ \hline 12 \end{array}$$

The groups of boys and girls look like this:

$$1111 \qquad 1111 \qquad 1111 \qquad = 12$$

Now rearrange the boys and girls into 4 groups of 3 in each group. How many groups? How many in each group? How many altogether? Write the number problem on the board:

$$\begin{array}{r} 3 \\ \times 4 \\ \hline 12 \end{array}$$

The groups of boys and girls look like this:

$$111 \qquad 111 \qquad 111 \qquad 111 \qquad = 12$$

Discuss with the class what has been done. Did any boys or girls leave any of the groups? Were any added? No, they were just grouped differently. Do this with other groups of boys and girls. Guide them toward the generalization that the numbers in a multiplication fact can be interchanged and not change the answer. Use other devices such as egg boxes, chairs, tables, books, and blocks.

2. Develop the understanding with problems and drawings. Show with a number line that 4 eights are equal to eight 4's. Also, five 3's are equal to 3 fives.

$$/// \quad /// \quad /// \quad /// \quad /// \quad = \quad ///// \quad ///// \quad /////$$

Six 4's equal four 6's.

$$oooo \; oooo \; oooo \; oooo \; oooo \; oooo = oooooo \; oooooo \; oooooo \; oooooo$$

Arrange three groups with four children in each group ready to play partners in tether ball at recess. Then use the same children in four groups of three each ready to work at the board.

Concept: Multiplication is a quick way of adding several equal addends

Procedures. 1. Give the pupils ten disks to use as counters. Have them separate them into five equal groups:

How many groups are there? (5)   How many in each group? (2)   How many altogether? (10)   How did you obtain the answer of 10? Counting 2 + 2 + 2 + 2 + 2 = 10; five 2's = 10.

$$
\begin{array}{cc}
2 & 2 \\
\underline{\times 5} & 2 \\
10 & 2 \\
 & 2 \\
 & \underline{2} \\
 & 10
\end{array}
$$

Number line:

_____ = 10

As the children explain how they got the answer, put the various ways on the board. Show that in each explanation the child added or multiplied. Now change the counters to look like this: ○○○○○   ○○○○○.

What does the problem now say?   5 + 5 = 10, 2 fives = 10. Set up other problems and their reverses to show that multiplication is a shorter way of adding several equal numbers.

2. Give the children twelve colored popsicle sticks and ask them to arrange them in rows with equal numbers in each row. See how many different groups they can get. Ask the children to put on the board in figures what they found. 4 + 4 + 4 = 12; 3 + 3 + 3 + 3 = 12; 6 + 6 = 12; 2 + 2 + 2 + 2 + 2 + 2 = 12.

Have each child read his problem and tell his number story. Three 4's = 12; four 3's = 12; two 6's = 12; six 2's = 12. Ask which is quicker. The children find that this quick way of adding several equal numbers is called multiplication. Explain that it can be written.   3 × 4 = 12; 4 × 3 = 12; 2 × 6 = 12; and 6 × 2 = 12.

3. A field trip is planned by the children in the class where a school bus will furnish the transportation. There are 38 pupils to go. The bus has 20 seats and each seat will hold 2 pupils. The children are to find out if one bus will be enough. The pupils are asked to draw a picture to show how many children could ride, then show with numbers. Again a discussion of the various ways of solution will follow showing that multiplication is quicker.

4. Count out 24 small blocks and place them in a group. A paper is placed near the group of blocks. A child is chosen to move the blocks in groups of three to the paper. The rest of the class are at the board or at their seats adding the number of blocks moved each time to the number previously moved.

Example:

$$3 + 3 + 3 + 3 + 3 + 3 + 3 + 3 = 24$$

$$3 + 3 = 6 + 3 = 9 + 3 = 12 + 3 = 15 + 3 = 18 + 3 = 21 + 3 = 24$$

Take note that this is a long process to get the desired answer. Count the number of 3's in the problem. (8)   Discuss another way in which the number problem could be shown.

$$\begin{array}{r} 3 \\ \times 8 \\ \hline 24 \end{array}$$ 3 blocks 8 times = 24 blocks

5. The following problem is presented to the class. Matt is building a doghouse. He has 6 boards on each side. Each board has 4 nails in it. How many nails has Matt used after he has nailed on each board? How many did he use altogether?

Have a group of children work at the board, the rest at their seats with paper. The children are to illustrate the problem with drawings, the side of the doghouse with the 6 boards on it, 4 nails in each board. Starting at the top, they count down by 4, adding at each board to show how many nails have been used so far.

```
   4  nails in the 1st  board
  +4  nails in the 2nd board
   8  nails in the 2    boards
  +4  nails in the 3rd  board
  12  nails in the 3    boards
  +4  nails in the 4th  board
  16  nails in the 4    boards
  +4  nails in the 5th  board
  20  nails in the 5    boards
  +4  nails in the 6th  board
  24  nails in the 6    boards
```

Again the discussion will show that $6 \times 4 = 24$ is a shorter way of solving the problem.

Concept: Introduction to regrouping in multiplication

Procedures. 1. Answering questions by the "discovery method." Write the answers to the questions in the examples. If you don't know the answer, make a drawing to show what the example tells in words.

Problem: Bananas were priced at 19 cents a pound. How much did Mother pay for two pounds of bananas?

Diagrams and number records that might be used:

19 cents	20
<u>19 cents</u>	<u>20</u>
38 cents	$40 - 2 = 38$

1 ten 9 ones	19 cents
<u> X 2 ones</u>	<u>X 2</u>
2 tens 18 ones	38 cents

2. *Problem situation*. Before our Valentine party it was decided to bring enough cookies so that each child could have three cookies apiece. There are 27 children in our class. Write the problem on the board in equation form.

$$3 \quad X \quad 27 \quad = \quad N$$

(No. of cookies   (No. of   (No. of cookies
for each child)   children)   needed)

Tens	Ones
‖	⎮⎮⎮⎮⎮⎮⎮
‖	⎮⎮⎮⎮⎮⎮⎮
‖	⎮⎮⎮⎮⎮⎮⎮
⎮⎮⎮⎮⎮⎮⎮⎮ ⎮	

81 cookies

Work out the computation on the board. Ask how much 3 sevens are and write 21 off to one side of the board. Have a child come to the board and write the one in the ones place. Recall that 3 groups of 2 tens is 6 tens, and add this to the 2 tens from the first multiplication (3 X 7), then write the 8 in the tens place, giving the answer 81.

Using the same process, find the cost of 3 cans of peas at 24¢ a can, 2 cans of beans at 25¢ a can, and other food items.

When working with cost problems use pennies and dimes (play money) Scotch-taped to cards. Some of the problems should not involve transforming (carrying). This is necessary so that children understand that they do not always have to transform ones to tens.

A device that can be used to advantage is half an egg carton. See that each child has one like the one shown.

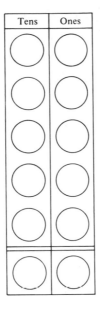

Use bright-colored round toothpicks which will stand up in these cups, and tie some in bundles of ten. Let the children use these to show story problems from the book before working them on paper.

Concept: In multiplication the second partial product has a larger value than the first partial product

Procedures. 1. *Emphasizing Place Value.* The children must understand fully the meaning of place value before multiplication by a two-digit number may have complete meaning. Write several two-digit numbers on the board and have such devices as colored sticks, plain sticks, beads, the abacus, and place-value charts for the children to use. Start with the number 23 and ask a child to show the value of the number 2, thereby showing what the number stands for. Have him count objects and show the one-to-one correspondence of the number and the object. Urge the child to look around him and find other objects to aid his understanding.

Now ask the meaning of the 2 in the number 23. Again have the children use many devices to show the meaning of 2 tens or 20 units. Bundle some of the objects together in groups of ten. Make two bundles of ten to represent the 2 tens. Then separate the objects in the bundles and count the single units. There are 20 units in two bundles of ten. Through demonstrations such as this the children learn to recognize:

2 tens as 20	4 tens as 40	6 tens as 60
3 tens as 30	5 tens as 50	7 tens as 70, etc.

Now write on the board an example such as this:

$$34$$
$$\times 24$$

Ask the meaning of the multiplier (24). The children should see that the 24 is 2 tens and 4 ones, that the 2 is actually 20, and the 4 is actually 4 ones.

Use drawings on the chalkboard or on charts to show these concepts.

△ = 1 ten   Therefore:
□ = 1 one   △△   □□□
△ = □□□□□□□□□□   2   3   or 23

All manner of shapes and figures can be used to picture the place-value concept. Children will want to make up their own codes for reference such as a square is equal to 1 ten and a triangle will stand for 1 unit. Then they can show what various numbers look like and mean to them.

2. *Breaking Down the Multiplier for Better Understanding.* Now write the completely solved problem on the chalkboard:

$$34$$
$$\times 23 \quad \text{(multiplier)}$$
$$\overline{102}$$
$$\underline{68}$$
$$782$$

Break the multiplication problem into 2 parts in order to show more clearly the partial products and the value that they actually represent.

$$34 \qquad\qquad 34$$
$$\times 3 \qquad\qquad \times 20$$
$$\overline{102} \qquad\qquad \overline{680}$$

Which partial product has the larger value? (680) Now add the two partial products to show that the total equals the same answer as before. Now do the example without breaking it up, as in the beginning.

$$34 \qquad\qquad 680$$
$$\times 23 \qquad\qquad +102$$
$$\overline{102} \qquad\qquad \overline{782}$$
$$\underline{680}$$
$$782$$

Always multiply first by the ones number. Also point out that the multiplier gives the *second partial product.* Emphasize further the representational value of the 2—that we multiply by 2 rather than 20, but the 20 is an unseen, understood quantity.

3. *Supplementary Work for Greater Understanding.* Have supplementary

demonstrations available. Many pupils are confused by the zero in the partial product as shown in the previous technique.

$$
\begin{array}{r}
34 \\
\times 20 \\
\hline
680
\end{array}
$$

Add twenty 34's to see if the answer (680) is correct and to see if the zero should be there.

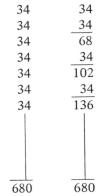

Next break up the multiplier into one-place multipliers to understand the process more fully, such as fives because 4 fives are equal to 20, thus:

$$
\begin{array}{cccc}
34 & 34 & 34 & 34 \\
\times 5 & 5 & 5 & 5 \\
\hline
170 & \overline{170} & \overline{170} & \overline{170} \\
170 & & & \\
170 & & & \\
170 & & & \\
\hline
680 & & &
\end{array}
$$

or, try 2 sevens and a six, thus:

$$
\begin{array}{ccc}
34 & 34 & 34 \\
\times 7 & 7 & 6 \\
\hline
238 & 238 & 204 \\
238 & & \\
204 & & \\
\hline
680 & &
\end{array}
$$

Try any other combination of single-digit numbers whose sum is 20. Do a more complicated method double multiplication—20 is equal to 4 × 5, thus:

$$
\begin{array}{cc}
34 & 34 \\
\times 4 & \times 5 \\
\hline
136 & 170 \\
\times 5 & \times 4 \\
\hline
680 & 680
\end{array}
$$

Through these later demonstrations the role of zero and why the 2nd partial product is actually larger is reinforced. For further demonstration, reverse the numbers and see if the 2nd partial product again comes out to be larger:

$$
\begin{array}{r} 23 \\ \times 34 \\ \hline 92 \\ 69 \\ \hline 782 \end{array}
\qquad
\begin{array}{r} 23 \\ \times 4 \\ \hline 92 \end{array}
\qquad
\begin{array}{r} 23 \\ \times 30 \\ \hline 690 \end{array}
\quad\text{(The 2nd partial}
$$

product is larger)

$$
\begin{array}{r} 690 \\ +92 \\ \hline 782 \end{array}
$$

Prove the findings by the same methods that were used before.

Concept: Multiplication is a quick check for division:

Procedures. 1. Ask 12 children to go to the front of the room. Have them divide into groups of three. Write the number story on the board: $3/\overline{12}$. By observation, we see that there are 4 groups:

$$
\begin{array}{r} 4 \\ 3/\overline{12} \end{array}
$$

Have the children add the 3 groups and see if they get 12 children in one group:

$$
\begin{array}{r} 3 \\ 3 \\ 3 \\ 3 \\ \hline 12 \end{array}
$$

Since all of the numbers are alike, we can multiply 3 (the number of children in each group) × 4 (the number of groups) = 12 (the total number of children, if all were in one group).

$$
\begin{array}{r} 3 \\ \times 4 \\ \hline 12 \end{array}
$$

Therefore, when checking a division problem, multiply the quotient by the divisor to get the dividend.

2. Write this problem on the board:

$$
\begin{array}{r}
7 \\
6\overline{)42}
\end{array}
\qquad \text{or} \qquad
\begin{array}{rl}
42 & \\
\underline{-6} & \text{(1 six)} \\
36 & \\
\underline{-6} & \text{(2 sixes)} \\
30 & \\
\underline{-6} & \text{(3 sixes)} \\
24 & \\
\underline{-6} & \text{(4 sixes)} \\
18 & \\
\underline{-6} & \text{(5 sixes)} \\
12 & \\
\underline{-6} & \text{(6 sixes)} \\
6 & \\
\underline{-6} & \text{(7 sixes)} \quad \text{7 sixes in 42} \\
0 &
\end{array}
$$

To prove that there are 7 sixes in 42, add or multiply.

$$
\begin{array}{lll}
\begin{array}{r} 6 \\ 6 \\ 6 \\ 6 \\ 6 \\ 6 \\ \underline{6} \\ 42 \end{array}
&
\begin{array}{r} 6 \\ \underline{\times 7} \\ 42 \end{array}
\quad
\begin{array}{l} \text{reverse is used as a} \\ \text{double check} \end{array}
&
\begin{array}{r} 7 \\ \underline{\times 6} \\ 42 \end{array}
\end{array}
$$

3. Write a problem and then break the tens number into ones so that it is easier to see how the answer is obtained.

$$
\begin{array}{r}
5 \\
7\overline{)35} \\
\underline{35} \\
0
\end{array}
$$

OOOOOOOOOO   OOOOO

OOOOOOOOOO

OOOOOOOOOO   = 5 sevens

Check by grouping 5 sevens and then drawing circles around every group of 10, ending with the original 35.

OOOOOOO   1 time

OOOOOOO   2 times

OOOOOOO   3 times   7

OOOOOOO   4 times   X5
                            ——
                             35

OOOOOOO   5 times
————————————————————
3 tens and 5 ones = 35

Another check would be to reverse the quotient and divisor and divide the 5 groups of seven into 7 groups of 5. Then the fives can be linked into tens and the result is the original 35 as before:

OOOOO

OOOOO

OOOOO   5

OOOOO   X7
            ——
             35

OOOOO   7 fives equal 35 or 3 tens and 5 ones = 35

OOOOC

OCOOO

4. Show by drawings or on the number line how many 3's equal 12.

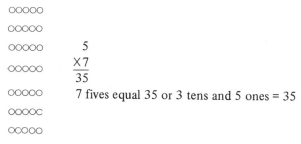

Four 3's = 12   3/12

In like manner show the following division facts:

How many 5's equal 15.

How many 3's equal 21.

How many 5's equal 20.

5. Show that multiplication of quotients in larger division problems by the divisor is a check for division.

$$\begin{array}{r} 32 \\ 3\overline{)96} \\ 9 \\ \overline{6} \\ 6 \\ \overline{0} \end{array}$$

          32   Check by multiplying 32 by three.
         X3   If the product is the dividend, the
         ——   work is correct.
         96

Show also by tally marks:

/////////////////////////// = 32
/////////////////////////// = 32
/////////////////////////// = 32
                            ——
                            96

6. When there is a remainder, add the remainder to the product of the quotient and the divisor.

$$
\begin{array}{r}
37 \\
2\overline{)75} \\
6 \\
\hline
15 \\
14 \\
\hline
1
\end{array}
\qquad
\begin{array}{r}
37 \\
\times 2 \\
\hline
74 \\
+1 \\
\hline
75
\end{array}
$$

Concept: Multiplication and division are related processes

Procedures. 1. Toy money is placed on the table. Have one pupil count out 25 pennies. Ask how else this might be expressed. (25 cents or a quarter) Have another child arrange the 25 pennies into groups of 5. How many groups are there? (5)

ooooooooooooooooooooooooo = 25 pennies

ooooo   ooooo   ooooo   ooooo   ooooo = 5 groups with 5 in each group.

Hence the fact: 5 fives are 25; 25 divided by 5 = 5.

2. Display several egg cartons. Some may have 3 rows with 4 compartments in each row. Some may have 6 compartments in each row.

oooo   oooooo
oooo   oooooo
oooo

Can you tell how many three 4's are? How many are 4 threes?

oooo   ooo
oooo   ooo
oooo   ooo
       ooo

Can you tell how many two 6's are? How many six 2's are?

oooooo   oo   oo
oooooo   oo   oo
         oo   oo

Can you tell how many threes there are in twelve?

ooo   ooo   ooo   ooo   12 divided by 3 = 4

Can you tell how many fours there are in twelve?

oooo   oooo   oooo   12 divided by 4 = 3

Record discoveries on the board:

Twelve is equal to four threes.   Twelve is equal to three fours.
Twelve divided by three = four.   Twelve divided by four = three.

3. Review with the children the idea that subtraction and addition are inversely related processes. It will be necessary to use several illustrations to reinforce and reteach this basic concept: $3 + 6 = 9; 9 - 3 = 6; 6 + 3 = 9; 9 - 6 = 3.$

Present the concept that since multiplication is a way of adding equal groups and division is a way of subtracting equal groups, multiplication and division are related in the same manner as addition and subtraction. Illustrate this relationship on the chalkboard, flannelboard, or with other devices: $2 \times 4 = 8$, 8 divided by 2 = 4, $4 \times 2 = 8$, 8 divided by 4 = 2.

Give multiplication and division work of the same type showing some pictorial or diagram problems which will allow slower pupils to divide groups with lines and then count the groups. Follow it with examples using the vertical symbols for multiplication and division after they have been presented on the board and discussed by the class:

$$
\begin{array}{cc}
4 & 2 \\
\underline{\times 2} & 4\overline{)8} \\
8 & \underline{8}
\end{array}
$$

Emphasize the checking of division by multiplying the divisor and the quotient to find the dividend.

4. Use small colored blocks for this technique. On the table place four groups of three blocks each. Each group of blocks should be a different color. Have the pupils find out how many blocks there are altogether. Bring all of the blocks into one group to check the answer. Separate them into their respective groups again to show the division aspect. Work on other combinations in the same way. The variety of colors of blocks should help the child see the individual groups in relationship to the whole large group. Other manipulative devices should also be used. These could include books, pencils, crayons, small balls, milk cartons, and paper cups.

DIVISION

Division, as a secondary operation, is defined in terms of multiplication. Thus division is the inverse or opposite of multiplication, as subtraction is the inverse of addition. Division "undoes" what multiplication "does."

In the usual multiplication operation, the two factors are known and the binary operation of these factors produces the product. In the usual division operation one factor is known and the product is known. The operation produces the second factor.

Teaching the basic structure of division should parallel the teaching of multiplication, and the concepts of subtraction can also be used to advantage here. Division has been defined traditionally in terms of dividend, divisor, and quotient. A dividend is divided by a divisor to obtain the quotient. But if modern-day logic is to be used as has been the case with the other operations, then division must be defined as the operation to find the missing factor. Therefore, in determining the missing factor in a problem such as $5 \times \triangle = 15$, rewrite the problem as $15 \div 5 = \triangle$. How many sets of 5 are there in 15? This question can be answered by successive equal subtractions of five until a difference of zero is obtained:

$$
\begin{array}{rl}
15 & \\
\underline{-5} & \quad (1) \\
10 & \\
\underline{-5} & \quad (2) \\
5 & \\
\underline{-5} & \quad (3) \\
0 &
\end{array}
$$

Three sets of 5 can be subtracted from 15, so that there are three sets of five in 15. The missing factor is 3.

There are basic division facts, just as there are basic subtraction facts. However, if children thoroughly understand multiplication and the inverse relation, they already know all the basic division facts. After acquiring an understanding of the properties of division, children should be given ample practice in using the basic division facts in order to learn to calculate efficiently.

After studying the basic division facts and solving a number of simple examples, children should be introduced to division involving larger numbers, which would also include ample practice in estimating trail quotients for division problems.

The Use of the Number Line in the Operation of Division

1. **Division–Measurement (no remainders).** In measurement division the size of each group is known and the number of groups is unknown. Thus in the problem $3\overline{)12}$, the size of each group is fixed at three and the number of groups of this size in 12 is sought.

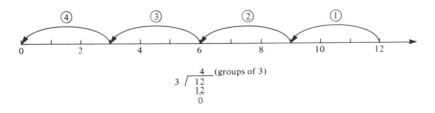

   2. **Division—Partition (no remainder).** In partitioning, the number of equal groups is known and the size of each group is sought. Thus in the illustration below the number of groups is fixed at 3, while the size of each equal group is unknown.

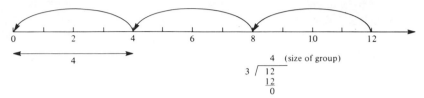

   Another schematic or number-line arrangement emphasizes more the sharing aspects of this phase of division. In dividing 12 by 3 each group along the number line should contain an equal part for each of the sharers:

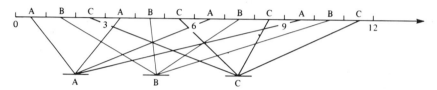

Thus we see that each sharer receives exactly 4 units, which is the quotient.

   3. **Division—Measurement (remainders).** There are $3\frac{2}{3}$ groups of 3 units each in 11:

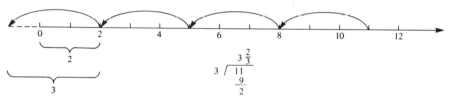

It may be correct to express the answer as "3 and 2 units remaining" as in the case where three cookies are to be given to each person and there are 11 cookies in all. The answer $3\frac{2}{3}$ is absurd, so only 3 boys may share the cookies.

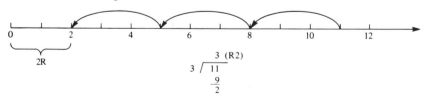

   In the case: "How many tables are needed to seat 27 persons at a party if no more than 4 persons may be seated at a table?" The remainder is "rounded off" to the next number. You cannot have $6\frac{3}{4}$ tables.

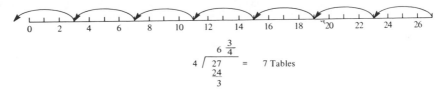

$$4 \overline{\smash{)}27} = 7 \text{ Tables}$$
$$6\frac{3}{4}$$
$$\underline{24}$$
$$3$$

4. **Division–Partition (remainders).** Interpreting partitive division using the more elaborate scheme used before, the problem $3\overline{\smash{)}11}$ shows 3 units each for those that share, with 2 units also being shared equally.

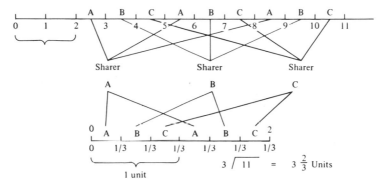

$$3 \overline{\smash{)}11} = 3\frac{2}{3} \text{ Units}$$

Remainders will require interpretation as in the examples given under measurement.

5. **Division–Circular Number Line.** Circular number line shows remainders 0, 1, 2, 3, 4 when number is divided by 5. Numbers whose remainders are 1 are listed near 1; other numbers are listed near their remainders.

Similar lines can be made for other divisors.

Children look for patterns and explore relationships rather than attempting to memorize the sets of dividends. *Exception*: The numbers which do not have remainders when divided by selected divisor.

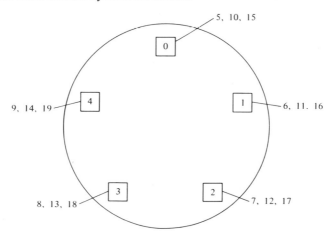

6. **Tests for Divisibility**. Twenty-four is divisible by 2 since it ends in a digit divisible by 2. Twenty-four is divisible by 4, since any number whose tens and units digits make a number divisible by 4 is divisible by 4.

Twenty-four is divisible by 3, since the sum of the digits is divisible by 3. $(2 + 4 = 6)$.

Other tests may be shown.

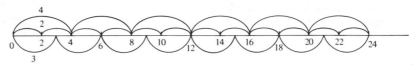

The specific division skills and understandings that should be developed include the following. The child should be able to:

Grade II

1. Through the use of sets and arrays and as an extension of multiplication discover how many 2's in 8, etc.

Grade III

1. Present methods of division.

   (a) Number Line:

$$20 \div 5 = 4$$

   (b) Arrays:

$20 \div 4 = 5$

5 rows of 4 in 20

   (c) Repeated subtraction:

$9 \div 3 = 3$

3 threes in 9

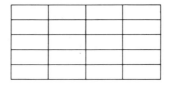

   (d) Long-division algorithm and subtractive algorithm:

2. Understand meaning and use of the division symbol (÷).
3. Use one-digit divisor with three-digit dividend and renaming.

$$\overset{30+\ 9}{4\overline{)156}} = 4\overline{)120+36} = 39$$

$$\overset{20+10+\ 9}{4\overline{)80+40+36}} = 39$$

4. Understand the use of remainders in division.
   (a) Determine how many equal sets there are in a number and how many are left over.

   $$17 \div 2 = 8 \text{ with 1 remainder}$$

   (b) Check (inverse operation).

   $$(2 \times 8) + 1 = 17$$

5. Divide by 10.

Grade IV

1. Review previous learning.
2. Use division algorithm.
   (a) Subtractive algorithm:

   $$
   \begin{array}{r}
   25\overline{)375} \\
   -100 \\
   \hline
   275 \\
   -100 \\
   \hline
   175 \\
   -175 \\
   \hline
   15
   \end{array}
   \quad
   \begin{array}{l}
   (4) \quad (4 \times 25 = 100) \\[1.2em]
   (4) \quad (4 \times 25 = 100) \\[1.2em]
   \underline{(7)} \quad (7 \times 25 = 175)
   \end{array}
   $$

   (b) Transitional (pyramid quotient):

   $$
   \left.\begin{array}{r} 5 \\ 10 \end{array}\right\} 15
   $$
   $$
   \begin{array}{r}
   25\overline{)375} \\
   -250 \\
   \hline
   125 \\
   -125 \\
   \hline
   \end{array}
   $$

   (c) Standard algorithm:

   $$
   \begin{array}{r}
   25\overline{)375} \\
   -250 \\
   \hline
   125 \\
   -125 \\
   \hline
   \end{array}
   $$

3. Use remainders in division.
4. Use zero in dividend and quotient.
5. Find averages.
6. Check division by multiplication (inverse operation).
7. Use the conventional vocabulary for division.

$$\text{Division} \overline{)\text{Dividend}}^{\text{Quotient}}$$

but make sure to include the terms:

$$\text{Factor} \overline{)\text{Product}}^{\text{Factor}}$$

(The basic rule for both multiplication and division is factor $\times$ factor = product.)

8. Use mathematical sentences in division process.
9. Show that problems with remainders are written thus:

$$(3 \times n) + r = 26 \qquad\qquad 26 = (3 \times n) + r$$

Also

$$(3 \times 8) + 2 = 26 \qquad\qquad 26 = (3 \times 8) = 2$$

10. Explain the two types of problem situation requiring dividing for solutions.

(a) Measurement division:

24 in. $\div$ 3 in.　　How many 3-inch strips can can be cut from 24 inches of ribbon? (Answer is an abstract number.)

(b) Partitioning division:

24 in. $\div$ 3　　Divide 24 inches of ribbon equally among three people. (Answer is a denominate number.)

11. Verify division facts by subtraction.
12. Divide one-, two-, or three-figure dividend by one-figure divisors—even and uneven division.
13. Express and label numbers "left over" as remainders.
14. Create a verbal situation that might apply to a given algorithm.
15. Divide a four-digit number by one- and two-digit number.

Grade V

1. Divide four- and five-digit numbers by one- and two-digit numbers.
2. Use division algorithm. (Many ways of arriving at an answer should be

presented.   No one way should be made mandatory during the learning stages.
The ultimate goal is to guide toward the use of the refined method.)

    (a) Subtractive

$$
\begin{array}{r}
23\overline{)3{,}335} \\
\underline{2{,}300} \quad\quad 100 \times 23 \\
1{,}035 \\
\underline{920} \quad\quad 40 \times 23 \\
115 \\
\underline{115} \quad\quad \underline{5 \times 23} \\
145
\end{array}
$$

    (b) Transitional

$$
\left.\begin{array}{r} 5 \\ 40 \\ 100 \end{array}\right\} \quad 145
$$

$$
\begin{array}{r}
23\overline{)3{,}335} \\
\underline{2{,}300} \\
1{,}035 \\
\underline{920} \\
115 \\
\underline{115}
\end{array}
$$

    (c) Refined method—short division

$$
\begin{array}{r}
145 \\
23\overline{)3{,}335} \\
\underline{23} \\
103 \\
\underline{92} \\
115 \\
\underline{115}
\end{array}
$$

(Note: Use short division only after a complete understanding of the division
algorithm.)

    3. Estimate quotients.

    4. Express remainders as fractions when appropriate.

$$
\begin{array}{r}
4\tfrac{5}{12} \\
12\overline{)53} \\
\underline{48} \\
5
\end{array}
$$

Grade VI

    1. Understand meaning of division.

    2. Review previous learnings.

3. Divide four- and five-digit numbers by two- and three-digit numbers.
4. Estimate quotient figures.
5. Express remainders as fractions, decimal numerals:

$$4\frac{5}{12} \\ 12\overline{)53} \\ \underline{48} \\ 5$$

$$4.41 \\ 12\overline{)53.00} \\ \underline{48} \\ 5\ 0 \\ \underline{4\ 8} \\ 20 \\ \underline{12} \\ 8$$

6. Use short-division form.
7. Check division by its inverse operation.

TEACHING SUGGESTIONS

Concept: Sets in division

Procedures. 1. Exhibit a set and give the children an opportunity to discover, by removing objects from the set, how many subsets of a given size are contained within the original set. For example: show a set of 20 and ask the children how many sets of 4 they can find in a set of 20. Have a child come up and remove the objects four at a time, and count the number of fours that he removes. When the children discover that five sets were removed, write on the chalkboard, "We can get 5 sets of 4 from a set of 20." Continue this type of demonstration until the children have grasped the concept. Follow this by exhibiting the corresponding division equations for each set demonstration. That is, for the example given above, write on the chalkboard $20 \div 4 = 5$. Call attention to the new operation, *division*; the phrase, *divided by*; and the fact that in this exercise 5 is the quotient. Repeat this discussion for other examples.

2. Hold up twelve 3-inch $\times$ 5-inch cards or slips of colored paper and tell the children you would like to have these twelve cards arranged in such a way that four cards are placed in each of several rows in the pocket chart. Say that you want to find out how many sets of four there are in a set of twelve. Have a child place the cards, four in a row, in the pocket chart. Have another child write the placeholder multiplication equation which relates to this activity: $\square \times 4 = 12$. Call on another child to write the related division equation:

$$\square \times 4 = 12 \qquad\qquad 12 \div 4 = \square$$
$$\square \times 3 = 12 \qquad\qquad 12 \div 3 = \square$$

Remove the twelve cards from the pocket chart and pose a different question. Tell the children you would like a set of twelve cards partitioned in such a way that three sets with the same number in each set would result. Write the equation $3 \times \square = 12$ on the chalkboard and ask a child to arrange the cards in three different rows in the pocket chart. After he has completed his assignment, ask another child to check to see that there are the same number of objects in each set and to give the number. Have the place-holder equation completed. Remind the children that they can also write a division equation to relate to this activity. Write $12 \div 3 = \square$ on the chalkboard. Refer back to the multiplication equation $3 \times \square = 12$. Point out that the product and one factor are known in this equation and that division can be used to find the missing factor. Ask another child to explain how he might use sets to help him find the number that is missing. Have him rearrange the set of felt cutouts into sets of four and tell how many such sets he has. Have another child complete the equation. Again place the equation $\square \times 4 = 12$ on the chalkboard. Tell the children to think about the meaning of each part of this equation. Point to each symbol in turn and ask the children to tell what it represents. The 12 represents the product in the problem; the 4 represents a known factor; the place holder holds the place for the missing factor. Review with the children the way they started with a set of twelve and partitioned it into sets of four. Explain that there is another way to show what happened: $\square \times 4 = 12$; $12 \div 4 = \square$. "Twelve divided by four equals some number." Help the children see that they can find this number in the same way that they found the missing factor in the multiplication equation. Have the children complete the *division* equation. (Started with the product and divided by the known factor to find the missing factor.)

3. Have the children use their plastic numerals and operation symbols to make related multiplication and division equations. Direct them to lay out the numerals 2, 3, and 6; and the $\times$, $\div$, = signs. Ask them to tell how many true statements they can make using these symbols. Have the children record the different equations they have made on the chalkboard:

$$2 \times 3 = 6 \qquad\qquad 6 \div 3 = 2$$
$$3 \times 2 = 6 \qquad\qquad 6 \div 2 = 3$$

Review the commutative property which relates the two multiplication equations and the inverse concept which relates the division equations to the multiplication equations. Discuss with the children whether division is commutative.

4. Place two columns of place-holder equations on the chalkboard. Put multiplication place-holder equations in the column on the left and division equations in the column on the right. Ask various children to complete the first multiplication equation. Have a second child draw a line from the completed equation to a division equation he thinks belongs with the multiplication equation. When the line has been drawn, have a third child complete the related division equation. Have the class discuss what they have discovered about the numbers that were used to complete the two equations. Have the equations read. Continue in this way to have all equations matched, completed, and read.

$$\square \times 4 = 16 \qquad\qquad 9 \div 3 = \triangle$$
$$\square \times 5 = 20 \qquad\qquad 12 \div 4 = \triangle$$
$$\square \times 2 = 8 \qquad\qquad 20 \div 5 = \triangle$$
$$\square \times 1 = 5 \qquad\qquad 16 \div 4 = \triangle$$
$$\square \times 3 = 9 \qquad\qquad 5 \div 1 = \triangle$$
$$\square \times 4 = 12 \qquad\qquad 8 \div 2 = \triangle$$

5. Develop story problems in which the children dramatize situations related to division.

Example: Mary had 12 books. She wanted to give two to each of several friends. "How many of Mary's friends would receive two books?" Have one child write the related division equation on the chalkboard: $8 \div 2 =$. Have one of the children dramatize the part of Mary. Have her distribute twelve books among several children to find how many children will get two books each. Finally have the place-holder equation on the chalkboard completed. Repeat with other stories which call for a division interpretation.

6. Use a classroom project in science or social studies as background material for creating story problems. Ask a child to write a story problem, exchange it with a classmate to compute, and return it to the writer for checking. Discuss the problems with the class to find errors in the information given in the stories and to check the computation.

Concept: Dividing is a short way of subtracting equal-sized groups

Procedures. 1. Let the first formal presentation develop from informal situations. Decide to have four people on each committee for the class newspaper. How many departments can we have in our classroom of 20 students? There are four different duties in the cafeteria. How many children will share each duty? Write the number 20 (representing the number of children in the classroom). Draw a number line to 20 and divide it into groups of four, then count the groups. Repeat the same technique with various children, marking the number line.

$$\begin{array}{c|c|c|c} \underset{0}{|} & \underset{10}{|} & \underset{20}{|} & \underset{30}{|} \end{array}$$

Use the flannelboard, beads on a string, clothespins and other manipulative material and take away groups of four at a time. Have the children count the number of groups taken away.

After the children have used such illustrative materials, the class should decide to check on what it is actually doing. Write the number 12 on the board and subtract 4, repeat subtraction of 4 from the remainder over and over until there is no remainder left. As you subtract the number of 4, a group of 4 should be divided off on the number line so that the children will see the two processes simultaneously as exactly the same action. Now count the number of groups divided off on the number line, and the number of times the subtraction process was repeated to prove that both processes will give the same answer.

After the subtraction-division is well established in their thinking, the children should be led to discover that the continued subtraction process is a long way to find out how many groups can be found in a large quantity.

Now present the abstract division form, tying in the division process with the multiplication facts which they have already used. Show that five 4's are 20, and 20 divided by 4 is 5. Show the picture way (numeral way) of writing the example:

$$\begin{array}{r} 5 \\ 4\overline{)20} \\ \underline{20} \\ 0 \end{array}$$

The final step in the process is in checking the division, which shows the relationship between multiplication and division.

2. Pass out 12 disks to each child to use at their desks as counters. Ask the pupils to arrange the disks in groups of 2's, 3's, 4's, and 6's.

In the formation of twos, ask the children to take away 2 disks, each time they do, have them count and tell how many are left. Try the other groups of numbers by taking away the numbers and counting how many are left.

Discuss if there is a shorter way to subtract the numbers? Write on the chalkboard the following examples:

$$\begin{array}{ccc}
12 & 12 & 12 \\
\underline{-2} & \underline{-4} & \underline{-3} \\
10 & 8 & 9 \\
\underline{-2} & \underline{-4} & \underline{-3} \\
8 & 4 & 6 \\
\underline{-2} & \underline{-4} & \underline{-3} \\
6 & 0 & 3 \\
\underline{-2} & & \underline{-3} \\
4 & & 0 \\
\underline{-2} & & \\
2 & & \\
\underline{-2} & & \\
0 & &
\end{array}$$

$$2\overline{)12}^{\,6} \quad 6\overline{)12}^{\,2} \quad 4\overline{)12}^{\,3} \quad 3\overline{)12}^{\,4}$$

$$12 \div 2 = 6 \qquad 12 \div 6 = 2$$

$$12 \div 4 = 3 \qquad 12 \div 3 = 4$$

3. Use a flannelboard: Arrange 10 red flannel apples on the flannelboard. Ask several children to come and take away groups of apples, then show that dividing is a shorter way of subtracting.

4. The children have 16 pictures to put on the bulletin board. There is space for 4 pictures across the board. The children are to find how many rows they will have by subtracting four for each row.

$$
\begin{array}{r}
16 \\
-4 \\
\hline
12 \\
-4 \\
\hline
8 \\
-4 \\
\hline
4 \\
-4 \\
\hline
0
\end{array}
$$

They discover four 4's in 16 or
$$
\begin{array}{r}
4 \\
4\overline{)16} \\
16
\end{array}
$$

They rearrange pictures into groups of 2 and subtract a 4 each time from 16. They discover 8 twos in 16.

$$
\begin{array}{r}
8 \\
2\overline{)16} \\
16 \\
\hline
0
\end{array}
$$

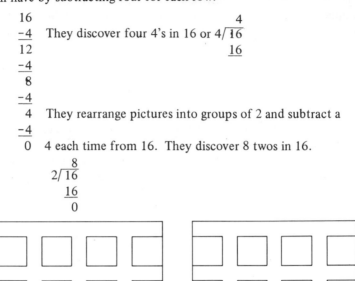

5. *Problem Situation.* We are having a room party and have 6 dozen cookies to divide between 24 children. How many cookies does each pupil get?

$$6 \times 12 = 72$$

$$
\begin{array}{r}
3 \\
24\overline{)72} \\
72 \\
\hline
0
\end{array}
$$

Each child receives 3 cookies. This should also be done in subtraction:

$$72 - 24 = 48 - 24 = 24 - 24 = 0.$$

6. Set out 30 small blocks. Explain that these blocks represent the players.

on a basketball team, and we want to see how many teams there can be if there are 5 players on a team. Do the problem by subtracting 5 until you have 6 (six) groups. Then do the problem by dividing 30 by 5. Have the children think up similar problems using small blocks, and have them come to the front of the room and work the problem out first with the blocks, and then let them work both the subtraction way and the division way on the chalkboard.

Concept: The quotient tells how many times the divisor can be subtracted from the dividend

Procedures. 1. Count off on the number line the example 6 divided by 3 = 2, as in the following illustration.

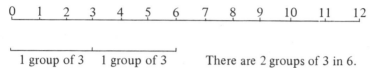

0   1   2   3   4   5   6   7   8   9   10   11   12

1 group of 3   1 group of 3   There are 2 groups of 3 in 6.

Discuss various ways to prove that your answer in the problem is correct. One of the ways would be to subtract 3 from 6 and 3 from 3. How many subtracted? (2) Therefore there are 2 threes in six or 6 divided by 3 = 2.

2. Present the following problem. Matt is making a toy train. He has 20 wheels. How many cars can he make if he needs four wheels for each car? Discuss the various ways that the answer could be obtained:

(a) By subtracting or taking away four wheels at a time from the 20 wheels. (With 5 groups of 4 wheels, Matt could make 5 cars.)

(b) Divide the 20 wheels by four. (20 divided by 4 = 5)

(c) Use the number line:

0   10   20

(d) Use the flannelboard: Separating the group of 20 wheels into groups of four: OOOOOOOOOOOOOOOOOOOO = OOOO + OOOO + OOOO + OOOO + OOOO.

3. The children are given bundles of sticks, using 28 sticks, divide them into groups of seven. How many groups of 7 are there in 28? The process to follow might be: Remove 7 sticks, how many are left? Remove seven more sticks, how many are left? Remove 7 more sticks, how many are left? Remove 7 more sticks? How many are there now? How many bundles of 7 sticks each do we have? Therefore there are 4 groups of 7 in 28, and 28 divided by 7 = 4.

Now write the abstract symbols on the board representing the above problem:

$$\begin{array}{r} 4 \\ 7\overline{)28} \\ \underline{28} \\ 0 \end{array}$$

Then write this on the board:

$$
\begin{array}{r}
28 \\
\underline{-7} \ \ (1) \\
21 \\
\underline{-7} \ \ (2) \\
14 \\
\underline{-7} \ \ (3) \\
7 \\
\underline{-7} \ \ (4) \\
0
\end{array}
$$

Compare the two processes. They will illustrate that the quotient tells how many times the divisor can be subtracted from the dividend.

Concept: The remainder in division indicates that there is not enough left over to make another group the size of the divisor

Procedures. 1. On the following illustration of 13 pennies, draw lines to show how many five-cent pencils you can buy for 13 cents.

ooooooooooooo

The drawing shows that for 13 cents, you can get _____ five-cent pencils and you will have _____ cents left over.

When you find how many 5's there are in 13, you will write the division in this manner:

$$
\begin{array}{r}
2 \ \text{R3} \\
5\overline{)\ 13} \\
\underline{10} \\
3
\end{array}
$$

The R3 means a remainder of 3. It tells that there are _____ left over.

2. Use the flannelboard: Place 6 large cardboard pennies on the flannelboard. Ask a child to group the 6 pennies to show how many nickels there are. The grouping will look like this: ooooo   o.   One nickel and a penny left over. Now place one more at a time until the children indicate that there are enough pennies to make another nickel. Each time a penny is added, discuss how many nickels there are and how many pennies are left over. Do this with several numbers.

Emphasize that the number left over is never larger or as big as the number in the group.

Now introduce the following examples: $5\overline{)6}$ $5\overline{)7}$ $5\overline{)8}$ $5\overline{)9}$. Give each child 10 or more counters. Have them group them on their desks and ask each child to write a division problem to go with the counters on the desk. The children first solve by counters the various examples and then the abstract examples themselves.

3. Development from the problem situation: Margaret and Pam had a party. Pam's mother put 7 cookies on a plate and passed the cookies to the girls. Each girl had three cookies. There was 1 cookie left over. Pam said, "Seven divided by 2 is 3 and 1 left over." Pam did a problem in uneven division. The problem can be written in this way:

$$\begin{array}{r} 3 \text{ cookies} \\ 2\overline{)\,7 \text{ cookies}} \\ 6 \\ \hline 1 \text{ cookie left over} \end{array} \qquad \text{or 7 divided by 2 = 3 and 1 over}$$

Seven cannot be divided by 2 evenly, so the next smaller number that can be divided evenly is 6. Since 6 divided by 2 = 3, the 3 is the quotient. Write the 6 under the 7 and subtract to find the remainder.

4. Divide each of the following numbers by 2: 2, 3, 4, 5, 6, 7, 8, 9, 10, 11, 12, 13, 14, 15, 16, 17, 18, 19. Which of these numbers can be divided by 2 having remainders of 0? Which numbers have a remainder more than 0 when divided by 2? When a number cannot be divided evenly, find the next smaller number that can be divided evenly. This next smaller number is sometimes called the "helper."

In the example 15 divided by 2, think that 14 is the next smaller number that can be divided evenly by 2. Fourteen divided by 2 = 7 and 15 – 14 = 1. So 15 divided by 2 equals 7 and 1 remainder:

$$\begin{array}{r} 7 \\ 2\overline{)\,15} \\ 14 \\ \hline 1 \end{array} \qquad \text{or 7 R1}$$

PRACTICE AND EVALUATION

Multiplication and Division of Whole Numbers:

1. Examine the sets, then answer each question:

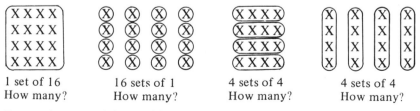

| 1 set of 16 | 16 sets of 1 | 4 sets of 4 | 4 sets of 4 |
| How many? | How many? | How many? | How many? |

2. Draw a ring around 4 sets of 3.

X X X X   4 × 3 = _____
X X X X
X X X X

Draw a ring around 2 sets of 5.

X X X X X   2 X 5 = _____
X X X X X

3. Use the number line to solve the equations:

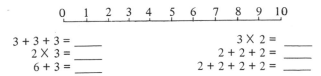

3 + 3 + 3 = _____   3 X 2 = _____
2 X 3 = _____   2 + 2 + 2 = _____
6 + 3 = _____   2 + 2 + 2 + 2 = _____

4. Fill in the blanks:

2 + 2 + 2 = _____   3 X 6 = _____
1 + 1 + 1 + 1 = _____   4 X 4 = _____
6 + 6 + 6 = _____   3 X 2 = _____
4 + 4 + 4 + 4 = _____   4 X 1 = _____

5. Show the correct symbol: (+, −, X).

3 ◯ 2 = 1   4 ◯ 2 = 6
4 ◯ 3 = 12   3 ◯ 2 = 6
4 ◯ 3 = 1   4 ◯ 3 = 7
3 ◯ 2 = 5   4 ◯ 2 = 8

6. Show the correct relation symbol: (<, >, =).

5 X 3 ◯ 3 X 5   5 X 4 ◯ 20 ÷ 4
3 X 5 ◯ 4 X 5   10 ÷ 5 ◯ 8 ÷ 4
12 ÷ 4 ◯ 16 ÷ 4   2 X 3 ◯ 3 X 4

7. Fill in the blanks:

15 ÷ 3   XXXXX XXXXX XXXXX
5 sets of 3   one set of 15
_____ X 3 = 15   15 ÷ 3 = _____

8. Fill in the blanks:

18 ÷ 6 = _____   _____ X 6 = 18
16 ÷ 2 = _____   _____ X 2 = 16
20 ÷ 4 = _____   _____ X 4 = 20

9. Rename each multiplication sentence as a division sentence, then find the missing factor

3 X △ = 12   △ X 3 = 18
12 ÷ 3 = _____
△ = _____
5 X △ = 20   △ X 4 = 16

10. Fill in the blanks:

_____ X 5 = 45   45 ÷ 5 = _____
_____ X 6 = 24   24 ÷ 6 = _____
_____ X 8 = 32   32 ÷ 8 = _____
_____ X 7 = 35   35 ÷ 7 = _____

11. For each of the multiplication equations, give the two related division equations.

$$5 \times 7 = 35 \qquad\qquad 4 \times 8 = 32$$
$$8 \times 6 = 48 \qquad\qquad 6 \times 9 = 54$$

12. Solve each problem:

$$8 \times 6 = (6 + 2) \times 6 \qquad\qquad 6 \times 9 = 6 \times (8 + 1)$$
$$= (6 \times 6) + (2 \times 6) \qquad\qquad = (6 \times 8) + (6 \times 1)$$
$$= \underline{\hspace{1cm}} + \underline{\hspace{1cm}} \qquad\qquad = \underline{\hspace{1cm}} + \underline{\hspace{1cm}}$$
$$= \underline{\hspace{1cm}} \qquad\qquad\qquad\qquad = \underline{\hspace{1cm}}$$
$$86 \times 4 = \underline{\hspace{1cm}} \qquad\qquad\qquad 54 \times 3 = \underline{\hspace{1cm}}$$

13. Complete each problem:

$$432 = 400 + 30 + 2 \qquad\qquad 432$$
$$\underline{\times\ 2} \quad \underline{\times \hspace{2cm} 2} \qquad\qquad \underline{\times\ 2}$$
$$800 + \underline{\hspace{0.5cm}} + \underline{\hspace{1cm}} \qquad\qquad 4$$
$$60$$
$$\underline{800}$$

$$634 = \underline{\hspace{0.7cm}} + \underline{\hspace{0.7cm}} + \underline{\hspace{0.7cm}}$$
$$\underline{\times\ 8} \quad \underline{\times \hspace{3cm} 8}$$
$$\underline{\hspace{1cm}} + \underline{\hspace{1cm}} + \underline{\hspace{1cm}} = \underline{\hspace{1cm}}$$

$$4 \ \square \ 2 \qquad 234 \qquad 654$$
$$\underline{\times\ \ \ 3} \qquad \underline{\times\ 5} \qquad \underline{\times 4}$$
$$1{,}296$$

14. Complete each equation:

$$8 \times 600 = 8 \times (6 \times 100)$$
$$= (8 \times 6) \times 100$$
$$= \underline{\hspace{1cm}} \times 100 = \underline{\hspace{1cm}}$$
$$400 \times 8 = \underline{\hspace{3cm}} 800 \times 9 = \underline{\hspace{1cm}}$$
$$264 \div 2 = (200 + 60 + 4) \div 2$$
$$= (200 \div 2) + (60 \div 2) + (4 \div 2)$$
$$= \underline{\hspace{1cm}} + \underline{\hspace{1cm}} + \underline{\hspace{1cm}}$$
$$= \underline{\hspace{1cm}}$$

$$2\overline{)\,264}$$

$\underline{\hspace{1.5cm}}$	100	$100 \times 2 = \underline{\hspace{1cm}}$
64		
$\underline{\hspace{1.5cm}}$	30	$30 \times 2 = \underline{\hspace{1cm}}$
4		
$\underline{\hspace{1.5cm}}$	2	$2 \times 2 = \underline{\hspace{1cm}}$
0		

15. Complete the table:

Factor	Product	Equation
2, 9	_____	$2 \times 9 =$ _____
6, 8	_____	_____
−, 4	_____	$- \times 4 = 28$
−, −		$5 \times 6 = 30$
7, −	56	$- \times - = -$

16. Find the missing factor:

$r \times 7 = 56$ $4 \times d = 20$
$t \times 9 = 63$ $8 \times n = 48$

17. Show each division equation as a related multiplication equation and find the product:

$n \div 6 = 3$ $a \div 5 = 9$
$b \div 8 = 7$ $c \div 7 = 4$

18. Show the correct relation symbol (= or ≠).

$72 \div 8 \bigcirc 70 \div 7$
$56 \div 7 \bigcirc 54 \div 6$
$64 \div 8 \bigcirc 63 \div 9$

19. Find the missing factor in each equation:

$39 \times n = 6,864$ $53 \times n = 7,208$
$11,316 = n \times 146$ $n \times 72 = 2,088$

20. Complete the following table:

	+	−	×	−
784 △ 19				
894 △ 36				
87 △ 26				
8756 △ 69				

21. Circle the numeral naming the greatest multiple of 10 that will make each mathematical sentence a true statement:

$3 \times r < 268$	50	60	70	80	90
$5 \times t < 193$	30	40	50	60	70
$8 \times w < 706$	50	60	70	80	90

22. Circle the numeral naming the greatest multiple of 100 that will make each mathematical sentence a true statement.

$3 \times y < 796$	100	200	300	400	500
$5 \times r < 943$	0	100	200	300	400

23. Use the largest multiple of 1, 10, 100, or 1,000 to fill in each blank below:

_____ X 40 < 100   _____ X 60 < 500
_____ X 40 < 800   _____ X 70 < 750
_____ X 20 < 2,600   _____ X 80 < 30,000

24. True-or-false mathematical sentences:

$4 \times 7 = 7 \times 4$ $(3 \times 4) \times 6 = (6 \times 3) \times 4$
$27 \times 46 = 46 \times 27$ $(51 \times 3) + (65 \times 107) = (107 \times 51)$
                                      $+ (3 \times 65)$
$2,478 \times 19,027 = 19,027 \times 2,478$ $(27 \times 456) \times 8 = 8 \times (456 \times 27)$

25. True-or-false mathematical sentences:

$8 \div 3 = 3 \div 8$ $2,567 \div 34 = 34 \div 2,567$
$24 \div 6 = 6 \div 24$ $(6 \div 3) \div 2 = 6 \div (3 \div 2)$

26. Complete:

```
46/ 74,567
   _____
     28,567          1,000 ←_____  1,000 X 46 _____
   _____
      5,567            500 ←_____   500 X 46 _____
   _____
        967            100 ←_____   100 X 46 _____
   _____
        507             10 ←_____    10 X 46 _____
   _____
         47             10 ←_____    10 X 46 _____
   _____
      1 |                1 ←_____     1 X 46 _____
              1,621
```

74,567   46 = (46 X 1,621) + 1

Use the same method with the following:

56/87,354   87/234,567   92/19,042

27. Use the distributive property and label each step in solving the multiplication problems below.

$13 \times 124 = n$
$13 \times 124 = 13 \times (100 + 20 + 4)$ renaming
           $= [13 \times 100] + [13 \times 20] + [13 \times 4]$ distributive property
           $= [(10 + 3) \times 100] + [(10 + 3) \times 20] + [(10 + 3) \times 4]$ renaming
           $= [(10 \times 100) + (3 \times 100)] + [(10 \times 20) + (3 \times 20)] + [(10 \times 4 +$
             $(3 \times 4)]$ distributive property
           $= [1,000 + 300] + [200 + 60] + [40 + 12]$ multiplication
           $= 1,000 + (300 + 200) + (60 + 40) + 12$ associative property
           $= 1,000 + 500 + 100 + 10 + 2$ addition
           $= 1,000 + (500 + 100) + 10 + 2$ associative property
           $= 1,000 + 600 + 10 + 2$ addition

$$= 1,612 \quad \text{addition}$$
$$19 \times 246 = r \qquad 29 \times 768 = n \qquad 89 \times 1,946 = t$$

28. Solve the following problems using vertical form:

$$
\begin{array}{r}
248 \\
\times 89 \\
\hline
72 \\
360 \\
1,800 \\
640 \\
3,200 \\
16,000 \\
\hline
22,072
\end{array}
\begin{array}{l}
\quad (9 \times 8) \\
\quad (9 \times 40) \\
\quad (9 \times 200) \\
\quad (80 \times 8) \\
\quad (80 \times 40) \\
\quad (80 \times 200)
\end{array}
$$

$$
\begin{array}{cccc}
345 & 785 & 6,789 & 456 \\
36 & 64 & 192 & 240
\end{array}
$$

29. Rename each multiplication problem below into a division problem, and find the quotient:

$$N \times 123 = 861 \qquad\qquad 784 \times D = 4,704$$
$$P \times 978 = 4,890 \qquad\qquad 937 \times N = 7,496$$
$$356 \times 9 = N \qquad\qquad 128 \times 5 = T$$

30. Use expanded notation to find the missing quotient:

$$
\begin{array}{l}
255 \\
200 + 50 + \quad 5 \\
200 + (40 + 10) + (4 + 1) \\
200 + \quad 40 + (10 + 4) + 1 \\
200 + \quad 40 + \quad 14 + 1 \\
5\overline{)1275} = 5\overline{)1,000 + 200 + \quad 70 + 5} \\
\qquad\quad \underline{1,000} \\
\qquad\qquad\qquad 200 + \quad 70 + 5 \\
\qquad\qquad\qquad \underline{200} \\
\qquad\qquad\qquad\qquad\qquad 70 + 5 \\
\qquad\qquad\qquad\qquad\qquad \underline{70} \\
\qquad\qquad\qquad\qquad\qquad\qquad\quad 5 \\
\qquad\qquad\qquad\qquad\qquad\qquad\quad \underline{5} \\
\qquad\qquad\qquad\qquad\qquad\qquad\quad 0
\end{array}
$$

$$4\overline{)\,847} \qquad 6\overline{)1,248} \qquad 8\overline{)3,208}$$

SELECTED READINGS

Multiplication and Division of Whole Numbers

Banks, Houston J. *Learning and Teaching Arithmetic*. Boston: Allyn and Bacon, 1959, pp. 83–85, 104–106, 139–155, 205–231.

Bell, Clifford, Cleia Hammond, and Robert Herrera. *Fundamentals of Arithmetic for Teachers*. New York: Wiley, 1962, pp. 8–9, 39, 54–77, 91–109, 110–126.

Brumfield, Charles, Robert Eicholz, and Merrill Shanks. *Fundamental Concepts of Elementary Mathematics*. Reading, Mass.: Addison-Wesley, 1962, pp. 69–79, 89–95, 112–115.

Brumfield, Charles, Robert Eicholz, Merrill Shanks, and P. G. O'Daffer. *Principles of Arithmetic*. Reading, Mass.: Addison-Wesley, 1963, pp. 75–93.

Dutton, Wilbur, and L. J. Adams. *Arithmetic for Teachers*. Englewood Cliffs, N. J.: Prentice-Hall, 1961, pp. 91–123, 124–149.

Educational Research Council of Greater Cleveland. *Key Topics in Mathematics for the Primary Teacher*. Chicago: Science Research Associates, 1962, pp. 40–44, 48–66.

Evenson, A. B. Modern Mathematics: *Introductory Concepts and Their Implications*. Chicago: Scott, Foresman, 1962, pp. 33–40.

Johnson, Donovan A., and William H. Glenn. *Sets, Sentences, and Operations*. St. Louis: Webster, 1960, pp. 30–34.

Morris, Dennis E., and Henry D. Topfer. *Advancing in Mathematics*. Chicago: Science Research Associates, 1963, pp. 65–78, 82–87.

Marks, John L., Richard C. Purdy, and Lucien B. Kinney. *Teaching Arithmetic for Understanding*. New York: McGraw-Hill, 1958, pp. 150–188.

Osborn, Roger, Vere DeVault, Claude Boyd, and Robert Houston. *Extending Mathematical Understanding*. Columbus, Ohio: Merrill, 1961, pp. 25–33, 41–49, 52–58.

Schaaf, William L. *Basic Concepts of Elementary Mathematics*. New York: Wiley, 1960, pp. 107–118.

School Mathematics Study Group. Studies in Mathematics, Vol. IX: *A Brief Course in Mathematics for Elementary School Teachers*. Stanford, Calif.: Stanford U. P., 1963, pp. 77–91, 93–105, 107–126, 203–217.

Shipp, Donald, and Sam Adams. *Developing Arithmetic Concepts and Skills*. Englewood Cliffs, N. J.: Prentice-Hall, 1964, pp. 40–43, 280–282.

Thorpe, Cleata B. *Teaching Elementary Arithmetic*. New York: Harper, 1962, pp. 132–142, 144–156, 160–162.

Williams, Sammie, Garland H. Read, Jr., and Frank L. Williams. *Modern Mathematics in the Elementary and Junior High Schools*. New York: Random House, 1961, pp. 48–50.

chapter 6

Rational Numbers

PROPERTIES AND RELATIONSHIPS

Most elementary schools' mathematics programs parallel the historical development of numbers. Man's need for a method to keep track of his possessions spurred the development of counting numbers. Recording numbers and computations were quite difficult without the use of the zero. The invention of zero gave us the set of whole numbers. As the need for measurement, partitioning, and division arose, man found the whole numbers inadequate. He then extended his number system by developing fractional numbers (rational numbers) to satisfy his needs.

Elementary school programs begin with the counting numbers. The next phase is the development of whole-number concepts and the arithmetic of whole numbers. The elementary child, like early man, soon discovers that whole numbers are inadequate to express the quantitative aspects of the physical world. It follows then that the next phase of learning must be that of fractional numbers and operations with them.

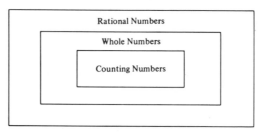

The diagram shows the *historical* development and extension of the number system. It shows the sequential development of numbers as taught in the elementary schools. The diagram also shows the continuity of mathematics. Each new system was developed as an extension of what was already known. We can see that the set of counting numbers is a subset of the set of whole numbers. That is, all counting numbers are whole numbers. *But* the set of whole numbers includes *one number* that *is not* a counting number—the zero. Thus the properties that belong to or hold for the counting numbers must also belong to or hold for the whole numbers. The set of whole numbers extended the number system to include zero and its properties.

The set of whole numbers is a subset of the set of rational numbers. Thus, all whole numbers are rational numbers. Since the set of rational numbers is an *extension* of the whole numbers, we know two things:

1. The set of rational numbers includes the whole numbers plus other numbers that are not whole numbers.

2. The set of rational numbers should obey some of the properties of the whole numbers.

Lets's examine (1) above—What are rational numbers?

The word rational stems from the word *ratio,* which means the relationship between two numbers a and b.

Given any two numbers a and b, a rational number is any number that can be written $\frac{a}{b}$ where a is any whole number and b is any whole number, except zero. The symbolism $\frac{a}{b}$ implies division. Division by zero is meaningless. Thus it is undefined and not possible in mathematics. For this reason, b cannot be zero.

Every Whole Number Is a Rational Number

The symbolism $\frac{a}{b}$ implies division; therefore any whole number a, can be written $\frac{a}{b}$ where $b = 1$ because any whole number divided by 1 yields that number:

$$\frac{a}{b} = \frac{2}{1} = 1\sqrt{2} = 2$$

NOTE:

$$\frac{4}{2} = \frac{10}{5} = \frac{16}{8} = \text{other names for the whole number } two$$

Some Rational Numbers Are Not Whole Numbers

Clearly $\frac{1}{2}$, .5, and 50% are not whole numbers. These numbers are rational numbers, however, because they can be expressed in the form $\frac{a}{b}$.

$$0.5 = \frac{5}{10} \qquad 50\% = \frac{50}{100}$$

These numbers are called fractional numbers. A fractional number is a number obtained by dividing any whole number by a counting number. Dividing by any counting number eliminates division by zero.

The following distinction is made between fractional numbers and fractions.

1. $\dfrac{\text{Number (abstract idea)}}{\text{Fractional number}}$ 2. $\dfrac{\text{Numeral (symbol)}}{\text{Fractions}}$

Fractions are symbols we use to name a fractional number.

Let's examine number two above. (The set of rational numbers should obey some of the properties of the whole numbers.)

A. The operations of addition, subtraction, multiplication and division are binary operations with respect to fractional numbers, just as they are with respect to whole numbers.

$$\frac{1}{4} + \frac{2}{4} + \frac{1}{4}$$

$$\frac{3}{4} + \frac{1}{4} = 1$$

B. Addition and multiplication of fractional numbers are commutative.

$$a + b = b + a \qquad\qquad a \times b = b \times a$$

$$\frac{1}{4} + \frac{2}{4} = \frac{2}{4} + \frac{1}{4} \qquad\qquad \frac{1}{4} \times \frac{1}{2} = \frac{1}{2} \times \frac{1}{4}$$

C. Addition and multiplication of fractional numbers are associative.

$$(a + b) + c = a + (b + c) \qquad\qquad (a \times b) \times c = a \times (b \times c)$$

$$\left(\frac{1}{4} + \frac{2}{4}\right) + \frac{1}{4} = \frac{1}{4} + \left(\frac{2}{4} + \frac{1}{4}\right)$$

D. Multiplication is distributive over addition with respect to fractional numbers.

$$\frac{1}{3} \times \left(\frac{1}{2} + \frac{1}{4}\right) = \frac{1}{3} \times \frac{1}{2} + \left(\frac{1}{3} \times \frac{1}{4}\right)$$

E. Zero is the identity element for addition.
   One is the identity element for multiplication.

F. Addition and multiplication are closed with respect to the whole numbers as well as rational numbers. This is not true for subtraction and division with respect to whole numbers:

$$3 - 4 \neq \text{a whole number}$$
$$3 \div 4 \neq \text{a whole number}$$

Extension of the number system to include rational numbers has added a major property.

Division is closed with respect to the rational numbers, with the restriction that division by 0 is still undefined.

$3 \div 4$ = some rational number
$4 \div 3$ = some rational number since all whole
numbers can be expressed as rational numbers

Proving that the above properties hold for fractional numbers is an excellent exercise for children.

Development of the fractional number concept begins very early in the primary grades. The young child constantly hears reference to halves and fourths, etc., but his idea of "half" is vague and imprecise. At this point we present enough material to satisfy the present needs of the child and to lay a *sound* foundation for the more complete explanation that will be developed later. The concept of rational numbers must be deferred until there is sound knowledge of fractional numbers. Use of the term "rational" could be confusing at this stage of development.

There are many opportunities in the daily activities in the primary grades for developing fractional-number concepts.

Examples:

Half the class is on each team for a game.
We have half a pint of milk for lunch.
Paper-folding activities.
Each child gets half a cookie

Throughout the development of the meaning of fractional numbers the various uses of fractions should be stressed. That fractional numbers imply division is a concept that should be given much attention. "One half of" should be synonymous with "divided by two."

Here are some of the many concrete and semiconcrete situations by which we can teach the uses and meaning of fractional numbers:

1. Fractions are used to name equal parts of a whole:

When a whole or unit has been divided into parts it is important to stress that each fractional part is exactly the same size.

2. Fractions are used to name parts of a set:

3 of the 5 objects in the set are red

$\frac{3}{5}$ of the set of objects are red.

2 of the 5 objects are triangles.

$\frac{2}{5}$ of the set of objects are tri-angles.

1 of the 5 objects is a square.

$\frac{1}{5}$ of the set is a square.

3. Fractions may be used to name a ratio (make a comparison).

The ratio of boys to girls is 2:3 (two boys to three girls). Then the fractional number telling the part of the group that are boys is $\frac{2}{5}$.

The ratio of girls to boys is 3:2 (three girls to two boys). Then the fractional number telling the part of the group that are girls is $\frac{3}{5}$.

4. Fractions indicate division:

$$\frac{4}{2} = 2\overline{)4} \qquad \frac{3}{4} = 4\overline{)3} \qquad \frac{3}{1} = 1\overline{)3}$$

5. A fraction is made up of two terms—numerator and denominator.

Writing Fractions

The two terms *numerator* and *denominator* are separated by a horizontal *fraction bar*.

$$
\begin{array}{ll}
3 & \text{numerator} \\
— & \text{fraction bar} \\
5 & \text{denominator}
\end{array}
$$

The *denominator* tells us the number of equal parts the whole or unit has been divided into.

The *numerator* tells how many of those parts we are concerned with.

The meaning of the denominator varies depending upon the use of the fraction. This should be pointed out to the children. In fact, this idea should cause no difficulty. The definition stated above is the first that is met by the child; once this is understood he can determine the meaning of numerator and denominator in other situations.

Reading Fractions

There are two acceptable ways to read the following fractions:

two over three $\qquad$ $\dfrac{2}{3}$ two thirds

five over sixty-nine $\qquad$ $\dfrac{5}{69}$ five sixty-ninths

nine over twenty-five $\qquad$ $\dfrac{9}{25}$ nine twenty-fifths

seven over twelve $\qquad$ $\dfrac{7}{12}$ seven twelfths

Notice that the numerals below the fraction bar are closely related and read in an ordinal sense.

Use of the number line to picture and compare fractions promotes further understanding.

Fractions less than one:

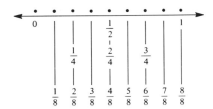

Ideas To Be Developed

The number line is only one way to develop the following meanings.

1. There is no next fraction as there is a next whole number. Between any two fractions there is always another fraction:

$$\text{Between } \frac{1}{4} \text{ and } \frac{1}{2} \text{ is } \frac{3}{8}$$

$$\text{Between } \frac{1}{2} \text{ and } \frac{3}{8} \text{ is } \frac{7}{16}$$

$$\text{Between } \frac{1}{2} \text{ and } \frac{7}{16} \text{ is } \frac{15}{32}, \text{ etc.}$$

2. The greater the number of parts (the denominator) the smaller the part.

$$\frac{1}{8}, \quad \frac{1}{4}$$

3. There are many different names for the same fractional number.
Fractions less than one:

$$\frac{1}{2} = \frac{2}{4} = \frac{4}{8} \qquad \text{(same point on number line)}$$

Fractions equal to one:

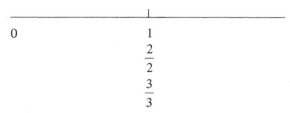

$$\begin{array}{ccc} 0 & & 1 \\ & & \dfrac{2}{2} \\ & & \dfrac{3}{3} \end{array}$$

Remember: Any nonzero number over itself is another name for one. One has many different names.

$$\frac{2}{2} = \frac{4}{4} = \frac{16}{16} = \frac{64}{64} = \frac{1}{1} = 1$$

Fractions greater than one:

$$\begin{array}{cccc} 0 & 1 & 2 & 3 \\ & \dfrac{5}{4} \quad \dfrac{3}{2} & \dfrac{4}{2} & \dfrac{6}{2} \\ \\ & & & \dfrac{9}{3} \\ \\ & \dfrac{6}{4} & \dfrac{6}{3} & \dfrac{12}{4} \end{array}$$

Understanding of Mixed Numbers and How They Can Be Expressed Using Different Names

$$1\frac{1}{2} = \frac{3}{2} = \frac{6}{4} = \frac{12}{8} \qquad 1\frac{1}{2} = \frac{2}{2} + \frac{1}{2}$$

Understanding What Is Meant by the Term "Improper Fraction"

The use of the term "improper fraction(s)" is discouraged by some writers of modern mathematics texts simply because there is nothing improper, logically, about such fraction(s). Any fraction with numerator larger than the denominator is a fraction greater than 1.

Comparing Fractions

Number lines or relationship charts such as the following can be used to deepen the understanding of fractions.

Unit		
$\frac{1}{2}$		$\frac{1}{2}$
$\frac{1}{3}$	$\frac{1}{3}$	$\frac{1}{3}$
$\frac{1}{4}$ $\frac{1}{4}$	$\frac{1}{4}$	$\frac{1}{4}$

Children can learn to picture solutions for the following types of activities using $>$, $<$, $=$.

$$\frac{1}{2} \;\square\; \frac{5}{8} \qquad \frac{2}{6} \;\square\; \frac{1}{8}$$

$$\frac{5}{7} \;\square\; \frac{15}{21} \qquad \frac{1}{4} \;\square\; \frac{3}{12}$$

Equivalent Fractions

Equivalent fractions are fractions that name the same fractional number, different names for the same number.

This idea has been pointed out with number-line activities. Thus the child's first experience with finding equivalent fractions is a visual one.

$$\frac{1}{2} = \frac{2}{4} = \frac{4}{8}$$

As soon as the child understands that $\frac{1}{2}$ and $\frac{2}{4}$ represent the same quantity,

we say that $\frac{1}{2} = \frac{2}{4} = \frac{4}{8}$.

Developing the fraction concept is best done by the use of concrete and semiconcrete instructional materials. The steps involve *identification*, *recognition* and *reproduction*, and the *comparison of fractions*. It must be made clear that fractions require two numbers; a numerator and a denominator.

The development of the fraction concept begins in the first grade where the student is introduced to fractions through the use of concrete informational materials. In the third grade the child learns to write fractions; in the fourth grade, the understanding of the meaning of fractions; in the fifth grade, addition and subtraction of fractions; and in the sixth grade, the multiplication and division of fractions.

If time is spent in the development of the meaning and understanding of fractions, the student will have little difficulty with the four fundamental operations involved. The fractions most commonly used in addition and subtraction have denominators which represent the number of units in various measures, such as 2, 3, 4, 5, 6, 10, 12, and 16. These constitute 99 percent of the denominators used.

Fractions are used to:

1. Express one or more equal parts of an object.
2. Express one or more equal parts of a group of objects.
3. Express a remainder.
4. Express relationship of numbers (ratio).

In comprehending a fraction attention must be given to two separate numbers, one of which indicates the size of the fractional part (denominator), and the other which indicates the number of parts (numerator). The numerator can tell us:

1. How many fractional parts have been taken.
2. The size of the unit to which the denominator refers.
3. What to use in reducing the fraction.
4. Whether to add, subtract, divide, or multiply.

On the other hand, the denominator of a fraction gives the size of the part under consideration. Other technical vocabulary which needs to be understood by the students include *proper fraction. improper fraction, mixed number, reduce, and invert.* All of these background concepts should be introduced before any formal abstract manipulation of numbers is undertaken.

There are two important generalizations that must be understood by the students in the study of fractions:

1. Both the numerator and the denominator of a fraction may be divided by the same number without changing the value of the fractional number $\left(\frac{3}{6} = \frac{1}{2}\right)$. In this case both the numerator and the denominator were divided by three. This is called *reducing a fraction to lowest terms*.

2. Both the numerator and the denominator of a fraction may be multiplied by the same number without changing the value of the fractional number. In the problem $\frac{1}{2} + \frac{1}{4}$, the fraction $\frac{1}{2}$ is changed to $\frac{2}{4}$ by multiplying the numerator and denominator by 2; the indicated operation is then completed since both of the fractions now have the same denominators (4).

The teaching of fractions does not begin with the teaching of the four fundamental operations. The foundations for the above begin in the first grade and through the use of many lifelike experiences the necessary concepts are built. In this way, when the actual manipulation of fractions occurs the students will have a firm background of the meaning and understanding of fractions.

Decimals

Decimals are encountered many times during the everyday use of mathematics. Actually, any number in our system is a decimal. This is because of the base-ten concept of our number system.

Among the many uses of decimals are, the measuring of distances, the measuring of volume and capacity, the density of population, all vital statistics, the amount of rainfall and snowfall, and the understanding of baseball and football averages.

The student finds that the computations performed with whole numbers using the same algorithms can be done with decimals. The only new difficulty is the understanding of where to place the decimal point in the various products and quotients. In the initial instruction a great deal of time needs to be spent in teaching the students how to write and read decimals.

In the teaching of decimals the common-fraction method is the approach often used. Decimal fractions do not differ in meaning from common fractions, they designate parts, ratios, and indicate division just as common fractions do. Through the use of common fractions the student is shown the various equivalents: $\frac{3}{10} = .3, \frac{3}{100} = .03, \frac{1}{4} = .25, \frac{1}{2} = .5$. The solution of a problem by the use of decimals can be checked by the use of common fractions.

Example: $.2 + .3 + .4 = .9$ or nine tenths; $\frac{2}{10} + \frac{3}{10} + \frac{4}{10} = \frac{9}{10}$.

Generally, some of the advantages of using decimals instead of common fractions include:
1. All four fundamental operations are done more easily.
2. Decimals are easier to write and to read.
3. The relationships between values can be more easily seen.

Generally, some of the advantages of using common fractions instead of decimals include:
1. The ratio between numbers can always be seen.
2. Common fractions are more easily visualized.
3. There is more need for common fractions in everyday life.

Decimal fractions written $\frac{7}{10}, \frac{7}{100}, \frac{7-}{1000}$, etc., are simply fractions with denominators of 10 or units of 10.

Decimal numerals or decimals written .7, .07, .007, etc., are an extension of the Hindu-Arabic numeration system.

It is important that the children realize that the only new understanding here is the manner in which tenths, hundredths, thousandths, etc., are written. The symbols $\frac{5}{10}$ and .5 are different names for the same number. The use of decimal numerals, is merely another way to write symbols for rational numbers.

Extending the place-value concept to include rational numbers (expressed in decimal notation) means the addition to the system of Hindu-Arabic numeration a way in which these numbers can be represented. Therefore, the basic principles governing the Hindu-Arabic system of numeration must apply to the decimal numerals as they do to the whole numbers. The following conclusions may be applied:

(a) Decimal numerals represent numbers less than one.

(b) Ten basic numerals (0, 1, 2, 3, 4, 5, 6, 7, 8, 9) called digits, are used to name decimal numerals.

(c) The value of each digit depends on its place or position in the numeral:

$$23.45$$
$$\longmapsto \text{5 hundredths (.05)}$$
$$\longmapsto \text{4 tenths (.4)}$$

The decimal point separates digit symbols which represent numbers less than one from digit symbols which represent whole numbers.

(d) Each place-value position has a name that tells its value in terms of powers of ten.

(e) Each place-value position has a value 10 times greater than the position to its right and $\frac{1}{10}$ of the value of the position to its left.

Tenths	Hundredths	Thousandths	Ten-Thousandths
$\frac{1}{10}$	$\frac{1}{100}$	$\frac{1}{1,000}$	$\frac{1}{10,000}$
$\frac{1}{10}$	$\frac{1}{10} \times \frac{1}{10}$	$\frac{1}{10} \times \frac{1}{10} \times \frac{1}{10}$	$\frac{1}{10} \times \frac{1}{10} \times \frac{1}{10} \times \frac{1}{10}$
$\left(\frac{1}{10}\right)^1$	$\left(\frac{1}{10}\right)^2$	$\left(\frac{1}{10}\right)^3$	$\left(\frac{1}{10}\right)^4$
10^{-1}	10^{-2}	10^{-3}	10^{-4}

The expanded notation of 123.456 can be written in either of the following ways:

(a) $(1 \times 100) + (2 \times 10) + (3 \times 1) + \left(4 \times \frac{1}{10}\right) + \left(5 \times \frac{1}{100}\right) + \left(6 \times \frac{1}{1,000}\right)$

(b) $(1 \times 10^2) + (2 \times 10^1) + (3 \times 10^0) + (4 \times 10^{-1}) + (5 \times 10^{-2}) + (6 \times 10^{-3})$

Percentage

The entire instructional program of decimals depends upon the pupil's understanding the placement of the decimal point. This is especially true in multiplication and division. The manner in which decimals are taught depends a great deal upon the background of the student as well as the teacher. Basically decimals are introduced, taught, and mastered in much the same way as addition, subtraction, multiplication, and division of whole numbers.

The difficulties encountered with the understanding and meaning of percentage stems from the language used to describe the operation rather than the computation. For this reason much of the instructional program needs to deal with developing the skill of interpreting percent as a ratio (9 percent means 9 out of 100). Have the children bring to class illustrations of percent from newspapers, reference books, magazines, and from their other activities. Discuss what is meant by percent and from this beginning proceed to the use of percent in solving problems.

Fractions, decimal numerals, and percents can be thought of as three ways to name the same set of numbers.

"%," the symbol for percent, means hundredths:

$$20\% = .20 = \frac{20}{100} = \frac{1}{5}$$

$$\text{percent} \quad \text{decimal} \qquad \text{fraction}$$

$$15\% = .15 = \frac{15}{100} = \frac{3}{20}$$

A fractional number implies division; thus $\frac{1}{4}$ means $1 \div 4 = 4\overline{)1.00} = .25$ or 25%

$\frac{1}{5}$ implies $1 \div 5 = 5\overline{)1.00} = .20 = 20\%$

Percents can represent numbers both equal to one and greater than one:

$$100\% = 1.00 = 1$$

$$300\% = 3.00 = 3$$

$$350\% = 3.50 = 3\frac{50}{100} = 3\frac{1}{2}$$

There are two common approaches to the teaching of percent—the equation method and the percent-formula method. Both are used extensively.

The specific skills and understandings regarding the various properties and relationships with rational numbers include the following. The child should be able to:

Grade I

1. Develop the concept that there are numbers other than whole numbers.
2. Develop an understanding of one-half and one-third of a whole and of a group.

Grade II

3. Review previous learnings.

Grade III

4. Understand use of positive rational numbers and zero.
5. Understand unit fractions as applied to whole and to a group.

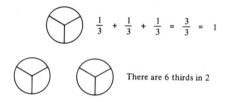

There are 6 thirds in 2

6. Understand the naming of nonunit fractions with reference to a whole and to a group.

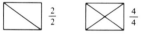

2 (¼ units) are the same as 1 (½ unit)

Grade IV

1. Develop fractions as part of a whole.

2. Develop fractions as part of a set.

$$\frac{1}{2} \text{ of the set } \left\{ \bigcirc \bigcirc \bigcirc \bigcirc \right\} \text{ is } \left\{ \bigcirc \bigcirc \right\}$$

3. Develop fractions as naming a ratio.

$$\left\{ \bigcirc \bigcirc \triangle \triangle \triangle \right\} \frac{2}{3}, \quad \frac{2}{3} \begin{matrix} \text{circles} \\ \text{to} \\ \text{triangles} \end{matrix}$$

4. Develop different names for 1 (whole).

$$1 = \frac{2}{2}, \frac{4}{4}, \frac{6}{6}, \frac{25}{25}, \frac{100}{100}.$$

5. Understand fractions and equivalent parts.

$\frac{1}{2}$ equivalent to $\frac{2}{4}$

6. Discover relationships between number and size of parts compared to whole.

7. Change fractions to simplest form.

8. Compare fractions.

Use number line and relationship charts to determine fractions = to, < than, > than.

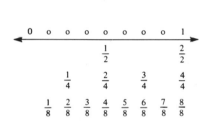

9. Develop commutative property regarding rational numbers.

10. Develop the multiplicative identity property.

11. Understand use of tenths, hundredths, (decimal numerals and percentage).

12. Develop relation of fractions and percents, decimal numerals and percents.

% (percent) means per hundred

$$50\% \text{ means } \frac{50}{100} \text{ or } \frac{1}{2}$$

$$5\% \text{ means } \frac{5}{100}$$

13. Know equivalent forms for fractions and decimals.

Grade V

1. Differentiate between common denominator; lowest common denominator, least common multiple, common divisor.

2. Simplify fractions and change fractions to mixed numerals.

3. Change terms of fractions.

    4. Determine if each of the whole number properties and relationships are true for rational numbers.

Grade VI

    1. Understand concept of an infinite (never-ending) set. For every fraction there is always one smaller or larger.
    2. Use common denominator, least common denominator, or least common multiple.

> (a) 12 is the least common multiple (least common denominator) of 3 and 4 because 12 is the smallest number that can be divided by both 3 and 4 with no remainder.
>
> (b) Common multiples are those numbers divisible by the given numbers. The common multiples of 3 and 4 are 12, 24, 36, ...

    3. Simplify and compare fractions.
    4. Understand and use ratio and proportion.

> (a) Ratio is a quotient of two numbers and is a means of comparing them.
>
> (b) Fractions are expressions of ratios.

$$\frac{1}{2} = \frac{2}{4}$$

Example:

If 2 pencils cost 5¢, how many pencils can you get for 10¢?

$$\frac{2}{5} = \frac{n}{10}, n = 4$$

    5. Define *rational number*.
    6. Determine if each of the whole number properties are true for rational numerals also.

    The specific skills and understandings regarding the various generalizations with rational numbers include the following. The child should be able to:

Grade I

    1. Develop concept that there are numbers other than whole numbers.
    2. Develop understanding of one-half, and one-third of a whole and of a group.

Grade II

    1. Develop understanding of one-half, one-third, one-fourth, one-fifth, two-thirds, and three-fourths, as applied to wholes and a group.
    2. Determine the size of a subgroup, if the subgroup is to be one-third, or

one-fourth of the original group, (Respond in like manner if told to find   the size of one part if the total number is divided into 3 or 4 equal parts.)

3. Demonstrate with concrete objects the number of halves, thirds, or fourths, in a unit quantity.

4. Break up a whole into equal parts so that each part is $\frac{1}{4}$ or $\frac{1}{3}$ of the unit quantity.

Grade III

1. Break up a whole into parts so that a part is $\frac{1}{5}, \frac{2}{3}, \frac{2}{4}$, or $\frac{3}{4}$ of a whole.

2. Break up a group of objects (whose cardinal number is a multiple of 3, 4, or 5 as the case may be) into groups so that each subgroup is $\frac{2}{3}, \frac{2}{4}, \frac{3}{4}$, and $\frac{1}{5}$ of the original.

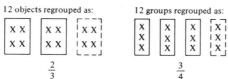

3. Demonstrate with counters the number of fifths in a unit quantity.

4. Compare one group of objects with another group and determine whether the larger is $\frac{2}{3}$, or 4 times the smaller.

5. Arrange counters or other materials into a given number of equal parts.

6. Find $\frac{1}{2}, \frac{1}{3}, \frac{1}{4}, \frac{1}{5}$ of a number by dividing respectively, 2, 3, 4, or 5.

Grade IV

1. Show by using drawings and fraction devices that taking two parts of a unit divided into fourths is equal to taking one part of the same size unit divided into halves.

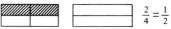

Grade V

1. Break up one group of objects into several smaller groups.

2. Compare smaller groups of objects with a larger group of objects.

3. Compare a larger group of objects with a smaller group of objects.

4. Recognize the unit fractional part of a whole becomes smaller as the denominator becomes larger.

5. Divide more than one unit (3) into different number of equal parts (4) and express the result as a single fraction.

6. Use the decimal point as a means of locating and fixing the *units* place which is the starting point of decimal notation.

7. Explain how decimals are related to the United States monetary system.

8. Construct diagrams showing place value of tenths and hundredths.

9. Write a fraction larger or smaller than the one given using the same denominator; then using the same numerator.

10. Change fractions to higher or lower terms by using pictures, objects, real-life situations, charts, then to abstract computation.

11. Change mixed numbers to improper fractions by using pictures, objects, real-life situations, charts, then to abstract computation.

12. Change improper fractions to mixed numbers by using pictures, objects, real-life situations, charts, then to abstract computation.

13. Change common fractions whose denominators are 10 or powers of 10 to equivalent decimal fractions.

14. Change decimal fractions to common fractions, when denominators are 10 or 100.

Grade VI

1. Write a fraction which is larger or smaller than the one given.
   (a) Use the same denominator given.
   (b) Use the same numerator given.
   (c) Use unlike denominators.

2. Find the common denominator of three or more unlike fractions.

3. Reduce fractions to lowest terms by dividing both numerator and denominator by the same number. (Discovery by manipulative device that dividing or multiplying both the numerator and denominator by the same number does not change its value.)

4. Change a decimal fraction to a common fraction and reduce to lowest terms.

5. Determine by inspection a three-place decimal fraction how many (a) tenths it contains, (b) hundredths it contains, (c) thousandths it contains.

6. Understand the meaning of percents.

7. Understand percents = to one, greater than one.

   (a) $100\% = \dfrac{100}{100} = 1.00$

   (b) $200\% = \dfrac{200}{100} = 2.00$

8. Understand percents of increases and decreases.

9. Understand formula:

$$10\% \text{ of } n = \frac{10}{100} \times n = .10 \times n$$

10. Understand repeating and terminating decimals.

11. Rank and compare decimals according to size.

OPERATIONS

In the initial instruction of the addition and subtraction of fractions, mixed numbers should be used $\left(Example:\ 3\frac{1}{4} + 2\frac{2}{4}\right)$. It is generally held that the familiar whole number part of the mixed number gives the child more confidence in his ability to solve the problem. As in all other cases, many illustrative problems are used as a means of introduction with the students solving the problems in any manner in which they can.

Addition of Fractions

There are four major types of problems involving the addition of fractions. The order of difficulty is as in the sequence given below. The types include:

1. Fractions having like denominators $\left(\frac{1}{4} + \frac{3}{4}\right)$.

2. Fractions having unlike but related denominators $\left(\frac{1}{2} + \frac{3}{4}\right)$. (These are called *related fractions* because one of the denominators is a common denominator.)

3. Fractions having unlike and unrelated denominators, but with a common factor present $\left(\frac{1}{4} + \frac{1}{6}\right)$. (The denominators are unlike—neither the 4 nor the 6 is the common denominator, but each of the denominators have the common factor of 2.)

4. Fractions having unlike and unrelated denominators with no common factors present $\left(\frac{1}{3} + \frac{1}{5}\right)$. (The denominators are unlike—3 and 5 are unrelated numbers, and there is no common factor contained in 3 and 5.)

Generalizations which should be understood before the student can add fractions in a meaningful manner include:

1. Fractions must have the same denominators before they can be added.

2. The numerator of the fraction in the answer is equal to the sum of the numerators of the fractions added.

3. The denominator of the fraction in the answer is the same as the denominator of the fractions added.

Generalizations involving mixed numbers include:

1. When the numerator is equal to or greater than the denominator, the

fraction may be changed to a whole number or a mixed number $\left(\dfrac{8}{4} = 2, \right.$
$\left. \dfrac{7}{5} = 1\dfrac{2}{5} \right)$.

2. An improper fraction is changed to a whole number or a mixed number by dividing the numerator by the denominator $\left(\dfrac{9}{5} = 1\dfrac{4}{5} \right)$.

3. The whole number found in the quotient when dividing the numerator of an improper fraction by the denominator represents the number of wholes and the remainder if any, is the fractional part of the whole remaining.

Example: $\dfrac{9}{5} = 1\dfrac{4}{5}$, the whole number is the 1 since 5 is contained in 9 once, the 4 represents the remainder of the division, and since you were dividing the 9 by 5, the fractional part becomes $\dfrac{4}{5}$.

Generalizations involving the addition of unlike, unrelated fractions include:
1. The product of the denominators is always a common denominator.

Example: $\dfrac{1}{4} + \dfrac{1}{6}$; the product of the two denominators is 24; this is a common denominator but not necessarily the lowest common denominator.

2. The numerator and denominator of each fraction are multiplied by the denominator of the other fraction.

Example: $\dfrac{1}{4} + \dfrac{1}{6}$; for our purpose we will assume that the common denominator used is 24; in order to do this, the 1 and the 4 are multiplied by 6 giving $\dfrac{6}{24}$; the 1 and the 6 are multiplied by 4 giving $\dfrac{4}{24}$, $\dfrac{6}{24} + \dfrac{4}{24} = \dfrac{10}{24} = \dfrac{5}{12}$.

3. The numerator of one of the two fractions must be greater than 1 if the sum of the fractions is to be greater than one. As long as both numerators are $1 \left(\dfrac{1}{3}, \dfrac{1}{5}, \dfrac{1}{13} \right)$ the sum will not be a whole number.

Subtraction of Fractions.

There are four major types of problems involving the subtraction of fractions. The order of difficulty is as in the sequence given below. The types include:

1. Subtraction of like fractions, no borrowing $\left(\dfrac{5}{8} - \dfrac{2}{8} \right)$.

2. Subtraction of like fractions, with borrowing $\left(3\frac{5}{8} - \frac{7}{8}\right)$.

3. Subtraction of unlike fractions, but related, borrowing included $\left(\frac{3}{4} - \frac{1}{2}, 3\frac{3}{5} - \frac{7}{10}, 15\frac{1}{4} - 7\frac{1}{2}\right)$.

4. Subtraction of unlike fractions, not related, borrowing included $\left(\frac{3}{5} - \frac{1}{3}, 11\frac{4}{5} - 4\frac{2}{3}\right)$.

Many of the generalizations included under the section concerned with the addition of fractions apply in the subtraction of fractions.

In the initial instruction of multiplication and division of fractions, whole numbers should be used. $\left(Example:\ 3 \times \frac{1}{4}, 8 \div \frac{1}{2}\right)$. Again, it is held that the familiar whole number gives the child more confidence in his ability to solve the problem. Once again, illustrative problems are used as a means of introducing the concepts with the students solving the problems in any manner in which they can.

Multiplication of Fractions

These are five major types of problems involving the multiplication of fractions. The order of difficulty is as in the sequence given below. The types include:

1. Fraction multiplied by an integer $\left(3 \times \frac{1}{2}\right)$.

2. Integer multiplied by a fraction $\left(\frac{1}{3} \times 4\right)$.

3. Mixed number multiplied by a whole number $\left(4 \times 2\frac{1}{2}\right)$.

4. Fraction multiplied by a fraction $\left(\frac{1}{2} \times \frac{3}{4}\right)$.

5. Mixed number multiplied by a mixed number $\left(3\frac{1}{2} \times 2\frac{1}{4}\right)$.

Generalizations which must be understood before the student can multiply fractions in a meaningful manner include:

1. Multiplying the numerator of a fraction increases the value or size of the fraction by that factor. *Example*: Multiplying a fraction or a mixed number by a factor $\left(4 \times 2\frac{1}{2}\right)$. Multiply the numerator by the factor and write the product

over the denominator $\left(4 \times 2\frac{1}{2} = 4 \times \frac{5}{2} = \frac{20}{2} = 10\right)$; change the fraction in the result to simplest form $\left(\frac{20}{2} = 10\right)$.

2. Both the numerator and denominator may be divided by the same number without changing the value or size of the fraction: $\frac{5}{10} \times \frac{4}{8} = \frac{20}{80} = \frac{1}{4}$ or $\frac{5}{10} \times \frac{4}{8} = \frac{5}{5} \times \frac{2}{8} = \frac{10}{40} = \frac{1}{4}$.

This is *cancellation*. It is the conventional concept used to represent the principle of reduction in multiplication of fractions.

Division of Fractions

This is a very difficult process for the students to understand. Much of the difficulty arises from the fact that there is very little lifelike application to this operation. The three major types of problems involved in the division of fractions are given below. The order of difficulty is the same as the sequence in which they are introduced. The types include:

1. Whole number divided by a fraction $\left(8 \div \frac{1}{4}\right)$.

2. Fraction divided by a whole number $\left(\frac{1}{4} \div 8\right)$.

3. Fraction divided by a fraction $\left(\frac{1}{4} \div \frac{1}{2}\right)$.

Most of us are familiar with the reciprocal method (invert and multiply) for solving these problems $\left(8 \div \frac{1}{4} = \frac{8}{1} \times \frac{4}{1} = 32\right)$. There is another method which in the opinion of the writer shows more clearly the divisional process and hence gives more meaning to the operation. This is called the common-denominator method. It is felt that the division of fractions might well be introduced by means of the introduction of the inversion (reciprocal) method. An example of the common-denominator method is given below:

$$8 \div \frac{1}{4} = \frac{32}{4} \div \frac{1}{4} = 32$$

Below are comparisons in the operations of the two methods mentioned: Inversion method:

$$\frac{2}{3} \div \frac{1}{3} = \frac{2}{3} \times \frac{3}{1} = 2 \qquad 1\frac{2}{3} \div \frac{3}{4} = \frac{5}{3} \times \frac{4}{3} = \frac{20}{9}$$

Common-denominator method:

$$\frac{2}{3} \div \frac{1}{3} = \frac{2}{3} \div \frac{1}{3} = 2 \qquad\qquad 1\frac{2}{3} \div \frac{3}{4} = \frac{20}{12} \div \frac{9}{12} = \frac{20}{9}$$

Addition of Decimals

Children have already studied fractions and should be able to apply the basic principles of place value and addition to the addition of decimals. In the addition of whole numbers, ones are placed in the ones column, tens in the tens column, and so on. This same principle applies to the addition of decimal fractions. Tenths are added to tenths and placed in the tenths column; hundredths are added to hundredths and placed in the hundredths column; and so on. With the understanding of place-value, children should discover that in addition of decimal fractions the decimal points are always aligned. Alignment of decimal points is comparable to finding a common denominator. The meaning of place-value should be reviewed and stressed as often as necessary in introducing children to *fractional numbers renamed in decimal form.*

If the basic addition facts are understood and known and the relationship of fractions and decimals is known, children will have little difficulty with the addition of decimals. This is just a different way of applying the basic structure of whole numbers and fractions.

Subtraction of Decimals

From a knowledge of addition of decimals, children should be able to discover some generalizations concerning the subtraction of decimals. Again children will see that decimal points are always aligned, that numerals must be expressed with proper place value, and that alignment of decimal points is associated with finding a common denominator. By alignment (tenths under tenths), we are subtracting numbers named with like denominators.

Multiplication of Decimals

There are two approaches to the teaching of multiplication of decimals that can be used. The first approach is based on the use of fractions; the other applies the basic idea of addition and subtraction of decimals to the multiplication of decimals.

To solve a problem such as $\frac{4}{10} \times \frac{2}{10} = \boxed{}$ by following the principles used in the multiplication of fractional numbers, the numerators are multiplied together to obtain the numerator of the product, and the denominators are multiplied together to obtain the denominator of the product.

Now consider the following example:

$$\frac{4}{10} \times \frac{2}{10} = \triangle N \; or \; .4 \times .2 = \square$$

Four-tenths times two-tenths is eight-hundredths. In decimal form this example is stated as .08; the 8 being written in the hundredths column to indicate its value.

$$\frac{4}{10} \times \frac{2}{10} = \frac{8}{100} \qquad \begin{array}{r} .4 \\ \times \; .2 \\ \hline .08 \end{array}$$

Now consider 2.3 multiplied by .8. Notice that 2.3 is another name for $2\frac{3}{10}$ and that

$$2\frac{3}{10} = \frac{10}{10} + \frac{10}{10} + \frac{3}{10} = \frac{23}{10} \qquad \begin{array}{r} 2.3 \\ \times .8 \\ \hline .24 \\ 1.6 \\ \hline 1.84 \end{array}$$

$$\frac{23}{10} \times \frac{8}{10} = \frac{184}{100} = \frac{84}{100}$$

$$\begin{aligned}
.8 \times (2.3) &= .8 \times (2 + .3) \\
&= (.8 \times 2) + (.8 \times .3) \\
&= 1.6 + .24 \\
&= (1 + .6) + (.2 + .04) \qquad \text{renaming} \\
&= 1 + (.6 + .2) + .04 \qquad \text{associative property} \\
&= 1 + .8 + .04 \qquad\qquad \text{of addition} \\
&= 1.84
\end{aligned}$$

Division of Decimals

This operation can be related to the child's knowledge of fractions. Consider the problem $.8 \div .2 = \triangle$. How many two-tenths are contained in eight-tenths. There are several approaches to the solution of this problem.

1. Repeated subtraction:

$$\begin{array}{r}
.8 \\
-.2 \rightarrow 1 \\
\hline
.6 \\
-.2 \rightarrow 2 \\
\hline
.4 \\
-.2 \rightarrow 3 \\
\hline
.2 \\
-.2 \rightarrow 4 \\
\hline
0
\end{array}$$

There are 4 two-tenths in .8.

2. Relating to fractions:

$$\frac{8}{10} \div \frac{2}{10} = \frac{\dfrac{8}{10}}{\dfrac{2}{10}} \times \frac{\dfrac{10}{2}}{\dfrac{10}{2}} = \frac{\dfrac{80}{20}}{1} = \frac{80}{20} = 4$$

3.

$$.8 \div .2 = \frac{.8}{.2} \times \frac{10}{10} = \frac{8}{2} = 4$$

| symbolism means division | multiplication by one | divide | quotient |

The above and the following methods are valid because multiplication by any name for one (the identity element for multiplication) results in an equivalent fraction.

$$.66 \div .11 = \frac{.66}{.11} \times \frac{100}{100} = \frac{66}{11} = 6$$

$$\begin{array}{r} 6 \\ 11\overline{)66} \\ \underline{66} \end{array}$$

THE USE OF THE NUMBER LINE IN THE OPERATIONS
OF RATIONAL NUMBERS

Common fractions are abstract symbols to represent rational numbers with a value less than one. Many devices have been used by man to picture his thoughts of numbers and to differentiate the partial value of one quantity from another. One of the most versatile of these techniques is called the number line.

The use of the number line for rational numbers is similar to the previous discussions in this respect concerning the natural numbers, except that each point on the line may now represent a fractional part of a natural number.

It is the purpose of the writer to show how the number line may be employed to give meaning to the rational numbers, but it is recognized that other schemes may be of equal importance to the individual teacher to give meaning to a particular process involving fractions.

This is a sample exercise in the introduction of fractions using the number line. Students may divide the line segments in many ways. Some of these methods are: (1) estimating, (2) folding the paper, (3) by the use of the ruler, (4) the geometric method.

A. _____

Divide into 2 parts
You now have _____ equal parts.
Each part is called_____.

B. _____

Divide into 3 parts.
You now have _____ equal parts.
Each part is called_____.

C. _____

Divide into 4 parts
You now have _____ equal parts.
Each part is called _____,

D. _____

Divide into 5 parts
You now have _____ equal parts.
Each part is called _____,

The exercise would include the dividing of a line into 6, 7, 8, 9, 10, and 12 equal parts.

Addition and Subtraction of Like Fractions

When the denominators of any two fractions are expressed with the same number we can add or subtract fractions in the same manner that whole numbers are added or subtracted. Thus

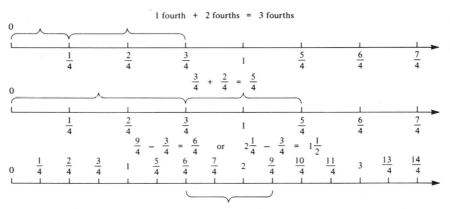

Least Common Multiple

One of the first concepts to develop in preparing to introduce work with fractions is the idea of finding common multiples of two or more numbers. The following number line will graphically demonstrate this concept.

Problem: Find the least common multiple of 3 and 4.

Procedure: Starting from *C*, picture the path of an object making jumps of 4 units each along the top of the line; also along the top of the line picture the path of an object making jumps of 3 units each. At whatever points on the scale these two paths coincide, we have common multiples of 3 and 4. The first such point, 12, is the least common multiple.

Sum or Difference of Unlike Fractions

We find it difficult to add or subtract two unlike fractions unless there is a further subdivision. In this example it becomes necessary to subdivide the fifths into halves.

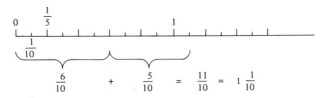

$$\frac{6}{10} \quad + \quad \frac{5}{10} \quad = \quad \frac{11}{10} \quad = \quad 1\frac{1}{10}$$

When we divide the fifths in half we find, by counting, the number of subdivisions to be equal to 10. We have divided the unit into 10 equal parts, each of these parts is called $\frac{1}{10}$. Therefore

$$\frac{1}{2} \text{ of } \frac{1}{5} = \frac{1}{10}$$

It follows then that by expressing $\frac{3}{5}$ in terms of tenths, and $\frac{1}{2}$ in terms of tenths, we can then add or subtract them, for they now have common denominators.

$$\frac{3}{5} = \frac{6}{10}; \frac{1}{2} = \frac{5}{10}; \frac{6}{10} + \frac{5}{10} = \frac{11}{10} = 1\frac{1}{10}$$

Addition of Unlike Fractions

$$\frac{2}{3} \qquad + \qquad \frac{1}{4}$$

$$\frac{1}{4} \qquad\qquad \frac{2}{3} \qquad \frac{11}{12}$$

Problem: $\frac{2}{3} + \frac{1}{4} = n.$

Procedure: To add $\frac{2}{3}$ and $\frac{1}{4}$, put 1 on the 12th point on the number line from 0, since 12 is the lowest common multiple of 3 and 4. Now it is merely a problem of adding $\frac{2}{3}$ of this line segment to $\frac{1}{4}$ of the line segment and show-

ing that the result is equal to $\frac{11}{12}$ of the unit 1.

Subtraction of Unlike Fractions

Subtraction of fractions is similar to addition of fractions except that we proceed in reverse order, beginning with the line segment representing the largest fraction and moving to the left a sufficient distance to represent the subtrahend. The remaining line segment is the difference.

Problem: $\dfrac{3}{5} - \dfrac{1}{3} = n$

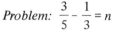

Multiplication of a Fraction by a Whole Number

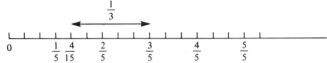

Problem: $\dfrac{1}{4} \times 2 = n;\; 2 \times \dfrac{1}{4} = n.$

Procedure: To find $\dfrac{1}{4}$ of 2, divide the two units into four equal parts on

the number line. One-fourth of 2 is shown to be equal to $\dfrac{1}{2}$.

Conversely, to find $2 \times \dfrac{1}{4}$, we must subdivide our number line into four

equal segments per unit. Two of these $\dfrac{1}{4}$ segments correspond to $\dfrac{1}{2}$ of a whole

segment.

Multiplication of a Fraction by a Fraction

Problem: $\dfrac{2}{3} \times \dfrac{3}{4} = n.$

Procedure: Let each segment of the number line represent $\dfrac{1}{4}$. Divide each segment into thirds, thereby letting each subdivision represent $\dfrac{1}{12}$. Now it is shown that $\dfrac{2}{3}$ of the $\dfrac{3}{4}$ segment is $\dfrac{6}{12}$ or $\dfrac{2}{4}$ or $\dfrac{1}{2}$.

Sometimes it is clearer for students to let the multiplicand be represented as a new unit as in the following problem.

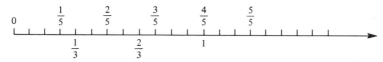

Problem: $\dfrac{2}{3} \times \dfrac{4}{5} = n.$

Procedure: The least common multiple of 3 and 5 can be shown to be 15 on the number line, so put 1 on the fifteenth mark from 0, thereby dividing the number line above into $\dfrac{1}{15}$'s. In finding $\dfrac{2}{3}$ of $\dfrac{4}{5}$, let the $\dfrac{4}{5}$ become the unit 1 on the underneath side of the line. Then by dividing the unit 1 into three equal parts it is easily shown that $\dfrac{2}{3}$ of $\dfrac{4}{5}$ is equal to $\dfrac{8}{15}$.

Division of Fractions

Problem: $\dfrac{2}{3} \div \dfrac{1}{8} = n.$

Procedure: By using the number line, 24 is found to be a common multiple of 3 and 8. It is convenient therefore to let each segment of the number line represent thirds and divide each segment into eighths so that the resulting segment represents one twenty-fourth. Since $\dfrac{1}{8} = \dfrac{3}{24}$, show by repeated subtraction that there are 5 one-eighths and $\dfrac{1}{3}$ of another one-eighth in $\dfrac{2}{3}$.

Division of a Mixed Number by a Fraction

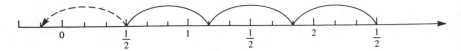

Problem: $2\frac{1}{2} \div \frac{2}{3} = n.$

Procedure: Since 6 is the common multiple of 2 and 3, divide each line

segment into sixths. By repeated subtraction of lengths equal to $\frac{2}{3}$, it is shown

that $2\frac{1}{2} \div \frac{2}{3} = 3\frac{3}{4}$.

Division of a Whole Number by a Decimal Fraction

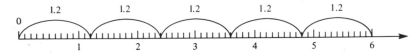

Problem: $6 \div 1.2 = n.$

Procedure: To divide 6 by 1.2, simply divide the number line into six equal parts (segments) and then subdivide each segment into tenths. By the process of measuring off segments equal to 1.2 it is shown that $6 \div 1.2 = 5$.

It is also wise to show that this is also the same as multiplying both numbers by 10, making the problem read $60 \div 12 = 5$.

Division of a Decimal Fraction by a Decimal Fraction

Problem: $.6 \div .05 = n.$

Procedure: To enlarge the units of measure on the number line multiply .6 and .05 by 10 to get 6 and .5, thereby making it obvious that $.6 \div .05 = 12$.

The specific operational skills and understandings regarding rational numbers include the following. The child should be able to perform.

ADDITION

Grade III

1. Discover that fractional parts may be put together or added just as whole numbers are added.

2 fourths and 1 fourth = 3 fourths

$$\frac{2}{4} + \frac{1}{4} = \frac{3}{4}$$

2. Demonstrate by manipulative devices addition of fractions pertaining to the common fractions.

Grade IV

1. Add fractions with like and unlike denominators.
2. Add with decimal point, exchange, rename. (Exchange means different forms .5 + .3 = .8, $\frac{5}{10} + \frac{3}{10} = \frac{8}{10}$.

Grade V

1. Add a whole number and one or two like fractions by some manipulative device. May also add two or three like fractions by the same method.
2. Add 2 or 3 mixed numbers with fractions having common denominators (like fractions) by using ruler or some other device.
3. Add mixed numbers with like fractions.
4. Add unlike fractions with no denominator larger than 12.
5. Add fractions not only in vertical position but also in equation form.
6. Add decimals through hundredths.

Grade VI

1. Add unlike fractions:
   (a) When lowest common denominator is the largest denominator given in the problem – $\frac{2}{4} + \frac{1}{4} = n.$
   (b) Least common denominator is the product of the denominators – $\frac{1}{2} + \frac{1}{3} = n.$
   (c) When common denominator is not present. (Add by use of concrete objects—measure on ruler, etc.)
2. Add mixed numbers with unlike fractions including regrouping.
3. Add fractions and mixed numbers when common denominator is not present.
4. Add mixed decimals that are carried out to thousandths.

SUBTRACTION

Grade III

1. Discover that fractional parts may be taken away or subtracted just as whole numbers are subtracted.

$$2 \text{ thirds} - 1 \text{ third} = 1 \text{ third}$$

$$\frac{2}{3} - \frac{1}{3} = \frac{1}{3}$$

2. Demonstrate by manipulative devices subtraction of fractions pertaining to the common fractions.

Grade IV

1. Subtract fractions with like and unlike denominators.
2. Subtract with decimal point, renaming, exchange. (Exchange means different forms.)

Grade V

1. Subtract fractions not only in vertical position but in equation form.
2. Subtract hundredths with renaming.

Grade VI

1. Subtract fractions when common denominator is not present.
2. Subtract with whole and mixed numbers as minuend with unlike fractions in subtrahend and including "regrouping."
3. Subtract fractions, involving all difficulties.
4. Subtract decimals, involving all difficulties.

MULTIPLICATION

Grade III

1. Use the concept of parts of a whole to parts of a set:

$$\frac{1}{5} \text{ of a set of 20}$$

Grade IV

1. Multiply whole numbers by fractions and fraction by whole number.

Grade V

1. Multiply a whole number by a mixed number, using money.
2. Multiply rational numbers named by fractions and mixed numerals with like and unlike denominators.
3. Multiply tenths and hundredths.

Grade VI

1. Multiply decimals involving thousandths.
2. Multiply a proper fraction by a whole number.
3. Multiply a whole number by a proper fraction.
4. Multiply a mixed number by a whole number.
5. Multiply a whole number by a mixed number.
6. Multiply a fraction by a fraction.
   (a) proper fraction by a proper fraction
   (b) proper fraction by a mixed number
   (c) mixed number by a mixed number
   (d) a mixed number by a proper fraction
7. Recognize that "of" may be interpreted as a multiplication sign in computation.
8. Multiply decimals, involving all difficulties.

DIVISION

Grade V

1. Divide rational numbers named by fractions and mixed numerals with like and unlike denominators.
2. Divide decimals—tenths and hundredths.
3. Find percents.
4. Find a percent of a number.

Grade VI

1. Divide a whole number by a fraction—see it as $2 \div \frac{1}{2} = n$, means how many halves are in 2.
2. Divide a whole number by a mixed number.
3. Divide a fraction by a fraction, either by changing to a common denominator or by inverting and multiplying.
4. Operation with decimals to thousandths.
5. Divide a fraction by a whole number, see it as a problem of dividing a fraction into a number of equal parts.

6. Divide a mixed number by a fraction.

7. Divide a mixed number by a mixed number.

8. Divide a fraction by a mixed number.

9. Divide a mixed number by a whole number.

TEACHING SUGGESTIONS

Concept: Fractions—one-half, one-third, one-fourth, two-thirds, three-fourths

Procedures. 1. Use the flannelboard to illustrate a pie or cookie and discuss the idea of sharing and giving one-half away. Use squares, candy bars, and other objects to teach one-half.

2. Draw pictures of squares and circles on the chalkboard and let the children come up and try to divide them in half.

3. Draw on the board a number of geometric shapes or objects. Use a dotted line to cut each shape into two parts. Divide some in even halves, others just cut in two segments. Children are asked to identify the objects that have been divided in half.

4. Draw on paper a number of geometric figures, then have the children write yes or no next to the figure telling whether it is divided in half or not.

5. Use flannelboard demonstrations for fractions.

6. Provide packs of cards showing fractions, and give a pack to each child. The children play in pairs. At a given signal each child turns the top card up showing the fraction. The one who has the fraction for the greater fractional number gets both cards. The winner is the one with the most cards.

7. Provide the children with numerous experiences in working with objects to demonstrate the ideas of one-half and one-third. Use both set collections and single objects. For example, show a set of six blocks and divide these between two children. Now point out that each child has half of the blocks. Now using this same set, divide them between three children. Point out that each child had one-third of the blocks. Now show a single object which the children can either take apart or cut apart to illustrate the ideas of one-third and one-half. Have the children actually divide this object.

8. Arrange six felt cutouts of the same size on the flannelboard. Then have a child loop a string around one-half of the cutouts, showing that one-half of six is three. Now ask the class if anyone can think of a way to show one-third of the cutouts. Help the children to see that if the set of six cutouts is separated into three equivalent subsets, there will be two cutouts in each subset. This will show that one-third of six is two.

9. Discuss the relative sizes of fractional parts of different shapes. Place a felt circle, two half-circles, and three one-third circles on the flannelboard. Compare the various parts of a circle. Develop the understanding that one-half is greater than one-third, that one-fourth is less than one-third, and that one-half is greater than one-fourth.

10. Review one-half and one-third by drawing shapes on the chalkboard and separating them into two or three parts of the same size. The children are to identify one-half or one-third of each shape. Relate the fractions $\frac{1}{2}$ and $\frac{1}{3}$ to these fractional numbers.

11. Show the children a large square of paper; fold the paper through the center to demonstrate halves. Fold the paper again so that four parts of the same size are formed. Ask the children the size of each of the portions. $\left(\frac{1}{4}\right)$ Discuss how many one-fourths there are in one whole. Repeat the demonstration with other shapes and sizes.

12. Have the children cut paper dolls from a piece of paper that has been folded into fourths. If the hands at the folded edge are not cut, the dolls will be joined and can be opened out to show one-half of a set of four or one-fourth of a set of four.

13. Display a large square of paper, then fold the paper through the center to demonstrate halves. The children name each part. Now fold the paper again so that four parts of the same size are formed. Explain that each of these parts is called one-fourth of the square. Develop the understanding of how many one-fourths there are in the whole piece of paper. Repeat this demonstration with other shapes and sizes.

14. Provide each child with a paper on which there are shapes or simple pictures. The children are to separate the pictures to show halves, thirds, and fourths.

15. To develop the understanding of three-fourths, draw a square on the chalkboard and mark it off in fourths. Shade one-fourth of the square and have a child write the numeral $\frac{1}{4}$ on the shaded part. Shade one more fourth and ask how many fourths are now shaded. Have a child write $\frac{1}{4}$ on the portion. Ask how many fourths have been shaded and how should two-fourths be written. After $\frac{2}{4}$ has been written, shade one more portion and have the children tell how many parts have now been shaded. Have a child write $\frac{3}{4}$. Ask how many fourths are not shaded and how many fourths are there in the entire square.

16. Develop the understanding of two-thirds by drawing different shapes on the chalkboard, dividing them into thirds, and proceeding as before. Introduce the fraction $\frac{2}{3}$ as representing two or three parts, all of which are the same size.

17. Cut rectangles, squares, and triangles into pieces like a puzzle and put them into envelopes. Each piece should be one-half, one-third, one-fourth, two-thirds, or three-fourths of the original figure. Have enough pieces in each en-

velope to form a whole shape. When the child has completed a puzzle he writes the fractional parts used as $\frac{1}{4}$, and $\frac{3}{4}$; or $\frac{1}{3}$ and $\frac{1}{3}$, and $\frac{1}{3}$.

18. Provide several demonstrations involving the concepts associated with the four fractions. Give the children an opportunity to work with set materials involving such things as half a set, a fourth of a set, as well as other fractional parts. Also provide demonstrations in which whole objects are marked or cut into a given fractional part.

Concept: A proper fraction—value less than one

Procedures. 1. Use a flannelboard for the introduction of this concept. On it have a rectangular piece of paper cut into five parts. Have one of the children remove two pieces and tell how many remain. Write the fractional part on the chalkboard. $\left(\frac{3}{5}\right)$ Write the fractional part that was taken away. $\left(\frac{2}{5}\right)$ Do the same thing with other rectangles cut into different-sized parts. Discuss the list of fractions on the chalkboard, noticing some likeness of them. (All of the fractions have numerators that are smaller than the denominator.) These fractions are called *common fractions*.

Have different children go to the board and tell what fractional part must be added to the ones on the board to make the numerator the same size as the denominator. $\left(\frac{2}{5} + \frac{3}{5} = \frac{5}{5} = 1\right)$ If each of the fractions needs another fraction to be added to it before it equals one, the fraction is a common fraction.

2. Each child has a pair of scissors and a sheet of rather heavy paper. Have a child write "one" on the board showing that each child has one "whole" piece of paper. Have the children fold the paper in half and cut it into two equal parts. The number now written on the board for one of the two pieces will be $\frac{1}{2}$.

Each of the two pieces of paper is now folded in half and cut. Each child now has four equal pieces of paper, each being $\frac{1}{4}$. Placing the four pieces together gives the original "whole" piece of paper. $\left(\frac{4}{4}\right)$ A common fraction has a numerator that is less than the denominator. Cut other pieces of paper into different fractional parts to strengthen the understanding.

3. Use sticks that are in bundles of 100 and are classified as "one" bundle. Take one, two, three, four, or more sticks from the bundle and write the fractional part remaining. Put the various number of sticks back into the bundle to make the "whole" bundle.

4. Draw a circle on the chalkboard, divide it into fourths. Erase one fourth.

Ask the class what part of the whole circle is shown on the board. $\left(\dfrac{3}{4}\right)$ Discuss whether or not this is more or less than the whole circle. Explain to the class that the number story for three-fourths is $\dfrac{3}{4}$ or a common fraction. Have some-one look up in the dictionary the definition of "fraction." Ask them what the two numbers that go to make up the fraction mean. What does the bottom number show? It is called a denominator. It tells how many parts the circle is divided into. What does the top number mean? It is called a numerator. It tells how many parts are being dealt with.

Draw another circle on the board and divide it into thirds. Erase one third. Ask the class if the remaining portion of the circle represents more than "one" or less than "one." Explain to the class that any fraction that has a value less than "one" is called a common fraction.

Draw circles on the board to represent $\dfrac{2}{3}, \dfrac{4}{4}, \dfrac{5}{8},$ and $\dfrac{1}{2}.$ Have the children explain and prove which of the circles represent common fractions and which do not. Do this same procedure with circles representing $\dfrac{4}{5}, \dfrac{1}{3}, \dfrac{2}{2},$ and $\dfrac{8}{7}.$

5. Draw a rectangular box 36" long and 2" wide on the board and label it "one whole." Have a pupil draw a similar box and divide it into two 18-inch pieces and label each part what fractional part it is of the whole. Have another pupil draw a box and divide it into thirds (12-inch pieces) and label each piece $\dfrac{1}{3}.$ Have the same done for fourths. The drawing on the board then looks like the illustration.

One Whole			
$\dfrac{1}{2}$		$\dfrac{1}{2}$	
$\dfrac{1}{3}$	$\dfrac{1}{3}$		$\dfrac{1}{3}$
$\dfrac{1}{4}$	$\dfrac{1}{4}$	$\dfrac{1}{4}$	$\dfrac{1}{4}$

Review the meaning of a "common fraction" and ask the children if $\dfrac{1}{2}, \dfrac{1}{3}$ and $\dfrac{1}{4}$ are common fractions and "how does a (or one) common fraction compare in size with a 'whole' or 1?"

6. Use an egg carton with 12 spaces for eggs. Place an object into each of the cartons and ask the children: "What common fraction of a dozen is represented by this many objects?" Write the fractional parts on the chalkboard under the heading "Of *one* whole dozen," e.g., "One object = $\frac{1}{12}$." When eleven objects have been handled in this manner, discuss: "How does each of these common fractions compare in size with the 'whole' or one?"

7. Use a clock face to develop the common fractions which would represent various parts of an hour. For example, fifteen minutes would be represented by $\frac{1}{4}$. Either draw the example on the chalkboard or have each student draw an appropriate drawing on his paper. Each of the drawings should be labeled with the appropriate common fraction. Ask: "How do all of these common fractions compare in size with one whole hour?"

Concept: An improper fraction—value always greater than one

Procedures. 1. Distribute to each child two strips of paper of different colors. Cut these strips into fractional parts, in this case perhaps thirds, then discard one third. How many thirds are left? (Five-thirds) Write five-thirds on the board in terms of a fraction. $\left(\frac{5}{3}\right)$ Have the children arrange their fractional strips according to color and determine if five-thirds is less than one, equal to one, or more than 1. Using the strips of the same color, it is shown that 3 thirds equal 1. Now cut the thirds in half to form sixths. Have the children make their own combinations of sixths and discuss and compare whether these fractions are equal to one, less than one, or greater than 1.

2. Break three pieces of chalk in half. Ask a child to pick up one of the pieces and then ask the pupil if he has picked up a whole piece of chalk. Have him pick up another piece of chalk. Again ask him to pick up another piece of chalk $\left(\frac{1}{2} + \frac{1}{2} = 1 \text{ whole piece of chalk}\right)$. Once more have him pick up another piece of chalk. Discuss the value of the chalk he now holds. $\left(\frac{1}{2} + \frac{1}{2} + \frac{1}{2} = \frac{3}{2}\right)$

3. Have the pupils cut up 8 circles from colored paper and divide two circles into halves. Ask how many halves equal a whole (2 halves = a whole). Then

take 3 halves. How many whole circles are contained in $\frac{3}{2}$?

Now divide the next two circles into fourths. Ask how many fourths are contained in a whole. (4 fourths = a whole)

Take seven-fourths and ask how many whole circles are contained in $\frac{7}{4}$.

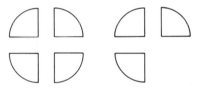

Show by manipulating the circles. $\left(\frac{7}{4} = 1\frac{3}{4}\right)$

Divide the last two circles into eighths. How many eighths equal a whole? (8 eighths = a whole) Now pick up $\frac{11}{8}$. Show how many circles are contained in $\frac{11}{8}$. $\left(\frac{11}{8} = 1\frac{3}{8}\right)$

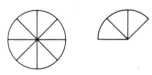

Discuss with the children the various fractional parts developed to further the understanding that an uncommon (improper) fraction has the value of 1 or more.

4. Have the children add $\frac{3}{4}$ and $\frac{3}{4}$ and discuss the answer $\frac{6}{4}$. Is this frac-

tion more or less than one in value, and if so how much more? Prove that $\frac{6}{4}$ is more than one by the use of the flannelboard or the chalkboard. Have various children explain their drawings and picture proofs.

5. Each child has two pieces of paper of equal size in front of him. Write "2" on the chalkboard to show that this is the number of "whole" items each child has. Ask the children to divide each of their papers into four equal pieces. Now have the children hold up $\frac{1}{4}$ of 1. Have a pupil write this fraction on the board and ask the children to hold up $\frac{2}{4}$ of 1. Then have a child write this fraction on the board. The same is done with $\frac{3}{4}$ of 1, and $\frac{4}{4}$ of 1. When $\frac{4}{4}$ of 1 is held up, discuss how else this fraction might be written.

Draw circles on the board, dividing them into parts of several sizes. Have children take turns shading parts and writing the fraction for which the shaded part stands. Develop the concept that when the numerator becomes the same as the denominator, a "1" is written to show that the equivalent of "one" has been reached. This fraction $\frac{4}{4}$ is called an uncommon (improper) fraction.

Continue with fractions that are greater than "one" in value. Discuss each fraction and have the pupils show by drawings and diagrams the meaning of these fractions. $\left(\frac{6}{4}\right)$ These are also improper (uncommon) fractions. Develop the overall concept that an uncommon (improper) fraction has a value equal to or greater than "one."

6. Have the children take their fraction kits and put three halves on their desks. Let the class decide whether they have more than one whole. Allow someone to write the abstract form of the fraction represented. $\left(\frac{3}{2}\right)$ Discuss this new fraction and discuss the term, *uncommon* (improper) *fraction*. Do this with different values, such as $\frac{2}{2}, \frac{4}{2}, \frac{5}{4}, \frac{4}{4}, \frac{9}{8}, \frac{6}{4}$, and $\frac{8}{8}$. Let the children compare these with "wholes." Allow them to write the abstract numbers representing the fractions under consideration and lead them to the generalization that uncommon (improper) fractions are equal to "one" or greater than "one."

7. Use a fraction chart that is divided from one "whole" to $\frac{16}{16}$. Have strips of paper that are equal to the halves, fourths, eighths, and sixteenths of the chart and have the children measure 3 halves. Let the class discover that 3 halves is more than 1 whole and have the abstract form written on the board. Do this

with 2, 3, 4, 5, halves, fourths, etc. Discuss when these various fractions are classed as "common" and when they are classed as "uncommon."

8. Use an enlarged ruler and provide each child with a ruler. Let the class find how many halves in one inch and have someone write this in abstract form on the board. Find how many halves in an inch and a half. Write this in abstract form on the board. Introduce the term *uncommon* (improper) *fraction*, explaining that this is what fractions are called if they equal one or are greater in value than one. Do this same procedure with fourths and eighths.

9. Use pictures or a flannelboard to show that uncommon (improper) fractions have a value equal to or greater than one. Objects on the flannelboard are used instead of actual objects.

Show that the first object in the following figure has six parts and that there are $\frac{6}{6}$ths in this object. The object is complete so that we may say that it is one whole object.

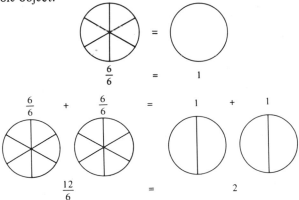

The figure above shows two objects with six parts in each object. Explain that there are $\frac{12}{6}$ths altogether which equals 2. A fraction should be written as a mixed number when the numerator is larger than the denominator.

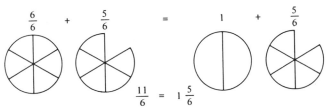

Show that there are $\frac{11}{6}$ths when one part (fractional) is taken away. The fraction then has the value of $\frac{11}{6}$ or $1\frac{5}{6}$, which is larger than one whole.

Combine the abstract numbers with the semiconcrete numbers so that the children will visualize how the abstract numbers are written.

Concept: Reducing a fraction does not change its size or value

Procedures. 1. Give each pupil three circles of colored construction paper. Have them divide one circle into halves by folding and cutting; one circle into halves, then into quarters; the third circle into halves, quarters, then eighths.

Present a problem similar to the following: Pam's mother divided a small pie into four pieces. Pam and Matt ate $\frac{1}{2}$ of the pie. How many of the four pieces did they eat?

Show your answer by laying the quarter circles on the half circle. How many fourths did it take to equal $\frac{1}{2}$? Write the equation: $\frac{1}{2} = \frac{2}{4}$ on the chalkboard. Ask: "Which is larger, smaller, or the same size; one-half of a pie or two-fourths of a pie?" Show by drawings and number equations.

Proceed in the same manner with $\frac{4}{8} = \frac{1}{2}; \frac{2}{8} = \frac{1}{4}; \frac{6}{8} = \frac{3}{4}$.

As a summation exercise, have the pupils make charts to put on the bulletin board, using circles and parts of circles to show the different equations. (Have each child choose a different equation to picture.)

At a given signal, have the children write all the equations they can find by looking at the charts. At the end of the time allotted, call on various students to put their equations on the board. Have the class study the equations on the board and formulate generalizations based upon their observations.

2. Use rulers to show that $\frac{2}{4} = \frac{1}{2}; \frac{2}{8} = \frac{1}{4}; \frac{4}{16} = \frac{1}{4}; \frac{8}{16} = \frac{1}{2}$, etc. Use the number line to show the findings from the rulers. Mark all the inch lines with a red pencil or crayon and all of the half-inch lines with a different color.

3. Have the class write stories in which they use words and illustrations to explain the understanding—when a fraction is reduced, its size or value remains the same, but its terms are smaller.

4. Cut out circles of paper and make clock faces with movable hands. Ask: "What part of an hour is used in the study of arithmetic?" Have each student show the starting time of the lesson (9:00 a.m.) and the closing time, (9:45 a.m.) How many minutes have elapsed? Write the 45 as a fractional part of an hour. $\left(\frac{45}{60}\right)$ Have the students observe the part of the clock face covered by the minute hand between 9:00 and 9:45. What part of an hour is covered during arithmetic class? $\left(\frac{3}{4}\right)$ Have them compare $\frac{45}{60}$ and $\frac{3}{4}$. Ask: "Do both mean the

same part of an hour?" Have various pupils explain their answers by means of graphic and oral portrayal on a large chalkboard representation of a clock face.

$\frac{45}{60}$ can also be made to equal $\frac{3}{4}$ by scaling down or reducing the numerator and denominator by the same number. What numbers are contained in both 45 and 60 evenly?

$\frac{45}{60} = \frac{9}{12} = \frac{3}{4}$, first 45 and 60 were both divided by 5, then 9 and 12 were both divided by 3. $\frac{45}{60} = \frac{3}{4}$, 45 and 60 were both divided by 15.

As 45 is reduced to 3 and 60 to 4, do the terms or numbers in the fractions get smaller? Does the value of both fractions remain the same? Use other periods of time such as 30, 15, and 20 minutes to show the same concept.

5. Give each child a 12-inch square of manila paper. Cut accurately into nine squares. Label with crayon as follows:

Square 1, 1 whole.

       2, divide into halves horizontally.

       3, divide into halves vertically.

       4, divide into fourths horizontally.

       5, divide into fourths as squares.

       6, divide into eighths (2 inches wide, $\frac{1}{2}$ inch deep).

       7, divide into eighths (2 inches deep, $\frac{1}{2}$ inch wide).

       8, divide into sixteenths (squares).

       9, divide into sixteenths (2 inches deep and $\frac{1}{4}$ inch wide).

The finished chart should look like this:

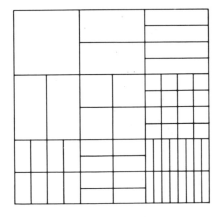

As each new figure is made, ask the children: "Into how many parts has the card been divided? What is each part called? One whole equals how many $\frac{1}{2}$'s, $\frac{1}{4}$'s, $\frac{1}{16}$'s? Two-fourths equal how many halves? Which is larger $\frac{1}{2}, \frac{1}{4}, \frac{1}{8}, \frac{1}{16}$; $\frac{1}{2}$, or $\frac{2}{4}$?" Develop other questions and comparisons which will show the desired understanding.

6. Have the children manipulate objects such as bottle caps, blocks, crayons, and pencils. Each object must be of the same size. Have them place 15 like objects in a group. It is learned that each object is $\frac{1}{15}$ of the group.

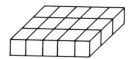

Have the children take away three objects from the group. They discover that they have taken away $\frac{3}{15}$ of that whole amount and that $\frac{12}{15}$ of the group remains.

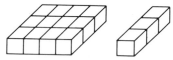

Explain that there are five groups of three and the children will realize that the remaining objects will amount to $\frac{4}{5}$ and the objects taken away to $\frac{1}{5}$.

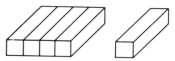

Show on the flannelboard or chalkboard that $\frac{12}{15}$ equals $\frac{4}{5}$ and $\frac{3}{15}$ equals $\frac{1}{5}$. Use different-shaped objects and illustrate with various fractional amounts such as twelfths, ninths, eighths, sixths, twentieths, etc.

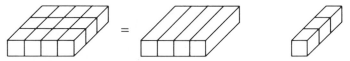

As you explain each example, stress that the size or value of the fraction remains the same, only the terms are smaller and easier to work with.

7. Use semiconcrete materials with the flannelboard and the children will obtain the same understanding as with the use of actual objects. This time combine the abstract numbers with the semiconcrete materials. Through the use of different colored semiconcrete objects, show that $\frac{3}{12}$ can be the same as $\frac{1}{4}$ and $\frac{9}{12}$ the same as $\frac{3}{4}$.

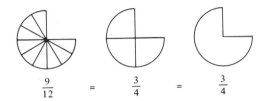

$$\frac{9}{12} \quad = \quad \frac{3}{4} \quad = \quad \frac{3}{4}$$

Compare these semiconcrete objects in several different manners so that a complete understanding is formed.

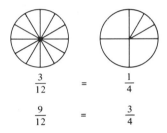

$$\frac{3}{12} \quad = \quad \frac{1}{4}$$

$$\frac{9}{12} \quad = \quad \frac{3}{4}$$

Again use combinations of fractions such as eighths, ninths, sixths, and fifteenths. Explain that fractions are reduced to their lowest terms and that a fractional part of the whole amount has been found in its lowest possible terms.

8. Have 10 play-money dimes on the table in the front of the room. Ask the class how much money is on the table. If all 10 dimes make one whole dollar, what part of a dollar would one dime be? How would you say and write it? Write $\frac{1}{10}$ on the board. Remove 8 dimes from the table and ask what part of a dollar remains. Continue adding dimes while writing the symbols for the fractions expressed on the chalkboard.

Bring out, through discussion, that all the fractions do not have to be expressed as tenths, that there are other ways to write $\frac{2}{10}, \frac{4}{10}, \frac{5}{10}, \frac{6}{10}, \frac{8}{10}$ and $\frac{10}{10}$. Have pupils suggest other ways and show with the dimes as they explain.

Have the children draw pictures of various groupings of dimes to show different fractions of a dollar. Possibly they could write the symbolic equations under their drawings.

Through discussion, bring out the reasons for working with the simplest fractions possible. Review and discuss vocabulary when and where necessary. Have some students write various fractions that they think can be reduced while the other students copy and attempt to reduce, using drawings, flannelboards, or other devices.

Concept: Fractions need to be changed to a common denominator before they can be added or subtracted

Procedures. 1. With the understanding of the value of parts of fractions, discuss how fractions can be grouped together and separated. Ask three boys and three girls to go to the front of the room. Can the 3 boys and 3 girls be added together? Can the answer be 6 boys or is it 6 girls? It is neither, because girls cannot be added to boys and the answer be in terms of girls or boys. There has to be a common name for the group, such as *children*.

3 boys	3 boys
3 girls	3 girls
(It can't be either boys or girls.)	6 children (common denominator)

The same principle applies with the adding and subtracting of fractions. Different fractions can be added or subtracted as long as they have a common name (denominator). Chairs and tables (common denominator = furniture,) dogs + cats + horses + cattle = animals (common denominator).

Using the fractional equivalence chart, have the children see how many ways they can express $\frac{1}{2}, \frac{1}{4}, \frac{1}{3}$.

2. Have the class work with their individual cut-out circles. With larger circles on the flannelboard, have one pupil demonstrate:

$$\frac{1}{2} + \frac{1}{4} = \frac{3}{4}$$

This could be done with other unit fractions. After adding halves to fourths and eighths, and thirds to sixths, discuss what they have been doing. Point out that before they could add $\frac{1}{2}$ and $\frac{1}{4}$, they first had to find out how many $\frac{1}{4}$'s equaled $\frac{1}{2}$. So then the problems read: $\frac{2}{4} + \frac{1}{4} = \frac{3}{4}, \frac{1}{3} + \frac{1}{6} = \frac{2}{6} + \frac{1}{6} = \frac{3}{6} = \frac{1}{2}$.

3. Example: $3\frac{1}{2} + 1\frac{1}{4}$. The actual addition may be illustrated by use of semiconcrete objects. It may also be illustrated with a concrete object such as a ruler. Have the pupils visualize the distance by manipulating their own rulers at their desks and finding the proper markings.

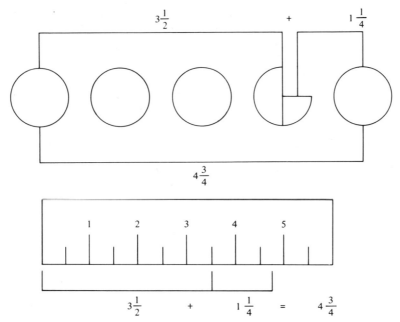

Show there is an easier way to find these solutions by changing the numbers to like fractions and then adding. Explain why the numbers must be changed. If $\frac{1}{2}$ and $\frac{1}{4}$ are added as they are, the answer would be $\frac{2}{6}$. The pupils already have realized the answer as $\frac{3}{4}$.

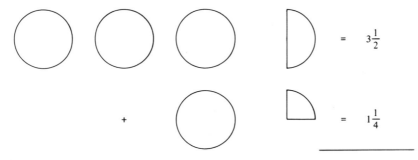

Impossible to add in this form

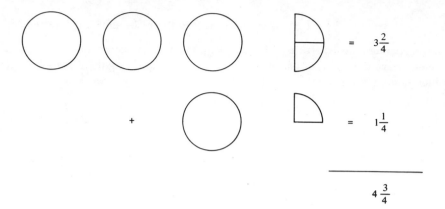

Show that there is an easier way to find solutions by changing the numbers to like fractions when subtracting. If $1\frac{1}{4}$ is to be subtracted from $2\frac{1}{2}$, explain that $\frac{1}{4}$ cannot possibly be taken away from $\frac{1}{2}$. Therefore, again a change to like fractions must be made.

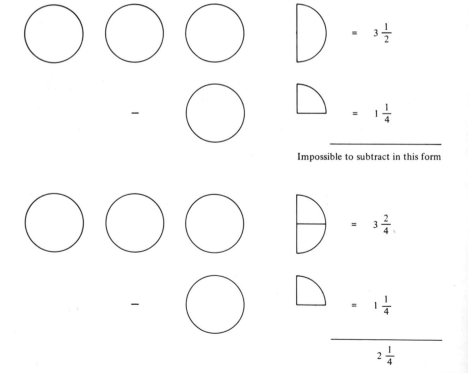

Call attention to the fact that the same process is used in both addition and subtraction. All fractions must have like denominators before they can be added or subtracted.

4. Before this skill can have complete meaning the child must understand that both terms of a fraction may be multiplied or divided by the same number without changing the value of the fraction.

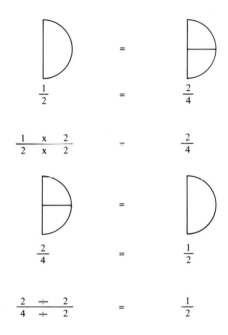

Explain why these fractions are called *unlike fractions*. The numbers (denominators) indicating the total amount are different or unlike. Show that adding $\frac{1}{3}$ and $\frac{1}{6}$ together could only give an answer of $\frac{2}{3}$ or $\frac{2}{6}$ or $\frac{2}{9}$. Place objects representing $\frac{1}{3}$ and $\frac{1}{6}$ together on the flannelboard so that the pupils can see that $\frac{2}{3}$ or $\frac{2}{6}$ or $\frac{2}{9}$ do not equal $\frac{1}{3} + \frac{1}{6}$.

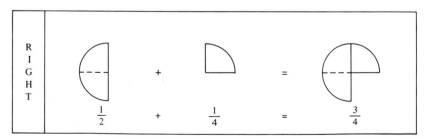

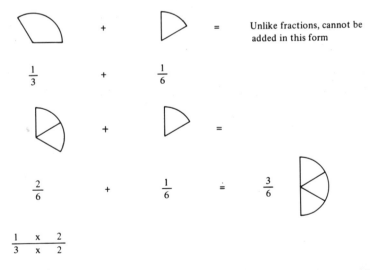

Show that unlike fractions cannot be added unless the fraction is changed by multiplying both terms of the fraction by the same number.

Let the pupils analyze various problems to clinch the understanding that unlike fractions cannot be added or subtracted until they are first changed to a common denominator.

5. After using the concrete and semiconcrete approaches, use abstract numbers to clinch the understanding. Ask the children if they could use the ruler to find how to add $\frac{1}{6}$ and $\frac{1}{3}$. They will find the ruler doesn't have these numbers, so it must be learned that the solution cannot always be solved by drawings, diagrams, or working with a ruler. By abstract numbers, show what process is used for adding such combinations as $\frac{1}{3} + \frac{1}{6}, \frac{3}{8} + \frac{1}{4}$, and $\frac{2}{3} + \frac{1}{9}$. (See examples below.)

$$\frac{1 \times 2 = 2}{3 \times 2 \quad 6} \qquad \frac{1 \times 2 = 2}{3 \times 2 \quad 6} \qquad \frac{3}{8} = \frac{3}{8} \qquad \frac{3}{8} = \frac{3}{8}$$

$$\frac{+1}{6} = \frac{1}{6} \qquad \frac{-1}{6} = \frac{1}{6} \qquad \frac{+1 \times 2 = 2}{4 \times 2 \quad 8} \qquad \frac{-1 \times 2 = 2}{4 \times 2 \quad 8}$$

$$\frac{3}{6} = \frac{1}{2} \qquad \frac{1}{6} \qquad \frac{5}{8} \qquad \frac{1}{8}$$

Explain that the number to which the fractions are changed is called a *common denominator*. More than two numbers can be added by changing the denominators to a common denominator. (See example below.)

$$\frac{1 \times 6 = 6}{2 \times 6 \quad 12}$$

$$\frac{1 \times 4 = 4}{3 \times 4 \quad 12}$$

$$\frac{+1 \times 3 = 3}{4 \times 3 \quad 12}$$

$$\frac{13}{12} = 1\frac{1}{12}$$

Concept: Multiplying the numerator of a fraction by a number increases the size of the fraction that many times

Procedures. 1. Each child takes from his fraction kit the fraction one-fourth. Have one of the children write the fraction on the board. Multiply the numerator 1 by three and the result is $\frac{3}{4}$. Determine from the use of the fraction kit that $\frac{3}{4}$ is three times greater than $\frac{1}{4}$. Do the same procedure with other fractions such as $\frac{2}{5} \times 2$, $\frac{2}{6} \times 2$, $\frac{1}{8} \times 7$ until the generalization can be developed that multiplying the numerator by a number increases the value of the fraction that many times.

2. Have the children draw two rectangles. Divide them into fifths and shade one-fifth of the first rectangle. Label the fractional part of the rectangle. Multiply the numerator by some number less than five and shade in the number of fifths that resulted from the multiplication. Verification of this concept is made by doing the same exercise with other fractional parts with either circles or rectangles.

3. Our room is having a program for the parents. The children decided that they would like the girls to make cookies for refreshments. However, the recipe that the children used made only enough cookies for the children themselves. They decided that the recipe would have to be increased three times in order to have enough cookies for the parents also. The original recipe looked like this:

$\frac{1}{2}$ cup butter	$\frac{1}{2}$ tsp soda	$1\frac{1}{8}$ cup flour
$\frac{1}{3}$ cup brown sugar	$\frac{1}{2}$ tsp vanilla	1 beaten egg
$\frac{1}{3}$ cup sugar	$\frac{1}{2}$ tsp salt	$\frac{1}{2}$ cup nuts

After the class had worked together and increased the recipe, it looked like this:

$\frac{3}{2}$ or $1\frac{1}{2}$ cup butter	$\frac{3}{2}$ or $1\frac{1}{2}$ tsp soda
$\frac{3}{3}$ or 1 cup brown sugar	$\frac{3}{2}$ or $1\frac{1}{2}$ tsp vanilla
$\frac{3}{3}$ or 1 cup sugar	$\frac{3}{2}$ or $1\frac{1}{2}$ tsp salt
$3\frac{3}{8}$ cup flour	$\frac{3}{2}$ or $1\frac{1}{2}$ cup nuts
3 beaten eggs	

The class had discussed many ways to increase the recipe. The flannelboard, fractional kits, and using the number line were among the devices that were used to solve and prove each of the increases of the ingredients.

4. *Problem situation.* If six girls were going to make aprons needing $\frac{3}{4}$ of a yard for each apron, how much material was needed?

$$\underline{} + \underline{} + \underline{} + \underline{} + \underline{} + \underline{} =$$

$$\frac{3}{4} + \frac{3}{4} + \frac{3}{4} + \frac{3}{4} + \frac{3}{4} + \frac{3}{4} = \frac{18}{4}$$

$$4\frac{2}{4} = 4\frac{1}{2} \text{ yards of material needed}$$

$$6 \times \frac{3}{4} = \frac{18}{4} = 4\frac{2}{4} = 4\frac{1}{2} \text{ yards}$$

Concept: Multiplying the numerator and the denominator by the same number does not change the value of the fraction

Procedures. 1. Discovering equal fractions in higher terms. Use a flannel-board or draw on the board the following:

Questions to be developed from the drawings:

Changing $\frac{1}{2}$ to fourths—how many times and how many parts are there now? (twice as many) $\frac{1}{2} = \frac{2}{4}$ (2)

Changing $\frac{1}{2}$ to eighths—how many parts and how many times are there now? (four times as many) $\frac{1}{2} = \frac{4}{8}$ (4)

What was done to the numerator and the denominator of the fraction $\frac{1}{2}$ in the first problem to get $\frac{2}{4}$? (Both the numerator and denominator were multiplied by 2.)

What was done to the numerator and the denominator of the fraction $\frac{1}{2}$ in the second problem to get $\frac{4}{8}$? (Both numerator and denominator were divided by 4.)

2. Discovering equal fractions without drawings or charts. To change $\frac{1}{2}$ to fourths, the denominator must be multiplied by 2 to make the new denomina-

tor. (4) Two times the numerator of one will be two. Hence $\frac{1}{2} = \frac{2}{4}$. Think: $\frac{1 \times 2}{2 \times 2} = \frac{2}{4}$ Write: $\frac{1}{2} = \frac{2}{4}$.

To change $\frac{1}{2}$ to eighths, the denominator must be multiplied by 4 to make the new denominator eight. Four times the numerator of one will be four. Hence $\frac{1}{2} = \frac{4}{8}$. Think: $\frac{1}{2} = \frac{1}{2} \times \frac{4}{4} = \frac{4}{8}$. Write: $\frac{1}{2} = \frac{4}{8}$.

3. Story problem: Matt ran 10 yards in $2\frac{1}{2}$ seconds. Randy ran the same distance in $2\frac{1}{4}$ seconds. What was the total time that it took the two boys to run 10 yards? Use circles or other objects to show the addition.

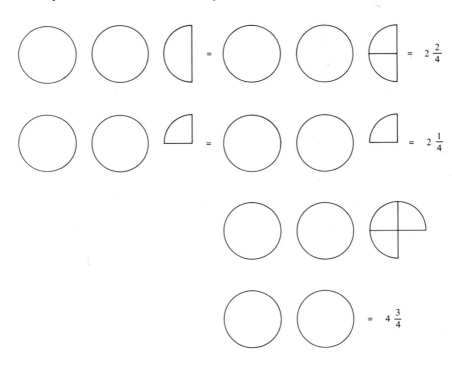

4. As a visual-demonstration technique to show this understanding, use a quart of colored water and two measuring cups. Fill one cup to the $\frac{1}{2}$-cup mark and place it so all can see it. Next write the fraction $\frac{1}{2}$ on the chalkboard and multiply both the numerator and the denominator by 3. The result will be $\frac{3}{6}$.

The fraction $\frac{1}{2}$ will represent the amount of water in the first cup and the $\frac{3}{6}$ will represent the amount that is put in the second cup. Fill the second cup to the $\frac{3}{6}$ mark. Compare the levels in both cups. They are the same. Discuss and have the children prove in as many ways as they can. (flannelboard, fraction-equivalence chart, etc.)

5. Have the children divide toothpicks into 6 groups of 3 and 6 groups of four each. Take one group of three and one group of four to represent the fraction $\frac{3}{4}$. Now multiply the fractions, $\frac{3}{4} \times \frac{4}{4}$. This is done by placing 4 groups of 3 and 4 in another pile making the fraction $\frac{12}{16}$. Through this procedure the children can see that the value has been unchanged. (The same number of groups were added to both the numerator and the denominator.)

$$\frac{///}{////} = \frac{3}{4} \qquad \frac{3}{4} \times \frac{4}{4} = \frac{12}{16} \qquad \frac{/// \times 4}{//// \times 4} = \frac{///\ \ ///\ \ ///\ \ ///}{////\ \ ////\ \ ////\ \ ////} = \frac{12}{16}$$

Concept: Both the numerator and the denominator of a fraction can be divided by the same number and not change the value of the fraction

Procedures. 1. Let the students discover the many fractions which are the same size (or equivalent value). Have the pupils make fractional kits containing whole, half, fourth, and eighth circles. Use these cutouts to show that $\frac{2}{4}$'s are the same as $\frac{1}{2}$ in size or value. Compare other equivalencies.

Have the pupils make 12-inch rulers from cardboard. Cut one ruler in halves, into fourths, one into sixths, and one into twelfths. By the use of these devices show that $\frac{3}{6}$ of a foot and $\frac{1}{2}$ of a foot are the same length. Continue with $\frac{6}{12}$ and $\frac{1}{2}$, $\frac{9}{12}$ and $\frac{3}{4}$, etc.

Using egg cartons, show that $\frac{1}{2}$ dozen eggs equals $\frac{2}{4}$ dozen eggs. Have the students show by a picture that $\frac{3}{6}$ dozen eggs and $\frac{1}{2}$ dozen eggs are the same number of eggs.

Discuss what can be done to change the terms of the fraction $\frac{3}{6}$ to $\frac{1}{2}$, seeing that both the numerator and the denominator are divided by 3. $\frac{3}{6}$ divided by

$\frac{3}{3} = \frac{1}{2}.$ $\frac{2}{4}$ divided by $\frac{2}{2} = \frac{1}{2}.$

Discuss why the terms of the fraction are divided. Would you ask a grocer for $\frac{3}{6}$ dozen or $\frac{1}{2}$ dozen eggs? Why?

2. Have the children draw a line 4 in. long and divide it into four equal parts. Label each part.

$\frac{1}{4}$	$\frac{1}{4}$	$\frac{1}{4}$	$\frac{1}{4}$

Have the children draw a similar line below this one and divide it into eighths as follows:

$\frac{1}{8}$	$\frac{1}{8}$	$\frac{1}{8}$	$\frac{1}{8}$	$\frac{1}{8}$	$\frac{1}{8}$	$\frac{1}{8}$	$\frac{1}{8}$

Discuss the two lines. Notice that they are both the same length. One line is divided into eighths and the other fourths. How many eighths are equal to one-fourth, using the two lines as reference? $\left(\frac{2}{8} = \frac{1}{4}\right)$ Write the equation on the board. How many fourths are contained in $\frac{6}{8}$'s? $\left(\frac{6}{8} = \frac{3}{4}\right)$ Discuss and compare various other equivalencies between fourths and eighths. Draw another line 3 inches in length and divide this line into thirds. Draw another line below it 3 inches in length and divide this line into sixths.

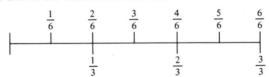

Compare as you did in the first lines drawn. From these drawings the children are led to discover that dividing both terms of a fraction by the same number does not change the value of the fraction involved.

Concept: Dividing a fraction by a whole number is the same as multiplying the fraction by a reciprocal of the whole number

Procedures. 1. The term "reciprocal" is explained to the children as being the number concerned with, made into a denominator of a fraction with a numerator of 1. For example, the reciprocal of 4 is $\frac{1}{4}$. Now show a fractional pie $\frac{1}{2}$. Have the children cut this portion into 2 equal parts, or actually dividing by

2. $\left(\dfrac{1}{2} \text{ divided by } 2 = \dfrac{1}{4}.\right)$ Now show them that $\dfrac{1}{2} \times \dfrac{1}{2}$ (the reciprocal of 2) $= \dfrac{1}{4}$.

2. Begin by using an illustration that most of the class can visualize. "Pamela had $\dfrac{2}{3}$ of a candy bar. She divided the piece of candy into 4 equal pieces. What part of the whole candy bar was each of these pieces?

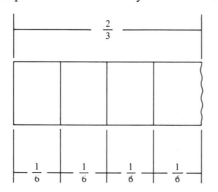 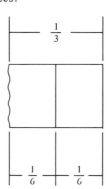

Divide the $\dfrac{2}{3}$ into four parts so that each of these parts is $\dfrac{1}{4}$ of $\dfrac{2}{3}$. But $\dfrac{1}{4}$ of $\dfrac{2}{3}$ means the same as $\dfrac{1}{4} \times \dfrac{2}{3} = \dfrac{1}{6}$. Therefore each piece of the candy was $\dfrac{1}{6}$ of the whole candy bar.

3. Now use this illustration with circles. Ask one of the children what number is represented by Diagram A? $\left(1\dfrac{1}{2}\right)$

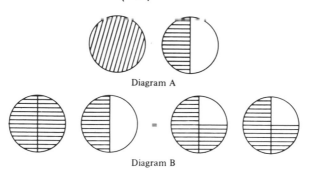

Diagram A

Diagram B

Diagram B shows the number in A divided by 2. To divide $1\dfrac{1}{2}$ into 2 equal parts (groups):

$$1\dfrac{1}{2} \text{ divided by } 2 = \dfrac{3}{2} \text{ divided by } 2 = \dfrac{3}{2} \times \dfrac{1}{2} = \dfrac{3}{4}$$

4. The children bring an apple or candy bar with which to work. Each child divides the apple he has into two equal parts and lays aside one part. Each of you has one-half of an apple or candy bar on your desk. Suppose you want to share with a friend. Into how many parts will you have to divide it? What part will each of you have? When you divided your half, what part did you give your friend? You gave $\frac{1}{2}$ of your $\frac{1}{2}$ which equals $\frac{1}{4}$. Dividing $\frac{1}{2}$ by 2 is $\frac{1}{4}$. $\left(\frac{1}{2}\text{ divided}\right.$ by $2 = \frac{1}{2} \times \frac{1}{2} = \frac{1}{4}.\Big)$

The children are given round, rectangular, and square pieces of paper. Have the children divide the rectangular piece of paper into four equal parts and shade in three of them. Each part is called $\frac{1}{4}$. Have them divide $\frac{1}{4}$ by 2. $\left(\frac{1}{4}\text{ divided}\right.$ by $2 = \frac{1}{4} \times \frac{1}{2} = \frac{1}{8}.\Big)$

Show the children how to write the examples:

$$\frac{1}{2} \div 2 = \frac{1}{2}\text{ of }\frac{1}{2} = \frac{1}{4}\text{ or }\frac{1}{2} \div 2 = \frac{1}{2} \times \frac{1}{2} = \frac{1}{4}$$
$$\frac{1}{2} \div 4 = \frac{1}{4}\text{ of }\frac{1}{2} = \frac{1}{8}\text{ or }\frac{1}{2} \div 4 = \frac{1}{2} \times \frac{1}{4} = \frac{1}{8}$$

Have the pupils look at the manner in which the examples are written in the illustration. Ask them if they notice what happened to the divisor in each example. They will probably say that the divisor (2) became $\frac{1}{2}$ because dividing something into 2 parts is the same as finding $\frac{1}{2}$ of it, and that the "2" became the denominator because that tells into how many parts the apple (or candy bar) was cut.

Concept: A decimal can be written as a proper fraction

Procedures. 1. The decimal fractions, .1, .01, .001, are written on the chalkboard and the pupils are asked to read them. The common fractions $\frac{1}{10}$, $\frac{1}{100}$, and $\frac{1}{1,000}$ are written on the board and the children are asked to read them. In this manner it is shown that .1 is merely another way to write $\frac{1}{10}$. The same is shown for .01 and $\frac{1}{100}$, .001 and $\frac{1}{1,000}$.

A line segment is drawn on the board and broken at even intervals into 10 segments. One of the smaller segments is designated to the children and they are asked to determine how much of the original line segment is represented by the smaller segment. Since the line has been broken in equal segments, each portion then becomes a fractional part of the whole, or $\frac{1}{10}$. Write $\frac{1}{10}$ above the smaller segment. Now write .1 and have the children identify it by name, $\frac{1}{10} = .1$. The relationship of common fraction to decimal becomes apparent.

Write the decimal fraction, .2345 on the board. The 2 is indicated as being in the tenths place, the 3 in the hundredths place, etc. The 2 then has a value of 2 tenths. Write the equivalent form as a common fraction. Do this for the rest of the parts of the decimal fraction, showing the equivalency between the common fraction and decimal fraction forms.

2. Review money values and correct symbols for $.01, $.10, $.02, and $.20. Ask the children to express each as a common fractional part of a dollar. For example, $.01 = $\frac{1}{100}$ of a dollar, $.10 = $\frac{10}{100}$ of a dollar. This can be further shortened to show: $.01 = \frac{1}{100}, .10 = \frac{10}{100}$ or $\frac{1}{10}, .02 = \frac{2}{100}.$

Have the pupils bring illustrative newspaper articles. Write fractionally such items as the following:

Time taken to run a race, 22.6 sec
Distance on speedometer, 45,678.9 mi
Speed, 127.236 mph
Batting average, .406
Amount of rainfall, 101.36 in.
Wind velocity, 13.75 mph
Hydroplane speed, 134.86 mph

Have the pupils note that two decimal places indicate the second power of 10 or 10 $\times$ 10 which is 100. Similarly, three places means the third power of 10 in the denominator or 10 $\times$ 10 $\times$ 10 = 1,000. Each time you multiply ten by itself, another zero is added—so the powers of ten become apparent. The decimal system is a way of expressing denominators as ten, one hundred, one thousand, etc. Each decimal place represents an added power or factor of 10 in the denominator. Therefore $.7 = \frac{7}{10}, .07 = \frac{7}{100}, .007 = \frac{7}{1,000}.$

Read the decimal as if it were a fraction and write in the numerator. Then note the number of decimal places used and use that power of ten as the denominator. For example, in the decimal .012, the number is 12. 12 is written as the numerator. The number of decimal places is three, so the third power of ten is the denominator. Therefore $.012 = \frac{12}{1,000}.$

3. Ask the children to add $\frac{1}{4}$ and .2 using any method that they can. Discuss ways of changing the fraction into a decimal and then ways of changing the decimal into a fraction. Develop the idea of .2 as being two parts of a whole which has been divided into ten equal parts. See illustration below.

Give other picture explanations of decimal fractions in the tenth power. Ask if any similarity can be drawn between decimal fractions and what is known about common fractions. Note the similarity of $\frac{2}{10}$ and .2.

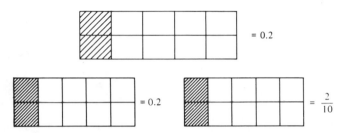

Change other decimal fractions in the tenth power to common fractions. Develop the idea of .02 as being two parts of a whole which has been divided into one-hundred equal parts. Show by similar methods decimal fractions in the thousandths and ten-thousandths power. Develop concept of .2 as being two parts of a group which has been divided into ten parts. Continue this concept in terms of hundredths and thousandths.

Concept: In a mixed decimal with identical digits (8.8), the digit in the tenths place has a value of one-tenth of the digit in the ones place

Procedures. 1. Problem situation: Matt's Dad drove Matt to the store to get some school supplies. When they got back, Matt told the family that he had been watching the speedometer and that it had been 1.1 miles to the store. Matt said that 1 mile was 10 times farther than $\frac{1}{10}$. Hence the .1 is a number $\frac{1}{10}$ the value of the 1 mile. Was Matt's reasoning correct? Prove your answer by drawing a diagram.

2. Draw diagrams representing 5 whole ones and .5 of one whole. Notice that there are 50 tenths in the 5 wholes. The whole number in 5.5 equals $\frac{50}{10}$. The decimal in 5.5 equals $\frac{5}{10}$. Therefore the digit 5 on the whole-number side is 10 times as great in value as the digit 5 on the decimal side.

3. The class has collected $4.44 for the Christmas party. How many dimes are represented in the $4.00? How many dimes in the 40 cents? The 4 on the

dollar side represents 40 dimes. The 4 on the decimal side represents 4 dimes. Therefore in $4.40 the first 4 is ten times greater in value than the second 4.

4. Distribute bundles of sticks (10 each), giving several bundles to each group of children. Assign board space (a column) for each group. Put various decimals in each column, such as:

Matt's group	Christy's group	Pam's group
2.2	3.3	4.4

Have each group show the quantity with sticks. Matt's group would show their quantity like this: ////////// ////////// //. The other groups would have similar layouts. Have Matt's group lay out their sticks in groups of twos: // // // // // // // // // // //. Have Christy's group lay out their sticks in groups of threes. Pam's group in groups of fours. Write on the board the results:

Matt's group	Christy's group	Pam's group
10 groups of 2	10 groups of 3	10 groups of 4
and	and	and
1 group of 2	1 group of 3	1 group of 4

Draw out the generalization: In a mixed number with identical digits (6.6) the digit in the tenths place has a value one tenth that of the digit in the ones place.

5. Write $6\frac{6}{10}$ on the board. Have a pupil write the decimal notation for it (6.6). Then put 6 in one place and .6 in another place on the chalkboard. Ask if the total is still 6.6. How much smaller is .6 than 6? Have several of the pupils divide 6 by various numbers. Circle the one:

$$10\overline{)6.0} \quad \begin{array}{r} .6 \\ \hline 6.0 \\ \underline{6.0} \\ .0 \end{array}$$

Repeat the procedure with 2.2, 4.4, and 9.9. This technique may be done with common fractions in similar fashion if multiplication and division of decimals have not been introduced.

Concept: The sum of two or more decimals can be found by changing them to proper fractions

Procedures. 1. It should be demonstrated that decimal fractions are a more convenient way of writing fractions whose denominators are 10, 100, 1,000, or any power of ten. Give the class mimeographed copies of a fraction-equivalency chart. Have them count by tenths and hundredths as they say the numbers. Record them both as common and decimal fractions. $\frac{1}{10} = .1, \frac{2}{10} = .2, \frac{3}{10} = .3,$

$\dfrac{1}{100} = .01$, $\dfrac{2}{100} = .02$, $\dfrac{3}{100} = .03$. By coloring parts of the diagram and by using both the common and decimal fractions to designate the colored parts, an understanding of the relationship between common fractions and decimal fractions can be gained.

2. Since problems involving mileage may be computed either by decimals or common fractions, give the class a problem and have the children work it by decimals first, then check their work by using common fractions. For example, Christy traveled the following distances: 16.8 miles, 29.1 miles, 42.7 miles, and 15.3 miles. Find the total number of miles Christy has traveled.

$$16\dfrac{8}{10}$$

16.8 $29\dfrac{1}{10}$
29.1
42.7 $42\dfrac{7}{10}$
15.3
103.9 miles $15\dfrac{3}{10}$

$$102\dfrac{19}{10} \quad \text{or} \quad 103\dfrac{9}{10} \text{ miles}$$

Concept: There are as many decimal places in the product as there are decimal places in the two numbers multiplied

Procedures. 1. Write a fractional multiplication problem, such as $4 \times \dfrac{4}{10}$, on the chalkboard and have the pupils work the example. Next substitute dimes for the tenths and show the product equals $1.60. Now write the problem on the board in decimal form: $4 \times .4$, and work it out (1.6). The 1 stands for the dollar and the .6 stands for the 6 dimes. Now approach problems where there is a decimal in the multiplier and the multiplicand. Write the fractional problem $\dfrac{6}{10} \times \dfrac{4}{10}$ on the board. Work out the problem. $\left(\dfrac{24}{100}\right)$ Now put the same problem on the board in decimal form: $.6 \times .4$. The answer is 24, but where does the decimal point go? Tenths times tenths have been multiplied, so the answer is in hundredths. The answer in decimal form becomes .24.

Write the problem $\dfrac{7}{10} \times \dfrac{46}{100}$ on the board. In fractional form the answer is $\dfrac{322}{1,000}$. ($.7 \times .46 = .322$.) Tenths times hundredths equals thousandths or three decimal places. Solve other examples with the decimal place in various positions in the multiplier and multiplicand. First solve by the common-fraction method, then by the decimal method. The generalization that should result: point off as many decimal places in the product as there are decimal places in the numbers being multiplied.

2. *Problem*: A boy walks a total of 2.7 miles a day going to and from school. How far would he walk in 5 days? Have the pupils solve the problem in any way that they can. Some will solve it by the use of a picture:

Home	2.7	School
Home	2.7	School
Home	2.7	School
Home	2.7	School
Home	2.7	School	Total 13.5 miles

Some will solve the problem in other ways:

$$2\frac{7}{10} \times 5 =$$

$$2 \times 5 = 10, \quad \frac{7}{10} \times 5 = \frac{35}{10} = 3\frac{1}{2} = 3.5$$

$$\begin{array}{r} 10 \\ 3.5 \\ \hline 13.5 \text{ miles} \end{array}$$

or

$$\begin{array}{r} 2.7 \\ 5 \\ \hline 13.5 \text{ miles} \end{array}$$

The reasoning was: by estimating the answer it was seen that 135 or 1.35 could not be right. The answer would have to be over 10 and less than 15. (2 X 5 = 10, 3 X 5 = 15) The answer would have to be 13.5.

3. *Problem*: If a motorist averages 17.5 miles per gallon, how many miles could he travel with 5.5 gallons of gasoline? Estimation shows that the answer is between 85 and 102 miles. (5 X 17 = 85, 6 X 17 = 102) Therefore

$$\begin{array}{r} 17.5 \\ \times 5.5 \\ \hline 875 \\ 875 \\ \hline 9625 \text{ or } 96.25 \text{ miles} \end{array}$$

The number multiplied is in tenths, the multiplier is in tenths. The product will be in hundredths since tenths X tenths = hundredths.

4. *Problem*: One Saturday Pam noticed that her bike meter recorded .6 of a mile for the trip to Sandy's house and back. She made 4 trips to Sandy's house that day. How far had she traveled? The students are directed to answer the problem in any way that they can.

Possible solutions:

$$\frac{6}{10} + \frac{6}{10} + \frac{6}{10} + \frac{6}{10} = \frac{24}{10} = 2\frac{4}{10}$$

or

$$\frac{6}{10} \times 4 = \frac{24}{10} = 2\frac{4}{10}$$

or

				Drawing
.6	.6	.6	.6	Numbers
six	twelve	eighteen	twenty-four	

Counts twenty-four tenths. "But how do I write it? .24? No, that would be less than one round trip. 2.4 miles—Yes, that's a reasonable answer."

or

.6 miles
4 trips
2.4 miles total for the day

5. Estimate the answer, work the example, then place the decimal point in the answer to make it like your estimate.

Example	Estimate	(a)	(b)	(c)
(a) 41.2 × 12	About 500 (12 × 40 = 480)	41.2	32.7	2.98
(b) 32.7 × 1.2	About 35 (1 × 32 = 32)	12	1.2	1.2
(c) 2.98 × 1.2	About 3 (1 × 2.98 = 2.98)	82 4	65 4	5 96
		412	327	29 8
		494.4	39.24	3.576

Concept: Both the divisor and the dividend may be multiplied by ten (or any power of ten) without changing the value of the quotient

Procedures. 1. Put the following explanation on the board: If the decimal point in .25 is moved 1 place to the right, the result is 2.5; 2 places to the right = 25; 3 places to the right = 250. Give the pupils a mixed-decimal number. (2.09) and have them practice moving the decimal point one, two, three, or four places. Illustrate your explanation by the use of the accompanying chart.

100's	10's	1's	10ths	100ths
	2	4		
2	4	0		
		3	4	6
	3	4	6	

When 24 is multiplied by 10 and becomes 240, the 2 originally in the tens place becomes 2 in the hundreds place—10 times as much. A zero has been supplied to show that there are no units to record. A similar thing happens when 3.46 is multiplied by 10. The 3 in the units place becomes 3 in the tens place, the 4 in the tenths place becomes 4 in the units place, and the 6 in the hundredths place becomes 6 in the tenths place. Each digit now has a value ten times as great as its original value.

This same device can be used for many other illustrations of multiplying by 10 and also for multiplying by 100 and 1,000. For example, if 2.4 is multiplied by 100, the 2 in the units place becomes 2 in the hundreds place, 100 times its original value; the 4 in the tenths place becomes 4 in the tens place, also 100 times its original value. A zero has been supplied to show that there are no units to record. Students have learned in previous years that to multiply by 10, they annex a zero; to multiply by 100 they annex 2 zeros, and so on. This concept applies to whole numbers. Now the pupil is shown the more general understanding, which applies to whole numbers as well as decimals, move the decimal point one place to the right when multiplying by 10, two places to the right when multiplying by 100, and so on, supplying zeros when necessary.

2. With the background skill introduced in the above technique, apply it in the division of decimals.

Problem: If the refreshments for a class of 25 comes to $4.50, how much will it cost for each person?

$$
\begin{array}{r}
\$\ .18 \text{ per person} \\
25\overline{)\,\$4.50} \\
\underline{2\,5} \\
2\,00 \\
\underline{2\,00}
\end{array}
$$

Now let's say that all ten upper classrooms totaling 250 pupils wished to buy the same kind of refreshments, and assuming no further reduction in cost due to quantity purchases, how would the $45.00 cost be divided among the pupils?

$$
\begin{array}{r}
\$\ \ .18 \text{ per person} \\
250\overline{)\,\$45.00} \\
\underline{25\,0} \\
20\,00 \\
\underline{20\,00}
\end{array}
$$

How are both of these problems alike? ($.18 per person cost for each problem.) Why, when two different sets of numbers have been divided, do we get the same answer? The reason: both the divisor and the dividend in the first problem were increased by 10. Our number system is based on ten and consequently this same thing will happen when any divisor and dividend are increased by 10 or any power of ten. The quotient will remain the same.

3. It has been previously learned that multiplying the denominator and the numerator of a fraction by the same number does not change the value of the fraction: *Example*:

$$\frac{1}{4} \times \frac{3}{3} = \frac{3}{12} = \frac{1}{4}$$

$$\frac{1}{2} \times \frac{5}{5} = \frac{5}{10} = \frac{1}{2}$$

$$\frac{1}{3} \times \frac{10}{10} = \frac{10}{30} = \frac{1}{3}$$

Since the fractional expression can also indicate *division* of the numerator by the denominator, $\left(\frac{1}{3} = 1 \text{ divided by } 3\right)$, then $\frac{1}{3} \times \frac{10}{10} = \frac{10}{30}$ could be written 1 divided by 3 = (1 × 10) divided by (3 × 10) = 10 divided by 30 or $3\overline{/1} = 30\overline{/10} = \frac{1}{3}$.

4. Consider the following problem. A scout troop brings 2 gallons of white gas on their weekend hike. If their camp lantern holds .3 gallon, how often can they fill it with their 2 gallons?

$$.2\overline{)2}^{\,?}$$

After much discussion one scout suggests that it would be the same situation if they had ten lanterns and ten 2-gallon cans of white gasoline, so they proceed to figure:

.3 gal per filling	2 gal per can
×10 lanterns	×10 cans
3.0 gal per filling	20 gallons available

$$
\begin{array}{c}
6 \text{ fillings} \\
3 \text{ gal}\overline{)20} \\
\underline{18} \\
2 \text{ gal. remaining}
\end{array}
\qquad \text{or} \qquad
.3/2 = 3.\overline{)20}^{\,6\frac{2}{3}}
\quad
\begin{array}{c}
\underline{18} \\
2
\end{array}
$$

The scouts find that they have enough gasoline to fill their lantern six and two-thirds times.

Concept: Introducing percent and the relationship between fractions, decimals, and percent

Procedures. 1. Make two-inch circles and divide them into the following fractional parts— $\frac{1}{2}$'s, $\frac{1}{4}$'s, $\frac{1}{3}$'s, $\frac{1}{5}$'s, $\frac{1}{6}$'s, $\frac{1}{8}$'s, $\frac{1}{10}$'s, $\frac{1}{12}$'s, and $\frac{1}{16}$'s —nine circles in all. Write the fraction, the decimal, and the percent in each part of the circle. Make a chart above each circle:

1 part	$\frac{1}{4}$	.25	25%
2 parts	$\frac{2}{4}$	.50	50%
3 parts	$\frac{3}{4}$	.75	75%
4 parts	$\frac{4}{4}$	1.00	100%

Use these to show the relationship between fractions, decimals, and percent.

2. Construct 100 empty thread spools of the same size on a heavy piece of string. Make several colored disks from heavy cardboard, place a hole in the center so that they will fit on the string. Use this device in introducing percent. Emphasize that percent means hundredths, and use the above device to demonstrate it. Use the disks to divide the spools into parts. Start with dividing the spools in the middle—50 percent—ask the pupils how many spools are on either side of the disk. (50) What would this be as a fraction? $\left(\frac{1}{2}\right)$ Ask them how this would be written if they were talking about money? ($.50) Therefore 50 percent can be written as $\frac{1}{2}$, $.50, or 50%. Do the same thing for $12\frac{1}{2}$%, $33\frac{1}{3}$%, and others. Ask a child to come and place a disk at $12\frac{1}{2}$ spools, how many $12\frac{1}{2}$'s are there in 100 spools? (8) Therefore $12\frac{1}{2}$ would be $\frac{1}{8}$ of the complete set. Use the procedure with all of the most common fractions.

3. Draw on the board a number line extending from zero to slightly past 1. (Or use a thread or wire with 100 beads on it.) On the number line mark off in hundredths. Have a pupil indicate half of the line, then one-fourth of the line, and three-fourths of the line. Ask how this would be read if pupils were reading it as hundredths. The pupils will see that $\frac{1}{4}$ of the line is the equivalent of 25

beads, or $\dfrac{25}{100}$; that $\dfrac{1}{2}$ of the line is equivalent to 50 beads or $\dfrac{50}{100}$. Lead

them to see that 1 part of the line, or 1 bead is equal to $\dfrac{1}{100}$ of the total line or

total number of beads. Now show that there is a different way to express $\dfrac{1}{100}$.

Call it $\dfrac{1}{100}$ or .01, or 1%. Percent implies counting by hundredths. Continue

with other fractional parts, showing that $\dfrac{1}{2}$ of the number line is 50 beads, or

$\dfrac{50}{100}$ or .50 or 50%.

4. Have the pupils bring to class various items, containing on the label a list of the contents and the sign "%," or assemble prior to class, items containing in their analysis the "%" sign.

Discuss with the class what the sign "%" means. For example, if a sweater is 50% wool, 25% rayon, and 25% mohair, lead the pupils to see that this means that half of the contents of the sweater are wool, $\dfrac{1}{4}$ of the contents are rayon,

and $\dfrac{1}{4}$ of the contents are mohair. $\left(50\% = \dfrac{50}{100} = \dfrac{1}{2}, 25\% = \dfrac{25}{100} = \dfrac{1}{4}\right)$ Demon-

strate this by blocking off a portion of a sweater and show how it would look if the fabrics weren't all mixed together.

5. Have prepared for class several boards, which can be made from acoustical tile or pegboard. The boards should have 10 rows of holes, 10 holes in each row. Explain to the class that today they are going to learn a new way to divide a whole number into its fractional parts. Have them count the number of holes in a row. (10) Have them count the number of rows. (10) Therefore, there are how many holes in the board? (100) Ask the pupils to cover half of the holes with their hands or a piece of paper. How many holes are covered? Of the 100

holes 50 or $\dfrac{50}{100}$ are covered. From this conclusion, lead the class to see that

$\dfrac{1}{2} = \dfrac{50}{100} = 50\%$. Explain to the class that when something is called percent,

you are simply dividing it into 100 parts, and talking about a certain number of those parts. Develop other fractional parts.

6. Have the pupils bring to school or prepare for the class a bulletin board containing various news items involving percent. Study should be directed toward the understanding that percent is a ratio of two numbers, with the denominator being 100. Use counting blocks, arrange them in a large square of 100

blocks. Have a pupil remove one block. This is $\dfrac{1}{100}$ of the entire square, or

1 percent. Have them remove other blocks and tell what fractional part of the square has been removed.

PRACTICE AND EVALUATION

Concepts of Fractions and Fractional Parts

1. What part of each of the figures has been shaded?

——————   ——————   ——————   ——————   ——————

2. Color the part of the set indicated by the numeral:

$\frac{1}{4}$ OOOOOOOOOOOOOOOO

$\frac{1}{2}$ OOOOOOOOOOOOOO

$\frac{1}{3}$ OOOOOOOOOOOO

3. Use the flannelboard or chalkboard for simple diagrams. Ask the child to draw a ring around (a) one-half, (b) one-fourth, (c) one-third.

```
x x   x x      x x x      x x x x
 x   x         x x x      x x x x
   (a)          (b)         (c)
```

4. Duplicate sheets with various shapes on them. Have the children draw lines dividing each shape into two parts of the same size. Encourage variety.

5. Draw a ring around the correct numeral:

$\frac{1}{2}$ $\frac{1}{3}$ $\frac{1}{4}$ $\frac{1}{2}$ $\frac{1}{3}$ $\frac{1}{4}$ $\frac{1}{2}$ $\frac{1}{3}$ $\frac{1}{4}$ $\frac{1}{2}$ $\frac{1}{3}$ $\frac{1}{4}$

6. Color $\frac{1}{2}$ of each picture:

7. Color $\frac{1}{3}$ of each set:

8. Write the correct numeral for the shaded part of each figure:

(a) _____   (b) _____   (c) _____   (d) _____

9. Color $\frac{1}{3}$ Color $\frac{3}{4}$ Color $\frac{1}{2}$ Color $\frac{2}{6}$

10. Write the correct numeral for the part that you did not color in each picture above.

(a) _____   (b) _____   (c) _____   (d) _____

11. State which is more:

$\frac{1}{2}$ or $\frac{1}{4}$ _____

$\frac{1}{4}$ or $\frac{1}{3}$ _____

$\frac{1}{3}$ or $\frac{1}{2}$ _____

12. State which is less:

$\frac{1}{2}$ or $\frac{1}{3}$ _____

$\frac{1}{6}$ or $\frac{1}{5}$ _____

$\frac{1}{4}$ or $\frac{1}{8}$ _____

13. Complete the statement:

There are _____ halves in a whole pie.
There are _____ thirds in a whole pie.
There are _____ sixths in a whole pie.
There are _____ fourths in a whole pie.

14. Write the fraction in figures:

There are eight boys playing together. Three boys have bikes.
_____ of the group have bikes.

One boy has a wagon. _____ of the boys have wagons.

Two boys have scooters. _____ of the group of boys have scooters.

Two boys are playing with trucks. _____ of the group of boys are playing with trucks.

15. Write the missing numerators:

$$\frac{2}{3} = \frac{}{6} \qquad \frac{1}{2} = \frac{}{4} \qquad \frac{1}{4} = \frac{}{16} \qquad 1 = \frac{}{3} \qquad \frac{6}{8} = \frac{}{4}$$

$$\frac{7}{8} = \frac{}{16} \qquad \frac{14}{18} = \frac{}{9} \qquad \frac{2}{6} = \frac{}{3} \qquad \frac{10}{12} = \frac{}{6} \qquad \frac{4}{5} = \frac{}{15}$$

16. Draw a circle around the largest fraction:

$$\frac{1}{2} \qquad \frac{1}{10} \qquad \frac{1}{5} \qquad \frac{1}{8} \qquad \frac{1}{6} \qquad \frac{1}{9} \qquad \frac{1}{7} \qquad \frac{1}{3}$$

17. Draw a square around the smallest fraction:

$$\frac{1}{2} \qquad \frac{1}{10} \qquad \frac{1}{5} \qquad \frac{1}{8} \qquad \frac{1}{6} \qquad \frac{1}{9} \qquad \frac{1}{7} \qquad \frac{1}{3}$$

18. Arrange the fractions according to value. Begin with the largest fraction:

$$\frac{1}{10} \qquad \frac{1}{4} \qquad \frac{1}{7} \qquad \frac{1}{9} \qquad \frac{1}{8} \qquad \frac{1}{5} \qquad \frac{1}{3} \qquad \frac{1}{6}$$

_____ _____ _____ _____ _____ _____ _____ _____

19. Change the fractions to lowest terms:

$$\frac{6}{16} = \underline{\hspace{1cm}} \qquad \frac{10}{12} = \underline{\hspace{1cm}} \qquad \frac{4}{12} = \underline{\hspace{1cm}} \qquad \frac{5}{20} = \underline{\hspace{1cm}}$$

$$\frac{14}{21} = \underline{\hspace{1cm}} \qquad \frac{8}{10} = \underline{\hspace{1cm}} \qquad \frac{18}{24} = \underline{\hspace{1cm}} \qquad \frac{7}{14} = \underline{\hspace{1cm}}$$

20. Write the missing numerator:

$$\frac{2}{3} = \frac{}{21} \qquad \frac{8}{12} = \frac{}{3} \qquad \frac{45}{54} = \frac{}{6} \qquad \frac{2}{3} = \frac{}{15}$$

21. Change to improper fractions:

$$3\frac{2}{3} = \underline{\hspace{1cm}} \qquad 5\frac{1}{2} = \underline{\hspace{1cm}} \qquad 4\frac{3}{4} = \underline{\hspace{1cm}} \qquad 2\frac{1}{4} = \underline{\hspace{1cm}} \qquad 2\frac{5}{9} = \underline{\hspace{1cm}}$$

22. Change to whole or mixed numbers:

$$\frac{30}{5} = \underline{\hspace{1cm}} \qquad \frac{7}{4} = \underline{\hspace{1cm}} \qquad \frac{15}{12} = \underline{\hspace{1cm}} \qquad \frac{10}{2} = \underline{\hspace{1cm}} \qquad \frac{11}{8} = \underline{\hspace{1cm}}$$

23. Find the lowest common denominator:

$$\frac{1}{2}, \frac{3}{4}, \frac{5}{8} \quad \underline{\hspace{1cm}} \qquad\qquad \frac{5}{6}, \frac{1}{5}, \frac{1}{4}, \frac{1}{2} \quad \underline{\hspace{1cm}}$$

$\dfrac{1}{3}, \dfrac{5}{6}, \dfrac{3}{5}$ _____

$\dfrac{5}{8}, \dfrac{3}{10}, \dfrac{3}{5}, \dfrac{1}{4}$ _____

$\dfrac{1}{2}, \dfrac{2}{3}, \dfrac{3}{4}$ _____

$\dfrac{7}{12}, \dfrac{3}{4}, \dfrac{3}{8}, \dfrac{1}{6}, \dfrac{2}{3}$ _____

24. Complete the patterns:

$\dfrac{3}{6}, 1, 1\dfrac{3}{6},$ _____ , _____ , _____ , _____

$1\dfrac{1}{2}, 3, 4\dfrac{1}{2},$ _____ , _____ , _____ , _____ , _____

8, 4, 2, 1, _____ , _____ , _____ , _____

25. Write 10 numerals you can think of for each fractional number:

$\dfrac{1}{6} \qquad \dfrac{2}{3} \qquad \dfrac{5}{8} \qquad \dfrac{8}{9} \qquad \dfrac{6}{6}$

26. Arrange the elements in the following sets of fractions in order from the least to the greatest:

$$C = \left\{ \dfrac{1}{3}, \dfrac{4}{5}, \dfrac{3}{4}, \dfrac{6}{6}, \dfrac{8}{4}, \dfrac{1}{6} \right\}$$

$$D = \left\{ \dfrac{3}{4}, \dfrac{1}{6}, \dfrac{4}{3}, \dfrac{1}{2}, \dfrac{1}{5} \right\}$$

27. Which of the following are names for whole numbers?

$\dfrac{14}{7} \qquad \dfrac{3}{9} \qquad \dfrac{7}{14} \qquad \dfrac{9}{3}$

28. True or false:

$\dfrac{3}{4} = \dfrac{75}{100} \qquad \dfrac{2}{3} = \dfrac{20}{30} \qquad \dfrac{1}{5} = \dfrac{5}{1} \qquad \dfrac{12}{4} = \dfrac{4}{1}$

29. Circle the greatest fractional number in each pair:

$\dfrac{6}{3}, \dfrac{5}{4} \qquad \dfrac{1}{1}, \dfrac{19}{18} \qquad \dfrac{3}{5}, \dfrac{5}{3} \qquad \dfrac{6}{9}, \dfrac{6}{8}$

30. Using a region, show the meaning of the fractional number $\dfrac{6}{7}$.

31. Using sets, show the meaning of the fractional number $\dfrac{4}{6}$ and indicate how $\dfrac{4}{6}$ can be renamed.

Addition and Subtraction of Fractions

1. Complete the equations:

$\dfrac{1}{4}+\dfrac{1}{4}=$ _____ $\dfrac{1}{4}+\dfrac{1}{3}=$ _____ $\dfrac{2}{4}+\dfrac{1}{4}=$ _____

$\dfrac{4}{6}+\dfrac{1}{6}=$ _____ $\dfrac{5}{6}+\dfrac{1}{6}=$ _____ $\dfrac{1}{3}+\dfrac{1}{3}=$ _____

2. Using the number line, find the sums:

0   1

$\dfrac{3}{10}+\dfrac{4}{10}=$ _____ $\dfrac{1}{2}+\dfrac{1}{5}=$ _____ $\dfrac{2}{5}+\dfrac{3}{10}=$ _____

3. Rename the number with a common denominator, then find the sum:

$\dfrac{1}{2}+\dfrac{1}{6}=$ _____ $\dfrac{3}{8}+\dfrac{1}{4}=$ _____ $\dfrac{2}{5}+\dfrac{3}{10}=$ _____ $+\dfrac{1}{6}=$ _____

4. Find the missing addends:

_____ $+\dfrac{2}{4}=\dfrac{3}{4}$ $\dfrac{2}{7}+$ _____ $=\dfrac{7}{7}$ $\dfrac{3}{5}-\dfrac{2}{5}=$ _____ $\dfrac{5}{5}-\dfrac{3}{5}=$ _____

5. Subtract and check by rewriting each problem below as an addition problem:

$\dfrac{5}{6}-\dfrac{1}{3}=$ _____ $\dfrac{6}{9}-\dfrac{2}{9}=$ _____ $\dfrac{9}{1}-\dfrac{1}{3}=$ _____

6. Draw diagrams to help you complete each question:

$\dfrac{1}{2}+\dfrac{1}{4}=$ _____ _____ $+\dfrac{1}{2}=\dfrac{4}{6}$ $\dfrac{2}{8}+\dfrac{3}{8}=$ _____

7. Solve each equation:

$2\dfrac{1}{4}+\dfrac{2}{4}=$ _____ $\dfrac{5}{8}+1\dfrac{3}{8}=$ _____ $\dfrac{2}{6}+4\dfrac{2}{3}=$ _____ $3\dfrac{4}{5}+2\dfrac{3}{5}=$ _____

8. Subtract and check by writing an addition equation for each subtraction equation:

$6\dfrac{5}{6}-\dfrac{2}{6}=$ _____ $4\dfrac{3}{4}-\dfrac{1}{2}=$ _____ $2\dfrac{1}{3}-1\dfrac{2}{3}=$ _____

9. True or false:

$\dfrac{2}{3}+\dfrac{1}{4}=\dfrac{1}{4}+\dfrac{2}{3}$ $\dfrac{5}{8}+\dfrac{2}{3}=\dfrac{2}{3}+\dfrac{5}{8}$ $\dfrac{3}{4}-\dfrac{2}{4}=\dfrac{2}{4}-\dfrac{3}{4}$

10. Find the prime factors of the numerator and denominator of each fraction:

$\dfrac{6}{8}$ $\dfrac{9}{12}$ $\dfrac{12}{15}$ $\dfrac{4}{8}$ $\dfrac{15}{25}$

11. Rewrite in lowest terms:

$$\frac{7}{30} \qquad \frac{10}{12} \quad \frac{4}{6} \quad \frac{15}{16} \qquad \frac{7}{8} \quad \frac{3}{12} \quad \frac{8}{12} \quad \frac{4}{10} \quad \frac{9}{12} \qquad \frac{4}{6}$$

12. Add or subtract as indicated:

$$6\frac{2}{3} + 8\frac{1}{8} = \underline{\quad\quad} \qquad 5\frac{1}{4} + 4\frac{2}{3} = \underline{\quad\quad} \qquad 6\frac{2}{3} + 2\frac{5}{12} = \underline{\quad\quad}$$

$$7\frac{11}{12} - 2\frac{3}{12} = \underline{\quad\quad} \qquad 5\frac{1}{2} + 3\frac{1}{3} = \underline{\quad\quad} \qquad 5\frac{5}{8} - 1\frac{3}{8} = \underline{\quad\quad}$$

13. Change each fraction to a mixed number or whole number:

$$\frac{3}{2} = \underline{\quad} \qquad \frac{5}{3} = \underline{\quad} \qquad \frac{8}{4} = \underline{\quad} \qquad \frac{4}{2} = \underline{\quad} \qquad \frac{6}{4} = \underline{\quad}$$

14. Change each fraction to a higher term:

$$\frac{1}{2} = \frac{}{8} \qquad \frac{1}{4} = \frac{}{8} \qquad \frac{1}{5} = \frac{}{10} \qquad \frac{3}{6} = \frac{}{12} \qquad \frac{1}{3} = \frac{}{3}$$

15. Solve:

$$32\frac{1}{7} - 19\frac{3}{8} = \underline{\quad\quad} \qquad 10\frac{1}{4} - 8\frac{5}{6} = \underline{\quad\quad} \qquad 41\frac{3}{12} - 26\frac{2}{3} = \underline{\quad\quad}$$

16. Solve:

Matt cut a piece $2\frac{2}{3}$ ft long from a board that was 8 ft long. How many feet were left?

Last weekend, Steve spent 5 hours helping his father in the garden. If he worked $4\frac{3}{4}$ hours on Saturday, how long did he work on Sunday?

Mr. Baker's farm has $27\frac{1}{2}$ acres of wooded land and the buildings take up 5 acres and the pasture $63\frac{2}{3}$ acres. The rest of the farm is planted with crops. How many acres of crops did he have?

17. Solve:

$$5\frac{3}{8} - \frac{2}{3} = \underline{\quad\quad} \qquad 6\frac{4}{9} - 2\frac{3}{10} = \underline{\quad\quad} \qquad 6\frac{7}{8} - 2\frac{2}{3} = \underline{\quad\quad}$$

18. Change to improper fraction:

$$3\frac{2}{3} = \underline{\quad\quad} \qquad 4\frac{3}{4} = \underline{\quad\quad} \qquad 8\frac{7}{8} = \underline{\quad\quad} \qquad 2\frac{1}{4} \underline{\quad\quad}$$

19. Change to a whole or mixed number:

$$\frac{20}{5} = \underline{\quad\quad} \qquad \frac{11}{8} = \underline{\quad\quad} \qquad \frac{42}{7} = \underline{\quad\quad}$$

$$\frac{9}{3} = \underline{\quad\quad} \qquad \frac{15}{12} = \underline{\quad\quad}$$

20. Solve the equations:

$$\frac{3}{4} + \frac{5}{8} + \frac{1}{2} = \underline{\hspace{2cm}} \qquad 2\frac{2}{3} + 3\frac{3}{4} + 1\frac{1}{8} = \underline{\hspace{2cm}}$$

$$\frac{1}{4} + \frac{1}{3} + \frac{3}{8} = \underline{\hspace{2cm}} \qquad 4\frac{1}{2} + 6\frac{3}{4} + 3\frac{5}{8} = \underline{\hspace{2cm}}$$

21. Find the lowest common denominator:

$$\frac{1}{2}, \frac{3}{4}, \frac{5}{8} \underline{\hspace{6cm}}$$

$$\frac{5}{6}, \frac{1}{5}, \frac{1}{4}, \frac{1}{2} \underline{\hspace{5cm}}$$

$$\frac{5}{8}, \frac{3}{10}, \frac{3}{5}, \frac{1}{4} \underline{\hspace{5cm}}$$

$$\frac{7}{12}, \frac{3}{4}, \frac{3}{8}, \frac{1}{6}, \frac{2}{3} \underline{\hspace{5cm}}$$

22. Solve:

$$9\frac{3}{8} - \frac{3}{4} = \underline{\hspace{1.5cm}} \qquad 7\frac{1}{3} - \frac{3}{5} = \underline{\hspace{1.5cm}} \qquad 4\frac{1}{3} - \frac{7}{12} = \underline{\hspace{1.5cm}}$$

$$5\frac{1}{2} - 3\frac{3}{4} = \underline{\hspace{1.5cm}} \qquad 6\frac{5}{12} - 2\frac{2}{3} = \underline{\hspace{1.5cm}} \qquad 3\frac{3}{4} - 1\frac{1}{8} = \underline{\hspace{1.5cm}}$$

23. Find the missing number:

$$1\frac{3}{4} + \underline{\hspace{1.5cm}} = 2 \qquad 12\frac{3}{4} - 2\frac{7}{8} = \underline{\hspace{1.5cm}} \qquad 3\frac{1}{8} - 1\frac{1}{4} = \underline{\hspace{1.5cm}}$$

$$\underline{\hspace{1.5cm}} - \frac{5}{16} = 3\frac{3}{8} \qquad \frac{4}{5} = \underline{\hspace{1.5cm}} \qquad \underline{\hspace{0.8cm}} + \frac{1}{2} \quad 8 - \underline{\hspace{1cm}} = 4\frac{7}{8}$$

24. (a) Write 2.3 as the sum of four (4) unit fractions. (b) Write $\frac{3}{4}$ as the sum of two (2) unit fractions.

Multiplication of Fractions

1. State answers in simplest form:

$$9 \times \frac{1}{3} = \underline{\hspace{1cm}} \qquad 6 \times \frac{1}{6} = \underline{\hspace{1cm}} \qquad 2 \times \frac{1}{3} = \underline{\hspace{1cm}} \qquad 8 \times \frac{1}{5} = \underline{\hspace{1cm}}$$

$$7 \times \frac{1}{9} = \underline{\hspace{1cm}} \qquad 1 \times \frac{1}{12} = \underline{\hspace{1cm}} \qquad 15 \times \frac{1}{13} = \underline{\hspace{1cm}} \qquad 6 \times \frac{1}{4} = \underline{\hspace{1cm}}$$

2. Solve:

Pamela needs $\frac{1}{3}$ cup of shelled nuts to make a batch of cookies. How many cups of nuts does she need for 6 batches of cookies?

Matt drinks $\frac{1}{2}$ pint of milk three times a day. How much milk does he drink each day?

Christy bought 4 candy bars. Each candy bar weighed $\frac{1}{3}$ of a pound. Find the weight of all the candy bars.

Andrew feeds his dog $\frac{1}{4}$ of a pound of beef every day. How many pounds of beef does he need to feed his dog a month? (Count the month as 30 days.)

3. State the products in the simplest form:

$2 \times \frac{1}{3} =$ _____ $6 \times \frac{5}{8} =$ _____ $4 \times \frac{1}{5} =$ _____ $16 \times \frac{3}{8} =$ _____

$7 \times \frac{5}{6} =$ _____ $9 \times \frac{2}{4} =$ _____ $3 \times \frac{4}{9} =$ _____ $4 \times \frac{7}{8} =$ _____

4. Solve:

Andrew earns $\frac{3}{5}$ cents for each advertisement he delivers. How much will he earn for delivering 150 advertisements?

If a hiker strides $\frac{5}{6}$ of a yard in one step, how far will he travel in 600 steps?

If each person at a banquet eats $\frac{2}{3}$ pound of turkey, how many pounds of turkey will be needed to serve 94 people?

How many grapefruit will be needed to serve 12 people if each person receives $\frac{1}{2}$ grapefruit?

5. State the products in simplest form:

$\frac{2}{3} \times 4 =$ _____ $5 \times \frac{9}{11} =$ _____ $6 \times \frac{2}{5} =$ _____ $3 \times \frac{9}{12} =$ _____

$4 \times \frac{9}{14} =$ _____ $\frac{1}{4} \times 5 =$ _____ $\frac{3}{8} \times 7 =$ _____ $\frac{4}{5} \times 6 =$ _____

6. State the products in simplest form:

$\frac{1}{2} \times \frac{1}{3} =$ _____ $\frac{1}{4} \times \frac{1}{6} =$ _____ $\frac{3}{4} \times \frac{1}{4} =$ _____ $\frac{1}{2} \times \frac{3}{5} =$ _____

$\frac{2}{3} \times \frac{4}{5} =$ _____ $\frac{5}{6} \times \frac{1}{4} =$ _____ $\frac{1}{4} \times \frac{1}{4} =$ _____ $\frac{1}{4} \times \frac{3}{8} =$ _____

7. Solve:

Shirley practices her piano for $\frac{3}{4}$ hour each day. If $\frac{1}{5}$ of her practice time is spent working on the scales, how many minutes will she have left each day for the remainder of her piano practice?

Bob walks $\frac{2}{3}$ mile to take his trumpet lesson, and Andrew walks $\frac{2}{3}$ as far to take his dancing lesson. How far does Andrew walk?

8. State the products in simplest form:

$\frac{5}{6} \times \frac{10}{10} =$ _____ $\frac{5}{8} \times \frac{2}{3} =$ _____ $\frac{1}{2} \times \frac{2}{3} =$ _____ $\frac{4}{5} \times \frac{1}{8} =$ _____

$\frac{1}{6} \times \frac{2}{3} =$ _____ $\frac{7}{8} \times \frac{a}{5} =$ _____ $\frac{5}{6} \times \frac{7}{10} =$ _____ $\frac{1}{3} \times \frac{3}{5} =$ _____

9. Change to improper fractions.

$2\frac{1}{2} =$ _____ $3\frac{2}{3} =$ _____ $7\frac{1}{6} =$ _____ $3\frac{5}{12} =$ _____

10. Change to mixed numbers:

$\frac{11}{3} =$ _____ $\frac{13}{10} =$ _____ $\frac{7}{2} =$ _____ $\frac{15}{9} =$ _____ $\frac{9}{5} =$ _____

11. State answers in simplest form:

$3 \times 1\frac{9}{10} =$ _____ $3\frac{3}{4} \times 8 =$ _____ $4\frac{1}{2} \times 7 =$ _____ $2\frac{2}{3} \times 3 =$ _____

$1\frac{5}{9} \times 4 =$ _____ $3\frac{5}{6} \times 4 =$ _____ $4\frac{1}{3} \times 6 =$ _____ $5 \times \frac{7}{12} =$ _____

12. Solve:

Pam took $2\frac{2}{3}$ hours to make a doll dress. If Christy made one in $\frac{3}{4}$ the time it took Pam, how long did it take Christy to make her doll dress?

Anna had $3\frac{1}{2}$ yards of material. She gave $\frac{1}{3}$ of it to Mabel. How many yards did she give Mabel?

13. State the products in simplest form:

$2\frac{1}{3} \times 1\frac{3}{4} =$ _____ $1\frac{6}{8} \times 5\frac{2}{4} =$ _____ $2\frac{2}{3} \times 6\frac{1}{2} =$ _____

$3\frac{6}{8} \times 6\frac{2}{3} =$ _____ $1\frac{1}{3} \times 9\frac{3}{5} =$ _____ $4\frac{1}{2} \times 2\frac{2}{3} =$ _____

14. Solve:

Mrs. Baker has a teakwood coffee table $4\frac{2}{3}$ ft long and $2\frac{1}{8}$ ft wide which she wants to cover with glass. The glass cost $2\frac{1}{5}$ per square foot.

(a) What is the area of the piece of glass? (b) How much would the glass cost Mr. Baker?

Christy's recipe for hot cocoa used $3\frac{1}{4}$ squares of dark chocolate. One evening Christy made cocoa twice and her mother made $1\frac{1}{2}$ times the recipe. How much chocolate did they use during the evening?

15. State the products in the simplest form:

$43 \times 3\frac{1}{2} =$ _____ $29 \times 21\frac{2}{3} =$ _____ $28 \times 17\frac{1}{2} =$ _____ $14\frac{1}{9} \times 50 =$ _____

16. State the products in simplest form:

$10 \times \frac{3}{4} =$ _____ $25 \times \frac{5}{6} =$ _____ $15 \times \frac{2}{5} =$ _____ $36 \times \frac{2}{9} =$ _____

17. Solve:

Lou read in the newspaper that the average rainfall for each month during the past year had been $\frac{9}{10}$ in. What was the total rainfall for the year?

Mary's cookie recipe calls for $\frac{3}{4}$ cup of sugar. How many cups of sugar did she use in the six batches of cookies she baked?

Division of Fractions

1. Solve by the common-denominator method and prove by the inversion method:

Common-denominator method	Inversion method
$6 \div \frac{2}{3} = \frac{18}{3} \div \frac{2}{3} = 9$	$6 \div \frac{2}{3} = 6 \times \frac{3}{2} = 9$

$5 \div \frac{1}{4} =$ _____ $10 \div \frac{2}{5} =$ _____ $6 \div \frac{1}{3} =$ _____

$\frac{7}{8} \div \frac{5}{8} =$ _____ $\frac{1}{2} \div \frac{1}{8} =$ _____ $\frac{3}{5} \div \frac{3}{8} =$ _____

$1\frac{1}{2} \div \frac{3}{5} =$ _____ $2\frac{1}{4} \div \frac{9}{10} =$ _____ $4\frac{1}{3} \div 2\frac{5}{8} =$ _____

$18 \div 2\frac{1}{4} =$ _____ $25 \div 3\frac{3}{4} =$ _____ $10 \div 7\frac{1}{2} =$ _____

$2\frac{1}{2} \div 4 =$ _____ $3\frac{1}{6} \div 4 =$ _____ $2\frac{1}{4} \div 5 =$ _____

$\frac{1}{2} \div \frac{1}{3} =$ _____ $\frac{3}{8} \div \frac{1}{3} =$ _____ $\frac{4}{5} \div \frac{2}{3} =$ _____

$$\frac{2}{3} \div 1\frac{3}{5} = \underline{\hspace{1cm}} \qquad \frac{3}{4} \div 2\frac{5}{8} = \underline{\hspace{1cm}} \qquad \frac{5}{6} \div 8\frac{1}{3} = \underline{\hspace{1cm}}$$

$$4\frac{1}{3} \div 3\frac{1}{3} = \underline{\hspace{1cm}} \qquad 4\frac{1}{8} \div 1\frac{1}{4} = \underline{\hspace{1cm}} \qquad 2\frac{1}{2} \div 3\frac{1}{4} = \underline{\hspace{1cm}}$$

2. Solve:

Anna Louise has 9 cups of flour. Her cake recipe calls for $2\frac{1}{4}$ cups of flour. How many cakes can she make?

Matt needs to know how many boards $1\frac{3}{4}$ feet long he can cut from a board 7 feet long. How many boards can he cut?

Christy took $2\frac{1}{4}$ hours to make 3 doll dresses. How long did it take her to make one dress? How many minutes is this?

Pamela has $2\frac{2}{3}$ yards of material to use in making 6 doll dresses. How much material can she use for each dress?

If $\frac{7}{10}$ of an inch of snow falls in $1\frac{1}{4}$ hours, what is the average snowfall per hour?

From $\frac{7}{8}$ ounce of yarn Mary knitted $2\frac{1}{4}$ flowers. Each flower took _____ ounces of yarn.

Concepts of Decimal Fractions and Decimal Parts

1. Write as a decimal:

$$\frac{3}{4} = \underline{\hspace{1cm}} \qquad \frac{3}{5} = \underline{\hspace{1cm}} \qquad \frac{1}{2} = \underline{\hspace{1cm}} \qquad \frac{8}{20} = \underline{\hspace{1cm}}$$

2. Write as a decimal correct to hundredths place:

$$\frac{7}{8} = \underline{\hspace{1cm}} \qquad \frac{5}{6} = \underline{\hspace{1cm}} \qquad \frac{3}{9} = \underline{\hspace{1cm}} \qquad \frac{3}{7} = \underline{\hspace{1cm}}$$

3. Write as a decimal correct to thousandths place:

$$\frac{4}{5} = \underline{\hspace{1cm}} \qquad \frac{1}{3} = \underline{\hspace{1cm}} \qquad \frac{1}{25} = \underline{\hspace{1cm}} \qquad \frac{1}{30} = \underline{\hspace{1cm}}$$

4. Write as a fraction in lowest terms:

$$.2 = \underline{\hspace{1cm}} \qquad .375 = \underline{\hspace{1cm}} \qquad .83\frac{1}{3} = \underline{\hspace{1cm}} \qquad .125 = \underline{\hspace{1cm}}$$

5. Which is larger?

$$\frac{9}{16} \text{ or } \frac{8}{15} \underline{\hspace{1cm}} \qquad .08\frac{1}{3} \text{ or } \frac{1}{12} \underline{\hspace{1cm}}$$

$\dfrac{1}{2}$ or .55 _____ $\dfrac{5}{6}$ or .85 _____

$\dfrac{9}{20}$ or .44 _____   .14 or $\dfrac{1}{7}$ _____

6. Change to decimal form:

$\dfrac{7}{100} =$ _____ $\dfrac{45}{100} =$ _____ $\dfrac{6}{1000} =$ _____ $\dfrac{305}{1000} =$ _____

7. Change to common fraction form in lowest terms:

.75 = _____   .6 = _____   .04 = _____   .80 = _____   .15 = _____

8. Change to decimal form:

$\dfrac{2}{3} =$ _____ $\dfrac{7}{8} =$ _____ $\dfrac{1}{15} =$ _____ $\dfrac{5}{12} =$ _____ $\dfrac{5}{40} =$ _____

9. Change to common fraction form in lowest terms:

$.12\dfrac{1}{2} =$ _____ $.37\dfrac{1}{2} =$ _____ $.91\dfrac{2}{3} =$ _____ $.06\dfrac{1}{4} =$ _____ $.22\dfrac{1}{2} =$ _____

10. Change to decimal form and round to nearest hundredth:

$\dfrac{2}{3} =$ _____ $\dfrac{7}{32} =$ _____ $\dfrac{19}{36} =$ _____ $\dfrac{8}{11} =$ _____ $\dfrac{7}{9} =$ _____

11. Write as fractions in simplest form:

.66 = _____   .875 = _____   .7 = _____   .003 = _____   .025 = _____

Decimals—Addition

1. Use one of these two methods to find the sums:

(a)   .87 + .38 = (.8 + .07) + (.3 + .08)   (b)   .87 = .8 + .07
          = (.8 + .3) + (.07 + .08)   +.38 = .3 + .08
          = 1.1 + .15   1.1 + .15 = 1.25
          = 1.25

.4 + .3 + .6   = ____   .66 + .74 + .37   = ____

9.64 + 9.67 + 7.48   = ____   7.90 + 5.73 + 4.82   = ____

9.84 + 3.3 + 27.1 + .8 + 75.3 = ____   69.23 + 14.29 + 6.30 + 45.89 = ____

1.2 + 1.5 + 2.4   = ____   7.39 + 632   = ____

Decimals—Subtraction

1. Use one of the two methods to find the missing addend as shown above:

7.3 − 4.5   = ____   50.4 − 6.5   = ____   16.35 − 8.06 = ____

14.605 − 8.295 = ____   8.82 − 4.79 = ____   8.5 − 6.8   = ____

73.1 − 26.5   = ____   9.09 − .59   = ____   60.04 − 4.89 = ____

Decimals—Multiplication

1. Use one of the two methods to find the missing product as shown above:

524 × .6 = _____	4,436 × .66 = _____
.43 × 1,894 = _____	2.6 × 4,275 = _____
1.009 × 11 = _____	20.40 × 702 = _____
15.45 × .09 = _____	.6874 × 7.14 = _____
.7904 × .510 = _____	.3094 × 4.26 = _____
.57 × 1,400 = _____	.9 × 704 = _____
6,340 × 8.9 = _____	.327 × 5 = _____
7.081 × 303 = _____	.740 × 6.3 = _____
.246 × .5 = _____	
7.093 × .409 = _____	

Decimals—Division

1. Find the missing factor:

$3\overline{)38.4}$ $45\overline{)19.35}$ $14\overline{)44.62}$ $71\overline{)63.19}$ $8\overline{)72.80}$

$5.4\overline{)448.2}$ $2.1\overline{)4.41}$ $7.7\overline{)64.68}$ $1.22\overline{)14.762}$ $.34\overline{)2.074}$

$.061\overline{)2,319}$ $.033\overline{)1,782}$ $6.1\overline{)2,501}$ $.14\overline{)84}$ $3.1\overline{)3,689}$

$5\overline{)3}$ $12\overline{)9}$ $20\overline{)4}$ $30\overline{)9}$ $28\overline{)7}$ $4\overline{)3}$ $5\overline{)3}$

Decimals—Problems (Addition and Subraction)

1. Solve:

During one day 4.26 in. of rain fell. This was .68 of an inch more than the record set in 1894. The 1894 record was how many inches?

From Springfield to Roseburg is 72.5 miles and from Roseburg to Myrtle Creek is 19.6 miles. How far is it from Springfield to Myrtle Creek by way of Roseburg?

Andrew's father is building a play yard for his younger sisters. How many feet of wire fencing will he need to enclose a rectangular space 42.5 ft by 14.75 ft?

Mr. Baker's farm is 456.126 acres. Mr. Sanderson's farm is 379.404 acres. How much larger is Mr. Baker's farm?

One day Rosanna rode her bike 1.7 miles. The next day she rode 2.3 miles. How far did she ride during both of these days?

Mr. Chatman raised 150.125 hundredweight of peanuts this year. Last year he raised 136.875 hundredweight. How many more hundredweight of peanuts did he raise this year than last?

Decimals—Problems (Multiplication and Division)

1. Solve:

Mr. Baker bought 15 gal of paint weighing 187.5 pounds. What was the weight of one gallon?

Matt worked at the grocery store during the summer. He earned $2 for every 4 hours of work. How much did he earn per hour?

The Taylors drove for 9 hours on a vacation trip. If they averaged 43.7 miles per hour, how far did they travel?

About .4 of Mr. Shirk's farm is woodland. The farm contains 860 acres. How many acres are woodland?

Percent

1. Change to percent:

   .75 = _____   .08 = _____   .125 = _____

   .185 = _____   .7 = _____

2. Change to decimal form:

   80% = _____   87.5% = _____   75% = _____

   4.3% = _____   37.5% = _____

3. Circle the correct answer:

   | 87.5% = | 8.75 | .875 | 875 | 87.5 |
   | 30% = | 30 | 3.0 | .3 | .003 |

   $12\frac{1}{2}\% =$ .125   1.25   12.5   125

   $16\frac{2}{3}\% =$ $1.6\frac{2}{3}$ $16\frac{2}{3}$ $.16\frac{2}{3}$ $.016\frac{2}{3}$

4. Change to decimal form, and then to percent:

   $\frac{4}{5} =$ _____ ,   _____ $\frac{3}{5} =$ _____ ,   _____

   $\frac{1}{3} =$ _____ ,   _____ $\frac{7}{8} =$ _____ ,   _____

5. Write as percent:

   $\frac{1}{8} =$ _____ $\frac{3}{4} =$ _____ $\frac{3}{8} =$ _____

   $\frac{3}{10} =$ _____ $\frac{2}{3} =$ _____

6. Write as a mixed number:

   225% = _____   112% = _____   109% = _____

   450% = _____   133% = _____

7. What percent is

   7 of 10 _____   15 of 12 _____   9 of 18 _____

   10 of 15 _____

8. What percent of

   28 is 21 _____   45 is 25 _____   14 is 9 _____

   80 is 10 _____   11 is 7 _____   100 is 30 _____

   15 is 10 _____   5 is 4 _____

9. Solve:

   6% of 70   8.5% of 30   90% of 25   16% of 49

10. Solve:

   Matt has $8.00. Andrew has 25% more than Matt. How much does Andrew have?

A shipment of milk contains 4.25% butterfat. How many pounds of butterfat are in 1,900 pounds of milk?

Peter earned 80¢ an hour. He got an increase of 22%. How much did he then earn?

Christy sold 180 boxes of greeting cards for $.75 a box. Her rate of commission was 20%. How much commission did she get?

When the department store held a sale, a $30.00 coat was reduced 25%. What was the sale price for this coat?

Mr. Smith owned 750 acres. He sold $16\frac{1}{2}$% of it. How many acres did he have left?

In 1959, there were about 3 million Americans 14 years or older who could not read or write. In all, there were about 122 million Americans in this age group. What percent of this group were illiterate? (Round to nearest percent.)

The price of eggs was increased from $12.00 to $14.40 per case. The increase was what percent of the original price?

The regular price of a radio was $49.95. The sale price was $37.50. What was the percent of reduction to the nearest whole percent?

SELECTED READINGS

Rational Numbers

Banks, Houston J. *Learning and Teaching Arithmetic.* Boston: Allyn and Bacon, 1959, pp. 242-243, 257-270, 271-279, 317-341.

Bell, Clifford, Cleia Hammond, and Robert Herrera. *Fundamentals of Arithmetic for Teachers.* New York: Wiley, 1962, pp. 9-11, 141-162, 163-176, 179-196.

Brumfield, Charles, Robert Eicholz, and Merrill Shanks. *Fundamental Concepts of Elementary Mathematics.* Reading, Mass.: Addison-Wesley, 1962, pp. 50, 63-68, 101-112, 141-148.

Brumfield, Charles, Robert Eicholz, and Merrill Shanks, and P. G. O'Daffer. *Principles of Arithmetic.* Reading, Mass.: Addison-Wesley, 1963, pp. 150-152, 163-172, 180-184, 211-251.

Dutton, Wilbur, and L. J. Adams. *Arithmetic for Teachers.* Englewood Cliffs, N. J.: Prentice-Hall, 1961, pp. 198-224, 225-238, 254-275.

Evenson, A. B. *Modern Mathematics: Introductory Concepts and Their Implications.* Chicago: Scott, Foresman, 1962, pp. 45-46.

Fujii, John N. *An Introduction to the Elements of Mathematics.* New York: Wiley, 1961, pp. 132-134.

Marks, John L., C. Richard Purdy, and Lucien B. Kinney. *Teaching Arithmetic for Understanding.* New York: McGraw-Hill, 1958, pp. 207-218, 227-249, 251-271.

Morris, Dennis E., and Henry D. Topfer. *Advancing in Mathematics*. Chicago: Science Research Associates, 1963, pp. 65-78, 82-87.

Schaaf, William L. *Basic Concepts of Elementary Mathematics*. New York: Wiley, 1960, pp. 131-136.

School Mathematics Study Group. *Studies in Mathematics*. Vol. IX: *A Brief Course in Mathematics for Elementary School Teachers*. Stanford, Calif.: Stanford U. P., 1963, pp. 219-228, 257-291, 293-314, 315-325, 456-479, 486-492.

Shipp, Donald, and Sam Adams. *Developing Arithmetic Concepts and Skills*. Englewood Cliffs, N. J.: Prentice-Hall, 1964, pp. 176-177, 281-287, 288-294.

Thorpe, Cleata B. *Teaching Elementary Arithmetic*. New York: Harper, 1962. pp. 177-183, 189-211.

Williams, Sammie, H. Garland Read, Jr., and Frank L. Williams. *Modern Mathematics in the Elementary and Junior High Schools*. New York: Random House, 1961, pp. 37-39.

chapter 7

Measurement and Geometry

MEASUREMENT

Children develop many basic measurement concepts before starting to school. The child learns that a thing is higher, lower, larger, or smaller than he is. The child knows that his glass is full, partly full, or almost empty. Most children have heard adults talk about weight and height. They have some concept of temperature, time, counting, one-to-one correspondence, and measurement by comparison.

In teaching the concepts of measurement the teacher does not assume a background of experience on which to build meaning, but instead provides experiences which definitely involve or lead to the achievement of the desired meaning. As children grow in their understanding of measurement, teachers provide them with the words and skills which they need in order to express and develop their discoveries about differences in size, weight, distance, quantity, position, temperature, time, and form.

The discovery method is used to develop basic concepts of measurement. For example, in developing the idea of a unit in linear measurement the teacher may lead the class to wonder about the size of things in the classroom. Short sticks of approximately the same length (about three inches) are used as a unit of length. With these sticks the children measure familar objects like books, pencils, notebooks, and desks. The children readily discover that some objects are shorter than the unit and other objects are longer than the unit. Thus they may determine that the units will not measure small distances accurately. If some of the unit sticks are of different lengths, the children may discover the importance of standard units of measure. The teacher helps the class develop the proper language needed to talk about and express measurements. Similar methods may be used to develop concepts of weight and capacity.

Defined and accepted units of measure such as an inch, foot, and mile are called "standard units." Nonstandard units of measure are improvised for indefinite units such as a "pinch of salt." The children are introduced to many of the nonstandard units of measurement. From this study the teacher can lead the children to a better understanding of the importance of standard units.

One of the earliest methods of measurement was putting things in one-to-one correspondence. This could be done without word symbols or numerals. A shepherd might place pebbles in a bag so that he would have one pebble for one sheep. When he took the sheep to the fold in the evening, he would take out one pebble as each sheep entered. By placing the sheep in one-to-one correspondence with the pebbles, the shepherd could tell if any of the sheep were missing.

Later men learned to correspond one thing with one symbol. He also learned to let one symbol stand for several things. With the development of numerals and counting, man was able to measure "how many" more efficiently. With counting, man could find out exactly how many sheep he had. He could count the number of discrete objects. In measuring, however, he could not be exact, since a smaller unit than the one employed can always be used. Therefore, all measurement of continuous quantities is approximate.

The measurement of a quantity by a direct comparison of the object with some standard unit of measure is called *direct measurement*. When the child measures a book with a ruler or water with a measuring cup, he is using direct measurement. Values obtained by using a measuring instrument like a ruler are called *continuous data*. Such measurements are never exact.

If the measuring instrument cannot be directly applied to the object to be measured, indirect measure is used. The clock for example is an instrument used to make indirect measurements. A thermometer is another example of an indirect-measuring device. When a thermometer is placed in hot water, the heat causes the alcohol in the thermometer to expand. Therefore, temperature is measured indirectly by measuring the expansion of the alcohol in the thermometer.

By way of comparison, if one-inch pieces of paper are cut and placed on a rectangle to find the area, direct measurement is being used. However, if the area is found by measuring the length and the width of the rectangle and multiplying, indirect measurement is being used.

The specific measurement skills and understandings include the following. The child should be able to:

Grade I

1. Make simple measures with a foot ruler and yardstick. (Error of measure plus or minus one foot.)
2. Use nonstandard units of measure for comparison in the classroom.
3. Use simple measures of cup, pint, and quart as total units of liquid measure.
4. Recognize on the clock the time of classroom activities; time for cafeteria, play time, etc.
5. Tell time when the hands of a clock indicate the hour.
6. Place hands on a clock face to show any given hour.

7. Observe the room thermometer and determine whether the room is "too hot," "too cold," or "a good temperature." (Where good room temperature has been indicated on the thermometer by marks.)

8. Use the cent sign (¢) when it is appropriate to do so.

9. Know the equivalence of coins in amounts to 10 cents.

    (a) Penny equals one cent.

    (b) Nickel equals 5 pennies.

    (c) Five pennies equal one nickel.

    (d) One dime equals 10 pennies.

    (e) Ten pennies equals one dime.

    (f) Two nickels equal one dime.

    (g) One nickel and five pennies equal one dime.

10. Make up story problems involving the use of pennies, nickels, and dimes.

11. Solve story problems which involve the use of pennies (10), nickels (5), and dimes (10).

12. Buy and make change in play situations with pennies, nickels, and dimes.

13. Use calendar to find specific data of the current month.

14. Copy current data from the calendar as needed.

Grade II

1. Choose the proper device and/or units for measuring the following quantities:

    (a) length—ruler, yardstick, mile, inches, foot, centimeter

    (b) liquid—cup, $\frac{1}{2}$ cup, pint, $\frac{1}{2}$ pint, quart, gallon, teaspoon, tablespoon

    (c) weight—pounds, $\frac{1}{2}$ pound

    (d) temperature—thermometer, degrees, freezing point, above and below zero

    (e) time—minutes, hours, days, weeks, months, year, clock

    (f) money—quarters, half-dollars, dollars

    (g) dry—teaspoon, tablespoon

    (h) quantity—dozen, $\frac{1}{2}$ dozen

2. Tell time when the hands on the clock indicate the hour and half hour.

3. Use dollar sign ($) when it is appropriate to do so.

4. Read cent point (.) as "and" when using dollars and cents.

5. Use cent point (.) when writing dollars and cents.

6. Use real coins to show equivalence to $1.00.

7. Tell month and day of birthday.

8. Use calendar in various ways.

Grade III

1. Write and read the following words as abbreviations, and vice versa:

foot	ft	gallon	gal
yard	yd	quart	qt
inch	in.	pint	pt
pound	lb	teaspoon	tsp
ounce	oz	tablespoon	tbl
hour	hr	minute	min
year	yr		

2. Measure quantities common to everyday experiences.

3. Measure an object to the nearest unit using appropriate standard measures.

4. Convert measures by computing or other means.

5. Tell and record own weight and height.

6. Tell time when large hand is pointing to 3, 6, 9, or 12, at any time of day.

7. Make change for a dollar by using a variety of coins and in a variety of ways.

8. Use calendar in appropriate ways.

9. Write correctly the names of the months of the year in sequence when names given in scrambled order (days of the week also).

10. Read temperature.

11. Use number operations involving dollars and cents.

12. Use fractional parts of measure.

13. Read charts involving measurement.

14. Find data involving measurement.

Grade IV

1. Understand that no measurement is precise, since all measurements are approximate measures.

2. Use time.

    (a) Use clock and calendar time.

    (b) Understand meaning of a.m. and p.m.

    (c) Know the days of the week and the months of the year.

3. Use measurement units of inch, foot, year, mile, and equivalents.

4. Use square measures for inches, feet, and yards.

5. Understand and use cup, pint, quart, and gallon.

6. Understand and use dozen and half dozen.

7. Use number operations involving dollars and cents.

8. Use fractional parts of measures.

Grade V

1. Add and subtract denominate numbers where a change of unit is not necessary.

2. Express measurements in different ways as they are needed.

3. Estimate quantities, check actual measurement.

4. Illustrate units of measure used in area.

5. Determine area and perimeter of a rectangle.

6. Illustrate fractions by using measuring devices.

7. Recognize measurements to the nearest $\frac{1}{2}, \frac{1}{4}, \frac{1}{16}$, in., etc.

8. Determine the best unit of measure to be used in a situation.

9. Understand the use of the number line.

10. Understand the use of graphs:
   (a) Read and construct bar, line, and circle graphs.
   (b) Read picture graphs and tables.
   (c) Understand scale drawings.

Grade VI

1. Understand that the smaller the unit of measure the more accurate the measurement.

2. Understand that the unit of measure must correspond with what is being measured.

3. Understand the use of the following time measures:
   (a) Time zone, daylight time, standard time
   (b) Date line
   (c) B.C. and A.D.
   (d) Scores of years, decades, centuries

4. Understand the use of length measures.
   (a) English units
   (b) Metric units

5. Understand and use square measure.

6. Understand and use volume measure.

7. Understand and use weight.

8. Understand and use fractional parts of measure represented by fractions and decimal numerals.

9. Understand and use conversions to linear, square, and volume measure.

10. Understand and use addition, subtraction, multiplication, and division with measure.

11. Understand and use the metric system.

12. Read and construct bar, line, circle, and picture graphs.

13. Use maps and scales.

14. Use tables.

15. Use estimation.

Concept: Understanding time

Procedures. 1. Discuss the usefulness of the clock. It helps us know when it is time to go to school, to go out to play, to go home, to eat, to rest, to go to bed, etc.

2. Discuss the number of days in a week, the number of days we attend school, the number of days we do not attend school. (Relation of time as related to the child's own activities.)

3. Have the children tell about the time of the day that they engage in certain activities. As an independent activity they can paint pictures of things they do at different times and tell about them. These pictures, perhaps with sentences dictated by the children, may be bound into a book.

4. Use a clock face with only the hour hand—one that is clearly the short hand—and move it to different positions. First call attention to its position when it is pointing directly at the numerals for the even hours. Then ask questions directed to time between the hours, example: a little after two o'clock, shortly after seven o'clock, almost five o'clock, etc.

Concept: Liquid measure—quart, pint, cup, gallon, half-gallon

Procedures. 1. For some time previous to the presenting of this concept, have a water table somewhere in the room. On it would be several pint milk cartons, and at least two quart cartons (have a large can, bent for easy pouring or a nonbreakable pitcher to keep the water in). Some other utensils of smaller size would also be on the table. Signs in color crayon with "big," "small," "one pint," "one quart" printed on them, would be on the table.

Write an experience story about going to the store and buy only things that come in pints, quarts, or gallons. This would of course, led up to social studies as well as other arithmetic lessons. Children will no doubt suggest things that cannot be purchased at the store in this size. Let them check at home if the members of the class do not catch the mistake.

Then have two children each fill a pint milk carton and have a third child hold an empty quart carton. Ask the following:

> Do we have enough water to fill the larger carton?
> What is this larger carton called?
> Pour one pint into the quart carton.
> How full is the quart carton? When answered, write one half or
> $\frac{1}{2}$ to show this fraction.
> Pour another pint of water into the quart carton.
> How many pints of water did it take to fill the quart carton?

Can all this water (in the quart carton) be poured back into the pint carton?

Can all this water be poured into a gallon can? Let them try any method of measuring they want.

Refer back to the reference chart and have the children discuss the things they mentioned that could be purchased in these sizes.

2. Show a pint bottle, labeled, and a quart bottle, labeled. Use a type familiar to the children, such as milk cartons or bottles. Write the words *pint* and *quart* on the chalkboard, calling attention to the labels on the containers. Are they the same size? Is one larger or smaller than the other? Which is smaller? Which is larger? How much more does the quart hold than the pint? How can we find out how many pints it will take to fill the quart container? If milk is suggested, point out that water or dry sand will do just as well.

Allow the children to fill and pour from one bottle to another. Provide one quart and two pint containers for the experimenting. As the pint-quart relationship is developed, have the children draw diagrams illustrating the concept. A flannelboard and appropriate cutouts may be used also. Replace the diagrams with numbers and words to show that two pints equal one quart. (2 pints = 1 quart, 1 quart = 2 pints.)

3. This concept can be developed, incidentally, by using the lunch situation at school. This can be initiated by a discussion about how much various thermos bottles hold. In this case, a quart one for the teacher and pint-sized ones used by the children. After lunch, allow the children to actually see how much each thermos holds. Use a large jug of water, a quart jar, a pint jar, a quart thermos, and a pint thermos. Ask the children how many have seen a pint jar and a quart jar. Some children will have seen these sized jars when their mothers were canning. Experiment to see how much water a quart jar will hold, and a pint jar. If we pour water into the pint jar and then pour it in one of the thermos bottles, we can measure how much the thermos bottle holds. (Have the children do the pouring and make sure that they know what "measures" means.) After a child has filled the pint, hand him the small thermos. When he pours the water from the pint jar into the pint thermos, it will be seen that the small thermos holds a pint. Now fill the small jar and pour the water into the large thermos. The large thermos is not filled. Either by suggestion of other children, or the teacher, have the child pour another pint of water into the thermos. It is now seen that the large thermos holds two pints. Suggest that the children find out how much water is held by the quart jar. Start again with the small jar and show that the quart jar holds two pints also. Finally, have the children pour the water from the large thermos into the empty quart. Both contain or hold a quart of water.

4. An occasion usually arises to use the pint and quart in filling the aquarium. The directions on the antichlorine tablets, stated that one pill should be used to every four quarts of water. Two people went to fill the aquarium, but

there was only a quart and a pint jar available. To see how much water the child with the pint jar should pour into the aquarium, fill the pint jar with water and then pour it into the quart jar. Since this does not fill the quart jar, fill the pint jar again and pour it into the quart jar. It is seen then that one quart is equal to two pints. One child will put in two quarts and the other will put in four pints of water.

5. Display quart, pint, and cup containers. Give demonstration of the relationships.

6. Let the children take turns making up oral problems concerning liquid measure. Start them off with these: "Mother had two pints of milk in the refrigerator. The milkman brought four more pints of milk. How many quarts of milk did Mother have then?" or "Mrs. Borbely had two quarts of maple syrup. How many pint jars would the maple syrup fill?"

7. Have the children bring pint and quart jars to class. Discuss the difference and relationship.

8. Have a party. Make a fruit drink to culminate learning about liquid meaures. Let the children choose from among lemonade, orangeade, and various colored drinks. Help them to decide on the number of cups they want to serve and help them determine how many pints and quarts this will be.

9. Provide opportunities for the children to review the relation between pint and quart. Ask them to show how many pints are needed to fill one quart container. Have them take turns pouring water from two pint bottles into one quart bottle. Write on the board "2 pints = 1 quart." Remind the children that this is read "two pints equal the same amount as one quart." Discuss the relation of pints to quarts by questions such as "Which is the greater amount, one pint or quart? Two quarts or three pints?"

10. Introduce the gallon and half-gallon as standard units of liquid measure. Have the children bring in half-gallon containers and gallon containers. Have the children fill the gallon container with quarts of water and count the number of quarts needed. Write on the chalkboard "4 quarts = 1 gallon." Then pour the water from the gallon container into two half-gallon containers. Write on the chalkboard, "1 gallon = 2 half-gallons." Provide many opportunities for the children to pour from the two half-gallon containers to the gallon container and in reverse. Lead them to further conclude that 4 quarts = 2 half-gallons.

Concept: Development of the inch, foot, and yard

Procedures. 1. Have the children draw lines of an inch long on the chalkboard. Then have them use their ruler to see how close to an inch they came. Introduce the foot in the same manner and allow the children to measure many items about the room. Introduce the advantage of using inches and feet in expressing the length of larger items such as the desk. Each child is given an opportunity to measure some items in the room. The relationship of one inch to 12 inches or 1 foot is introduced.

Prepare a chart in feet and inches, and in small numerals, the equivalent inches. Hang the chart up so that the children can measure their height.

2. Each child puts his ruler on the top of his desk. Attention is called to the inch marks on the ruler, its length, and the total number of inches on the ruler. Have the children count the number of inches on their rulers. They will find that the ruler has 12 inches, or we can say that it is 12 inches long. Have the children use their rulers to find out how many inches long their crayons and pencils are.

Have some of the children stand against the wall. Mark their height and let other children figure the height of the children measured. Approximate or estimate first, then measure to see how close various children were to estimating the correct height.

As the children measure, have them tell the length in inches or feet.

3. Have the children compare the height of different objects in the classroom. Provide each child with a ruler for measuring.

4. Provide opportunities for the children to estimate and compare measures of length. Have them guess how long a book or the chalk tray is in inches and in feet. Then have them measure to see how accurately they estimated. Have a child draw a line 3 inches long on the chalkboard. Have him measure his line to see whether he is correct. Have other children try to draw lines of other given lengths.

5. Draw a line four inches long on the chalkboard. Ask a child to measure the line and name its length in inches. Ask a second child to draw a line 3 inches longer than the given line. Have another child tell how long this line should be and measure to see that the second child drew a line of the correct length. Continue the activity, drawing lines which are longer or shorter than each given line.

6. Give each child a foot ruler which has been marked off in inches. Through discussion of the use of the foot ruler have them conclude that it is easier to measure some objects in terms of feet. On some occasions a measure may be given in terms of both feet and inches, as 2 feet, 7 inches.

7. Develop the concept of comparative length. Ask, "Which is longer: ten inches or one foot?" Then have the children draw lines 10 inches long and one foot long on their paper and discuss again which length is greater and which is less. Ask other questions: "Would it be better to buy two inches or two feet of ribbon for a hair bow?" "Why?" "Which is longer?" "Matt had two sticks, one eight inches long and one five inches long. If he put them end to end, would they be longer or shorter than a foot ruler?"

"If I had a piece of string one foot long, how many ways can I cut it so that each of the two pieces can be measured in whole inches?"

8. Draw a line 5 inches long on the chalkboard. Have a child measure the line and give its length in inches. Have another child draw a line 4 inches longer than the given line. Have still another child tell how long this line should be and measure it to see that the second child drew a line of correct length. Continue

this activity having the children draw lines which are longer or shorter than the given lines.

9. Provide the children with several experiences in measuring objects in the classroom.

Concept: Recognition of money—penny, nickel, dime

Procedures. 1. Teach the children to recognize the coins and the difference between them in such activities as milk money, party money. When money is brought in for milk, lunch, or other purposes, such questions as the following might be asked: "How much does the carton of milk cost? How many pennies is that? Can you buy your milk with a nickel? What coins are exactly enough money to pay for your milk? How much does lunch cost?"

2. Provide experiences for children which will help them understand the value of money. *Example*: "A nickel will buy as much as five pennies," "A nickel is worth five pennies," "A dime is worth two nickels," "A dime is worth ten pennies," etc.

3. Have a toy store and use buying and selling experiences to help teach the use and value of money.

4. Let the children examine real coins. Use a magnifying glass.

5. Provide the children with collections of play or real coins and give them the opportunity to determine the values of various groupings of these coins.

6. Write the symbol "5 cents" on the chalkboard, then spread a group of pennies and nickels on the table. Have the children read the symbol on the chalkboard and then select a coin or coins which have that value.

7. Children usually like to play store and you can help them set up a store in one corner of the room. Display several items on a low table, and show the children how to make price tags for these items. Use the word "cents" in making the tags with prices from one cent through nine cents. Choose a child to be the storekeeper and another as the customer. For this activity the customer enters store, selects an item, and counts out the coins she would use to buy it. The storekeeper must decide whether the coins have the correct value. If the cost is five cents or greater, call on a third child to show another set of coins which might be used in the purchase.

8. Play a game, Who Will Trade? The child who is "it" offers to trade a set of coins. He says, for example, "I have two nickels and one penny. Who will trade with me?" He calls on a child who has raised his hand. This child may offer him one dime. If "it" refuses the offer, he may have another turn. If he accepts, he loses his turn because he has accepted coins of less value than his set of coins. The other trader then becomes "it" and the game continues.

9. Have the children develop charts to show the different sets of coins that have the same value. The children should record in the columns the number of dimes, nickels, and pennies they might use for each given amount.

10. Provide opportunities to work with coin collections in a classroom situation. (*Example*: milk money, lunch money, party money.) It is very important that children have the opportunity to handle money and count out various amounts specified in real-life situations.

11. Ask a child to choose two coins and give their combined value. Continue this with varying numbers of coins to review finding the value of a set of coins. Ask the child to state a value less than twenty-five cents and pick up a set of coins of that value. Continue this activity with several children to develop the ability to choose a set of coins of a given value.

12. Play the game, I Have—. Have a child pick up some coins secretly. Then he should turn to the group and say, "I have three coins and they have the same value as fifteen pennies. What coins do I have?" The child who answers correctly then chooses some coins and repeats the procedure.

Concept: Recognition of money—extension to include quarters, half-dollars, one dollar

Procedures. 1. Have the children count the total amounts in various collections containing quarters, dimes, pennies, and nickels.

2. Give children more opportunity to play store.

3. Hold up a quarter for identification. Write the word "quarter" on the chalkboard. Have the children look at the quarter closely. Ask: "Does the word 'quarter' appear on the coin?" Ask if anyone knows the value of a quarter. When it has been established that one quarter has the value of twenty-five cents, ask a child to choose a set of three or more coins that have the same value of twenty-five cents. Ask a child to find different coin combinations that have the same value as a quarter. Have a child record these choices on the chalkboard:

$$1 \text{ quarter} = 2 \text{ dimes} + 1 \text{ nickel}$$
$$1 \text{ quarter} = 1 \text{ dime} + 3 \text{ nickels}$$
$$1 \text{ quarter} = 2 \text{ dimes} + 5 \text{ pennies}$$
$$1 \text{ quarter} = 1 \text{ dime} + 15 \text{ pennies}$$

As the list grows, develop the understanding that one quarter has the same value as any group of coins that has the value of twenty-five cents.

4. Prepare cards picturing sets of coins whose value ranges from one cent to forty-nine cents. Hold the cards up one at a time. The children should determine the value.

5. Ask ten children to bring in small toys that cost less than 50 cents. If necessary, use pictures of inexpensive toys. Assign a toy to each child and ask him to make a price tag. Attach the tags to the toys. Arrange the toys on a table. Provide another table with coins on it. Let one child be the storekeeper and another the customer. The customer must choose one toy and ask the cost.

The storekeeper will reply, and the customer goes to the "money table" to get a set of coins which has the same value as the cost of the toy. The coins are given to the storekeeper who counts out the value of the coins orally. He will either accept or reject the sale. Choose other pairs of children to buy and sell other toys.

6. Hold up a half-dollar for identification. Establish that it has the value of fifty cents. Have the children choose other sets of coins that have the same value as the half-dollar. Have the children list these sets of coins on the chalkboard.

7. Draw four price tags on the chalkboard. Ask the children to draw a picture of four toys and put one of these price tags on each picture. Direct them to draw under each picture a set of coins which could be used to purchase the toy.

8. Put sets of coins into envelopes. Each set should contain six or more coins with a total value of less than one dollar. Let one child choose an envelope and empty its contents on the table. Have him count orally and write the value on the chalkboard using the symbol (¢). Continue this activity with several different envelopes.

9. Draw a set of coins on the chalkboard. Do not arrange them in order of their value. Have a child come to the chalkboard and identify the coin with the greatest value, the next greatest, and so on. Then have him find the value of the set shown. Continue this activity using different combinations of coins.

10. Develop the idea of one dollar and exhibit the notation for one dollar. Explain that the dot or period is the symbol that separates the number of dollars from the number of cents. (*Avoid* using the term "decimal point" for this notation. The idea of decimals will be developed more carefully at a later time.)

11. Conduct class activities in which the children find the value of coin collections, compare collections, and put collections together.

12. Cut up several newspaper advertisements picturing articles priced at less than one dollar (food ads are best). Provide each of two children with a set of coins. Have another child reach into a container, pull out an ad and read it aloud. "Peas, two boxes for thirty-nine cents." The two children then compete for speed and accuracy in selecting a set of coins which has that value.

Concept: Recognition of money—making change

Procedures. 1. Develop the idea of *change* as the difference in value between a set of coins and the price of something which has been purchased. *Suggestion*: Have each child write an individual story about change. Each story must ask a question. Have the children read their stories for the group to solve.

2. Have the children bring pictures of toys, clothes, or sports goods and write prices less than fifty cents on each picture. Have each child put out coins which measure fifty cents. Then have them exchange pictures with their neighbors, read the prices, and put the correct amount of change from the fifty cents on the picture. Have each child check his own picture and see that his neighbor

gave the correct change. If he is correct, he should change with another neighbor; if not, he should try again.

3. Each child puts out fifty cents on his desk using different coins. As he is called he tells a short story about change that he has made. For example: "I had fifty cents. I bought a ball for 46 cents, and I have four cents left." Another child checks the story of the first child. Give the children time to get stories and change ready while others are telling stories and checking answers.

4. Provide additional experiences in working with coin collections.

Concept: Recognition of money—dollar-and-cent notation

Procedures. 1. Encourage the children to think of adding numbers and then interpreting the answer according to the amount of money. Do not elaborate on the decimal point in such exercises. Simply indicate that this is a dot that separates the dollars from the cents. The children should understand this readily and it is not likely that it will cause any difficulty.

2. Hold up a silver *dollar*. Ask for the name of the coin. Let a child inspect the coin to see if the name appears on it. Ask if anyone knows the value of this coin, and establish this as one hundred cents.

Display a dollar *bill*. Establish its value as one hundred cents. Display a five-dollar bill and a ten-dollar bill. Establish the value of each.

Direct the children at their seats to make a set of half-dollars which will have the same value as one dollar. Continue with quarters, dimes, nickels, and pennies, and finally sets containing different coins. Summarize the activity with the statement that one dollar has the same value of any set of coins which has the value of one hundred cents.

3. Prepare several envelopes containing money having a value from less than one dollar to less than five dollars. Begin with an envelope containing coins measuring a value less than one dollar. Have a child remove the contents, count to determine the value of the coins, and record the value on the chalkboard. Opposite the value recorded, write the same value with the *dollar sign* and *separating point*. Explain that amounts less than one dollar may be recorded either way, but that amounts of one dollar or more are recorded with the dollar sign and separating point.

27¢	$ .27
3¢	$ .03
229¢	$2.29

In using the symbols ($) and (.), the numeral before the separating point shows the number of dollars and the numeral after the separating point shows the number of cents. The first digit to the right of the separating point could be thought of as representing the number of dimes, and the second digit to the right of the separating point as representing the number of pennies.

4. Make cards made of tagboard with various values recorded on them. Place the cards in random order along the chalk tray. Ask a child to pick up the cards which name the least amount of value and place them in one row in the pocket chart. The next child should select the cards which name the next least amount of value, and so forth.

5. Provide children with activities involving the dollar-and-cent notation.

PRACTICE AND EVALUATION

Measurement—Length: Inch, Foot, and Yard

1. Use your ruler to measure these lines. How long are they?

_____   _____ inches

_____   _____ inches

_____   _____ inches

2. Draw lines 3 inches long, $5\frac{1}{2}$ inches long, and $6\frac{1}{4}$ inches long.

3. Write the following words the short way:

   feet _____ inch _____ foot _____
   inches _____ yard _____

4. Fill in the blanks.

 1 foot = _____ inches 1 yard = _____ inches 1 yard = _____ feet

5. Tell the longer measure which each of these equals.

     12 inches = _____
      3 feet = _____
     36 inches = _____

Measurement—Liquid: Gallon, Quart, Pint, and Cup

1. Draw a line to the equal amount:

     4 quarts   1 pint
     2 cups   1 gallon
     2 pints   1 quart

2. Draw a ring around the correct answer.

      Which is less?
     1 cup, or 1 pint
     1 gallon, or 1 quart
     1 pint, or 1 quart

3. Draw a ring around the correct answer.

      Which is more?
     1 gallon, or 3 quarts
     1 quart, or 3 pints
     1 pint, or 3 cups

4. Solve the problems:

Mr. Baker used a gallon and two quarts of paint to paint a shed. He used how many quarts of paint in all?

Pamela has a quart and a pint of ginger ale. She has enough ginger ale to fill how many cups?

Matt wanted to buy 3 quarts of red paint. The store had no quart cans of red paint, but it had pint cans. How many pint cans should Matt buy?

Common Measure—Change Form

1. Find the missing numbers.

3 ft 7 in. = _____ in.
6 hr 4 min = _____ min
17 mo = _____ yr _____ mo
10,000 ft = _____ mi _____ ft
1,280 rd = _____ mi
2 lb 14 oz = _____ oz

Money—Equivalents

1. A nickel = _____ pennies.
2. A quarter = _____ pennies or _____ nickels. It also = _____ dimes or _____ quarters.
3. A half dollar = _____ pennies or _____ nickels or _____ dimes or _____ quarters.
4. Fill in the blanks:

23 cents = _____ dimes plus _____ pennies
62 cents = _____ dimes plus _____ pennies
84 cents = _____ half dollar plus _____ quarter plus
nickel plus _____ pennies

5 Solve the problems—addition and subtraction

Christy had 5 pennies, and 1 quarter. How much money did she have? _____ cents.

Pam bought a pair of shoes for $5.25, and a new skirt for $3.50. How much did she spend?

Mother bought some shirts for Matt for $4.69. She also bought a blouse for Christy for $2.15. How much more did the shirts cost than the blouse?

Matt bought a baseball bat for $3.20 and a toy truck for $1.68. How much did he spend?

6. Use figures to write each of these amounts:

2 dollars and 35 cents _____   3 dollars and 78 cents _____
8 dollars and 3 cents _____   5 dollars and 9 cents _____

7. Write the figure that is in the dollar place and in the cents place in each of these amounts.

$2.35 equals _____ dollars and _____ cents

$7.93 equals _____ dollars and _____ cents
$5.64 equals _____ dollars and _____ cents
$1.23 equals _____ dollars and _____ cents

8. Find the sums:

$$\$5.24 + \$1.39 + \$4.20 + \$3.98 = r$$
$$\$1.69 + \$\ .23 + \$2.14 + \$\ .89 = t$$
$$\$5.08 + \$2.45 + \$\ .14 + \$\ .37 = a$$

9. Find the differences:

$$\$11.84 - \$6.52 = b \qquad\qquad \$29.45 - 17.20 = c$$
$$\$\ \ 5.34 - \$2.22 = r \qquad\qquad \$19.01 - \$9.98 = a$$

10. Find the product:

$$\$15.60 \times 4 = a \qquad \$32.37 \times 3 = b \qquad \$9.38 \times 2 = c$$

Ratio and Scale Drawings

1. Solve:

A table is 6 ft wide. It is 14 ft long. What is the ratio of its width to its length? (Express as a fraction.)

Anna Louise made a drawing of her room. She let $\frac{1}{4}$ in. stand for 1 ft. The drawing was $3\frac{1}{2}$ in. by 4 in. What is the size of her room?

The diameter of a Ferris wheel is 42 ft. The circumference is 132 ft. What is the ratio of the circumference to the diameter? (Express as a fraction.)

If you make a scale drawing of the Ferris wheel in the above problem, using 1 in. = 84 ft, what should be the length of the diameter? _____ The circumference? _____

Ratio and Proportion

1. A fruit punch is made from 1 part fruit punch concentrate and 3 parts of water. From these facts find the missing amounts.

Concentrate	Water	Fruit Punch Drink
2 pt	_____	_____
_____	15 glasses	_____
_____	_____	12 pt
_____	12 oz	_____

Metric and English Systems of Measure—Equivalents within system

1. Use the following table of U. S. equivalents of metric measures to complete the problems. Round your answers to the nearest hundredth.

1 g = .0352 oz   1 m = 39.37 in.   1 kg = 2.2046 lb
1 m = 1.093 yd   1 liter = .264 gal   1 liter = 1.056 liquid qt
1 hl = 2.837 bu   1 cc = .061 cu in.   1 km = .621 mi

1 sq cm = .155 sq in.   1 sq m = 1.196 sq yd   1 cu m = 35.314 cu ft
1 kg = _____ oz   1 liter = _____ cu in.   1 hl = _____ gal
3 kg = _____ lb   50 km = _____ mi   30 sq m = _____ sq yd

2. Use the following table of metric equivalents to U. S. measures to complete the problems. Round your answers to the nearest hundredth.

1 yd = .9144 m	1 ft = .3048 m	1 in. = .0254 m
1 mi = 1.609 km	1 lb = .4536 kg	1 oz = 28.35 g
1 liq qt = .946 liter	1 gal = 3.785 liter	1 cu yd = .764 cu in.

1 pt =_____ liter   1 lb =_____ g $\frac{1}{2}$ cup = _____ dl

1 pt =_____ cc   1 fl oz = _____ ml   10 lb   _____ kg

3. Solve:

A jet passenger plane averaged 920 km per hour on a trip from Paris to Oslo. How many miles per hour was this?

Jim weighs 132 lb. Sam weighs 65 kg. Who weighs more? How much? (Give answer in pounds and kilograms.)

Denominate Numbers—Equivalents

1. Write answers only:

5 wk = _____ days   1 hr, 15 min = _____ min   6 ft = _____ yd

8 pints = _____ qt   4 gal, 1 qt = _____ qt $\frac{1}{2}$ lb = _____ oz

2 gal = _____ qt   2 lb 10 oz = _____ oz   21 da = _____ wk

2. Solve:

Christy brought lemonade to a picnic. She filled 3 quart jugs and 1 pint bottle. How many pints of lemonade did she bring?

A quart of milk costs 31 cents. How much will Matt have to pay for 3 gallons?

Mr. Baker bought $\frac{1}{4}$ gross of pencils. How many pencils did he buy?

Andrew and his friends laid out a race track which was $\frac{1}{3}$ of a mile long. How many feet is this?

Denominate Numbers—Addition and Subtraction

1. Follow the signs and state in simplest form:

| 3 hr 30 min | 2 yr 9 mo | 15 wk 2 da |
| +2 hr 25 min | +6 yr 11 mo | +9 wk 7 da |

| 54 gal 3 qt | 1 lb 12 oz | 1 peck 5 qt |
| -13 gal 1 qt | +5 lb 3 oz | +4 pecks 4 qt |

| 3 ft 1 in. | 6 yd 9 in. | 59 min 32 sec |
| -2 ft 11 in. | -2 yd 27 in. | -47 min 53 sec |

2. Solve:

The height of the tallest boy in Lou's class is 5 ft 4 in. The height of the shortest boy in the class is 4 ft 6 in. What is the difference in their heights?

Mrs. Smith planted a row of radishes 22 ft 10 in. long and a row of green onions 12 ft 6 in. long. How much longer was the row of radishes than the row of onions?

Matt's best broad jump was 13 ft 6 in. His jump was how much greater than Lou's jump of 11 ft 9 in.?

3.

4 ft 6 in.	15 da 19 hr	10 hr 45 min
3 ft 9 in.	9 da 15 hr	7 hr 60 min
8 ft 10 in.	12 da 23 hr	13 hr 16 min
7 ft 8 in.	8 da 14 hr	5 hr 9 min

4. Solve:

2 lb 9 oz	6 ft	8 wk 6 da
− 15 oz	− 9 in.	−4 wk 4 da

5. Solve:

Pam walked for 2 hr 24 min. Christy walked for 1 hr 55 min. How much longer did Pamela walk?

Andrew rode his bike two miles in 4 min 10 sec. The school record was 2 min and 6 sec, for the same distance. What was the difference between the two times?

Elaine bought 1 yd 17 in. of red ribbon, 2 yd 30 in. of blue ribbon, and 1 yd 11 in. of white ribbon. How much ribbon did she buy altogether?

The morning session at school is 3 hr and 10 min long, and the afternoon session is 2 hr and 55 min long. How long is the school day?

Denominate Numbers—Multiplication

1. State answers in simplest form:

4 yd 2 ft	3 gal 2 qt	4 min 50 sec
×3	×5	×6

8 ft 8 in.	8 hr 30 min	8 bu 3 pecks
×7	×9	×6

2. Solve:

Christy is in school 5 hr and 35 min a day. How long is she in school during 5 days?

Mary weighs 42 lb 7 oz. Her father weighs 4 times as much. How much does her father weigh?

Mr. Jones's pickup truck can carry about 16 five-gallon cans of paint. If each can weighs 62 lb 9 oz, what is the weight of a full load on Mr. Jones's truck?

Pam caught a fish that was 1 pound 14 oz. Christy caught one that weighed three times as much. How much did the fish that Christy caught weigh?

Each of seven campers took 1 pound 10 oz of bacon on their hike. How much bacon was taken in all?

3. Solve:

$$
\begin{array}{ccc}
\text{8 lb 4 oz} & \text{10 ft 11 in.} & \text{8 wk 5 da} \\
\underline{\times 4} & \underline{\times 3} & \underline{\times 4} \\
\\
\text{5 yd 2 ft} & \text{6 hr 30 min} & \text{5 da 14 hr} \\
\underline{\times 5} & \underline{\times 3} & \underline{\times 6}
\end{array}
$$

Denominate Numbers—Division

1. State answers in simplest form.

$$
\begin{array}{ccc}
4\overline{)\text{6 yd 2 ft}} & 6\overline{)\text{34 yr 6 mos}} & 7\overline{)\text{15 lb 5 oz}} \\
6\overline{)\text{28 ft 6 in.}} & 7\overline{)\text{31 yd 4 in.}} & 5\overline{)\text{9 gross 7 doz}}
\end{array}
$$

2. Solve:

For four days Anna Louise spent the same amount of time practicing her violin. In all she spent 5 hr and 40 min practicing. How much did she practice per day?

Matt ran 4 miles in 18 min and 24 sec. What was his average time per mile?

Lou used 5 gal and 2 qt to paint the outside of his house with two coats. What was the average amount per coat?

After a heavy rain, the Raritan River rose 3 ft 9 in. in 2 hr. What was the average rise per hour?

Mrs. Baker made 6 dishtowels of equal length from a piece of material 8 ft 6 in. long. How long was each towel?

GEOMETRY

Nearly all authorities on mathematics education recommend a greater emphasis on geometry. As a result, from the very beginning of the child's study of a modern mathematics program he will have certain experiences with geometry. Just as numerals are the representations of abstract ideas called numbers, so the pictures the child draws of points, lines, and planes are simply representations of abstract ideas. They are classified with the study of plane geometry at the secondary level.

Through his early and continued experiences with algebra and geometry, the child is taught to define in a correct and precise way. He is thus provided with a rich background as well as *definitions and understandings that will not need to be unlearned at a later date.*

Let us take a look at the vocabulary and precise definitions students of today are being exposed to. Almost everyone will agree that the definition of a building would include a house, garage, store, barn, school, and factory. Most of us will also agree that children of primary school age should be able to distinguish the various types of buildings as house, garages, schools, etc. In modern mathematics language we would have said that houses, garages, stores, etc., are *subsets* of buildings.

With the possible exception of metropolitan areas, most of us live in an environment where we are exposed to the various types of buildings mentioned above, and we therefore expect our children to be able to use precise language in naming these types of buildings. However, since geometry is also a part of everyday life and various geometric shapes are part of our normal environment, is it any more unreasonable to expect a child to be able to distinguish a triangle from a hexagon than a factory from a house?

In modern elementary school mathematics, children learn to recognize and name basic geometric shapes: the square, the circle, the triangle, the rectangle, etc. Geometry is not presented in its classic form in the elementary grades. However, the child is given an introduction to the study of points, lines, shapes, their names and relationships. As geometry is a part of modern mathematics, many textbook publishers have incorporated geometry with the earlier studies in modern mathematics, including set language and set symbols. However, this is an area where the authorities have not yet come to an agreement, and many other textbooks do not incorporate set language and geometry. It would seem logical to incorporate set mathematics where the students have had the appropriate background.

We will now look at some of the basic concepts of geometry as they are being taught in the elementary grades. A point, a line, and a plane are ideas; *they cannot be drawn*—in fact they cannot be mathematically defined, and are therefore referred to as undefined terms. However, we can represent these ideas in an observable way—by physical representations or symbols, mainly dots and lines drawn on paper or the chalkboard. Therefore, a geometric *point* is an idea of a precise location in the universe of geometric space, and can be represented by a dot. However, it must be pointed out that our dot, no matter how small, actually covers many points in space. *Space* is a set of all points, and points do not move. Our representations of points are labeled with capital letters.

A *curve* is a particular set of points passed through in moving from one given point to another. Therefore all lines are curves, including the so-called "straight line," which of course is only part of a great circle.

A *line segment* is the most direct path between two points. It is also a set of points in a line. Line segments begin and end at particular points called "end points."

The symbol for the curve or line segment from point A to point B, and from point C to point D, (the endpoints) is $\overline{AB}$ and $\overline{CD}$ or $\overline{BA}$ and $\overline{DC}$. In working with primary children, using $\overline{AB}$ is recommended since they learn that a line segment has a first and last point, the above symbol is easier to associate with the meaning of line segment.

The *line* is an undefined term in geometry. Like the point, the line is also a subset of the universal set space. Although we cannot define a line, we can describe it as a series of line segments which extends without limit in two directions.

To represent a line, we place arrowheads at each end to indicate that the line has no endpoints, but extends endlessly in both directions; it is written $\overleftrightarrow{AB}$.

Using set language, we can draw some relationships: $\overline{AB} \subset \overleftrightarrow{AB}$. Line segment AB is a subset of line AB. Also: $\overleftrightarrow{AB} \supset \overline{AB}$. Line AB contains line segment AB.

A *ray* is a subset of a line that includes an endpoint and all points on the line that lie to one side of the endpoint. In short, a ray has an endpoint or beginning but no ending. A ray is the union of the endpoint and all the points in one direction from the endpoint. An infinite number of rays may have the same endpoint.

An infinite number of rays can have the same endpoint.

A ray is written using the endpoint and another point on the ray. $\overrightarrow{AB}$

The intersection of two distinct rays forms a new set containing a common end point. $\overrightarrow{AB} \cap \overrightarrow{AC} = A$

The union of two opposite rays form a line: $\overrightarrow{BA} \cup \overrightarrow{BC} = \overleftrightarrow{AC}$

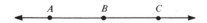

Also, line AC contains rays:

$$\vec{BA} \subset \overleftrightarrow{AC} \text{ or } \overleftrightarrow{AC} \supset \vec{BA} \text{ and } \overleftrightarrow{AC} \supset \vec{BC} \text{ or } \vec{RC} \supset \overleftrightarrow{AC}$$

Set relation symbols $\left\{ \begin{array}{l} \subset \quad \text{is a subset of} \\ \supset \quad \text{contains the subset} \end{array} \right.$

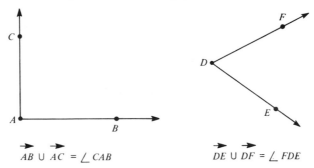

Like a line, a ray contains an infinite number of line segments.

$$\vec{AB} \subset \overline{AB},\ \overline{AC},\ \overline{AD},\ \overline{AE},\ \overline{BC},\ \overline{BD},\ \overline{BE},\ \text{etc.}$$

Ray AB could also be called $\vec{AC}$, $\vec{AD}$, or $\vec{AE}$, but it must always start with the endpoint, namely point A.

An *angle* is generally defined as the union of two rays having a common end-point. The intersection of the rays (common endpoint) is called the *vertex*, and each ray is called a *side* of the angle. The symbol for angle is $\angle$, and angles are designated with three capital letters, usually A, B, C, the middle letter A always being the vertex or endpoint of the two rays.

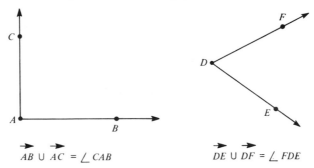

$$\vec{AB} \cup \vec{AC} = \angle CAB \qquad\qquad \vec{DE} \cup \vec{DF} = \angle FDE$$

Since rays extend indefinitely, we can think of the plane containing the angle as having three parts: (1) the two rays that form the angle, (2) the set of points forming the inside of the angle, (3) the set of points forming the outside of the angle.

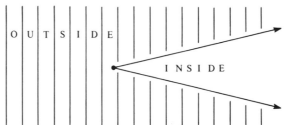

If two lines share a common point, that point is the point of intersection. Two intersecting lines form a set of four rays and a set and four angles.

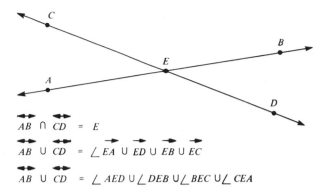

$$\overset{\leftrightarrow}{AB} \cap \overset{\leftrightarrow}{CD} = E$$

$$\overset{\leftrightarrow}{AB} \cup \overset{\leftrightarrow}{CD} = \angle\, \overrightarrow{EA} \cup \overrightarrow{ED} \cup \overrightarrow{EB} \cup \overrightarrow{EC}$$

$$\overset{\leftrightarrow}{AB} \cup \overset{\leftrightarrow}{CD} = \angle\, AED \cup \angle\, DEB \cup \angle\, BEC \cup \angle\, CEA$$

The tool or instrument most commonly used to measure angles is a protractor. Naturally, when we say "measure angles" we mean to measure the representations of angles we have drawn. The measure of an angle will refer to the amount of opening (inside) between two sides. The standard unit of angle measure is called a degree, written °. A complete rotation of any ray would be 360°, so a degree is 1/360 of a rotation. Therefore a perfect circle would contain 360°, a straight line 180°, and an $\angle$ from 0° to 360°.

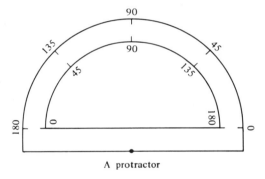

A protractor

Angles are classified according to their degree measure. A *right angle*, sometimes called "square corner" angles in the primary grades, are angles that measure exactly 90°.

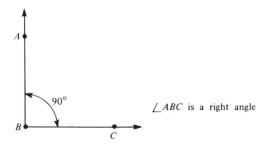

$\angle\, ABC$ is a right angle

An *acute angle* has a degree measure more than 0° but less than 90°.

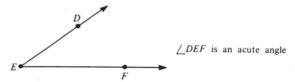

$\angle DEF$ is an acute angle

An *obtuse angle* is one which measures more than 90° but less than 180°.

$\angle GHI$ is an obtuse angle

A *straight angle* is formed when two rays extend in opposite directions from the same point. The degree measure of a straight angle is always 180°.

$\angle JKL$ is a straight angle

Elementary school children should learn to recognize and be able to name these types of angles by visual observation. In the intermediate grades, they should learn to use a protractor and be able to measure various angles.

By using their protractors students will discover that two or more angles may have the same degree of measure. However, they cannot be called equal, because equal means "the same," and two angles cannot occupy the identical set of points in space. When two geometric figures have the same size and shape, they are *congruent*, the symbol for congruence is ≅.

Two angles are congruent, if the models of one can be placed exactly over the model of the other and the rays of the first angle lie exactly along the rays of the second; in short, if they have the same degree measure, the picture of the rays may or may not be the same.

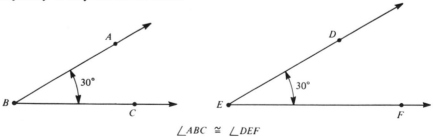

$\angle ABC \cong \angle DEF$

An examination of angles can lead to the introduction of a *simple closed plane* figure and a *plane*. Before discussing a closed plane figure, we should first attempt to describe a plane. Like a point and a line, a *plane* is a mathematically undefined term.

A set of points suggested by a flat surface is a *plane*. When you look at a flat surface such as a floor, a desk top, a window, or a wall, you are looking at a good representation of the mathematical idea of a plane. Like a line, a plane extends indefinitely in all directions without limit. As a line contains an infinite number of points, a plane contains an infinite number of lines, and there are an infinite number of planes in space.

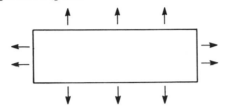

Through two points an infinite number of planes can pass.

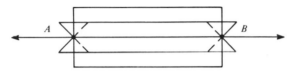

Through three points *not on a line*, there can be only one plane.

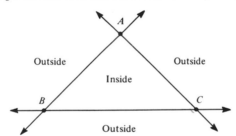

A *closed plane figure* is a geometric figure composed of a set of points in space which separates space or a plane into 3 sets of points: (a) the set of points inside the figure, (b) the set of points outside the figure, and (c) the set of points that make the figure, or the sides of the figure. Some examples of closed plane figures are:

A simple closed curve is a curve that returns to its starting point without crossing itself at any point. The following figures are examples of closed curves, but *not* simple closed curves.

A *polygon* is a special type of simple closed curve that is the union of line segments. ("Poly," from Greek, meaning many; and "gon" from the Greek "gonia," meaning angle.)

The prefixes for the names of particular polygons are:

tri	+ angle	=	3-sided figure,		3 line segments	
quad	+ rilateral	=	4- "	" ,	4 "	"
penta	+ gon	=	5- "	" ,	5 "	"
hexa	+ "	=	6- "	" ,	6 "	"
hepta	+ "	=	7- "	" ,	7 "	"
octa	+ "	=	8- "	" ,	8 "	"
nona	+ "	=	9- "	" ,	9 "	"
deca	+ "	=	10- "	" ,	10 "	"

Another special type of a simple closed curve is a circle. A circle is a closed plane figure all of whose points are at the same distance from a given point in the same plane. A *radius* is any line segment joining the center point with any point on the circle. The term radius is also used for the name of the line segment; therefore all radii of the same circle are the same length. The line segment joining any two points on the circle is called a *chord*. If the chord passes through the center point, the chord is designated a *diameter*. A portion of the circle bounded by any two points on the circle is an *arc*.

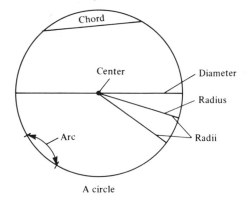

A circle

The *interior* of a simple closed curve is the set of points inside the curve. The points on the curve are not included.

The *exterior* of a simple closed curve is the set of points outside the closed curve. Again, the points on the curve are not included.

The union of a simple closed curve and its interior is called a *plane region*.

Therefore, a triangular region would include the interior of the triangle, plus the sides of the triangle.

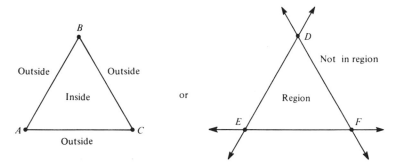

Let us now examine a triangle and make some general observations.

1. A triangle is a simple closed curve.
2. A triangle is a closed plane figure.
3. Every triangle is made up of three line segments.

$$\triangle ABC = \overline{AB} \cup \overline{BC} \cup \overline{AC} \qquad \triangle DEF = \overline{ED} \cup \overline{DF} \cup \overline{EF}$$

4. The triangle is made up only of those points that are elements of the line segments.

5. A triangle has an inside and an outside.

6. A triangle is a subset of a plane.

7. The sum of the degree of measure of the angles of any triangle is always $180°$.

8. When we say two triangles are congruent, we mean, they have exactly the same size and shape.

Introduction to three-dimensional, or *solid*, geometric shapes should be developed by drawing the child's attention to geometric forms or shapes in our daily environment—for example, a book, an eraser, a globe, waste basket, and the room itself.

A rough sketch of a room shows that it is a physical representation of a particular kind of geometric solid, namely a *prism*.

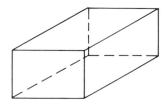

At the elementary level we are not concerned with the complexities of geometric solids such as volume. However, along intuitive lines we should strive to show a relationship among various geometric forms as well as develop a useful and precise vocabulary. For instance, we should be able to recognize that *geometric solids are a union of closed surfaces*, four or more.

Let us now examine and name the parts of a prism.

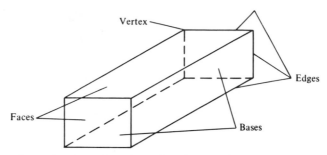

In the above drawing of a prism, the plane surfaces are called *faces*. The intersection of these faces (line segments) are called *edges*. Two faces, called *bases*, must be congruent and in parallel planes. Each end point of each edge (corner) is called a *vertex*.

Prisms are named according to the plane figure forming the base. The above base is rectangular, therefore, we call it a *rectangular prism*. Other types of prisms could be triangular, pentagonal, hexagonal, and so on depending on geometric form of the base.

Pyramids are a special kind of solid with *one* base (a simple plane region), and three or more sides in the form of triangles. As with prisms, the shape of the base would determine the type of pyramid.

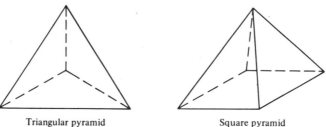

Triangular pyramid   Square pyramid

A *cylinder* is a simple closed surface consisting of two bases and the lateral surface between the two bases. A tin can is a cylinder. A prism by this definition is a cylinder.

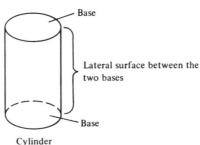

Cylinder

A *cone* has one face, the base, and a lateral surface that is the set of all points on the segments between the vertex and every point on the edge of the base.

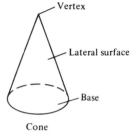

Cone

A *sphere* is a set of points in space such that all points in the set are an equal distance from a given point called the *center*. A good example of a sphere is a globe of the earth or a basketball.

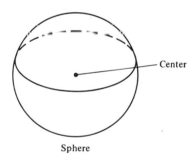

Sphere

Geometry is not a mystery, and should not be turned into one. It should be treated as a series of perceptual discoveries, especially on the introductory intuitive level. There is an important need to describe objects that are part of our physical world. Geometry becomes a descriptive discipline at the elementary school level.

The following discussion is an example of how geometry might be taught at the elementary level.

EXPERIENCES FOR UNDERSTANDING THE PROPERTIES OF THE RECTANGULAR PRISM

Related Teaching Suggestions	Related Geometric Concepts
I. Unstructured block play A. Provide geometric solids of different shapes and sizes such as:	The teacher does not attempt to develop concepts during unstructured block play. This is to be a period of discovery by the child.

Rectangular prism

Cone

Pyramid

Cylinder

Triangular prism

Cube

    B. Provide the children with geo-
       metric solids of various materi-
       als such as:
       1. wooden blocks
       2. a variety of cardboard boxes:
          oatmeal boxes (cylinder), shoe
          box (rectangular prism), hexag-
          onal hatboxes
       3. plastic containers
       4. art gum and chalkboard
          erasers
       5. bricks
       6. metal containers
       7. paper cups (cones and cut cones)
       8. rubber balls, baseballs
    C. Adequate time should be pro-
       vided for playing with geomet-
       ric materials. (Teacher observes
       without commenting or direct-
       ing.)
II. Introduction of structure based on   Geometric solids are of many
  teacher observation.   shapes and sizes.
    A. Discuss the experiences which   Teacher identifies geometric
       occurred during block play.   solids by name.
    B. Reenact block-play situations

through which geometric concepts can be derived.

1. Which solids can be added
   vertically? Why?
2. Which solids roll? Why?
3. Which solids have only flat
   surfaces?
4. Which of these solids look
   like a box?

Continuous addition of solids requires that the solids have two flat
parallel surfaces. The nearer the
solids come to a curved surface, the
easier they roll.

This concept leads to the child's
recognition of rectangularity.

C. Help children to become aware
   of the existence of geometric
   shapes in their world, particularly of the rectangular solid.
   1. rooms, buildings
   2. books, lunch boxes
D. Record experiences through the
   development of a cooperative
   story.
E. Have the children make drawings which represent solids in
   two dimensions. (Encourage
   attempt at three-dimensional
   representation.)

The concept of a two-dimen-
sional figure is differentiated from
a three-dimensional object.

III. Planned study of geometric solids.
   A. Examine geometric solids by
      counting faces, vertices, and
      edges.

Understand the terms *face*, *vertex*, *vertices*, and *edge*.

   B. Record findings in table form.

Recognize the relationship of the
faces, edges, and vertices to its
solid. Euler's formula for poly-
hedra: $F + V = E : 2$

Name of Solid	Faces	Vertices	Edges
Rectangular prism	6	8	12
Cube	6	8	12
Pyramid (square base)	5	5	8
Pyramid (triangular base)	4	4	6
Triangular prism	5	6	9

C. Consider one of the faces of the
   rectangular prism.
   1. Have children measure the
      pairs of opposite sides of many
      rectangles.

Line segments opposite each
other are equal in length.

2. Construct a model of a rectangle with nonrigid corners,
using an erector set or any
other suitable material.

  (a) Show through demonstra-   This is the definition of parallel
      tion that opposite sides are   lines. This concept holds true re-
      the same distance apart.   gardless of the change in opposite
                                        angles.

  (b) Have the children observe
      this change in angles.

  (c) Using the nonrectangular
      parallelogram ask the chil-
      dren. "Is this the usual ap-
      pearance of forms in the
      world around you?"
      (doors, walls, buildings,
      etc.)

  (d) Introduce the concept of   Right angles are formed by per-
      the right angle and perpen-   pendicular lines.
      dicularity.

3. Summarize the properties of
the rectangle which have been
developed.

  (a) Cite the special case: the   All sides of a square are equal.
      square.

D. Reexamine the rectangular prism.

1. Observe that all the faces are
rectangles.

2. Show by measurement that op-   Introduce the concept of con-
posite faces have the same di-   gruences.
mensions.

3. Observe also that the faces are
perpendicular at the edges.

4. Observe that the edges are perpendicular at the vertices.

5. Show by measurement that opposite faces are parallel.

6. Summarize the properties of
the rectangular prism.

  (a) Cite the special case: the   All edges of a cube are equal; all
      cube.   its faces are squares.

7. By means of a drawing of a
rectangular prism and its mapping, have pupils construct

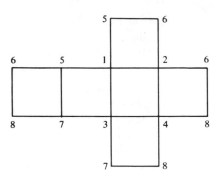

This is a mapping of a cube.

similar ones. (If mapping is
done by the pupil, graph paper is an excellent aid.)

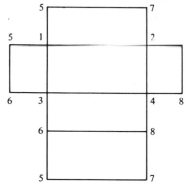

This is a mapping of a
rectangular prism.

IV. Planned experiences involving the
volume and area of a rectangular
prism.

A. Volume
1. Compare.
    (a) Compare the volume of
      different size boxes filling
      them with appropriate ma-
      terials.
      1. sand
      2. water
      3. marbles
      4. rice
      5. beans
      6. unit blocks

Volume is expressed in comparative terms.

Establish the concept of a unit
block.

(b) Compare volumes by weighing different containers filled with or made of the same material.

2. Measure volume in terms of unit blocks.
   (a) Select boxes whose measurements are a multiple of the unit block.
   (b) Fill the box with unit blocks in an orderly manner.
   (c) Empty the box and count the number of unit blocks.

   The total number of unit blocks will represent the volume of the box.

3. Develop the formula for volume.

   Children's ability to handle multiplication is a limiting factor.

   (a) Fill the bottom layer of the box and count the number of unit blocks.
   (b) Determine the number of layers.
   (c) Develop the relationship of volume to the number of unit blocks in a layer and the number of layers in the box.
   (d) Develop the generalization for obtaining volume.

   Develop the formula: volume is equal to the length times the width times the height ($V = L \times W \times H$).

   1. How do you determine the number of blocks in a layer without completely filling the box?

   The number of unit blocks in each layer is equal to the number of blocks in the length times the number of blocks in the width.

   2. How do you determine the number of unit blocks that are needed to fill the box without completely filling the bottom layer?

   The number of unit blocks needed to fill the box is equal to the number of blocks in the length times the number in the width times the number in the height.

- (e) Repeat this experience
  with many different size
  boxes.
4. Determine the volume in
  terms of standard units. (Use
  of the ruler.)
  (a) Measure the boxes whose
    volume has previously
    been determined in unit
    blocks.
  (b) Show the relationship of
    the unit blocks with mea-
    sured volumes.
  (c) Extend the generalization
    with many experiences.
B. Surface area of a rectangular prism
  1. Develop the formula for the
    area of a face.
    (a) Review the properties of a
      face of the rectangular
      prism.
    (b) Cover the face of the   The area is the total number of
      rectangle with unit squares.   unit squares in the surface.
      (For convenience use a
      square with a side dimen-
      sion of one inch.)
    (c) Determine the number   The area of the rectangle is the
      of unit squares in the face.   product of the number of units in
      the length by the number of units
      in the width. Express this: $A = L \times W$.

    (d) Develop the formula for
      area from the children's
      findings.
    (e) Determine the area of the
      rectangle using a standard
      unit.
  2. Develop the formula for the
    surface area of a rectangular
    prism.
    (a) Apply the formula for
      area to each face of the
      rectangular prism.

(1) Do we have to mea-
sure all faces?
(b) Have the children develop   The surface area of a rectangular
their own formula for de-   prism is equal to the sum of the
termining surface area.   areas of all six faces.

DEVELOPMENT OF GENERALIZATIONS IN ELEMENTARY
SCHOOL GEOMETRY

It is possible and practical to provide many opportunities for the discovery of geometric generalizations in the upper elementary grades, once a minimal background and vocabulary has been achieved by the average class. In the following examples, the necessary preparation is listed at the beginning of each "discovery project." No brief is made here for any particular example. The basic object of this type of work with children is not to cover some actual content (although the content should be intrinsically interesting to children), but rather to develop a variety of techniques for generalizing and a habit of using these techniques, an appreciation that "sweet are the uses of generality."

That ordinary (not just "gifted") elementary school children are quite capable of reaching a fairly high ability to generalize in different contexts, and enjoy it greatly, is being demonstrated every day in classroom experiments. The teacher can expect very gratifying success in using "discovery projects" *if he or she becomes thoroughly familiar with the material beforehand* and introduces it in the classroom with a light touch. Although the activity described below is hard mathematical work in fact, the children consider it a delightful "game" and literally play at it the way they play at baseball. The essence of a "discovery-project" technique is to refrain from hinting wherever possible, but the children must know at what they are aiming, i.e., the general idea of the problem but not given procedures or intermediate-end results. Indeed, one of the main advantages of the method used below is that the children produce far more imaginative and diverse solutions and new problems than any teacher could devise on her own.

Example 1: Generalization of the Degree Measure of an Angle of a Regular Polygon
Preparation. This project could come naturally after a discussion of angles, angle measure, and polygons. Recognition of common polygons could be the discussion leading into the topic. Regular polygons are polygons which have equal sides and angles. The children should have already discovered that the sum of the measures of the angles of any triangle is always the same, $180°$. Material developed in the SMSG Elementary Program leads to this knowledge by several cutting and folding experiments with triangles.
Problem. What is the measure of an angle of an equilateral triangle? Of a square? regular pentagon? hexagon? n-gon? (An n-gon is a polygon with n sides).

Suggestions for teaching. Give the class the problem to think about. Test the guesses about the triangle by measurement if appropriate, but many children will probably see the solution as $180°/3$ or $60°$, since they know that the measures of the three angles are equal and their sum is $180°$. If, after extensive discussion of the square and the pentagon, the class has not gone beyond measurement as a technique, suggest that they try to divide their polygons into simpler sections. It would be desirable if the teacher did not have to suggest specifically that the sections be triangles, or that these triangles should be formed by diagonals from one vertex of the polygon to all the other vertices. Perhaps the children may come up with a variety of interesting different solutions to the problem at this stage. For example, a child might cut out the four corners of the square and show that they exactly fill a complete 360-degree rotation about one vertex (see following illustration). It won't do him any harm to make this particular digression.

It is extremely important for the teacher to be sufficiently familiar with possible solutions so that she may use the innate originality of the children to advantage. Discovery projects should not be introduced by teachers who are unwilling to make this considerable extra effort of preparation. For example, a child might discover that he can take a point anywhere inside a polygon and make the same number of triangles as the polygon has sides (see following illustration). This is not what the teacher is looking for, but it would be very bad if she rejected this solution and others like it because *she* didn't expect it. In fact, one can derive the formula for the measure of the sum of the angles of a polygon from such a figure just as well as from the more conventional one shown in the illustration given below. The important point is that the

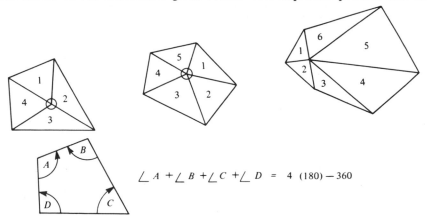

$$\angle A + \angle B + \angle C + \angle D = 4\,(180) - 360$$

teacher be prepared *in advance* to recognize a possible fruitful approach and give it the credit it deserves. No original attempt at a solution should ever be rejected out of hand. Perhaps a child will think of taking more than one point inside a polygon and construct quadrilaterals and even more complicated sec-

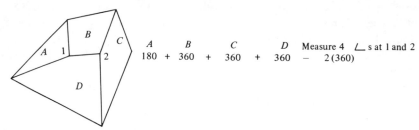

tions as shown here. Such solutions offer the teacher an excellent opportunity to analyze in a class discussion the advantages of one technique over another. Eventually the children will discover, or be tactfully led to discover that all polygons, including regular ones, can be divided into triangles as shown.

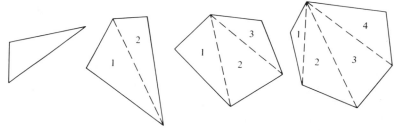

Meanwhile, some children, by other means of their own device may have gathered sufficient data to fill out a table similar to that shown. It is possible for many children to generalize from this table that the degree measures in line 2 go up by multiples of 180. This could suggest to them that a geometrical solu-

Number of sides	3	4	5	6	...
Total degree measure	180	360	540	720	
Measure of one $\angle$ (Regular Polygons)	60	90	108	120	

tion to the problem would be to cut polygons into triangular sections. Teachers should not be surprised if children at this point make a generalization about the degrees of a polygon related to the degrees of a triangle and even justify the claim that their measure is the same as that of two less triangles. Some children, however, will need to see the relationships of the following table before

Number of sides	3	4	5	6	...n
Number of triangular sections	1	2	3	4	...$n-2$

they understand the reasoning of their classmates that an n-gon can be sectioned into $(n - 2)$ triangles.

The important point to remember is that no one can predict the precise order of these discoveries and each child may see it differently. The fewer hints the better. Teachers are frequently guilty of underestimating the ability of ordinary children to generalize successfully and too often step in where angels fear to tread. Discovery is time-consuming, but well worth the time. Also, teachers are usually amazed at the rapidity with which children make many of these generalizations. Indeed, the problem is to keep the faster two-thirds of a class from going too rapidly for the rest. Often the teacher has a very difficult time keeping up with her fastest students.

Most children will discover for themselves that the sum of the measures in a triangular section is equal to the measure of all the angles of the polygon under investigation. To generalize for the n-gon is not at all difficult for children who have had some practice in generalizing number patterns. Many experimental programs currently under development use such practice in place of old-style "drill." (See W. W. Sawyer, "Why Arithmetic is not the End," *Arithmetic Teacher*, March 1959.) If they have already had this type of experience with numbers it will be natural for them to phrase the solution algebraically as $(n - 2)$ times 180. If not, something like "the measure of the sum of the angles of an n-gon is 2 less than the number of sides times 180" will do just as well.

Teachers should not expect completely accurate verbalizations too soon and can be satisfied with much less sophisticated explanations at first. After a class has struggled with the convolutions of attempted verbalizations they will appreciate all the more the elegance of algebraic notation and will come to prefer the expression $\dfrac{(n - 2)\,180}{n}$ as meaning "the measure of the sum of the angles of an n-gon is 2 less than the number of sides times 180."

Note on Example 1: With an average class, these discoveries may occur for a majority of the group within a single class period. However, it is well to play it lightly and allow plenty of time for the ideas to percolate and really be "discoveries." Children learn more out of school than in, and there is a real advantage to both teacher and child when the discovery comes at the dinner table (as it often does). It is always fatal to rush discovery. One way to reinforce the relationship discovered in this example, if class discussion has not already led to it, is to observe the relation as one builds up polygons out of triangles. In the next illustration, we see that when a triangle replaces the side of another triangle, we lose one old side but gain two new ones for a net gain of one side. But as we gain one more side we also gain one new triangle with all of its 180 degrees. The simplest polygon, the triangle, has three sides and starts with a measure of $180°$. Hence the measure of the angles of any n-gon is $(n - 2)$ times $180°$.

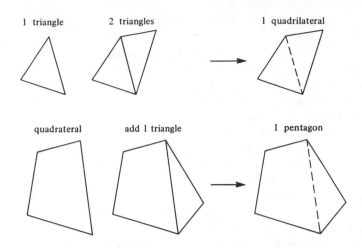

Example 2: The Tesselation Problem
Preparation. Example 1
Problem. What is the shape of the linoleum tiles used to cover floors? Can you always cover a floor with squares or rectangles? Can you do it with regular (equilateral) triangles? How about other regular polygons? How about combinations of regular polygons? Can we generalize?

Suggestions for teaching. Present the problem and give the class time to think about it. Triangular and rectangular solutions will be easy for most children.

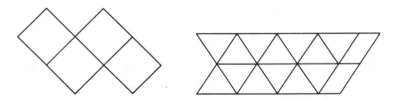

It will be natural for the children to try pentagons. Why won't pentagons work? Children can discover by experiment that when they put three pentagons together at a common vertex there will be a space unfilled which is too small for another pentagon. It may take more thinking and discussion to arrive at the reason—that each angle of the pentagon measures 108 degrees so that when three are put together there are 3 times 108 or 324 (degrees) which is short of 360 by 36. Is this because the measure of a pentagon angle is too big? What about the honeycomb? The hexagon angle measures 120°. Let the children experiment with hexagons and see how three of them exactly fill the angular measure about a point (360°). It's not that pentagon angle measures are too big, it's just that they don't fit evenly into a circle.

How about angles of a seven-gon (heptagon)? How big can the measure of an angle of an *n*-gon get? What does an *n*-gon start to look like when it has many

many sides (such as a 100-gon)? Children will see the important relation with circles, and also the fact that if the angle measure of an n-gon becomes 180°, the n-gon would be a straight line and never "close up." What combinations of polygons with more than six sides will fill the circular measure about a point? Heptagons won't work. Neither will octa-gons. Do we need to try all of them out? What condition has to be met? The class should get the understanding here that no three n-gons of more than six sides can fit about a point so only two at most could fit. But if two fit exactly they must have angles which measure 180°. But (as stated above) you can't have polygons with angles that big (because they would be straight lines and not closed up).

Now that the children have satisfied themselves that only regular triangles, rectangles, and regular hexagons will cover a floor if you have to use tiles all of the same shape, they will be ready to cope with the harder problem of the possibilities when you may use regular polygons of different shapes. (The case where the polygons are irregular is trivial, since infinitely many easy solutions are possible). The important discovery they have already made is that the polygons about one point or vertex must have angles whose measures add up to exactly 360. However, this was discovered, it can be rediscovered by experimenting with a variety of regular polygons and listing some of the combinations that work (see table titled "Some Solutions"). Making a table of polygon angle measures will help suggest solutions.

Sides of n-gon	3	4	5	6	7	8	9	10	11	12.....
Measure of an angle	60	90	108	120	$128\frac{4}{7}$	135	140	144	$147\frac{3}{11}$	150...

Experiment first with regular polygon cutouts and then introduce the idea of an angle-measure table if the children do not suggest it first.

SOME SOLUTIONS

Polygon Combinations	Angle Measures	Sum
2 hexagons and 2 triangles	2 (120) and 2 (60)	360
2 octagons and 1 square	2 (135) and 1 (90)	360
3 triangles and 2 squares (Two patterns are possible with the above combination)	3 (60) and 2 (90)	360
1 hexagon, 2 squares, and 1 triangle	1 (120, 2 (90) and 1 (60)	360
1 hexagon and 4 triangles	1 (120) and 4 (60)	360
1 dodecagon, 1 hexagon, 1 triangle	1 (150), 1 (120) and 1 (90)	360
2 dodecagons and 1 triangle	2 (150) and 1 (60)	360

These eight solutions together with the three simple ones are not exhaustive. Such tessellation patterns which have the same polygon combination about each vertex are called *homogeneous,* and there are six more of them. For example, try an 18-gon, a 9-gon, and a triangle. A good project for a bright child would be to find the rest. (Suggestion to the teacher: First find them yourself!)

If the same vertex pattern is not required (see following illustration), the tessellation is called nonhomogeneous and there are infinitely many patterns. (Why?) Some of them are extremely beautiful. In fact, one good reason for a project on tessellations is to give the children an opportunity to see the beauty inherent in geometric configurations.

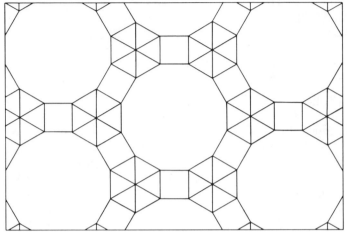

(From Steinhaus, *Mathematical Snapshots,* New York 1950. p.67.)

Example 3:Regular Polyhedrons

Problem. Construct regular polyhedrons. Regular polyhedrons have equal regular polygonal faces which are equidistant from the center of the solid. They may be inscribed in a sphere, just as regular polygons may be inscribed in a circle. They may also be circumscribed about a sphere. How many regular polyhedrons are there? Can you prove it?

Suggestions for teaching. This problem may be too difficult for some sixth-grade classes. It is a good project to give to a bright child and follow through individually. The main generalization to be made is that the number of regular polygonal faces of the solid at any vertex is limited. At least three faces must meet at any vertex (why?), but the sum of their angle measures may not equal or exceed 360° (why?) After this is seen, all of the possible combinations with triangular, square, and pentagonal sides can be worked out. They will yield the five regular solids—the tetrahedron, the cube, the octahedron, the dodecahedron, and the icosahedron (20 sides each an equilateral triangle). Children in any class will enjoy making regular solids as well as solids made up of combinations of regular polygons. A study of Euler's relation, "Vertices plus faces equals edges plus two," may be a discovery project for average groups. This relation is used in the standard proof that there are only five regular solids. The demonstration above is more intuitive and probably more suitable for upper elementary grade children.

Example 4: Networks

Problem. How can you tell whether or not you can trace any figure, however complex, without lifting your pencil off the paper or retracing any line? Many puzzles use this rule, discovered by Euler, and a general solution is well within the reach of upper elementary grade children.

Suggestions for teaching. Set up a series of simple networks of increasing complexity as shown in the figure. Have the children experiment until they notice certain regularities in the problems they can solve. It may be necessary to call their attention to the idea of even and odd vertices (an even vertex has an even number of paths leading away from it; an odd vertex, an odd number.) The teacher of course, should make the discovery herself before giving the problem to the children. Treatments of this topic are found in many texts (for example, *Topology*, pamphlet, Webster Publishing Co., 1960); but usually too many hints are given so that true discovery is not possible if you follow the text too closely.

SIMPLE NETWORKS

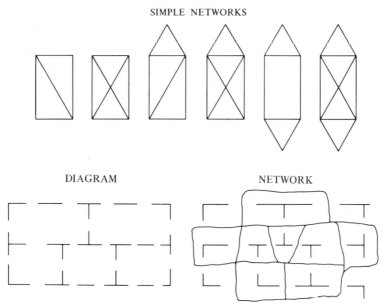

DIAGRAM   NETWORK

Can you walk through all the "doors" once, but not go through any door more than once in one trip.

Example 5: Points, Lines, and Plane Partitions

Problem. In how many ways can you draw lines through a given number of points when no set of three points lie on the same line? Into how many regions, finite and infinite, will these lines separate the planes?

Suggestions for teaching. This topic is rich with generalizations, some of which are listed in the chart on page 338. Start out with two points and construct a table similar to the one on page 338 based on the following drawing.

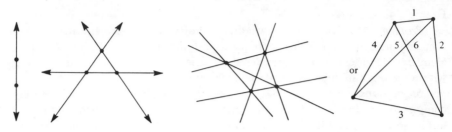

4 points, 6 lines

An easier way (see following table), is to count the diagonals and sides of 2-, 4-, 5-, . . . , n-gons.

Number of points	2	3	4	5	. . . n
Number of lines	1	3	6	10	. . . $\dfrac{n(n-1)}{2}$

Now take 1, 2, 3, 4, . . . , n lines and experiment with the number of ways they can be drawn on the plans. For example two lines can be parallel or they can intersect:

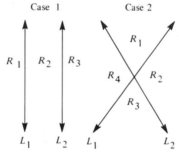

With three lines there are four possibilities: all parallel, two only parallel, none parallel intersecting in three points, and none parallel intersecting in one point. Count the maximum and minimum number of regions for the sets of 2, 3, 4, . . . , n lines. In the figure, the minimum number of regions is 3 (Case 1) and the maximum, 4 (Case 2). Now an elaborate chart may be constructed as follows.

Number of lines	L	1	2	3	4	5	n
Maximum intersections.	i	0	1	3	6	10	$n(n-1)/2$
Maximum regions	R	2	4	7	11	16	$[n(n+1)/2] + 1$
Minimum regions.	r	2	3	4	5	6	$n + 1$
Finite regions (max.) . .	r_f	0	0	1	3	6	generalize
Infinite regions (max.) .	r_i	2	4	6	8	10	$2n$
Number of possibilities .	P	1	2	4	7	11	$\tfrac{1}{2}n(n-1) + 1$

This project should not be attempted by a teacher or a group unfamiliar with the technique of making algebraic generalizations. The teacher not only should be thoroughly familiar with methods for doing this but should enjoy doing this sort of thing. If this is the case, then Example 3 will be a very rewarding experience. Lest skeptics believe this example is far above the heads of sixth-grade children, it should be noted that a sixth-grade class working with Mrs. Rasmussen of the Miquon School developed the following generalizations from the table on the bottom of page 332 in addition to those listed:

$$R \text{ equals } N + i + 1$$
$$N \text{ equals } R - i - 1$$
$$i \text{ equals } R - N - 1$$
$$R - i \text{ equals } r \text{ equals } N + 1$$

Experience with sixth-graders shows that children of this age enjoy a challenge such as this one as much as they enjoy playing baseball.

Example 6: How many squares?

Problem. How many squares can you find on a checkerboard? How many squares can you find by connecting points in a square array of four points, nine points, 16 points, ... n^2 points.

Suggestions for teaching. A "geoboard," constructed from patterns developed by C. Gategno and available from the Cuisenaire Company of America, is very useful in this project.

Take the simple problem of the checkerboard. There are 64 small squares, 49 squares made from four little squares at a time, 36 squares of size 3 × 3, 25 4 × 4 squares, 16 5 × 5 squares, 9 6 × 6 squares, 4 7 × 7 squares and one 8 × 8 square (the checkerboard itself). Thus there are 204 squares in all. Children enjoy this game and also get in some useful computational practice.

If one examines square arrays, a number of new possibilities enter the picture with squares formed from diagonal line segments as shown.

Generalizations about the number of squares of various sizes in such arrays can become quite complex, and the teacher should experiment with these herself before trying to discuss them with a class.

CONCLUSION

These six examples are a small sample of the use of geometric topics to provide experiences in generalization for elementary-school children. Of course, some of them would be equally suitable in junior-high or high-school work. Indeed, adults are not above such games. Teachers can think of many more "discovery projects" and of different approaches to those listed here. One can take a variety of solid blocks, perhaps cut out of wood in the shape of stairs, prisms, etc., and have the children count the number of vertices, edges, and faces, and develop Euler's formula for solids (faces + vertices equals edges + 2). Or simpler yet, one can have children connect points by lines in various ways to develop Euler's rule for plane figures (regions + points = lines + 1).

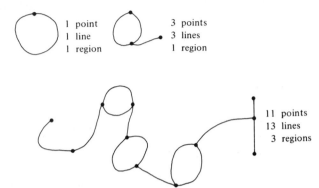

1 point
1 line
1 region

3 points
3 lines
1 region

11 points
13 lines
3 regions

Topics from the geometry of *n*-dimensions have been successfully introduced in the lower grades. The field is a wide open one and well worth developing.

CONSTRUCTION OF SIMPLE MODELS

Show the intersection of two planes in a variety of ways.
A. Folding a piece of paper,

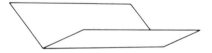

then relating this to an open book,

The intersection of the walls of a room, etc. Many techniques are developed in the SMSG materials. Intersections of lines with line, lines with planes, and planes with planes are treated extensively.

B. Models of plane figures,

(1) Draw and cut out triangular regions of varying shapes. Include isosceles, equilateral, right, scalene, obtuse, acute, and varying combinations.

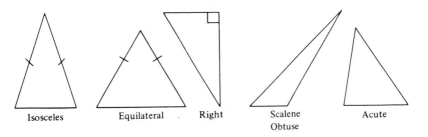

Isosceles   Equilateral   Right   Scalene Obtuse   Acute

(2) Construct triangles using rubber bands on a pegboard or "geoboard."

(3) Draw and cut out all kinds of quadrilaterals.

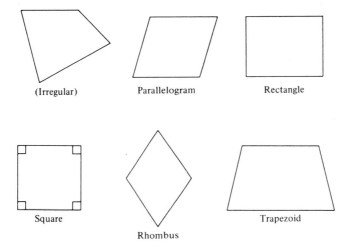

(Irregular)   Parallelogram   Rectangle

Square   Rhombus   Trapezoid

Then cut these figures into simpler and/or smaller sections, deriving other shapes than the original and also similar shapes: The "geoboard" may also be used for this purpose. (A good classroom project would be to have the children make a collection of shapes culled from their environment.)

(4) Draw and cut out other polygons and combinations of polygons of varying shapes and sizes. Experiment with breaking them down into smaller sections.

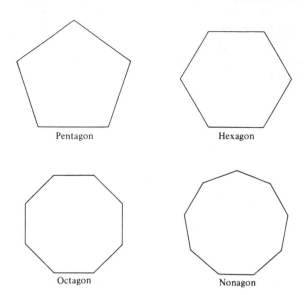

(An excellent classroom project is to cut polygons out of folded paper and then attempt to predict the resultant shapes.)

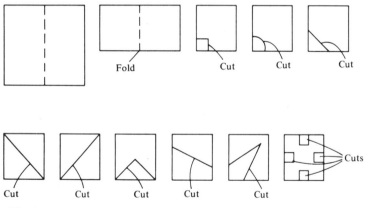

(5) Construct plane figures on squared (graph) paper of different shapes but of the same area, then of the same shape but of different areas. (See Robert B. Davis, Madison Project Workbook, 1st Course, Syracuse, 1959, pp. 279-289 [mimeo].)

C. Construct models of solid figures. Children may construct all sorts of polyhedrons, regular and irregular, and combinations of these.

   (1) Models made of sticks or wire are useful for studying the vertices and edges of polyhedrons and they may also be used on the study of perspective.

   (2) Models made of Plasticine or similar materials are useful for study-

ing the intersections of planes and solids. An unusual effect may be obtained by drawing a taut, thin wire through the model in various ways. The sections then formed may be carefully examined.

(3) Models constructed from stiff paper or cardboard are useful for studying the surfaces and the relations of faces, edges, and vertices of polyhedrons. Color may be used to illustrate relationships and may lead to the study of maps of solids.

(A good classroom project would be to make a collection of solid shapes and to construct objects familiar to the child. These objects might be constructed using combinations of polyhedrons.)

D. Make plane maps of solid figures.

(1) If a cube is made of paper and then flattened out on a plane surface, a map of the cube results. This may be done in many ways, some of which are shown below. A class could experiment to see how many ways this could be done with a variety of maps of solids.

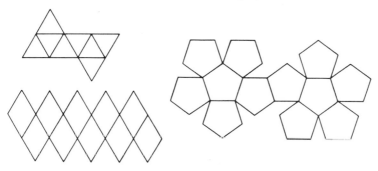

The maps cannot be understood unless the child is able to label the vertices of the resulting cube on the map directly without making the actual solid itself. Note the first example.

Examples of the maps of other polyhedrons are shown below:

Identifying the vertices of the solid forms from the maps becomes increasingly difficult. (Be sure to assign the same number to the equivalent vertices.) Good classroom projects can be based on finding the shortest paths from a point on the surface of a solid to a point on another face of the same solid. These paths may be constructed on the map and then applied to the solid. A classic example is shown below:

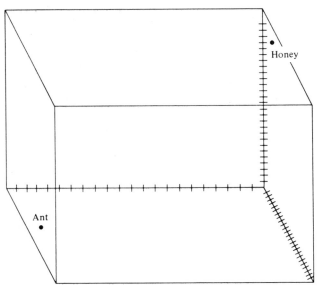

The Ant and the Honey

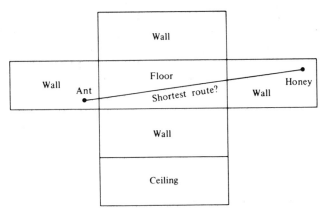

Which is the shortest route for the ant to take?

(2) Maps of odd solids.

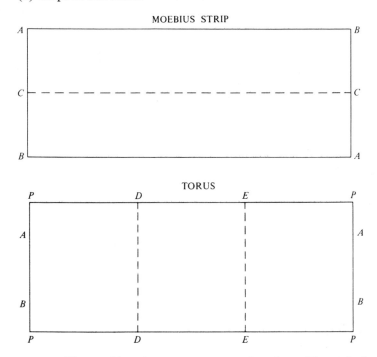

The problem is to try to guess what the solids might be when they are constructed from maps. (See *Topology*, Webster Publishing Co., 1960.)

The specific geometry skills and understandings include the following. The child should be able to:

Grade I

1. Place objects on an indicated line.
2. Attach orally the names to circles, squares, and triangles.
3. Match forms of circles, squares, and triangles when they are seen in drawings, or in the immediate surroundings.

Grade II

1. Point to north, south, east, and west.
2. Indicate left and right in reference to oneself.
3. Trace on a large neighborhood map the route from home to school or school to home and indicate north, south, east, and west.
4. Use *left* and *right* as a position in a situation. *Example*: The store is on the left side of the street as you go toward town.

5. Describe and draw a line, circle, triangle, square, and rectangle as forms in descriptions, directions, and basic designs.
6. Orally describe a situation, group, or object by using the following.
   Follow directions correctly when the following words are used:

here	there	in	the middle
up	down	high	low
over	under	around	across
above	below	out	

Grade III

1. Understand the following geometric concepts:

   A •————————————————————————• B

   (a) A line segment is a part of a line that has two endpoints.

   ←————————————————————————→

   (b) A line is a set of points that go on and on in both directions.

   •————————————————————————→

   (c) A ray is a part of a line that has one endpoint.

   (d) Angles are made of two rays that have the same endpoint.
   (e) With closed figures; points inside, outside, and on the figure can be established.
   (f) There are both open and closed plane figures.

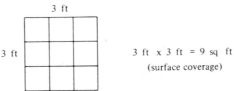

Open   Closed

2. Recognize the following forms:
   (a) Triangle
   (b) Square
   (c) Rectangle
   (d) Circle
   (e) Rectangular prism (cube)
3. Understand and use the concept of square measure.

3 ft

3 ft   [grid diagram]   3 ft x 3 ft = 9 sq ft
                          (surface coverage)

4. Locate general regions on the map.
5. Use map legends and scale of miles.

6. Reproduce in drawings or materials these forms: straight line, circle, triangle, square, rectangle, sphere, and globe.

Grade IV

1. Develop understanding of points, lines, planes, and angles:
   (a) Points are locations and the dot is a symbol for point " . "
   (b) A line is a set of points. It has infinite length and no endpoints.
   (c) A line segment is a part of a line or set of points with two endpoints.
   (d) A ray is a part of a line or set of points with one endpoint.
   (e) An angle is a set of points in two rays with the same endpoint.
2. Develop understanding of plane figures and space figures:
   (a) Points may be shown inside, outside, and on a closed figure.
   (b) Know the definitions of and recognize the following shapes:
       1. Triangle
       2. Four-sided figures (parellelogram, rhombus, rectangle, and square)
       3. Circle (radius, center, diameter)
       4. Right prisms and cubes
       5. Cylinders
       6. Spheres
3. Use measurement in determining:
   (a) Linear units for measuring line segments
   (b) Perimeter of polygons
   (c) Area of squares and rectangles
   (d) Surface area of cube
4. Locate directions north, south, east, and west indicating directions in classrooms, on playground, in community, and on maps.
5. Give directions in drawing a map of the room, bus route, and community.
6. Locate directions by the use of a compass.

Grade V

1. Recognize and understand concepts of points, lines, planes, and angles.
   (a) Understand points are locations in space represented by a symbol (.) the dot.
   (b) Recognize and describe:
       1. Line as a set of points
       2. Space as a set of all points, all locations
       3. Line segments and endpoints
       4. Ray as a set of points with one endpoint
       5. Angle as two rays with common endpoint
       6. Plane as represented by a table top

(c) Differentiate between:
1. Intersecting lines, parallel lines, perpendicular lines
2. Perpendicular lines, right angles
3. Intersecting lines and angles
4. Opposite and supplementary
2. Recognize closed plane figures:
(a) Understand concept of inside, outside, and on closed figures
(b) Recognize and describe:
1. Equilateral triangle
2. Four-sided figures: squares, rectangles, parallelograms, and trapezoid
(c) Recognize and describe:
1. Circle (central angle, radii, diameter, sector)
2. Right prism and cube (edge and faces)
3. Pyramid and cone (base and vertex)
4. Cylinder
5. Sphere (center and radius)
3. Understand measurement of:
(a) Line segments with linear units
(b) Closed figures (perimeter and area)
1. Circle using circumference formula
2. Surface area of right prism and cylinder
4. Construct and copy:
(a) Line segments and angles (labeling)
(b) Perpendicular lines
(c) Angles and bisectors
(d) Congruent line segments; polygons; angles—congruent figures are the same in shape and size
5. Show the line of the equator on the globe.
6. Locate meridians, to read longitude and latitude of a point on a globe.
7. Know the meaning of "elevation"—of buildings, it is the height above the street, or mountains, it is the height above sea level.

Grade VI

1. Review previous learnings in regards to points, planes, lines, and angles.
2. Recognize and describe angles formed by one or more intersecting lines:
(a) Vertical angles
(b) Corresponding angles
(c) Alternate interior angles
3. Recognize and describe plane figures, space figures:
(a) Understand 2–dimensional, 3–dimensional figures
(b) Three-dimensional figures related to square, rectangle, triangle, and circle

      (c) Set of points inside, outside, and on closed figures

      (d) Recognize, classify, describe:

         1. Triangles (right, isosceles, equilateral)

         2. Quadrilaterals

            (a) Parallelograms, rectangle, rhombus, square

            (b) Trapezoid

      (e) Recognize and describe:

         1. Circle (central angles)

         2. Right prism, cube

         3. Cone, pyramid, right cylinder

   4. Understand and use congruency in constructing:

      (a) Geometric figures are congruent when they are in the same shape and size.

      (b) Make figures congruent by copying figures and constructing new figures.

      (c) Construct and copy:

         1. Parallel lines and intersecting lines

         2. Line segments and angles

      (d) Determine congruency of:

         1. Line segments

         2. Angles

         3. Triangles

         4. Polygons

   5. Trace water routes and air routes in a great circle on the globe. To measure the great circle, rotate and compare its length with that of the parallel of latitudes.

TEACHING SUGGESTIONS

Concept: Recognition of geometric figures—points and lines

Procedures. 1. Place a dot on the chalkboard and ask the children if they know another name for this dot. Anticipated response is a "point." Let the children experiment making points. Then discuss other points. For example, point of a needle, pencil point, pen point, the end of the pointer.

2. Introduce a line segment by drawing two points on the board. Ask the children how they can join the two points. Anticipated response is to connect the two points with a line, from one point to the other. Have the children draw lines connecting two points.

3. Introduce the terms "straight" and "curved" by using a piece of yarn or heavy string. Hold the yarn tight. Drop one end of the yarn and ask if it's straight now. Also illustrate straight and curved lines on the flannelboard with the string or yarn. Discuss other lines about the classroom.

4. Have the children fold paper to see that when a paper is folded in two, the crease results in a straight line.

5. Create string pictures by dipping varicolored yarn in thin paste and arrange the yarn on a piece of construction paper to make an array of straight and curved lines.

Concept: Recognition of geometric figures—squares

Procedures. 1. Point out a square region that has four sides and four corners. Show materials that are square in size. Use other classroom media available. *Example:* floor tiles, picture, window glass, etc.

2. Use squared manila paper and have children color square regions.

3. Let the children make pictures of square regions and objects having a square shape.

4. Draw large circular regions and square regions on paper, and have the children color all the circles red and all the squares blue.

5. A comparison could be made of the square regions and the rectangular regions, pointing out that both have four sides and four corners but one pair of opposite sides may differ from the other pair in length in a rectangle.

Concept: Recognition of geometric figures—quadrilateral

Procedures. 1. Quadrilateral regions are introduced through the use of pictures. Have the children draw a rectangular region and experiment with the sum of the angles for a rectangle. The children will soon see that the angles are all right angles.

2. Have the children draw a quadrilateral region and experiment with the sum of the quadrilateral's angles by pasting them around a point.

3. Have the children discuss the properties of quadrilateral regions.

Concept: Recognition of geometric figures—triangle

Procedures. 1. Put a triangular region on the flannelboard or chalkboard and compare the shape with the circle and the square. See if the triangle shape can be found anywhere in the classroom.

2. Use and observe the rhythm-band instrument called the triangle.

3. Make different pictures using the shape of the triangle. *Example:* the top of a house, a Christmas tree, points on a star, etc.

4. Draw various shapes on the chalkboard. Ask the children how many sides you drew to show a triangle, a square, a rectangle.

5. Use name cards in the shape of triangles. Use rectangular and circular regions in the same way. These shapes may also be varied as to size and color.

6. Use perception cards, flannelboard materials, and construction paper to make visual aids as the following:

Discuss with the children to see what shapes they see, and why.

Concept: Recognition of geometric figures—circle

Procedures. 1. Display a circular region of felt or paper and discuss its shape. *Example:* "It's round," and "it looks like a plate." Use different-colored circles. Lead the children to identify the shape and name.

2. Beginning with the circular region, have the children run their fingers around the rims or edges of objects, making a circle, a square, a triangle. Ask the children to place a piece of string around each of these, then remove the object, and discuss the shape of the figure remaining.

3. Develop games in which children must form a circular region.

4. Have the children experiment in drawing a circular region.

5. Make pictures of circular shapes. *Example:* colored balloons and balls, bears, snowmen.

6. Provide children with compasses and discuss thoroughly with them how this instrument should be used and cared for. Demonstrate its use on the chalkboard or on large white newsprint.

7. Guide the children to see that a circle is thought of as a black thin outline only and that it is different from the inside or the outside, which are different from the inside or the outside, which are different regions of the plane.

8. Have the children experiment making circular regions with their compasses.

9. Have the children make patterns of circular regions and color them.

10. Develop the skill of learning how to make circular regions of different size using the compass.

11. After the children have experimented in making circular regions with compasses, provide rulers. Have the children then make a point on their paper with the compass tip and then draw a straight line through it. Follow this with making a circle from the point. Experiment with making many circular regions by placing the tip of the compass at different places on the circle.

12. Let the children draw circles with their compasses and find the radii. Write on the chalkboard the size radius you wish and have the children draw circular regions with a radius the size you specified.

Concept: Area of the rectangle or square

Procedures. The steps in the use of measures of area are the same as have been used throughout this discussion of teaching arithmetic in a meaningful way. Area is one of the hardest mathematical concepts for children to understand and hence a great deal of time must be spent in building this concept. Area is coverage. To be more exact, it is the surface coverage of an object. All questions concerning area are answered by the question: "How much surface is covered?" The units of measure used to describe this answer are in terms of square inch, square foot, and square yard.

The understanding of these measures comes from the actual manipulation of these units. Using these units to actually measure surfaces, the pupil develops the concept of area and comes to realize why areas are labeled as square units rather than in inches, feet, or yards. The following discussion will show this development of understanding.

In working with area, it is important that emphasis be placed not on the formula $A = LW$ or $A = L \times W$, but on the understanding that in area you are working with square units.

1. Prior to class, cover a large flannelboard with napkins. When the flannelboard is covered, discuss with the class, the number of paper napkins required to evenly cover the flannelboard. After counting the napkins, remark that the area of the flannelboard is 10 paper napkins (or whatever the number might be).

Following this demonstration, have the students suggest other materials which could cover the flannelboard. Notebook paper, books, blocks, and many other objects will be mentioned. Develop the need for *a standard measure* that can be used to find the area of any rectangular object. Introduce the unit "square inch." Have the pupils mark off the flannelboard in square-inch units. Count the number of squares. Discuss how else the number of square units could be gotten. A meaningful way to work the problem would be to count the squares in each row and count the number of rows and multiply. Therefore the area of a rectangle is found by the formula: A (Area) = L (number of squares in each row) $\times$ W (number of rows) or $A = L \times W$.

2. Provide the pupils with square-foot units of cardboard or tagboard. Ask them to use their rulers to measure the sides of the cardboard units. They will discover that each side is one foot long. Develop the understanding that when area is measured, units that are square, or equal on all four sides are used.

Have them mark off the square foot into square inches, and discover the number of square inches contained in a square foot. Have them count, each individual square inch; the number of squares in each row, the number of rows, then multiply. Prove to see that there are 144 square inches in a square foot.

Mark off a portion of the classroom floor with chalk and have the children find the area of this portion by placing their individual square-foot cards within the portion. Count the number of cards. Find the number of rows, the number of cards in each row, and multiply the two numbers. Compare the two answers. Are they the same?

3. Begin with the following problem: A neighbor wishes to build a play yard for his dog, but he only has 28 ft of wire. What is the shape of the largest rectangle that he could make to obtain the greatest amount of space?

Give the pupils a length of string 28 ft long and several pieces of Scotch tape. Have them lay out their dog pens on the classroom floor, making pens that will cover the greatest area. Suggest that they might want to make sketches first on paper. After various-sized pens have been laid out, have the students compare the space inside, by counting the number of square feet in each dog pen. This can be done by chalking off the interior of the pen into square feet. Develop the formula Area = length × width.

Concept: Area of a parallelogram

Procedures. 1. Supply each pupil with a piece of paper and a pair of scissors. Have each one draw a set of parallel lines on the paper and then draw another set of parallel lines at an angle to the first set.

The name of this figure is a *parallelogram.* (Two sets of parallel lines.) Cut out the figure. Now cut a triangle from one end cutting on the dotted line. Be sure that this cut is perpendicular to the long set of parallel lines. Place this cut triangle on the other end of the figure so that a rectangle is formed. Check to see that all pupils are following directions. Have a pupil place on the board, the formula for the area of a rectangle. This is the same formula as used to find the area of a parallelogram. But usually different symbols are used. Substitute the B for L and the letter H for W. Does this change the formula? Why would it be better to use B for base and H for height in this formula ?

2. With a piece of $\frac{1}{2}$-inch squared paper in front of each pupil, have them draw a parallelogram on the sheet which is three squares high and five squares long.

There are three rows of squares or parts of squares. For each row, combine the half squares to make a full square as shown in the drawing above by the dotted lines. You now have how many rows and how many squares in each row? Can you find the total number of squares in the figure? To find the area, take the number of rows and multiply by the number of squares in each row. Using B to represent the number of squares in each row and H to represent the number of rows, the formula $A = BH$ is developed.

3. On a squared section of chalkboard, draw a parallelogram and label the base B and the height H. With dotted lines, add a triangle to one end of the figure to make a rectangle of the figure and use dotted lines to show the end of the figure you would erase. Looking at the large figure point out that the triangle that was erased and the triangle added are of the same size. What was actually done, was substituting the triangle from one end and placing it at the other to make the figure a rectangle. The area of a parallelogram becomes the base × height.

Concept: Area of a triangle

Procedures. 1. Begin by considering the area of a right triangle first because the relationship is easier to grasp. When one attempts to measure the size of the triangle by applying the unit of square measure, he finds that the unit of square measure will not apply exactly. To show this, have a pupil draw a triangle on squared paper and attempt to count the units. It will be readily seen that counting squares is not an accurate method. Due to its shape, some of the squares are cut in thirds, or fourths at the vertex of the angle.

2. The next step is to show how the triangle can be changed to a rectangle, to which the unit of square measure can be applied. Proceed as follows:

3. Draw a triangle like *ABC* on tagboard.

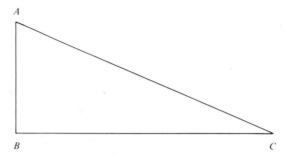

4. Cut this triangle out along the lines *AC, AB,* and *BC.* Draw another triangle that is exactly the same size and cut it out also. Show the class how the two triangles can be placed together to form another figure as shown in illustration.

Now ask the pupils the name of the new figure? How long is it? How wide is it? How do you find the area?

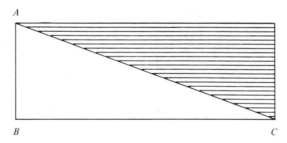

How does the size of the triangle with which we started, compare with the size of the rectangle that is now shown? If the area of the rectangle can be found, the area of the triangle which we started with can be found. The area of the triangle can be found, since it is exactly one-half the size of the pictured rectangle. Write this statement in formula form:

$$A = \frac{L \times W}{2}$$

The area of the rectangle is found by multiplying the length times the width, since the triangle is one-half the size of the rectangle, its area would be one-half that of the rectangle. Converting this formula to simpler terms would result in the formula: Area of triangle = one-half base × height, or $A = \frac{1}{2}BH$.

Now show the class how rectangles can be made from other types of triangles. See illustration.

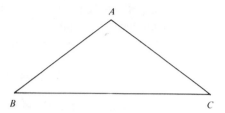

Draw and cut the triangle out of tagboard. Draw another exactly like it and cut it out. Cut the second triangle as shown in the following illustration and place the two parts as shown.

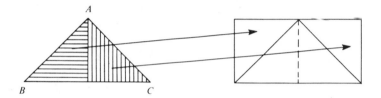

Ask the class to identify the new figure that has been formed and discuss whether the formula worked out above, holds true for all triangles.

5. Before the concept of area is introduced, the pupils should have understood the formula for the area of the rectangle and parallelogram. They should also understand and be able to identify the various shapes of triangles.

To start, the development of the concept of area of a triangle equaling one-half the base times the height, pass out paper 8 inches by 11 inches to the pupils. Have them measure the paper and label the measurements on the paper. Have them find the area of the rectangle. Now have them cut or fold the rectangle so that two right triangles are made. Find the area of the two triangles. At this point, discuss with the pupils what has happened and arrive at the formula $A = \frac{1}{2}LW$. Bring out the fact that in all triangles "base" is used to denote length. Instead of width, the term used is "height" or "altitude." This is the height from the base to the vertex. Substituting these terms, the formula reads $A = \frac{1}{2}BA$ or $A = \frac{1}{2}BH$. It is quite important that pupils understand altitude or height. Have them tell where the altitude occurs from models or drawings.

Concept: Total area of a pyramid

Procedures. 1. Show the class a pyramid and discuss some of the general characteristics of the object:

(a) It has only one base.

(b) The sides are triangles.

(c) The sides slope to the top (or vertex).

2. After a thorough discussion, have the pupils construct a pyramid or show them a pyramid that can be taken apart or collapsed, with the slant height clearly marked on the pyramid. The base should be shown at this time and have the pupils observe that the base area is found by multiplying the side times the side or S.

The triangular sides can be placed on the chalkboard or flannelboard as shown in the illustration. (Be sure that the triangle with the slant height marked is placed in the number one position.)

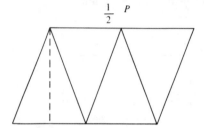

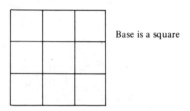

Base is a square

3. Have the pupils observe and discuss the object that is now represented (a parallelogram). If the triangles are of a different color, both on the collapsible pyramid and the same colors on the triangles placed on the chalkboard or flannelboard, it is much easier to comprehend the concept.

Using P as the perimeter of the base of the pyramid, the children see that the base of the parallelogram is equal to one-half of the perimeter of the base of the pyramid, and the slant height K is equal to the height of the parallelogram H. By substituting $\left(\frac{1}{2}P\right)$ for B in the formula $A = B \times H$ (area of a parallelogram), and K (slant height of the pyramid) for H in the formula, it is found that the lateral area of a pyramid equals $\frac{1}{2}PK$. Adding this $\frac{1}{2}PK$ to the base area formula S, the total formula for the area is found. Area $= S + \frac{1}{2}PK$.

Concept: Circumference and the meaning of "pi"

Procedures. 1. Discuss with the class the meaning of circumference. Most of the students will know the meaning. "Circumference" is the distance around a circle. "Diameter" should also be discussed with the students. It is the distance through the center from one side of the circle to the opposite side. After this discussion, pass out various circles with different diameters made from heavy cardboard. Each student should have a ruler and a piece of string. Have the pupils answer the following questions, using only the materials at hand (circle, ruler, and string).

(a) Distance (circumference) around their respective circle.

(b) What is the relationship between the diameter and circumference of their circle?

(c) What is wrong with this method of measuring the circumference of a circle that you have just completed?

2. Later, when the class has had an opportunity to answer the questions, a discussion should follow. Some of the class will have found the circumference of the circle by rolling the circle on the ruler. Others will have wrapped the string around their individual circle and then measured the string. The pupils will discover that the circumference is slightly over three times that of the diameter. Measuring a circle this way is awkward and will not work for large circles. With these findings in mind, explain the meaning of "pi." It is approximately equal to $3\frac{1}{7}$ (or more accurately, 3.1416) and is the ratio of the radius of any circle to its circumference. In other words pi or π = circumference ÷ radius = $3\frac{1}{7}$. The relationship will never be even.

3. Another technique to use for the explanation of "pi" is as follows: Using a circle with a diameter of 7 in., have pupils rotate this circle on a line drawn on the chalkboard. Measure the distance traveled with a yardstick. The distance covered should be approximately 22 in. Have the pupils do this same demonstration with various circles of different diameters. Write the diameter and the distance traveled on the board. Compare the diameter and the distance traveled of each circle. The distance traveled will be approximately 3 times the diameter of the circle. Divide the distance traveled by the diameter and check. The quotient should be approximately $3\frac{1}{7}$ or 3.14.

(a) The value of $3\frac{1}{7}$ or 3.14 will never come out as an even quotient,— therefore it is approximate.

(b) This value of $3\frac{1}{7}$ or 3.14 is called "pi." The symbol for "pi" is π.

Concept: Area of a circle

Procedures. 1. Draw a rectangle on the board and review. The area of a rectangle is the product of the length times the width. Now draw a circle on the board, and divide it into pie shapes and rearrange as shown in following illustration. Divide into 12 parts, then 24 parts, and show that the smaller the pieces the closer the figures resemble a rectangle, and when it gets so small that the eye can not discern the shape it will very closely resemble a rectangle.

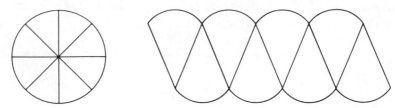

2. It is known that the area of a rectangle can be found by $A = L \times W$ and that the width of the rectangle would be the same as the radius of the circle. Futhermore, the length of the rectangle is equal to $\frac{1}{2}$ the circumference of the circle. (Refer to the original division of the circle into pie shapes.) The relationship between the circumference and the diameter, (the circumference of any circle is $3\frac{1}{7}$ times as large as its diameter, or $C = \pi D$), would be stated as $\pi\, 2R$ because $D = 2R$. Then the length which is $\frac{1}{2}$ of the circumference could be stated as $\frac{\pi}{2}2R$, and dividing $\pi\, 2R$ by 2, we get πR. Substituting πR for L (length of rectangle) and R for W (width of rectangle) and multiplying them together to find the most condensed formula for finding the area of a circle, the formula $\pi \times R \times R$ or πR^2 is obtained.

Concept: Total area of a cylinder

Procedures. 1. Show the class a cylinder, made of wood or in the form of a can, then ask the class to identify the object. Characteristics of a cylinder include:
   (a) It has a top and a bottom.
   (b) The bases are circles.
   (c) It has a base and lateral areas.

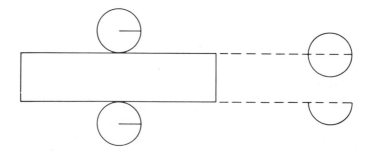

2. Draw the illustration on the board. The base area will be $2 \pi R^2$, because there are two bases made up of circles. Have the pupils take a piece of paper and form a cylinder, (so that the ends do not overlap). Now unfold the paper and what object is represented?(a rectangle) The lateral area of a cylinder is represented by a rectangle. Now have the pupils mark L for length on one side and W for width on the other side. From previous learning it is known that the area of a rectangle $= L \times W$. Have the pupils form the cylinder again and mark P for the circumference (or perimeter of the base) and H for height of the cylinder. Unfold the cylinder again and now it will be seen that the side marked L is the same side as marked H. Knowing that the area of a rectangle can be found by using the formula $A = L \times W$; by substituting P from the cylinder for L of the rectangle, and by substituting H of the cylinder for W of the rectangle, the lateral area of the cylinder can be found (PH). Then adding PH (lateral area of the cylinder) to $2 \pi R^2$ (the base area), the formula reads: Total area of a cylinder $= 2 \pi R^2 + PH$.

Concept: Total area of a sphere and hemisphere

Procedures. 1. Show the class a real sphere and a solid hemisphere at the same time. Then ask what they are, and what are some of the characteristics of each? Such responses will be:

(a) Both are related to a circle.

(b) The sphere has no base.

(c) The hemisphere has a base.

(d) The base of the hemisphere is a circle, while the rest is dome shaped.

2. Having previously studied the area of a circle and with the knowledge that the area of a circle is found by the use of the formula $A = \pi R^2$, the pupils will note that the base area of a hemisphere can be found by using the same formula. Thus, if the total area formula for a hemisphere is $3 \pi R^2$, and the base area is πR^2, this would mean that the lateral area (or dome) would be $2 \pi R^2$, which would be twice as much area as the base, which is πR^2.

3. A croquet ball may be cut in half to form a solid hemisphere, and driving a nail into the center of the curved part of the hemisphere, wind string around it until all the curved area is covered. Now remove the string and measure its length. Record this measurement. Now drive a nail into the center of the flat part of the hemisphere and wind the string around the nail until the flat area is covered. Unwind the string and measure its length. Compare the two measurements, finding that the string covering the curved area is twice as long as the string covering the flat part of the hemisphere.

4. Therefore, the formula for the base is πR^2, the lateral area (or dome area) is $2 \pi R^2$, and the total area of the hemisphere is $3 \pi R^2$.

Since the total area of the sphere has no base area, the total area equals that of the lateral area of the two hemispheres. The formula for the total area of the sphere would be $4 \pi R^2$.

Concept: Area of a cone

Procedures. 1. Show the class a solid cone, and ask what it is. What previously studied objects does the cone resemble? Some may answer "a pyramid" and some may answer "a cylinder." In some ways, it resembles each of these objects. Therefore, the formula for finding the area of a cone is developed from each of the above-mentioned objects.

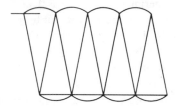

The characteristics of a cone include:
(a) It has only one base.
(b) The base is a circle.
(c) The sides are slanted like a pyramid.
(d) The sides are round like a cylinder.
(e) The sides taper to a point, called vertex.
(f) The altitude is like the altitude of a pyramid. (Bring out the difference between the altitude and the slant height because the altitude is necessary when finding the volume of a cone.)

2. Show the base area on the board to demonstrate that the base is a circle, and show that the area of the base can be found by the formula πR^2. Show then the slant side which could be cut into pie shapes and arranged to form a parallelogram as the illustration. Do this either on the chalkboard or with colored cutouts on the flannelboard. This shows that the length of the base of the parallelogram is the same as one-half of the circumference of the base of the cone. If $C = \pi D$, $\frac{1}{2}C$ would be $\pi \frac{D}{2}$ or πR. The slant height of the cone K would be shown by the height of the parallelogram H. Substitute K (slant height of the cone) for H (height of the parallelogram). The area of the parallelogram is $B \times H$, the lateral area of the cone would be πR times K or πRK. If the base area is πR^2 and the lateral area is πRK, by adding the base formula and the lateral area formula together we would get the formula for the total area of the cone: $A = \pi RK + \pi R^2$.

Concept: Introduction to the study of volume

Procedures. 1. In the primary grades children become acquainted with the measures of volume through the use of liquid and dry measure. In the intermediate grades, the children must develop an understanding of cubic units as a means of measuring the volume of solid figures, as well as further understanding and use of the standard measures encountered, such as quarts, pints, and gallons.

The need for discussing and understanding "volume" comes about through the situations described by or materials bought by cubic units. These materials which may be used for introducing this concept include: top soil, fertilizer, ready-mix concrete, some kinds of fuel, and soil taken from an excavation. A need for a "space-occupying" standard measure is developed. This "space-occupying" standard unit becomes "volume."

Pupils in the sixth grade can learn much from a few introductory exercises in the measurement of volume and cubic contents. Start from the concrete and proceed to the semiconcrete or visualization, and finish with the abstract.

2. Start with a cube the size of a cubic inch. Discuss how many dimensions a cube has. A cube has length, width, and height (depth). Discuss the differences between the dimensions of a cube and a rectangle or square.

3. Arrange the cubes in a line and count to see how many there are. (Place 8—10 cubes in a line.) After emphasizing there are so many cubes, bring out a box and arrange one layer of cubes in the box. Tip the box so that the pupils can see the cubes. Ask how many cubes are in the box. Develop the word "capacity." (All that the box can hold).

Discuss with the class at this point, what the capacity of the box is. (It should be pointed out that the cubes that you are putting in the box must be 1-in. cubes. This will keep the confusion of how large a cubic inch is at a minimum.)

Discuss with the class the possibility of finding some way that would be easier to find how many cubes were contained in a rectangle, than by counting every cube in the box. The discovery might be made that counting the number in each layer and then multiplying by the number of layers would give the capacity of the box. It could be discovered that by counting the number of squares in length and multiplying the number of squares in width and then multiplying the number of squares high would also give the capacity.

Develop the understanding that volume is measured in cubic units larger than cubic inches. Discuss the various uses for cubic feet and cubic yards. This is the basic foundation to the understanding of volume.

4. Now develop volume from the semiconcrete standpoint and have the pupils draw a cubic inch on paper. It would also be advisable to have a cubic foot (made from cardboard, $\frac{1}{4}$ -in. plywood, or any other material) to show the children. Draw a cubic foot on the board and compare with the actual cubic foot.

Now develop the abstract understanding. How is the volume of a rectangle or square found? The volume of a rectangle is found by multiplying the area of the base ($L \times W$) by the height H. $A = LWH$. To reinforce this understanding do the following problem:

5. Have cubic construction blocks on the table. Construct a rectangular solid with a base of 3 units by 4 units. The area of the base of this solid is 3 × 4 or 12 square units. The volume is 3 (width) × 4 (length) × 1 (height) or 12 cubic units. What is the volume of this object? (See the illustrations.)

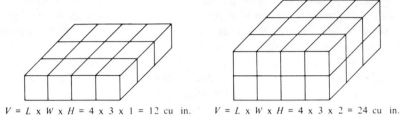

$V = L \times W \times H = 4 \times 3 \times 1 = 12$ cu in. $V = L \times W \times H = 4 \times 3 \times 2 = 24$ cu in.

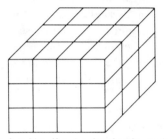

$V = L \times W \times H = 4 \times 3 \times 3 = 36$ cu in.

Concept: The study of scale

Procedures. Many of the techniques discussed here are close to one another, with the exception of devices and methods used. The classroom teacher might wish to use several or all of these to convey the ideas of scale drawings.

1. The teacher relates an incident to the class, seen while watching a carpenter at work. He was beginning a new building and wished to get the corners square. To do this, he took a board 8 ft long, one 6 ft long, and one 10 ft long. He laid the 8-ft board along one line, then laid the other two boards in such a way that he had a square corner. How would he do this? Suggest that they make boards and try it. Since it would be cumbersome and expensive to have each child in a single room, each with an 8-, 6-, and 10-ft board, suggest that the boards be cut to scale, out of paper. Discuss scale as we have used it in map work. Decide what a good scale will be. (Probably the pupils will mention one inch equals one foot, written $1'' = 1'$.) Let them proceed with the problem, then continue with discussion of how we use scale drawings in building. Some pupils may volunteer to bring blueprints to class.

2. Prior to class, prepare a 6-in. length of elasticized tape by stretching it to the length of one foot, then fastening it to a board so that it is one foot long. Mark off the tape as you would a ruler, with inch markings. Develop the con-

cepts through the use of maps in the social studies class. Ask the pupils what method is used to make a map an accurate picture of a particular area of the earth. Discuss meaning of scale on a map. Then show the pupils the board with the elasticized tape attached. Ask them to estimate the length of the tape. Measure the tape and show that it is a foot in length. Unfasten it and measure. Lead pupils to the conclusion that $\frac{1}{2}$ in. on the stretched tape is equal to 1 in. on the unstretched tape. Ask them what scale is being used. Lead them to the decision that the scale being used is $\frac{1''}{2} = 1''$.

3. Discuss meaning of the term "scale drawing." Have class tell what it means as related to a map in a geography book, or to a road map of a known area. Discuss the meaning of ($''$) and ($'$). Progress from the map reading to a discussion of how we could make a "map" of the classroom. Show how a scale would have to be developed for use. Have students measure the room. Suggest that different scales be tried. Some pupil will propose the scale that $1'' = 1'$ in the drawing. Lead the class to see if this scale would be a practical scale for a large room. Show how fractional parts of an inch can be used to represent a foot. Have part of the class make their drawings using $\frac{1}{4}''$ scale and part of them use $\frac{1}{8}''$ scale. Have the pupils realize that scale drawings are the same shape, even though they are different in size.

PRACTICE AND EVALUATION

Angles—Measurement and Drawing

1. Measure the following angles with a protractor. Under each angle write the number of degrees in the angle. State whether the angle is right, acute, straight, or obtuse.

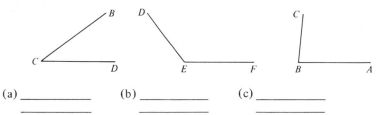

(a) _____   (b) _____   (c) _____
    _____   _____   _____

2. Draw the following angles and state whether the angle is right, acute, straight, or obtuse.

(a) Angle = $150°$ (b) Angle = $90°$ (c) Angle = $45°$
    _____   _____   _____

Triangle—Measurement and Drawing

1. Using a protractor and ruler, draw triangles with the angles and included sides equal to the angles and lines given below.

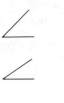

_____

Triangle *ABC* is an (acute scalene, obtuse scalene, isosceles right) triangle.

_____

Triangle *JKL* is an (right isosceles, obtuse isosceles, equilateral) triangle.

2. Draw triangles with given angles and base of 1 inch.

Triangles—Measurement and Construction

1. Construct triangles with sides equal to the lines given below. Letter each side. Measure the angles and write the number of degrees within the angle. In the blanks given, write whether the triangle is right, acute, or obtuse: and whether it is scalene, isosceles, or equilateral.

   (a) _____
   (b) _____
   (c) _____

   _____   _____

2. Sides M, N, and O, each equal to $1\frac{1}{2}$ in.

3.. Two sides P and Q each equal to $1\frac{3}{4}$ in. Third side R equal to $1\frac{1}{2}$ in.

Circles—Radius, Diameter, and Circumference

1. Find the circumference $\left(\text{use } \pi = 3\frac{1}{7} \right)$:

(a) _____ (b) _____ (c) _____ (d) _____

2. If you double the radius of a circle, you _____ the diameter.
3. If you double the diameter of a circle, you _____ the circumference.
4. If you double the radius of a circle, you _____ the circumference.
5. Find the circumference of these circles (use $\pi = 3.14$):

Diameter	Circumference	Radius	Circumference
900 in.	_____	$5\frac{1}{2}$ in.	_____
27.9 in.	_____	27 ft	_____
300 rd	_____	6 ft	_____
36.4 in.	_____	36 ft	_____
10 mi	_____	14 in.	_____

6. Complete the table below. Follow Example 1.

You Want to Find	You are Given	Process or Formula
Diameter	Radius	Radius $\times$ 2 ($d = 2r$)
Radius	Diameter	_____
Circumference	Diameter	_____
Pi	Circumference and Diameter	_____

7. Complete the following table $\left(\text{use } \pi = 3\frac{1}{7} \right)$:

Radius	Diameter	Circumference
_____	35 ft	_____
$4\frac{1}{2}$ in.	_____	_____
_____	_____	176 yd

8. Figure the ratio and tell whether the measurements indicate true circles $\left(\text{use } \pi = 3\frac{1}{7} \right)$:

Circumference	Diameter	Ratio	Yes or No
66 in.	21 in.	_____	_____
100 ft	35 ft	_____	_____
72 yd	18 yd	_____	_____

Perimeter—Rectangles and Squares

1. Find the perimeter of these rectangles.

Length	Width	Perimeter
14 in.	3 in.	_____
7.9 mi	4.3 mi	_____
19 rd	13 rd	_____

2. Solve:

Nobel School has a rectangular paved playground about 250 ft long and 165 ft wide. Matt and Ronney ran a race all around the edge. How many yards did they run?

The floor plan of a department—store warehouse is a square, $114\frac{1}{2}$ ft on a side. Workmen have finished digging 184 ft of trench for the foundation. How many more feet will they have to dig to complete the square?

A football field is 160 ft by 120 yd (including the end zones). What is the perimeter? (Give your answer in feet.)

Mrs. Woods dining room table top is 72 in. long and 48 in. wide. She wants to put a binding around a tablecloth pad exactly the size of the top. How many yards of binding will she need?

Triangles—Perimeter

1. Marks Park is a triangle formed by three intersecting streets. Along Forest Avenue the park is 140 ft long, along Hemlock Street 96 ft, and along Ironwood Avenue 108 ft. What is the perimeter of the triangle?
The owner of the parking lot at Washington Terrace Shopping Center is building a low concrete wall around the lot. The lot is a triangle with sides 375 ft, 236 ft, and 375 ft. About how long is the wall?

2. Find the perimeter of each triangle:

Side A	Side B	Side C	Perimeter
8' 6"	7' 10"	5' 11"	_____
$5\frac{1}{2}$ ft	$4\frac{1}{8}$ ft	$6\frac{2}{3}$ ft	_____
16 in.	14 in.	8 in.	_____
9.7 mi	8.2 mi	6.4 mi	_____

3. Solve the following problem:
Bud's Service Station is on a triangular island, 130 ft by 160 ft by 110 ft in the middle of the street. Mr. Chatman is painting the curbing around the lot. How many feet of curbing will he have to paint?

Area—Circles

1. Write the formula for the area of a circle _____,
then find the areas of the circles shown below $\left(\text{use } \pi = 3\frac{1}{7} \right)$:
Area P = _____   Area Q = _____   Area R = _____

2. The following measurements are for circles. Find the areas $\left(\text{use } \pi = 3\dfrac{1}{7} \right)$:

Radius	Area	Diameter	Area
13 yd	_____	28 in.	_____
27 rd	_____	31 yd	_____
$7\dfrac{1}{4}$ in.	_____	$17\dfrac{1}{2}$ ft	_____

3. The following measurements are for circles. Find the areas (use $\pi = 3.14$). Give answers to nearest hundredth.

Radius	Area	Radius	Area
9.7 in.	_____	14.9 rd	_____
10.5 in.	_____	30 yd	_____
15 ft	_____	13 yd	_____

Area—Rectangles

1. Find the areas of the following rectangles:

Length	Width	Area	
60 ft	34 ft	_____	sq ft
12 ft	9 ft	_____	sq ft
21 yd	7 yd	_____	sq yd

2. Solve:

The playroom in Andrew's house is 24 ft long and 12 ft wide. How many square yards of linoleum must be used to cover the floor?

A rectangle one-half mile long and 900 ft wide has an area of _____ sq ft or _____ sq yd.

Matt has three boards, each 36 in. long and 8 in. wide. Has he enough wood to make a floor for his doghouse if the area of the floor must be 6 sq ft?

A cattle ranch is 4 miles wide and 28 miles long. How many square miles are there in the ranch?

Find the area of a square patio whose sides measure $7\dfrac{3}{4}$ yd.

Pam has a writing tablet $8\dfrac{1}{2}$ in. by 11 in. Christy has one 9 in. by 10 in. Which has more space on which to write? How much more?

Area—Parallelogram

1. In the drawing below of the parallelogram, what is the measurement of the base? _____ The height? _____ Find the area. _____

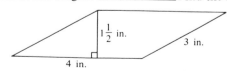

4 in. $1\dfrac{1}{2}$ in.   3 in.

2. Find the areas of these parallelograms:

Base	Height	Area
28 ft	19 ft	_____
$9\frac{1}{2}$ yd	6 yd	_____
18 in.	$7\frac{1}{4}$ in.	_____
8.7 ft	6.4 ft	_____

3. Solve the following problems:

   Mr. Kaye has a concrete patio which is shaped like a parallelogram with a height of 14 ft and a base of 24 ft. He wants to paint it to blend with the new outdoor furniture. How many square feet will he have to paint?

   The restricted area of a military testing ground is shaped like a parallelogram with a height of 35 miles and a base of 50 miles. What is the area of the testing ground? If the population ratio is one person per 40 acres, what is the approximate population of the area?

Area—Trapezoid

1. The following measurements are for trapezoids. Find the areas.

Base a	Base b	Height	Area
36 ft	24 ft	10 ft	_____
14.6 mi	13.4 mi	9.8 mi	_____
9 in.	8 in.	13 in.	_____
8 ft	$6\frac{2}{3}$ ft	4 ft	_____

Area and Perimeter—Review Rectangles, Squares, Triangles

1. Find the area of each rectangle:

   $L = 14$ ft $l = 12.4$ in.
   $W = 13$ ft $w = 9.6$ in.
   $A =$ _____ $a =$ _____

2. Find the perimeter of each rectangle:

   $l = 32.7$ in. $L = 5\frac{3}{4}$ yd

   $w = 27.9$ in. $W = 4\frac{5}{8}$ yd

   $p =$ _____ $P =$ _____

3. Find the perimeter of each triangle:

   $a = 12\frac{1}{2}$ in. $A = 4.75$ ft

   $b = 9\frac{3}{4}$ in. $B = 9.25$ ft

   $c = 5\frac{7}{8}$ in. $C = 12.50$ ft

   $p =$ _____ $P =$ _____

4. Find the area of each triangle:

$B = 9$ ft
$H = 7$ ft
$A =$ _____

$b = 14.6$ yd
$h = 7.8$ yd
$a =$ _____

5. Find the perimeter and area of each square:

$S = 14.5$ yd

$P =$ _____
$A =$ _____

$s = 5\dfrac{5}{6}$ ft

$p =$ _____
$a =$ _____

Lateral Surface and Total Area—Rectangular Solids and Cubes

1. Complete the problems:

Length	Width	Height	Lateral Surface	Total Area
10 ft	8 ft	6 ft	_____	_____
14 in.	16 in.	10 in.	_____	_____
14.4 in.	12.1 in.	8 in.	_____	_____
$15\dfrac{1}{2}$ yd	$11\dfrac{1}{4}$ yd	9 yd	_____	_____

2. Solve these problems:

Mrs. Starr is painting the interior of a wardrobe with inside measurements $5\dfrac{1}{2}$ ft high, 8 ft long, and 3 ft deep. If she paints the total interior area, how many square feet will be painted?

Bonnie has 6 white boxes, 18-in. cubes, which she is covering with gold paper. Three must be covered on all sides; the rest are to have two opposite faces left white. How many square feet of gold paper will Bonnie use?

Lateral Surface and Total Area—Cylinders: (base measurements and height given)

1. Complete the table $\left(\text{use } \pi = 3\dfrac{1}{7}\right)$:

Diameter	Height	Lateral Surface
6 ft	4.5 ft	_____
8 ft	7 ft	_____
28 yd	10 yd	_____
12 ft	6 ft	_____

2. Complete the table (use $\pi = 3.14$):

Radius	Height	Total Area
6 ft	7 ft	_____
14 ft	10 ft	_____
6 in.	9 in.	_____
3 in.	30 ft	_____

3. Solve:

How much would it cost to paint the total outside area of a horizontal cylindrical oil tank 8 ft in diameter and 21 ft long, if the cost of the paint is estimated at $2\frac{1}{2}$ cents per square foot?

Volume—Rectangular Solid

1. Find the volume of a rectangular solid measuring:

4 in. × 3 in. × 2 in.	_____ cu in.
3 in. × 4 in. × 1 in.	_____ cu in.
7 ft × 4 ft × 8 ft	_____ cu ft
5 yd × 7 yd × 2 yd	_____ cu yd

2. Solve:

How many cubic yards of cement are needed to make a driveway 14 ft by 24 ft, if the concrete is poured to a depth of 4 in.?

Since there are $7\frac{1}{2}$ gallons in a cubic foot, how many gallons of fuel are needed to fill a tank 6 ft long, 2 ft wide, and $1\frac{3}{4}$ ft deep?

How many cubic yards of sand are needed to fill a sandbox 10 ft square and 2 ft deep?

3. The following measurements are for rectangular solids. Find the volumes.

Length	Width	Height	Volume
9 ft	7 ft	6 ft	_____
14 ft	8 ft	16 ft	_____
7.6 in.	8.4 in.	9.9 in.	_____
$7\frac{5}{6}$ ft	$6\frac{3}{4}$ ft	$4\frac{2}{3}$ ft	_____

4. Solve:

The inside measurements of Mrs. Borbley's refrigerator are 16 in. by 24 in. by 42 in. What is the capacity in cubic feet?

The Bells have a deep freezer which is 6 ft by 4 ft by $3\frac{1}{2}$ ft, outside measurements. Allowing an average of 3 in. on all sides for wall thickness, about what would be the actual capacity for storage?

Volume—Right Prisms

1. The following measurements are for rectangular solids. Compare the tables.

Length	Width	Height	Volume
6 ft	4 ft	10 ft	_____
4 rd	6 rd	5 rd	_____
85 ft	4 ft	14 ft	_____
3.8 in.	2 in.	4.7 in.	_____

2. The following measurements are for triangular prisms. Complete the table:

Base of Prism		Height	Volume
Height	Base	of Prism	
2 in.	3 in.	18 in.	_____
5 ft	$2\frac{1}{4}$ ft	$9\frac{1}{2}$ ft	_____
6 in.	8 in.	7 in.	_____
15 ft	30 ft	60 ft	_____

Volume—Sphere (radius or diameter given)

1. Complete the chart:

Diameter	Volume
14 ft	
6 in.	_____
10 in.	_____
5 ft	_____

2. Solve:

What is the volume of a spherical raindrop with a diameter of $\frac{1}{8}$ in.? How many such raindrops would fill a cylindrical glass with a diameter of 2 in. and a height of $3\frac{1}{2}$ in.?

The average radius of the earth is about 3,960 miles. Approximately what is the volume of the earth in cubic miles? (nearest whole mile)

The average diameter of the moon is 2,160 miles. Find its volume in cubic miles. (nearest whole mile)

Comparing the volumes, the earth is equal to about how many moons? (nearest whole moon)

Volume—Pyramid and Cone (base measurements and height given)

1. The following measurements are for square pyramids. Complete the table:

Side of Base	Height	Volume
5 ft	10 ft	_____
4 in.	9 in.	_____
4.6 in.	7.4 in.	_____
4 yd	6 yd	_____

2. The following measurements are for cones. Complete the table $\left(\text{use } \pi = 3\frac{1}{7}\right)$:

Diameter	Height	Volume
12 ft	5 ft	_____
6 ft	13 ft	_____
$\frac{1}{2}$ in.	22 in.	_____

Volume—Cylinder (base measurements and height given)

1. Complete the table (use $\pi = 3.14$):

Radius	Height	Volume
12 in.	10 in.	_____
9 ft	13 ft	_____
4.8 in.	9 in.	_____
9 in.	13 in.	_____

2. Complete the table $\left(\text{use } \pi = 3\frac{1}{7}\right)$:

Diameter	Height	Volume
28 in.	16 in.	_____
14 ft	28 ft	_____
10 in.	24 in.	_____
5 ft 3 in.	8 ft	_____

3. Solve:

An oil storage tank base has a diameter of 56 ft. The tank is 35 ft high. What is its volume? How many gallons of oil will the tank hold?

The Wygant's have a cylindrical plastic wading pool with a diameter of 72 in. and a depth of 3 ft (inside measurement). How many gallons of water does it take to fill the pool to 6 in. from the top?

Formulas—Identification

Match the following statements with the correct formulas by placing the correct letter in the blank to the left of the statement.

_____ 1. Perimeter of a regular hexagon	a.	$A = s^2$
_____ 2. Interest formula	b.	$A = \dfrac{bh}{2}$
_____ 3. Area of a triangle	c.	$1 = \dfrac{A}{W}$
_____ 4. Area of a circle	d.	$i = prt$
_____ 5. Area of a rectangle	e.	$v = \pi x^2 h$
_____ 6. Circumference of a circle	f.	$p = 4s$
_____ 7. Volume of right circular cylinder	g.	$p = 6s$
_____ 8. Perimeter of a square	h.	πR^2
	i.	$A = lw$
	j.	$C = \pi D$

Geometry—Questions

1. How many degrees are there in three-fourths of a circle? _____
2. What is the name of the triangle with three equal sides? _____
3. What name is given to lines that are neither horizontal nor vertical? _____
4. A triangle with a 90° angle is called a _____triangle.
5. The interior angles of any triangle total _____ degrees.

6. A square is a rectangle with _____

7. A cube is a rectangular solid with _____ as faces.

8. The lateral faces of a pyramid are _____

9. The base of a cone is a _____

10. A parallelogram is a four-sided figure with_____ pairs of sides parallel.

11. The lateral surface of a right-circular cylinder forms a_____

12. In a trapezoid, how many pairs of sides are parallel?_____

SELECTED READINGS

Measurement and Geometry

Banks, Houston J. *Learning and Teaching Arithmetic.* Boston: Allyn and Bacon, 1959, pp. 342-357.

Bell, Clifford, Cleia Hammond, and Robert Herrera. *Fundamentals of Arithmetic for Teachers.* New York, Wiley, 1962, pp. 238-247, 302-342.

Brumfield, Charles, Robert Eicholz, and Merrill Shanks. *Fundamental Concepts of Elementary Mathematics.* Reading, Mass.: Addison-Wesley, 1962, pp. 237-252, 253-270, 277-287.

Brumfield, Charles, Robert Eicholz, Merrill Shanks, and P. G. O'Daffer. *Principles of Arithmetic.* Reading, Mass.: Addison-Wesley, 1963, pp. 273-286.

Dutton, Wilbur, and L. J. Adams. *Arithmetic for Teachers.* Englewood Cliffs, N. J.: Prentice-Hall, 1961, pp. 150-154, 334-345.

Marks, John L., C. Richard Purdy, and Lucien B. Kinney. *Teaching Arithmetic for Understanding.* New York: McGraw-Hill, 1958, pp. 273-287.

Morris, Dennis E., and Henry D. Topfer. *Advancing in Mathematics:* Chicago: Science Research Associates, 1963, pp. 183-214, 259-270, 276-296.

Osborn, Roger, Vere DeVault, Claude Boyd, and Robert Houston. *Extending Mathematics Understanding.* Columbus, Ohio: Merrill, 1961, pp. 156-174, 184-192.

Peterson, John A., and Joseph Hashisaki. *Theory of Arithmetic.* New York: Wiley, 1963, pp. 238-246.

Schaaf, William L. *Basic Concepts of Elementary Mathematics.* New York: Wiley, 1960, pp. 203-220, 240-244.

School Mathematics Study Group. *Studies in Mathematics,* Vol. IX: *A Brief Course in Mathematics for Elementary School Teachers.* Stanford, Calif.: Stanford U. P., 1963, pp. 139-202, 327-388.

Shipp, Donald, and Sam Adams. *Developing Arithmetic Concepts and Skills* Englewood Cliffs, N. J.: Prentice-Hall, 1964, pp. 142-144, 232-236, 263-265.

Thorpe, Cleata B. *Teaching Elementary Arithmetic.* New York: Harper, 1962, pp. 233-243, 257-260.

Index